Ellsworth Bunker

Ellsworth

Howard B. Schaffer

Bunker

Global
Troubleshooter,
Vietnam
Hawk

An ADST-DACOR Diplomats and Diplomacy Book

The University of North Carolina Press   *Chapel Hill & London*

The ADST-DACOR Diplomats and Diplomacy Series is cosponsored by the Association for Diplomatic Studies and Training in Arlington, Virginia, and Diplomatic and Consular Officers, Retired, Inc., of Washington, D.C. The Institute for the Study of Diplomacy at Georgetown University also supported the work on this book.

Set in Sabon type by Tseng Information Systems
Manufactured in the United States of America

Library of Congress Cataloging-in-Publication Data
Schaffer, Howard B.
Ellsworth Bunker: global troubleshooter, Vietnam hawk / Howard B. Schaffer.
    p. cm.
"An ADST-DACOR Diplomats and Diplomacy Book."
Includes bibliographical references and index.
ISBN 0-8078-2825-4 (alk. paper)
    1. Bunker, Ellsworth, 1894–1984.   2. Ambassadors—United States—Biography.   3. United States—Foreign relations—1945–1989.   4. Vietnamese Conflict, 1961–1975—Diplomatic history.   I. Title.
E840.8.B845 S33   2003
327.73′0092—dc21   2003010307

cloth   07   06   05   04   03   5   4   3   2   1

To my mother,

MINNIE R. SCHAFFER,

who turned 100 as this book

headed for publication

CONTENTS

ILLUSTRATIONS

PREFACE

Working on my first book, *Chester Bowles: New Dealer in the Cold War*, whetted my interest in the writing of biography. After I completed it, I looked for another prominent practitioner of foreign policy, my own professional field, whose life I could detail and assess. In Ellsworth Bunker I found someone who deserved serious study.

Bunker was one of the stars of postwar American diplomacy. He served with distinction as ambassador to five countries, including most notably a six-year assignment to Saigon at the height of the Vietnam War. At the request of a long succession of presidents, he undertook many troubleshooting negotiations climaxing with the successful completion of new treaties governing the security and management of the Panama Canal. His story is the more remarkable because he began his twenty-five years in diplomatic affairs when he was already fifty-six and had become a leading figure in the American sugar refining industry.

To my surprise, I learned that no systematic effort had been made to examine Bunker's career in diplomacy or any other aspect of his fascinating life. He had been the subject of numerous press commentaries, which usually appeared at the beginning or end of one of his many important assignments. But no one had ever set out to write a full-scale biography of the man.

Bunker was not himself a prolific writer, except of classified official documents. He gave many lectures and interviews, provided personal recollections and documents for studies of several of his negotiations, and collaborated on a book, never published, on his Vietnam experiences. But unlike many other American diplomats of his day, he did not write an autobiography or a volume that set out his thoughts on the conduct of postwar U.S. diplomacy and foreign policy.

I had met Ambassador Bunker many times in South Asia and Washington, but never worked directly with him. I was better acquainted with his second wife, Ambassador Carol Laise, like me a State Department specialist in U.S. South Asia policy. Before she died in 1991, Carol strongly encouraged me in my interest in writing about Bunker and offered to make available files of his personal letters and other memorabilia. She was pleased when I decided to go forward with the biography.

In writing it I have tried to show how varied Bunker's diplomatic experiences had been. Although his Saigon and Panama Canal assignments brought him to the center stage of U.S. foreign policy—and domestic politics—for the first time, he had earlier performed many other valuable services for the nation. His activities often involved problems that seemed outside the mainstream of U.S. Cold War diplomacy. But these problems, unless effectively resolved or managed, as Bunker proved able to do so well, could have posed serious challenges to U.S. regional interests.

I have received valuable support from the Association for Diplomatic Studies and Training (ADST) in preparing this volume for publication. The association has included it in its Diplomats and Diplomacy series, which it cosponsors with the Diplomatic and Consular Officers, Retired (DACOR). The series seeks to increase public knowledge and appreciation of the involvement of American diplomats in world history. It demystifies diplomacy by telling the story of those who have conducted our foreign relations, as they saw them, lived them, and reported them. I'm delighted that ADST has added this study to its impressive list of works on diplomacy.

I am also grateful to the Institute for the Study of Diplomacy (ISD), part of Georgetown University's Edmund A. Walsh School of Foreign Service. The institute rightly prides itself on being the university's window to the world of the foreign policy practitioner. Appropriately, Ambassador Bunker became its first board chairman when it was founded in 1978. ISD's current director, Casimir A. Yost, who made me his deputy and institute director of studies in 1996, has consistently encouraged me to pursue this study and has been generous in helping to fund it.

At Yost's suggestion, a number of people who knew or worked with Bunker have contributed to a special ISD fund to support its publication. They include the late Roy Atherton and his wife Betty Atherton, Sheridan Collins, William K. Hitchcock, J. Jefferson Jones, Barnett B. Lester, James L. O'Sullivan, David H. Popper, Harry W. Shlaudeman, Allan Wendt, Barry Zorthian, and the late Betty Lee Berger and Charles S. Whitehouse. Several of these donors were also generous in sharing with me their recollections of Bunker and his work. Allan Wendt, Charlie Whitehouse, and Barry Zorthian were especially helpful in offering their views of Bunker's activities in Vietnam. Harry Shlaudeman, who was his deputy in Santo Domingo, provided valuable insights into Bunker's efforts to bring about a resolution of the Dominican crisis of 1965–66. Roy Atherton vividly recalled for me the role Bunker played in Secretary of State Henry Kissinger's

Middle East shuttle diplomacy, when Bunker and Atherton were fellow passengers.

Many other associates of Bunker were also interested in discussing his diplomatic role. Men who had worked with him on Argentine affairs a half-century ago included Henry Dearborn and the late Lester Mallory. Among those with whom he had collaborated in the crafting and passage of the Panama Canal Treaties were Douglas Bennet, Sol Linowitz, and Ambler Moss. Space constraints rule out my mentioning all of those who provided insights into Bunker's activities between these two bookends to his diplomatic career. But they should know that I am most grateful to them.

Many of those I have mentioned above reviewed chapters of the draft manuscript dealing with episodes in Bunker's professional life in which they were involved. Among others who willingly carried out this onerous chore were Fred Brown, Sam Bunker, George Elsey, Charles Hill, Eva Kim and George McArthur, Roger Kirk, Robert Lincoln, Winston Lord, Edward Masters, Michael Newlin, Gilbert Sheinbaum, Michael Sterner, Galen Stone, and Stephen Young. All of them gave me many useful suggestions.

Ambassador Bunker's three children, Ellen, John, and Sam, were helpful both in making his records available to me and in providing their unique personal recollections of his long and colorful life. When I went through these records, I came across a letter in which Bunker had asked that his papers be given after his death to the Lyndon B. Johnson Presidential Library. After I had reviewed them, representatives of the National Archives collected them from me and sent them on to Austin. They are cited in the book's endnotes as "Bunker Collection." The Bunker family also provided copies of the ambassador's correspondence with Carol Laise when he was in Saigon and she was ambassador in Nepal, as well as the final draft of the unpublished manuscript on Vietnam that he prepared with Stephen Young.

I want to single out Margery Boichel Thompson for particular thanks and praise. At ISD, Margery had given me major assistance in the editing and publishing of my book about Chester Bowles. As ADST publishing director, she has been similarly helpful in shepherding this volume to publication. I'm also grateful to Albert Decie Jr., who as a Georgetown graduate student worked with me in the early stages of my research, and to Michael Rizzi, Michael McVicar, and Niels Melius, Georgetown undergraduates who helped in its final phases. My thanks go too to the staffs of the National Archives; the Dwight D. Eisenhower, John F. Kennedy, Lyndon B. Johnson, and Gerald R. Ford presidential libraries; the Office of the Historian of the State Department; the Lauinger Library at Georgetown University; and the ADST Oral History Project. With their assistance, I have been able to use important, recently declassified material which has never before appeared in a published work.

I am grateful to Charles Grench, Pamela Upton, and all the others at the University of North Carolina Press who worked so skillfully and congenially with me on this biography.

Finally, I want to thank my wife, Ambassador Teresita C. Schaffer. Tezi has provided enormous help to me in the drafting and editing of this manuscript with an expertise few professionals in the field can match. She has also given me the loving support without which I could not have completed this work.

Howard B. Schaffer
Washington, D.C.
April 15, 2003

Ellsworth Bunker

When Ellsworth Bunker accepted the invitation of his old Yale rowing coach and friend Secretary of State Dean Acheson to leave a successful business career and take on the difficult assignment of ambassador to Juan Perón's Argentina in 1951, neither man anticipated that the appointment would lead to Bunker's becoming one of the outstanding American diplomats of the Cold War decades.

Already in his late fifties, Bunker had seen the Buenos Aires embassy as a brief stop on the way to a quiet, retired life, not as the start of a full-fledged, highly distinguished second career in public service. But before he finally left the diplomatic frontlines in 1979 at the age of eighty-five, he went on to become ambassador to Italy, India, Nepal, and, most famously, South Vietnam. As special diplomatic negotiator and troubleshooter, he helped resolve major challenges to U.S interests in such far-flung places as Indonesia, Yemen, Panama, and the Dominican Republic. When no diplomatic appointments were available, he served as the first full-time, salaried president of the American Red Cross. His years in diplomacy and public life climaxed with the complex negotiations and arduous domestic political effort that resulted in the signing and ratification of controversial treaties governing the operation and security of the Panama Canal.

Acheson has rightly called Bunker a *rara avis*, a natural professional in diplomacy. Dean Rusk has said that he considered himself blessed to have Bunker's services. Both of these secretaries of state joined many others in the foreign policy world, not least seven presidents, from Harry Truman to Jimmy Carter, in prizing him as an accomplished diplomatic craftsman, perhaps the most skillful of his time. He won similar respect from foreign leaders as different from one another as Prime Minister Nehru of India and President Sukarno of Indonesia.

A man with no political axes to grind or personal ambitions to satisfy, Bunker considered his public service a responsibility that a patriotic American should willingly shoulder. He brought to his assignments the classic skills and qualities that are vital to the successful conduct of diplomacy: integrity, creativity, realism, precision, and an ability to step into the shoes of his negotiating partners and understand their priorities. He had seemingly infinite patience, an innate courtesy, and a talent for convincing the foreign leaders and officials he dealt with that he was genuinely interested in helping them reach settlements that would satisfy their needs as well as his own. His impressive physical appearance and his gentlemanly, seemingly aristocratic manner contributed to his effectiveness.

Bunker proved unusually adept in carrying out specific diplomatic tasks. Like all good ambassadors and special negotiators, he sought to influence strategy and tactics. Surprisingly for someone of his recognized diplomatic achievements, he rarely challenged the main contours of U.S. policy toward the countries he dealt with. Nor did he seek a significant part in shaping America's role in the world or in crafting diplomatic architecture to promote this. What was important to him were the issues for which he was immediately responsible. He was masterly in dealing with these in resourceful ways that achieved the objectives Washington laid out.

Bunker's place in the annals of American diplomatic history has been distorted by his assignment to Saigon, where he served as ambassador for six crucial years during the Vietnam War. Caught up in the bitter antagonisms the war generated, he became for the first time in his public life both a widely recognized figure and a controversial one. He is now remembered, ironically, more for what he did or failed to do as Lyndon Johnson's and Richard Nixon's representative in South Vietnam than for any of his other diplomatic assignments.

The prominence of Bunker's role as a "hawk" in wartime Saigon and the controversies that still surround it should not obscure the major contributions he made to the successful practice of American diplomacy. Many of his accomplishments in promoting U.S. interests in areas of continuing significance to our national security remain relevant now, almost a quarter century after he retired from public life. Perhaps most important, the way Ellsworth Bunker went about achieving the difficult goals assigned him can teach our generation a great deal that is as useful to the conduct of foreign policy in these very different times as it was in his day.

I

The Years before Diplomacy

Like so many prominent members of the American foreign policy establishment in the Cold War years, Ellsworth Bunker came from a well-to-do white, Protestant, Ivy League background. The first of his ancestors to reach America was George Bunker, who landed in Boston and settled in Ipswich, Massachusetts, in 1634. According to Ellsworth, George was the son of a French Huguenot refugee, and the family name had originally been Boncoeur ("good heart" in English). "It had been corrupted by the British into Bunker," Ellsworth once told Member of Parliament Philip Goodheart, "so we really must be cousins."[1] But for all his well-merited reputation for candor at the negotiating table, Ellsworth was given to weaving tall tales and embroidering others, and this genealogy may have been an effort on his part to romanticize his family background and make the seventeenth-century Bunkers more important and interesting than they actually were. A genealogical study published in 1965 traced the family tree back to ordinary English forebears in early sixteenth-century Bedfordshire, and is probably a more accurate version of Bunker's real Old World ancestry.[2]

English or Huguenot, the Bunkers made their way from Ipswich to Topsfield, Massachusetts, then to Nantucket. There they became seafaring people. "Lay me on, Captain Bunker, for I'm hell with the long dart," was a line in an old Nantucket whaling song, according to the curator of Old Mystic Seaport.[3] Ellsworth loved to tell tales about his seafaring, early nineteenth century great-grandfather, Thomas Gorham Bunker. Thomas, he would relate, was returning from a two-year whaling voyage on a packet he owned when the ship was captured by the British in the War of 1812. The Yankee whaler subsequently spent two years as the Royal Navy's guest at Dartmoor Prison. This story, too, seems somewhat fanciful, if not wholly invented: Thomas was only seventeen when a treaty of peace was signed in December 1814, and packets were never used to hunt whales. The most charitable construction is that he was one of the many American ordinary seamen impressed by the British during the war. In any event, Ellsworth never held his real or invented detention against Thomas's British hosts. "To have exchanged Dartmoor prison for the cramped quarters and appalling fare on an American merchantman of those days, not to mention the rigors of the North Atlantic winters, must have seemed to the young man almost providential," he genially told a gathering of British naval officers when he was ambassador to Argentina.[4]

Following his repatriation, Thomas became the family's first "off-islander" when he left Nantucket for Manhattan to become a shipbuilder. For the next century and a half the Bunkers lived mostly in the New York City area. George Raymond Bunker, Ellsworth's father and Thomas's grandson, followed several other family members into the sugar refining business in the 1860s. Eventually he participated in organizing the National Sugar Refining Company of Yonkers, then a small and quiet Hudson River town just north of New York City, and served as a senior official in the firm and its larger successor corporation, the National Sugar Refining Company of New Jersey, until his death in 1927.[5] George paved the way for Ellsworth's own long and successful career in the sugar business and seems to have been very much a role model for him. Father and son were similar in their quiet, low-key temperaments, and shared many of the same values although the worlds they lived in were separated by a half century.

George played a prominent role in civic, philanthropic, and religious affairs in Yonkers in the manner of wealthy and public-spirited businessmen of his day. A sepia photograph in the *Cyclopedia of American Biography* depicts him as a slim, rather stiff, neatly bearded gentleman in pince-nez, dark three-piece suit, and watch-chain, the very embodiment of a respectable turn-of-the-century pillar of society. In 1882, while living in Philadelphia, he married Katherine Lawson Uhler, a chemist's daughter there. They had one son, Raymond, before Katherine died in 1886.

Ellsworth's mother, Jean Polhemus Cobb, married George in 1893. She was the daughter of Oliver Ellsworth Cobb, a member of the Yale Class of 1859 and, like many of the Cobbs, a minister of the Dutch Reformed Church. In contrast to the Bunkers and their Massachusetts origins, Jean Cobb's family traced their American connection to the days when New York was Dutch New Amsterdam. According to family history, the first Cobb to reach the Dutch colony had come there from Brazil, where he had ministered to a congregation when the territory was ruled briefly by the Dutch West India Company. Reverend Cobb was returning to Holland after the Portuguese regained control when a storm forced his boat to put in at New Amsterdam. He decided he liked the place and stayed on.

(One of Ellsworth's sons suspects that his father's invention of a Huguenot background for the Bunkers may have been piqued by a desire to
make them as interesting as the Cobbs.) Three centuries later Ellsworth's
daughter Ellen married a Brazilian and moved to São Paulo, restoring the
family's brief connection with the country.

The union of Cobb religious piety and Bunker business success
produced three children. Ellsworth, born on May 11, 1894, when George
was almost fifty, was the eldest. Arthur followed a couple of years later,
and Katherine three years after that.

In later years, Ellsworth looked back on his childhood as an extraordinarily happy golden age. The Yonkers of those days, caught in the 1964
musical *Hello, Dolly!*, was a wonderful place to grow up, especially if you
were well-to-do and lived on fashionable North Broadway in a four-story
house with its own apple orchard, stables, tennis court, and woods sloping
down to the New York Central railroad tracks along the Hudson. It also
helped to have a close-knit and loving family, and in George Bunker a
father you could admire and seek to emulate. Ellsworth spoke of George
later as "one of the greatest men I've known, a man of superb intellect,
judgment, wisdom."[6] A rather formal gentleman very much a product of
the Victorian age, "he was always looked to and accepted as the dominant
figure in the family, not because of any egotism on his part, but because
of his qualities and nature."[7]

Ellsworth's mother was devoted to George and wanted it that way. A
tall, elegant woman, Jean Cobb Bunker became very much a patrician
figure in her later life, much involved in the Episcopal Church and social
work. She had what Ellsworth later described as an enormous circle of
friends, the result of her attractive personality and broad interests, including some mildly intellectual ones. "I remember them," he wrote about his
father and mother to his own wife Carol much later, "as an unusually devoted couple, each having qualities that complemented the other and both
having a wonderful sense of humor."[8] He did not suggest that he had inherited that sense of humor, but it would have been a reasonable claim
(though the elder Bunkers would not have fully appreciated Ellsworth's
occasional bouts of ribaldry). "What a wonderful family life we had," he
recalled to his sister Katherine in one of the lively letters they exchanged
when he was an ambassador. "I think back so many times to the fact that
it has been due so much to the kind of life and atmosphere that father and

mother created for us, surrounded as we were with affection and love, but also instilled in us a sense of discipline and responsibility."[9]

Ellsworth flourished in this secure and privileged setting, long since vanished as the big houses in Yonkers were torn down, subdivided, or put to commercial and institutional use, and the pleasant and attractive turn-of-the-century city became the dingy, run-down suburb of today. George taught him to handle a boat at Watch Hill in Rhode Island when he was six, stimulating what became a lifelong love of the sea and a devotion to sailing and competitive racing. He also took him to Pinehurst in North Carolina on Easter vacations to improve his golf game, apparently (to judge from Ellsworth's later handicaps) with limited effect. Under his parents' watchful eye, Ellsworth became an avid reader, an interest he kept for the rest of his life. The Leatherstocking Tales of James Fenimore Cooper and the novels of Charles Dickens were early favorites. Cooper's stories stimulated an interest in learning more about American history; Dickens led him to read a wide range of English authors. As he grew older he became fascinated by Joseph Conrad and read all of his novels, beginning with *Lord Jim*. W. H. Hudson's *Tales of the Pampas*, *Green Mansions*, and *Far Away and Long Ago* were also high on his adolescent reading list. He later said that Conrad and Hudson, along with Willa Cather, were his favorite modern authors.

Unlike many of the golden youth of those days, Ellsworth was not sent to Andover, Exeter, or the "St. Grottlesex" boarding schools favored by the sons of well-to-do northeastern families. Instead, he attended a private day school in Yonkers, then went on to the Mackenzie School in Dobbs Ferry, a few miles further up the Hudson. Dr. Mackenzie, its head, had been headmaster at the famous Lawrenceville School in New Jersey before founding his own preparatory school, now long defunct. Ellsworth took a standard course—"Latin, German, history, mathematics—pretty much across the board."[10] He was something of an athlete, captaining the track team and playing fullback in varsity football. He assumed at the time, as he did when he was at college, that he would be going into business as a matter of course. The idea that he might have an extensive career in public service never occurred to him.

Looking back, Bunker agreed with Dean Acheson's remark that people of their generation had grown up in the golden age of childhood. As he wrote his sister on his sixtieth birthday, the world seemed quieter and more composed.[11] "There was little reason to think that things would not continue much as they had been," he later reflected. "'Manifest Destiny' had defined a role of expanding influence and power for the United States, which it would continue to exert largely from a self-sufficient and self-contained base."[12]

Public affairs and partisan politics were very much on the agenda at the Bunker family dinner table. George was a Republican but a pretty independent one, Ellsworth recalled, and an admirer of Theodore Roosevelt. Ellsworth himself does not seem to have taken as a hero any of the prominent political leaders of his adolescent years. He was able to get a glimpse of the world outside the northeastern United States twice. On the first occasion, his father took him on a month's tour of Cuban sugar plantations. A few years later, in 1912, the whole family boarded the White Star liner S.S. *Baltic* for Liverpool and spent the summer touring southern England, Wales, and France.

There seems to have been no question that Ellsworth would go on to Yale. Aside from his maternal grandfather, his Yale connections included his half-brother Raymond and his cousin George H. Bunker. The family tradition was carried on by Ellsworth's younger brother Arthur, both of Ellsworth's sons (to whom he used to say half-jokingly that it was the only college they could attend), and one of his grandsons. He remained a fondly loyal Eli throughout his life, participating in university functions in New Haven, promoting Yale clubs abroad, and avidly following the Bulldogs' varying fortunes on the gridiron. Yale awarded him an honorary doctor of law degree in 1959.[13]

Entering the college in September 1912 as a member of the Class of 1916, Ellsworth majored in economics and took a minor in history. He enrolled in a broad array of courses, including mathematics, physics, chemistry, English, and anthropology. Giving up his prep school German, he switched to Spanish, taught at Yale by what were then considered pioneering "modern" methods emphasizing conversation. He thought the language might be useful in business, particularly if he decided to work for his father, whose sugar company had extensive Latin American connections. He was especially drawn to courses given by the many academic stars who flourished on the New Haven campus in the 1910s. He studied English under Chauncey Tinker, William Lyon Phelps, and Edward Bliss Reed, economics with Irving Fisher, and history with Charles Seymour, later president of the university. A particular favorite was constitutional law, offered to seniors by William Howard Taft, a Yale graduate who had recently been president of the United States and would soon become chief justice. The course was popular, Ellsworth recalled, not only because the ex-president was a wonderful lecturer but also because he was an easy grader. Bunker's friendship with his classmate Morris Hadley also brought him into what was unusually close contact for an undergraduate with Morris's father, Arthur Twining Hadley, the president of Yale. But while he held Hadley and many of his professors in affectionate regard, none of them seems to have come close to rivaling his father's powerful influence on him.

His academic record at Yale was good but not spectacular. According to the 1916 class yearbook, "Elly" or "Bunk" received second degree honors in his freshman and junior years. He maintained later that he had only barely missed winning academic distinction. "In my time," he wrote his Yale undergraduate grandson many years later, "for some reason, God knows why, they used a scale of 400 for grades. 200 was passing. . . . To join Phi Beta Kappa one had to have an average of 330 for two consecutive years. To my father's great disappointment I ended up with a grade of 327 and he always felt that with a little more effort and a little less fun I could have made Phi Beta Kappa." [14] But after reading a 1961 *New Yorker* magazine article on Yale admissions procedures, Bunker surmised that he was lucky to have got into Yale forty-nine years earlier. "I should never have made it past the Admissions Committee today," he concluded. [15]

Life at Yale was quite different in those days, long before it became the cosmopolitan university it is now. Although the college always accepted a few bright, "poor but honest" New Haven "townies" of various ethnic backgrounds, most of its students were drawn from well-to-do white Protestant families and had gone to private preparatory schools. Boys from the Northeast predominated. Among those Bunker knew were some who later won prominence in public life, including Averell Harriman, governor of New York in the 1950s and an architect of Cold War U.S. foreign policy, and his brother Roland Harriman, Bunker's predecessor as head of the American Red Cross; Robert Lovett, another major foreign-policy-establishment figure who served as under secretary of state and secretary of defense; and banker Prescott Bush, Republican senator from Connecticut in the 1950s, father of one president of the United States and grandfather of another.

Accommodations in 1912 were much less comfortable than they became after the university established residential colleges in the early 1930s. As a freshman, Bunker lived in Pierson Hall, an old five-story building just off the campus, long since torn down. It "resembled nothing so much as a county jail, and [its] conveniences were about of the same order," he recalled in remarks he made to the much better housed students of Yale's Davenport College years later.[16] Confined and frustrated, the young Pierson residents soon took to throwing bottles out of their windows. Bunker recalled that the dean promptly put the whole lot on social probation, the axe falling on participants and nonparticipants alike on the logical grounds that those who were out and hadn't taken part were unintentionally innocent. In his sophomore year, he moved into less Spartan quarters on the campus where he shared a three-room suite with two roommates from the New York area and a third from Honolulu. The four young men remained together for the rest of their time at Yale. As juniors, they were admitted as a group to the Zeta Psi fraternity. One of them, Herman Von Holt of Hawaii, also became a member of Skull and Bones, but Bunker himself was not tapped for that select secret society.

As he had in prep school, Bunker tried his hand at athletics, though with less success. Handicapped by poor eyesight, he was forced to give up his bid for the freshman football team. He switched to rowing, hoping to make the freshman crew, only to run afoul of sophomore Dean Acheson, its amateur coach, who moved him from starboard to stroke and then dropped him from the boat altogether. Bunker later contented himself with rowing number seven on the class of '16 crew. Averell Harriman, who coached the varsity crew, later reportedly claimed that it was he who had taught Bunker how to row. The Old Crocodile professed himself distressed that the young oarsman had gone on to promote unacceptably hawkish policies in Vietnam a half century later.

Herman Von Holt told an interviewer in 1987, when he claimed to be Yale's oldest living graduate, that he had not been wrong in choosing Bunker as a roommate. From the start, he said, he had found Ellsworth "a very fine, gentlemanly, decent fellow and the kind of guy I would like to room with . . . a delightful person, very kind, very calm, very considerate. . . . We never had a cross word the whole time." Bunker would be described by many others in very similar terms throughout his life. Von Holt recalled visiting the Bunker family at Yonkers and inviting Ellsworth to travel to Hawaii. "I think it would be nice if he came out to Hawaii because he's never really been west," he told George Bunker. "Oh, I've been west," Ellsworth chimed in, "I've been out to Buffalo, New York."[17] The visit to the islands included an expedition to Kauai for goat-hunting. Shooting was not the near-sighted, pince-nezed Ellsworth's forte. According to Von Holt, Ellsworth needed to wear glasses even to shave, and the Hawaiian had to do the shooting for both of them.

World War I broke out a few weeks before Bunker entered his junior year. He recalled being pro-Allies, like most of the Yale student body. Although the war seemed far away, he tried to enroll in Yale's Reserve Officer Training Corps program, but his poor vision disqualified him. Soon after he graduated in June 1916, two of his roommates who *had* enrolled telegraphed him in Yonkers urging him to make another try. The Yale ROTC expected to be sent to the Mexican border to help Major General John Pershing track down the insurgent Pancho Villa following Villa's raid on Columbus, New Mexico, and they wanted Bunker to join them in the expedition. Ellsworth hurried back to New Haven and memorized an eye examination chart his roommates had filched for his benefit. Though briefly baffled by having to pretend to read one line backward, he managed to pass. But he never saw any fighting. The Yale unit was mustered into the Connecticut National Guard and did not come any closer to Mexico than a training camp at Tobyhanna, Pennsylvania. When it became clear that Pershing intended to take on Villa's insurgents without Yale's help, university president Hadley decided that the student warriors would be better off returning to New Haven. They were demobilized in September 1916.

When the United States declared war on the Kaiser's Germany seven months later, Bunker tried to enlist in a regular unit but was again turned down because of his poor eyesight. He went to Canada and tried to get into the army there, but was rejected for the same reason. Apparently in neither place were there accomplices available with purloined eye charts.

After graduating from Yale, Bunker began his long association with the sugar industry as a trainee at his father's refinery in Yonkers. At George's insistence, he learned the business from the bottom up. Initially this meant handling such menial tasks as hand-trucking raw sugar to the refinery from boats moored at the National's Hudson River dock. Ellsworth recalled that his starting salary in 1916 was ten dollars a week. His father thought he was overpaid.

He remained in the manufacturing end of the company until the end of the 1920s. It was a good time to be on the payroll of the National, as it was generally called. Although the company's independent existence had been threatened in 1924 by a takeover bid mounted by the larger American Sugar Refining Company, the U.S. attorney general had disallowed the deal—much to the distress of the National's directors, who favored the arrangement. Accepting its unwelcome survival with apparent good grace, the National then tried to improve its competitive position by acquiring other sugar companies or making marketing arrangements with them. In 1927 it bought the Warner Sugar Company's large refinery at Edgewater, New Jersey, across the Hudson from Manhattan. The acquisition boosted the National's refining capacity over 50 percent and made the company and its Jack Frost brand a very close second to American Sugar, which marketed the Domino brand. Bunker, who had moved up the ladder in Yonkers, was named refinery manager, a considerable feather in the cap of a man then only thirty-three.[18]

George Bunker died at about that time at age eighty-two. He had remained in harness to the end, a much respected figure in the business. The whole sugar industry in downtown New York closed on the morning of his funeral and workers trooped from the Yonkers refinery he had helped found to his home on North Broadway to pay him homage. Ellsworth took his place as a director of the National. The outdated refinery, the starting point of Ellsworth's own career, was torn down in 1936 when the company concentrated its New York refining operations at Edgewater and another refinery in Long Island City.

Ellsworth remained at Edgewater for only two years. In the summer of 1929, he suffered a severe attack of arthritis. He had to quit the business and for some time was uncertain whether he would ever be able to return to it. Fortunately, a year of rest and physiotherapy restored his health. But when he went back to the company, it was to the National's headquarters in the New York financial district, not to Edgewater. His days on the manufacturing end of the sugar business were over.

Although the National improved its competitive position in the late 1920s against its U.S. rivals, like the rest of the industry it began to suffer from the competition of refined cane sugar from outside the then forty-eight states. Imports from Cuba, Puerto Rico, Hawaii, and the Philippines rose sharply, costing domestic refiners an estimated 15 percent of their market. The industry was also hit hard in the early Depression years by declining consumption, increased distribution of beet sugar, and protective tariffs imposed by other countries. Between 1925 and 1933 domestic refined cane sugar output shrank approximately one-third as a result. The protectionist Smoot-Hawley Tariff of 1930 failed to remedy the situation.

Against this unpromising background, Bunker became the domestic cane sugar refining industry's leading spokesman while he was secretary of the National, then, after 1934, as its vice president and treasurer. Persuading Washington to help the industry deal with its critical situation, though a difficult assignment, proved to be the opening act in Bunker's long performance during the 1930s and 1940s as the industry's principal political operator. It brought him into close contact with key congressional figures and senior officials in the Agriculture Department and other federal agencies and led to his spending much of his time in Washington. In 1933 he became a key member of a committee the secretary of agriculture convoked to develop stabilization agreements covering sugar imports and production. When these "voluntary" agreements were overturned by the Supreme Court the following year, Bunker directed his formidable lobbying skills at Capitol Hill. He proved a forthright and capable advocate as he argued forcefully before Senate and House committees for limitations on the import of refined cane sugar from low-cost offshore island producers, reasonable protection for the domestic refining industry, and establishment of raw sugar quotas for other producing countries.[19]

These efforts were important in the drafting and passage of the Jones-Costigan Act of 1934. The legislation incorporated the basic provisions of the 1933 "voluntary" agreements. It greatly enhanced the role of the federal government in the operation of the sugar business by giving it sweeping authority to set quotas for production, processing, marketing, and imports of raw and refined cane and beet sugar. One student of the sugar industry has written that Jones-Costigan, in effect, "[turned] the sugar-industry into a government-regulated public utility."[20] Bunker agreed that "the industry gave up in the Jones-Costigan Act a large measure of economic freedom for economic security."[21] Although the act failed to stem the decline in the domestic refiners' gross income, he concluded later that it had "offered a reasonably good method of bringing about . . . a balanced system" and had been in the public interest.[22]

Bunker's colleagues in the refining business highly valued his performance, so much so that they arranged a testimonial dinner for him at the Waldorf-Astoria Hotel in New York in July 1934 to express their appreciation. The refiners also chose him to be the first chairman of the U.S. Cane Sugar Refiners' Association when it was organized two years later to replace the earlier Sugar Institute, an industry public relations and lobbying group that had been dissolved after running afoul of the Justice Department.[23] As association chairman he continued to speak for the industry in its dealings with officials, legislators, and the press. The main thrust of his arguments continued to be that domestic cane refiners were getting a raw deal compared to others in the business. To remedy the situation, he urged the Agriculture Department to set higher quotas for domestic cane sugar refining output, limit refining in Hawaii and Puerto Rico, and reduce and eventually eliminate refined product imports from Cuba.[24]

Bunker's experience as a Washington lobbyist was highly important in setting the stage for his successful second career in diplomacy. It gave him a good knowledge of the ways of Capitol Hill and the executive branch of the federal government, honed his negotiating skills, and won him the respect of members of Congress and administration officials. His dealings in New York in those years were another major stepping stone to his diplomatic service. They brought him into frequent contact with top-flight lawyers in establishment firms who represented the National and other sugar companies in negotiations with the Justice Department over alleged violations of the Sherman Anti-Trust Act. Among them were future secretaries of state Dean Acheson and John Foster Dulles and others who participated in postwar foreign policymaking and who would in their government roles be on the lookout for fresh recruits from the legal and business worlds to join them. These connections made Bunker a prime candidate for a diplomatic assignment when he left the sugar industry in the early 1950s.

His experience as a labor negotiator for the National in the 1930s also helped him in his diplomatic career. As a management representative in those years, he had to deal with the leaders of the tough, aggressive packing-house workers' union. He would shout back at them, sometimes walk out of meetings. Although his style as a diplomat differed markedly from the manner he adopted to bargain for the National, the experience no doubt prepared him for his later encounters with similar loud and blustering men across international negotiating tables.

By comparison, Bunker's exposure to Latin America was less important in paving the way to his later diplomatic success. His contact with the region, though much ballyhooed later (especially by Bunker himself), was actually rather limited. Like other senior officials of the National, he served on the boards of Latin American companies that supplied raw sugar cane to its refineries in the United States. But the meetings of these boards ordinarily took place in downtown Manhattan, not south of the border, and Bunker had little occasion to travel to the companies' Latin American holdings. His only significant personal financial venture in Latin America was the Potrero Sugar Company, a Mexican refinery and plantation property he rarely visited. He became a director and major stock-holder in Potrero when it was organized in 1927 and, later, its president and board chairman. The venture ended in financial disaster for Bunker when the Mexican revolution of 1938 led to land reforms that broke up the plantations supplying the refinery, sharply reducing the availability of raw cane. He later realized only five cents on the dollar from his investment.

Bunker was not one to let his limited exposure to Latin American sugar operations stand in the way of his spinning good yarns about it. In his romanticized tales of his trips south he often focused on a visit he had made to Santa Lucrezia, a little town on the Isthmus of Tehuantepec where he and one of his brothers had tried to start up a plantation in the early 1920s. By Bunker's dramatic account, the trip led to an unexpected en-counter with the Mexican revolution of 1923. Barricaded in his room in a rundown hotel when rebels raided the town, he narrowly avoided get-ting shot in the melee that followed Santa Lucrezia's brief "liberation." He eventually made his way to the dingy harbor of Puerto México on the Caribbean, where he bribed a ship captain with twenty pesos to take him up the coast to Vera Cruz. He got back to New Orleans just in time to head off a search for him. It would have been a minor display of 1920s gunboat diplomacy: according to Bunker, his father had arranged for a U.S. Navy warship to proceed to Puerto México on a rescue mission.

Beginning in the early 1930s, Bunker supported the Democratic Party. Abandoning his family's longtime Republican allegiance, he voted for Franklin D. Roosevelt in the 1932 presidential election and in all of his later races. It is unclear why Bunker registered as a Democrat. He told an interviewer much later that he hadn't thought much of Republican presi-dent Herbert Hoover and had made his decision to switch to Roosevelt as an "intellectual choice."[25] Bunker's son Sam has speculated that Bunker's Democratic orientation—never either ardent or rigid—stemmed from his humanitarian concern and an empathy for ordinary people, which con-trasted with the views of the dyed-in-the-wool, ordinarily Republican Wall Street businessmen of his day.[26] His older son John has suggested that he may have been influenced by the fact that in the 1930s the Democrats were more sympathetic than the Republicans to the sugar business and more willing to provide the kind of assistance the industry sought. According to the biographer of sugar magnate Horace Havemeyer, one of Bunker's close business associates, when arthritis caused Bunker to retire temporarily he got involved in New York Democratic politics and was much influenced by the liberal economic policies of Roosevelt, then New York's governor.[27] Bunker never mentioned this connection when queried by historians.

Bunker met Roosevelt several times when lobbying for the sugar refining industry. In the 1930s he became closely acquainted with Postmaster-General James A. Farley, then the powerful national chairman of the Democratic Party. Bunker was briefly active himself in partisan politics in 1936, when he served as a member of the Democratic National Committee's finance committee and raised funds for Roosevelt's race against Governor Alfred M. Landon of Kansas. As he wryly recalled, "It put me in a minority on Wall Street."[28]

Minutes of finance committee meetings in Bunker's files indicate that his volunteered quota was $25,000, which he tried to raise largely among his sugar industry colleagues.[29] Bunker himself contributed $2,000 to the Roosevelt campaign, not a small sum in those days. The minutes also report that at the committee's October 22 meeting, Farley predicted to Bunker and other committee members that in his opinion Roosevelt would not lose more than six states, possibly only two, Maine and Vermont.[30] To Bunker's pleasure, the more optimistic forecast was borne out in the election two weeks later.

Bunker strongly backed Roosevelt's efforts to help Britain in its struggle against the Axis powers. His first significant foreign policy role came when he was chosen to chair the finance committee of the Committee to Defend America by Aiding the Allies, the analogue on the interventionist side of the anti-interventionist America First Committee. Organized in May 1940 by Kansas editor William Allen White as Nazi armies were overwhelming France and the Low Countries, the committee advocated aiding the British short of war. Measures it proposed included transfer of overage destroyers and other equipment, stepped-up production in the United States of war materiel for export, generous financial grants, increased anti-German activity by the U.S. Navy in the North Atlantic, and changes in U.S. neutrality legislation. In the latter part of 1941 the committee also urged strengthening U.S. measures against Japanese expansionism. Committee members included many with what would now be called "Eastern establishment" credentials, Bunker among them. As his title suggests, his activities focused largely on fund-raising, as they had in the 1936 Roosevelt campaign. He continued to serve as finance chairman until the committee was disbanded after Pearl Harbor.

Despite his earlier allegiance to Roosevelt and his support for the president's pro-British foreign policy, Bunker was unenthusiastic about his 1940 third-term bid and did not participate in the campaign or in subsequent presidential elections. Much later, in 1958 when he was ambassador to India, he was briefly tempted to enter electoral politics on his own behalf. The chairman of the Vermont Democratic Committee urged him that year to run for the United States Senate. Bunker recalled having no illusions that a Democrat could be elected from the state and concluded that he ought to remain in New Delhi. Moreover, he was reluctant to contest against the incumbent, Republican senator Ralph Flanders, an old friend. He sent the exchange of letters to Flanders thinking it would amuse him. The senator replied cryptically, saying he was glad Bunker had decided to stay on at the embassy. A month later, Flanders decided not to run, and 1958 turned out to be a year of sweeping Democratic congressional victories. Although Vermont remained faithful to its traditions and elected the GOP nominee, his share of the vote was a scant 52.2 percent, an extraordinarily low margin for a Republican senatorial candidate in the state in those days.[31] Bunker, who might well have won, complained to Flanders that the senator had done him out of a seat. Discussing the episode in an interview in the late 1970s, he declined to speculate whether as senator he might have joined the anti–Vietnam War Democrats led by Foreign Relations Committee chairman J. William Fulbright and thus emerged as a dove rather than the hawk he became as ambassador in Saigon.[32]

When he first went to work for the National, Bunker lived at home in Yonkers. A nearby neighbor was Harriet Allen Butler, one of the eight children of a wealthy and well-connected businessman, George Prentiss Butler. Four years younger than Ellsworth, Harriet had attended Miss Porter's School in Farmington, Connecticut, with his sister Katherine and had known him for many years, though they were never childhood sweethearts. They became romantically attached after Bunker graduated from Yale and were married in Yonkers in April 1920.

As newlyweds, the young Bunkers lived in a house built on a small lot George Bunker carved out of his property and presented to them as a wedding present. The house was designed by Harriet's brother George Butler, a Columbia University architectural school graduate, and Harriet's widowed mother Ellen Butler paid for its construction. The family lived there when Ellsworth's and Harriet's daughter Ellen and their two sons, John Birkbeck and Samuel Emmet, were born. They moved to a Manhattan brownstone in 1927 following Ellsworth's transfer to Edgewater. Ellsworth's widowed mother remained on in the family's big North Broadway residence until she died in 1942. The house was sold soon afterwards, ending the Bunkers' half-century link with Yonkers.

Ellsworth and Harriet were a devoted couple over their forty-four years of married life. A strong, likeable, somewhat reserved woman, Harriet was every bit Ellsworth's intellectual equal, though like most young women of her background in those days she had not gone to college. She was forthright in her opinions and shared Ellsworth's good sense of humor. But she was much more quick-tempered than he was and did not always value his legendary patience and meticulousness. A family story has it that during World War II, when Ellsworth served as an air raid warden, Harriet used to tease him for taking forty-five minutes to dress in his customary, impeccable way after the sirens had signaled a drill (by which time the exercise was over). She saw her role in the family in the traditional way of those times. This meant providing personal support for her husband and taking part in social life. It also meant ensuring that the children were well brought up, developed a strong sense of right and wrong, and enjoyed a stable home atmosphere.

Harriet did not pursue a career of her own and took no particular interest in Ellsworth's business affairs. The only somewhat unorthodox aspect of her approach to life in the Manhattan of the 1930s was her attitude toward churchgoing. George Butler, her father, had stormed out of his Episcopal church one Sunday and never gone back. He told his children he was tired of being called a sinner when he wasn't one. Although Ellsworth himself remained an Episcopalian all his life and became a devoted parishioner in his old age, the family did not belong to a church during their New York days. Once a year they might go to the Church of the Heavenly Rest on Fifth Avenue. None of the Bunker children was christened or confirmed and only John became an Episcopalian.

The family's place on 95th Street was a narrow but very comfortable, typical East Side brownstone row house with a small back garden. Close to Harlem, the old Jacob Ruppert Brewery, and the run-down tenements that lined the elevated train tracks along Third Avenue, it was in a livelier, more diverse neighborhood than other similar brownstone residences of prosperous New Yorkers farther south and west. The family lived well, though contrary to later legend, Bunker was not a rich man. He depended for his income largely on the salary he received as a senior National Sugar official. The children attended local private schools, the boys toughing it out en route on the sidewalks of New York, until they were sent off as teenagers to the Putney School in Vermont. Bunker was not stern in his dealings with them, nor much of a disciplinarian. But, as Sam Bunker has recalled, "We listened to what he had to say and did what he wanted us to do. . . . It never really occurred to us not to do what he asked us to do."[33] Although Ellsworth made it a practice to have dinner with them every night once they were older, and was always around and available to them, he and the children were not really close. In part, the relationship reflected the times, when Upper East Side New York fathers were not ordinarily intimate and informal with their sons and daughters.

The 95th Street brownstone was a convenient place for Ellsworth. He traveled back and forth by taxi in the morning and evening to the National's financial district headquarters at 129 Front Street, his place of business from 1930 until he retired from the firm in 1951. In his routinized and disciplined way, he arranged for the same taxi driver to carry him to and from the office every day. In the summer time, he similarly tried to have the same Pullman porter on the train between Grand Central and Brattleboro, Vermont, when he joined the family at the house he and Harriet had bought in nearby Dummerston in 1930.

The decision to buy the house followed the severe attack of arthritis Bunker suffered in 1929. Uncertain of the future and needing a place to regain his health, he had wanted to buy a property on the Eastern Shore of Maryland where he could indulge his love of the water. Harriet preferred a place in New England, knew what she wanted, had Butler money, and prevailed. The Bunkers looked at many possibilities and one day talked to a friend who had a home in Dummerston in the southeastern corner of Vermont. Entranced by an old house there owned by Ransom Laughton on what came to be called Bunker Road, they were told by a real estate agent that it was not for sale. Bunker persisted. Would the Laughtons change their minds? "They might, and they might not," was the laconic reply. Negotiations followed, and as a newspaper article in a local Vermont paper put it the year before Bunker died, "Negotiations? Whether the Laughtons knew it or not, they were in the hands of a master craftsman."[34]

Both Ellsworth and Harriet were Anglophiles and loved the west country of Thomas Hardy. When they found the Laughton house in Vermont, they named it Dummerston Downs because the area reminded them of the English downs. It was always Harriet's place. She had her architect brother George rebuild the old Laughton house into something approaching a "Connecticut River mansion." She saw to the construction of a horse barn and a cow barn—and then filled them with animals. She had pigs, chickens, horses, Ayrshire cows, apple and peach orchards, a vegetable garden, and an "old-growth" wood-lot. Ellsworth was more or less a guest at the farm. He was not much of a country man. Though in his romantic way he liked to think of himself as connected with the soil, he never learned to milk a cow or mow a hayfield. He graphically—and embarrassingly—disclosed his preference for the sea when on finding the horse he was riding heading in the wrong direction, he shouted, as if coping with an errant sail, "This horse wants to come about." As was the custom among prosperous New Yorkers in those days, he came up to the country on most summer weekends, arriving by train late on Friday night and returning on Sunday afternoon, and also spent a week or ten days at the place when he took his own holiday. Toward the end of these vacations he always seemed anxious to get back to his business. The Manhattan house was usually "closed" for the summer. Ellsworth stayed on weekdays with his mother in Yonkers or at the Yale Club on Vanderbilt Avenue if he was not lobbying in Washington.

It was only after he had entered the diplomatic world, and, even more, when Harriet's death in 1964 left him with no place else to go, that he came to value the farm more and to regard it as his real home. He made many friends in the neighborhood both among the year-round residents and the summer people who came up from New York and Boston. The Dummerston house also provided the setting in which he cultivated, during his diplomatic career, the persona of the upright "flinty Vermonter" of Yankee twang and cool demeanor. Few who knew him in those later years were aware that he was really a product of the New York City area who had reinvented himself as a New Englander late in life. What led him to adopt this Yankee image remains a mystery to his family and others. John Bunker has suggested the possibility that the press picked up the idea of the Yankee Vermonter when it was looking for ways to describe him, and that Bunker concluded that it would be useful for him to cultivate this image—the stern, upright, but honorable negotiator—as he pursued his diplomatic work.

The image was never a perfect one, in any event. It certainly never extended to his handling of money. Unlike the stereotypical Vermonter, Ellsworth was no tightwad. Quite the opposite. He spent money freely and was generous to the point of always being "broke," to use his own term. Harriet would become exasperated at his "helping out" some down-and-out acquaintance when he was himself the victim of the financial disaster of the Potrero Sugar Company. Moreover, he was always a natty dresser, again in contrast to the accepted Vermont image. He went well beyond the Brooks Brothers tastes of many of his business associates by ordering custom-tailored suits from London or from Twyfforts on Fifth Avenue, a store his father had patronized. He would spend hours there getting just the right look. Even the gray flannels and Harris tweed jackets he wore in Vermont were from Twyfforts.

When the Japanese attacked Pearl Harbor, Bunker was forty-seven, too old to go on active service even if his eyesight had permitted him to take a commission. He had become president of the National the year before. During the war he became deeply involved in efforts to deal with the serious disruptions the conflict had caused the sugar industry. He served as chairman of the U.S. Cane Sugar Refiners' War Committee and held several positions as a consultant to the government, including special advisor to the secretary of agriculture. His activities on behalf of the industry won him rare praise from Professor John Kenneth Galbraith, who was deputy administrator for price in the Office of Price Administration in the early war years. According to Galbraith, who succeeded him as ambassador to India in 1961 and became a Vermont neighbor and friend, "Bunker was one of the businessmen we could rely on to say what was right from the point of view of the public, not the industry."[35]

The industry's wartime problems stemmed mainly from distortions in supply and demand, the result of the loss of the Philippines, Nazi submarine activity off the Atlantic coast, heightened use of sugar for food and industrial purposes, and, in too many cases, federal government bungling. Despite various government programs, including early, strict rationing and the lifting of quotas on imports, by the summer of 1943 the situation had deteriorated to a point where further consumption cutbacks seemed imminent. Facing a critical situation, President Roosevelt established a secret committee of industry and government sugar experts with Bunker as chairman. Secretary of Agriculture Clinton Anderson later described its findings—the "Bunker Report"—as the most careful general survey of the sugar situation he had ever seen.[36] *Business Week* called it "dynamite."[37]

Bunker was outspoken and direct in laying the blame on those the committee considered responsible for "the sugar mess." The report condemned the War Food Administration for inept policies that had led to a decline in beet sugar output. It was also highly critical in its assessment of U.S. representatives on the Combined Food Board for failing to protect American interests and allowing themselves to be outmaneuvered by superior British talent. Its lengthy recommendations for administrative and policy changes to remedy the situation had an important impact in Washington and helped make Bunker a well-known figure there.

With the end of the war in 1945, Bunker's business career had only six more years to go. The National Sugar Refining Company was then under the control of Horace Havemeyer, who for years had been the leading figure in the industry. Havemeyer had been impressed by the younger Bunker's effective lobbying efforts in the early 1930s. His biographer has speculated that Bunker's presence at the National as executive vice president probably played a large part in Havemeyer's decision to take over the company in 1940.[38] It was Havemeyer who made Bunker company president at that time, and the two became cordial friends. Together with Bunker's father George and (later) Dean Acheson, Havemeyer can be considered one of the most important people in determining the course of Bunker's life.

In 1948, Bunker moved up again, this time to become chairman of the National board. He continued to lead the U.S. Cane Sugar Refiners' Association, and in that role acted as industry spokesman in the lobbying and public relations effort leading to the passage of the Sugar Act of 1948. The act in effect restored with some modifications the principles and practices of earlier sugar legislation, such as limiting the import of refined sugar and granting authority of the Department of Agriculture to determine fair wages and prices for sugar cane and beet growers. These had been largely suspended during the war. Bunker vigorously defended the legislation against criticism that it reestablished a sugar cartel for the benefit of U.S. refiners at the very time the United States was seeking freer trade through negotiations under the International Trade Organization. The *New York Times* was especially vitriolic, alleging that the Sugar Act had been written, "by the sugar industry for the sugar industry."[39] Despite these charges the act, as amended, continued to govern the operation of the sugar business until 1974.

During these postwar years Bunker was also named director of a lengthening list of companies, many of them in businesses related to sugar refining. He also stepped up his interest in civic, educational, and philanthropic activities. As early as the 1920s, he had succeeded his father as president of St. John's Hospital in Yonkers. At the end of the 1940s, he had become a member of the board of trustees of the New School for Social Research in New York and of Marlboro College, a small institution near his Vermont home. He was also treasurer and a trustee of the Union Settlement, an interracial nonsectarian neighborhood house in East Harlem.

By 1951 Bunker had long been recognized both in business and government circles as the preeminent political expert and operator of the cane sugar refining industry. Although the National had suffered a disastrous strike in 1948 from which it never fully recovered, he retained the confidence of Horace Havemeyer and could have continued as the company's board chairman and chairman of the Cane Sugar Refiners' Association for many years.

But there would have been few new fields for him to conquer. He had no interest in emulating his father's record of sixty years plus in the sugar business. Instead, in his mid-fifties, with thirty-five years of service to the National, he was considering retiring. He and Harriet would spend summers, he thought, at Dummerston Downs and winters in Brazil with their daughter and her family.

In any event, he was ready for a change, but with no real inkling of the direction that change would take him. Then a call came from his old friend Dean Acheson, now secretary of state. Acheson asked him to become President Harry S. Truman's ambassador to Argentina.

2

A "Correct" Year with the Peróns

Dean Acheson and Ellsworth Bunker had remained in contact in the four decades following their years together at Yale. The ties between the two men were professional as well as personal: Acheson had represented the National Sugar Refining Company as a partner at the prestigious Washington law firm of Covington and Burling. The quiet, self-contained Bunker greatly admired his imperious former rowing coach and his admiration grew during the twenty months they worked together in foreign affairs. As Acheson prepared to step down as secretary of state in January 1953 after four extremely trying years, Bunker would hail him as an example of Christian character and courage. "To see the unswerving devotion with which you have held to your principles in the face of unprecedented difficulties and of unwarranted and often base criticism has been an inspiring experience. I shall never forget it."[1]

Acheson reciprocated Bunker's admiration. According to his son David Acheson, he had been eager to recruit Bunker for some time before the possibility arose of assigning him to Argentina.[2] The secretary credited the idea to Edward G. Miller Jr., a close associate who was assistant secretary for inter-American affairs.[3] Like Acheson and Bunker the product of a well-to-do family and Yale education, "Eddie" Miller had been a partner at Sullivan and Cromwell, John Foster Dulles's Manhattan law firm, when Acheson brought him to Washington in 1949 to take responsibility for U.S. relations with Latin America. Miller had known Bunker well in New York and shared Acheson's high regard for him.[4] The two men kept in unusually close touch during Bunker's tenure in Buenos Aires through candid "official-informal" letters in which they exchanged assessments of developments in Argentina and considered ways the United States could most effectively deal with the difficult situation it faced there in the early 1950s.[5]

Bunker later recalled that Acheson turned to him for the Argentine assignment because he wanted "somebody who knew the Latins, had done business with them, and who spoke Spanish" at a time when Washington was having problems with the government of Juan Perón.[6] Acheson and Miller were also no doubt attracted by Bunker's position in the New York business community, his experience as a government consultant, and his Democratic Party credentials (though his appointment was not a payoff for campaign contributions). They probably also recognized that his physical presence would serve him well as a diplomat. Tall, slender, ramrod straight, always immaculately dressed, Bunker had become a smooth-shaven mid-twentieth-century version of his father and looked the part of an American ambassador of that era.

He also had the personal traits that made for an effective diplomat. He was cool and unflappable under pressure. Though not a particularly outgoing man, he was able in his affable, understated way to develop easy relations with the many different types of people a senior diplomat encounters. He had developed negotiating skills during the many years he had dealt with a diverse mix of businessmen, trade union leaders, government officials, and politicians, and had demonstrated an ability to win their confidence as a man of character and integrity. Perhaps most important, his secure family life and steady success in the business world had given him an inner confidence that allowed him to disregard distracting considerations of prestige and popularity. As Acheson wrote later in a much quoted assessment of Bunker's performance in Buenos Aires, "He could not have cared less about the public's attitude toward him."[7] Bunker was similarly disinclined to worry about the shrill noises emanating from Washington that are the bane of U.S. officials overseas.

Acheson's offer apparently came as a complete surprise to Bunker, and for some time he was uncertain about accepting it.[8] The prospective appointment entailed substantial financial sacrifice and a difficult sorting out of his business affairs. To prompt a favorable reply, Miller sent to New York his desk officer for Argentine affairs, Henry Dearborn, with instructions to talk encouragingly to Bunker about the work of the Foreign Service and the challenges and opportunities he would face if he accepted the Buenos Aires offer. The young Latin America specialist spent a couple of enjoyable days with Bunker in his office and his Manhattan brownstone and returned to Washington an enthusiastic devotee. "It was love at first sight. He was such a great person, such an easy person to be with," Dearborn recalled with much pleasure forty years later.[9]

Bunker came to Washington and discussed the assignment with Miller. He then called on President Truman at the White House.[10] Bunker could not resist recalling to the president his encounter with Acheson on the

Yale freshman crew. He told Truman he held the currently beleaguered secretary in great esteem but said it had been different in their college days. He remembered getting a very Truman-like rejoinder. "How do you know?" the president had remarked, "Perhaps he showed good judgment even then." [11]

Bunker had consulted closely with Harriet. He told a business associate that they had decided that "with [world] conditions as they are today it is difficult to say no to a request for service." [12] He later traced this sense of public duty to his college days. "One of the things that came out of my experience at Yale," he told an interviewer in the 1970s, "was the obligation for public service—that everyone ought to devote at least some part of his life to public service whether in government or out of government, whatever the form might be." [13]

The special features of the Argentine assignment no doubt added to the appeal a stint in diplomacy had for Bunker. He liked Latin America, and though Acheson had overstated his familiarity with the region, it was the part of the world outside the United States he knew best. The problems in bilateral relations that Dearborn had discussed with him in New York surely suggested that he would have more to do in Buenos Aires than attend fancy diplomatic receptions and enjoy the prestige of an ambassadorial title. The prospect of working with Eddie Miller was also important. And geography added a further dimension to Argentina's appeal: although the Bunkers would have to postpone at least temporarily their plans to spend the winters of their retirement years with their daughter Ellen and her family in São Paulo, a posting to Buenos Aires offered easy access to Brazil.

Bunker regarded his posting to Buenos Aires as a strictly one-shot essay in diplomacy. Though he did not rule out the possibility of returning to active management of the National, he figured he would probably retire—this time for good—after a couple of years at the embassy. He did not foresee, nor could Acheson or anyone else, the long succession of diplomatic assignments that lay ahead of him.

Bunker presented his credentials to President Juan Perón on May 8, 1951. His arrival in Buenos Aires to begin what turned out to be an unusually short (ten-and-a-half-month) ambassadorial assignment came at a difficult point on the rocky path that U.S.-Argentine relations had followed during World War II and afterwards. A few weeks earlier, the Argentine government had shut down the world-renowned daily, *La Prensa*, the only newspaper in the country still independent and courageous enough to criticize Perón's increasingly dictatorial regime. The closing of the newspaper dramatized for Americans the sorry state of affairs in Peronist Argentina. Washington considered it the hardest blow to U.S.-Argentine relations since the war.[14]

By the time he suppressed *La Prensa*, Perón had dominated the Argentine scene for over five years.[15] A strong, vigorous and charismatic leader a year younger than Bunker, he offered to the working masses — the *descamisados*, "shirtless ones" — a program of revolutionary change. His glamorous wife, Maria Eva Duarte Perón, a onetime actress universally known as Evita, played a powerful role in his regime and more than matched him in demagogic capability.

The closing of *La Prensa* was the latest step in Perón's effort to eliminate and subvert institutions that could challenge his increasingly broad control over Argentine life. He had already purged the supreme court and the universities of independent-minded judges and academics and amended the Argentine constitution to give himself greater power to carry out his economic and social programs. The constitutional changes also permitted an incumbent president to run for a second term. This made possible Perón's bid for re-election in November 1951, an important milestone in Bunker's tenure.

To prepare for that contest, Perón had created a new party under his tight control. Other parties remained legal but were so harassed that Argentina became for all practical purposes a one-party state. Although many Argentines deplored Perón's destruction of their country's democratic institutions, which he carried out largely under legal guise, the government enjoyed broad support, especially from the military, the *descamisados*, and important elements in big business and the Roman Catholic church. The president and his wife had large popular followings.

The problems in U.S.-Argentine relations were far broader and of longer standing than the concern of Washington and the American public over Perón's repressive measures. Many of these difficulties reflected the fundamental clash between U.S. and Argentine views of the hemispheric roles of the two countries. Historically, Argentina's intense national pride and ambition for leadership in South America had often brought its policies into conflict with U.S. positions. The Argentines resisted Washington's efforts to develop regional security arrangements and considered the growing political and economic power of the colossus of the north an imperialist threat to their own national interests and aspirations. Argentina's pro-Axis policies during World War II, pursued under the guise of its traditional neutralism, had evoked great antagonism in the United States. Despite its eleventh-hour declarations of war against Germany and Japan, recollections of this pro-Axis tilt remained an obstacle in Argentine relations with the United States and other Western countries for years afterward. They also added to concern about Perón's repressive measures, which U.S. opinion associated with his earlier sympathies for the Axis cause.

In the Cold War era that began in the late 1940s, the Argentine government's reluctance to support the West despite its own frequently expressed opposition to communism caused further difficulties for Washington. Perón's touting of a vaguely defined "Third Position" between the United States and the Soviet Union, which he tried to use as a bargaining chip to bolster Argentine nationalist aspirations, made matters worse. Problems in the economic area, including the treatment of American investments in Argentina, had further strained bilateral ties. Perón's blatant use of Argentine Yankeephobia for political advantage was another irritant. So was his effort to extend his influence in other Latin American countries by promoting his "justicialist" ideology and stirring up anti-U.S. sentiment.[16]

During and after World War II, the United States put Argentina at the top of its list of problem countries in the Western Hemisphere. The way it dealt with Buenos Aires varied over those years. The hard-line approach was exemplified by the policies of Spruille Braden, who was ambassador to Argentina for three months in 1945 before becoming assistant secretary of state for inter-American affairs. Braden's blatant, ham-handed effort to influence Argentine voters against Perón in the 1946 election played into the president's hands and proved disastrous.[17] Washington then adopted a strategy that the historian Arthur Whitaker aptly described as "one of intermittent conciliation for limited objectives."[18] Pursuing it, Truman successively appointed two businessmen as ambassadors.[19] Their pandering to Perón in what another observer termed "the salesman's approach" was roundly denounced as appeasement by liberals in the United States.[20] The policy achieved little success in promoting U.S. political, security, and economic interests. As Acheson later succinctly put it, "Successive ambassadors had approached Perón either with a challenge to combat, which they lost, or bearing gifts, which they lost also."[21]

The *La Prensa* affair triggered a tougher U.S. approach to Argentina. Although the Perón government's crackdown on the newspaper was by the standards of the 1950s Argentina's own affair, Assistant Secretary Miller recognized that its powerfully negative impact on American opinion required a change in Washington's course. He unveiled a new posture of "correctness" or "masterly inaction" during a visit to Buenos Aires in early March 1951 soon after Perón had closed the paper. As defined by Chargé d'Affaires Lester Mallory, the new policy meant that "we should be correct; reasonably pleasant but formal; we should not make any requests and we should not accede to major requests except where very clearly necessary and in our interest. . . ." Mallory noted that the approach called for an ambassador "endowed with large quantities of perseverance and patience."[22] He hoped Bunker would meet these requirements.

A State Department policy statement approved in late October 1951 spelled out the approach more formally: "The general U.S. policy believed best fitted to cope with the special problems of U.S.-Argentine relations is [to carry] on friendly but firm and frank relations. Within the scope of this broad policy we allow ourselves leeway between a liberally friendly approach and an approach which may be described as 'correct,' depending on the temper of relations in general." The statement noted that at the time "the United States is limiting itself to being 'correct,' among other lesser factors, because of the strain put upon our relations by the Argentine Government's expropriation of . . . *La Prensa*, by severe attacks on the United States by Argentine officials and the Peronista press, and by U.S. press and labor attacks on Argentina." It forecast that while these conflicting forces appeared to preclude a close friendship between the two countries, "it also seems likely that mutual interests will cause them to remain on moderately-friendly-to-cool terms and to work together in practical ways."[23]

Miller and Bunker discussed this new "correct" approach when Bunker was preparing to leave for Buenos Aires, and Bunker accepted it. Later, when Henry Dearborn sent him a draft of the formal policy statement, Bunker wrote Miller that with minor changes it looked fine to him. He was prepared to conduct himself as "correctness" called for, difficult as Miller knew this would be.[24] In a long message to Miller in mid-June in which he provided his first comprehensive assessment of U.S.-Argentine relations, Bunker wrote: "I am sure that during the next year we shall be angry and exasperated many times. Attacks on us may increase or wane depending on the internal political situation here. I think we should not let it worry us too much but should possess our souls in patience, and, as far as possible, maintain our equanimity. In the meantime we can do our best to represent American interests, insisting that obligations be lived up to, and that our citizens be accorded non-discriminatory treatment."[25]

Bunker meticulously hewed to this course, for which his personality and temperament perfectly suited him. Unlike his predecessors, he did not try to ingratiate himself with the Peróns. When Bunker presented his credentials, the president told him that he would be happy to work with him personally. As a non-diplomat, Perón said, he did not believe in protocol. If the ambassador had serious problems he should raise them with him directly.[26]

Displaying far more restraint than the businessmen-ambassadors who had preceded him, Bunker decided that the best interests of the United States and its masterly inaction posture called for him to decline the offer. He rarely saw Perón on substantive business during his assignment, despite hints from influential Argentines that the president would welcome private sessions. At the same time, he carefully developed cordial, professional relations with senior Argentine officials. They had given him a friendly reception and he never complained about his ability to conduct government business with them. But no evidence is available that he developed particularly warm ties with any of these officials during his short tenure.

Bunker expressed concern that in its dealings with the Argentines the United States had failed to demand sufficient reciprocity. "It seems to me," he wrote Dearborn, "that somehow the British, French, and Belgians always manage to get something in return for anything that they give, and I fear that sometimes we may give a good deal without much return to ourselves."[27] He was pleased when the Argentines became perturbed by Washington's deliberate posture of ignoring their provocations. This had "gotten under their skin a bit," he advised Miller. "The report in *Democracia* [a Buenos Aires newspaper Perón frequently used to criticize Washington], that no one could be found in the State Department to comment about *Democracia*'s article, which covered the waterfront from Braden down to the present time, is all to the good."[28]

As he pursued the "correct" posture, Bunker became concerned that Miller and others in Washington might be taking too hard a line with the Perón government when this was not warranted. Part of the problem seemed to stem from Miller's sensitivity to Argentine criticism of the United States and its leaders, which included personal attacks on the assistant secretary himself as the principal U.S. policymaker for Latin America. As Bunker had foreseen, this anti-U.S. line in the government-controlled media had escalated as the Argentine presidential election neared and the United States became an even more attractive political whipping boy for Perón and his supporters. Miller admitted that "it is extremely difficult for us to take this continual pounding from the Argentine press without reacting in some way along the lines of a stiffening in attitude."[29] He assured the thicker-skinned Bunker that this did not signify any change in U.S. policy.

Following the election, which Perón won easily, Bunker's differences with Miller and others in Washington took a new form. Bunker reported at that time that the victorious president wished to improve relations with the United States. He urged that Washington not close the door to better ties, or give the impression it was doing so. While agreeing with Bunker, Miller expressed skepticism that anything would come through the door if it were kept open.[30]

Bunker recognized early in his tenure that however laudable and appropriate, "correctness" or "masterful inaction" was a tactic rather than a policy. He wrote Dearborn, "They are really maneuvers which may be more or less temporary within a policy which is rather more broad or more permanent."[31] He dealt with the issue more formally in a January 1952 message. "Correctness," Bunker asserted, "is not an end in itself nor does it contain an end in itself. Rather, it is for the purpose of allowing disturbed waters to become calm, of indicating to Argentina that we are not concerned with their often petty aberrations and in the expectation that the progress of events in the world may demonstrate that Argentina has considerably greater need of the United States than the United States has of Argentina."[32]

In his messages to Washington, Bunker adopted a dispassionate view of the Perón government. Although he deplored many of Perón's policies, he regarded with some sympathy the social and economic changes the president was trying to bring about in Argentina. He thought it a wonder that the changes had not been more radical and violent given the attitude of the former ruling class. He scorned these deposed oligarchs and became convinced that their lack of social responsibility had been the principal cause of their downfall. Their newfound profession of support for democracy struck him as insincere and ineffectual.

Bunker did not try to justify Perón's repressive actions but sought to put them in perspective. The Latin view of democracy and civil liberty differed from the North American, and Latins had less experience in self-government. "What I'm trying to say," he told Miller, "is that they aren't like us and we'll butt our heads against a wall trying to make them [become] like us quickly—some day it may come but it will be a long slow process, and full of disappointments on the way." [33] In Bunker's view, the United States should not let the differences worry it too much. Where actions are taken that do not concern it, it should keep its hands off even though it may dislike what is being done. He put *La Prensa* in the hands-off category: Argentina's handling of the matter might have been less short-sighted had its pride not been injured by official U.S. comments and attacks in the American press. The United States needed to apply in Argentina and other Latin American countries a more practical standard of friendship and cooperation, in contrast to an ideological one. But he recognized that American public opinion made this difficult.

Bunker's attitude toward what is now called public diplomacy reflected this approach. He traveled extensively around Argentina and, as an old sugar industry hand, took special delight in visiting cane plantations and refineries. On these trips and in Buenos Aires, he used speeches—ordinarily speaking in Spanish despite his limited command of the language—to explain U.S. policies and practices and stress American values rather than to criticize Argentine moves. A favorite theme, both in his public addresses and private encounters, was the changed nature of American business. He had planned to strike this note from the start of his tenure and considered himself especially qualified to do so. "As one who has worked on capitalistic enterprises and who would probably qualify in Argentine eyes as a capitalist [then a dirty word in Argentina's political vocabulary], I find that the characterization given here is far from the truth," he wrote Dearborn a few days after presenting his credentials. "These people simply do not know what American capitalism is. They talk about it as though it were the old 19th Century laissez faire system." [34] He held that an explanation of the gradual evolution of the U.S. economic system could probably be as useful in creating good relations as anything the embassy information program was doing.

Bunker developed effective if not close working relations with his staff. They were the first group of Foreign Service officers he had encountered, and the high regard he came to have for them foreshadowed the esteem he developed for most career people he dealt with during his years in diplomacy. The embassy functioned well under his leadership. He was no novice at running a large organization, of course. But unlike many other

ambassadors who come from outside the Foreign Service, he wisely recognized that he needed assistance in dealing with unfamiliar terrain. He
was capably assisted throughout his time in Argentina by Lester Mallory
and looked to him to supervise the day-to-day operation of the embassy.
Mallory proved the first of many strong deputies he worked with as ambassador over the years. With Bunker's support, most of them went on to
become chiefs of mission themselves.[35] The embassy and the State Department enjoyed easy and productive relations. Frequent and candid contacts
between embassy officers and middle and lower levels of the Washington
bureaucracy usefully supplemented Bunker's warm ties with Miller.

Harriet ably supported Bunker in his activities. She had had misgivings
about diplomatic life, but soon adjusted easily to it. She enjoyed the enormous embassy residence, with its huge ballroom and large staff of servants,
and used it effectively as a setting for the entertainment that was an important aspect of Bunker's work. She seems to have done all the many things
an ambassador's wife was expected to do in those days. These even included uncharacteristic (for her) attendance at the American church. "We
go regularly every Sunday as an example, as well as for inspiration," she
wrote her sister-in-law Katherine Parsons.[36] She found particularly moving
Ellsworth's reading of the lesson at a Memorial Day service; it reminded
her of his maternal grandfather and the clerical traditions of the Cobb
family. When Ellen and her family came from Brazil for the Christmas
holidays, Bunker put her husband Fernando Gentil, a prominent Brazilian
surgeon, in touch with Argentine doctors to learn about the medical condition of Evita Perón. Señora Perón had been operated on for cancer a few
weeks earlier by the American surgeon George Pack, a former associate
of Gentil's in New York. Bunker had quietly helped arrange Pack's travel
from the United States to Argentina.

For all his self-confidence and ability to control his feelings,
Bunker felt increasingly frustrated in his final months in Buenos Aires. The
worsening state of U.S.-Argentine relations were to blame. Despite earlier
indications, Perón did not seek to improve ties following his re-election,
and after a brief lull the Argentines resumed their barrage of provocative criticism. Faced with a deteriorating economic situation, the president
tried to tighten further his control at home. He also sought to extend his
influence abroad, to the detriment of U.S. interests.

Sensing Bunker's mood, Miller urged Under Secretary of State James

Webb to tell the ambassador how well Washington regarded him: "Since Mr. Bunker is going through a very difficult period in U.S.-Argentine relations and now and then exhibits a feeling of frustration over his inability to do more about improving relations with Argentina, I believe a letter from you . . . would be helpful."[37] Such hand-holding testimonials are not uncommon in the Foreign Service. If one ever reached Bunker, it did little good. In January 1952, as word reached him of his early transfer from Buenos Aires to a European post, he wrote Miller of his continuing frustration and seemed concerned that in time he would be blamed for the sorry state of U.S.-Argentine ties. He wondered "if it is not an appropriate time to bow out before the brickbats and dead cats start coming this way."[38]

Since Bunker had been in charge at Buenos Aires for only eight months, he had not expected the transfer. The sudden reassignment was part of a musical-chairs series of shifts triggered by Webb's resignation and the selection of David Bruce, the ambassador to France, to replace him as under secretary. Secretary Acheson's first thought appears to have been to move Bunker to Paris as Bruce's successor. The secretary eventually decided to shift Ambassador James Dunn from Italy to France and send Bunker to Rome in his place.

Despite the difficulties in U.S. relations with Perón and the need for a highly competent ambassador to handle them, Rome was considered a much more important post than Buenos Aires in those early Cold War years. Acheson believed Bunker had earned the promotion. He wrote later, "Ellsworth Bunker's work and conduct in Argentina had so impressed the President and all of us in the Department that I was eager to try him in a different and even more difficult setting. In a remarkably short time Bunker had shown the qualities of that *rara avis*, a natural professional in diplomacy."[39]

Bunker prepared for his departure with mixed emotions. "I feel in a way I am just beginning to get hold of the job, and I am reluctant to give up at this point," he wrote Miller. "I have a feeling also that my accomplishments to date have been quite unsubstantial. . . . On the other hand, I know how you felt about the post at Rome, and consequently we [Harriet and himself] concluded that under the conditions we could only make the decision to go."[40]

He remained thoroughly involved until he left Buenos Aires, making the rounds of Argentine officials, American businessmen, and his fellow diplomats, and reporting his findings as carefully as before. In his farewell call on Perón, Bunker found the president unusually frank and open in replying to his question about the health of Evita, whose recovery from surgery had been slow.⁴¹ (She died in July 1952.) But as was usually the practice in Bunker's conversations with Perón, little substantive business seems to have been discussed.

A couple of days before he left Argentina on March 12, 1952, Bunker sent to the State Department a comprehensive and far-reaching memorandum outlining suggestions for U.S. policy.⁴² The message was prompted by his conviction that Argentine foreign policy had significantly shifted during his time in the country. The "Third Position," once equidistant between capitalism and communism, had become instead a policy of striking almost exclusively at the United States. "It now appears compelling to recognize," Bunker found, "that . . . efforts to extend Argentine influence are now fundamentally and aggressively anti-U.S. and represent a potential threat to the program of hemispheric unity" that the United States was strongly promoting.

To counteract the challenges posed by Perón's aspirations, Bunker recommended that the United States continue a "generally correct policy" towards Argentina but also take stronger measures to counter anti-U.S. propaganda and alert Latin American countries to the Peronist danger. He called for increased U.S. economic assistance to the other Latin American nations. But he also urged that the U.S. mission in Buenos Aires establish more effective working relations with the Argentine government and suggested that "the time seems to be approaching when such relations will be possible." Although Bunker did not explain why he thought so, he may have believed that the less agitated state of domestic political affairs in Argentina following Perón's reelection could be a positive factor. Ironically, he recommended that his successor be someone who would be able to cultivate better ties with the Peróns, something that he said had not been possible during his own tenure because of the disturbances caused by the Argentine elections and the illness of Señora Perón.

Back in Washington for consultations on his way to Rome, Bunker met Acheson and other State Department officials to review his findings and assess the state of affairs in Argentina. Despite his recommendations for a stronger line and the misgivings he had expressed earlier, he concluded that recent U.S. policy had been effective. The future would show some results in Washington's favor. Although he stressed again the anti-U.S. features of Argentine policy and practice, he found some bright spots, including the presence in high places of officials who were friendly to Washington, such as the foreign minister. He believed that following the failed army coup in September 1951 and the election two months later, the Perón regime was firmly rooted, though Evita's failing health could be important.[43]

Bunker went on to Rome highly regarded by his colleagues in Washington and Buenos Aires. Secretary Acheson's tribute in his autobiography is often cited.[44] But a less dramatic private letter he wrote about Bunker in 1954 catches even better the flavor of his performance as viewed from the upper reaches of Foggy Bottom: "When I was Secretary of State we induced Ellsworth to go to Argentina as our Ambassador. The times were difficult and the relations between the two countries difficult. He combined a quiet reserve and forcefulness, which maintained the position and dignity of the U.S., with a friendliness and hard business sense which accomplished far more with the Argentine authorities than lectures or bluster."[45] Lester Mallory, closer to the scene, probably reflected the sentiment of the embassy staff when he wrote, "we have a lot of Grand Old Men, but we don't have many that I would characterize as full-scale ambassadors."[46]

3
On, Briefly, to Rome

Bunker had never been in Italy before he went there as American ambassador in early May 1952. During his long diplomatic career, Rome was his only assignment in Europe, nor did any of his special negotiating missions involve European issues.[1] By all available contemporary accounts he performed well in leading the huge U.S. mission during the eleven months he was in charge. But his short tenure and lack of familiarity with Europe and the political-military dynamics of the Cold War limited his impact. Dwight Eisenhower's victory in the 1952 presidential election proved a further handicap; as a Truman-appointed Democrat, Bunker became a lame duck only six months after he took charge. Accurate reports circulating early in 1953 that the new president would replace him with Clare Boothe Luce, a glamorous, outspoken, and influential playwright and former congresswoman who was the wife of Henry Luce, the publisher of *Time* magazine, aroused great interest in Italy and highlighted Bunker's status as a short-timer, to his disadvantage.

Bunker presented his credentials to Luigi Einaudi, the president of Italy, on May 7, 1952. His record in Argentina and the high regard they knew Acheson had for him helped ensure a warm reception from Italian officials. The American press greeted his appointment enthusiastically. Anne O'Hare McCormick, the influential foreign affairs columnist for the *New York Times*, was especially laudatory. Although she reported that many observers thought that shifting American diplomats at that point "was like swapping horses in the middle of a peculiarly turbulent stream," she praised Bunker for his dealings with the Perón government and took in stride his inexperience in European affairs.[2] In her view, a man of Bunker's diplomatic temperament and warm interest in human problems was just what the American embassy needed in that difficult phase of postwar U.S.-Italian relations.

In the spring of 1952, the dominant feature of international relations in Italy and the rest of Western Europe remained the Cold War stalemate between the Western powers and the Communist bloc. The launching of the Marshall Plan in 1947 and the establishment of the North Atlantic Treaty Organization (NATO) two years later had led to impressive progress in rebuilding Western European countries and strengthening their defenses against potential Soviet attack. But important issues remained, especially in the security area. The West needed a politically acceptable way to have the Federal Republic of Germany contribute to European defense. Washington held that the best approach was to establish a unified Western European army—the European Defense Community (EDC). The French had proposed this two years earlier as a means of enlisting the Germans without reviving a national German military force. The Truman administration considered the EDC concept a further step in integrating Western Europe, a major advantage in its view. But despite U.S. prodding, negotiations among the proposed European partners proceeded fitfully and political uncertainties in France and elsewhere clouded the EDC's future.[3]

The EDC was to include Italy, along with France, West Germany, and the Benelux countries. Premier Alcide de Gasperi had led its government since 1945. A strong but personally unassuming moderate, he dominated a cabinet comprising members of his own center Christian Democratic Party and a few representatives of the small left-of-center Republican Party.[4] Bunker, for whom de Gasperi was "one of the great Europeans of our time," believed that without him Italy might well have gone Communist. He described the premier as "a man of extraordinary ability, yet a very modest person, deeply religious, quiet, but who nevertheless gave the impression of great spiritual, moral strength, as well as being a pretty acute politician."[5] The two men developed excellent working relations, if not close personal ties, during Bunker's short tenure.

Although Italy, like the Benelux countries, was concerned about potential Franco-German domination of the EDC, the de Gasperi government eventually became a firm supporter of the proposal. It saw greater European military and economic integration as Italy's best hope for security and prosperity following the severe physical and moral damage of the war. After some hesitation, the government had taken a strong role in the development of NATO, and it actively participated in other recently organized regional institutions. The Truman administration welcomed de Gasperi's policies. It had long considered the premier and his center coalition a critical bulwark against Communism that deserved strong support. Substantial American economic assistance provided through the Marshall Plan had been crucial to Italy's postwar recovery.[6]

Along with funds for economic and security assistance, Washington provided clandestine financial and other support to de Gasperi in his political battle against the Communists and their leftist allies. The Central Intelligence Agency's secret funding of the centrist parties in the Italian parliamentary election of 1948 has been called the most successful covert U.S. intervention in postwar Western Europe.[7] As a 1952 National Security Council study delicately put it, "The U.S. has used and is continuing to use both its influence and its resources wherever possible to strengthen democratic anti-Communist elements and to weaken Communist organizations within Italy. Arrangements have been made for continuing consultation in Rome between the American Ambassador and Prime Minister de Gasperi regarding common action the two governments may take against the internal Communist threat."[8] Never officially acknowledged, the covert program was widely known among Italians. There was some unfavorable nationalistic reaction to American intervention in general when U.S. officials publicized it, as Ambassador Luce did in warning that there would be unfavorable consequences in terms of American support if the coalition of centrist parties lost the 1953 parliamentary election. But these parties—the principal beneficiaries of clandestine U.S. funding—apparently had no qualms about receiving assistance.[9]

Unlike some northern Europeans, the Italians did not feel a need to advertise their independence from American influence in conducting foreign policy, and bilateral ties were generally warm and friendly. But Italy's earlier readiness to accept U.S. leadership and advice almost without question had begun to wane, and the conduct of U.S.-Italian relations required greater American sensitivity than before. Washington's awareness of this probably contributed to Bunker's selection as ambassador. The Italians resented what to them seemed America's practice of acting unilaterally in matters vital to their national interests. They believed it had done so in its policy toward the Free Territory of Trieste, a highly emotional issue for almost all Italians.[10]

Bunker accepted the conventional Washington wisdom that the most effective way to keep Italy in the Western camp—the overriding objective of U.S. policy—was to support de Gasperi's coalition. His recommendations focused on making this long-standing policy more effective, especially in the run-up to the Italian 1953 parliamentary elections. Bunker was personally comfortable in carrying out Washington's instructions and seems to have suffered none of the frustrations sparked by differences with senior U.S. officials that marred his time in Buenos Aires. Not surprisingly, he found the Italian democratic framework much less daunting than the Peronist system.

Bunker similarly accepted the overall policies the United States had adopted to contain Communist power in Europe. His cautious temperament and an awareness of his own limited exposure to the East-West confrontation in its European setting encouraged this. He was, after all, the new boy on a block well supplied with Wise Men.[11] For advice on Cold War matters, he relied heavily on his successive deputies, Llewellyn Thompson and Elbridge Durbrow, both able and experienced Foreign Service officers who had dealt extensively with the Soviet Union. Like many of Bunker's deputies, they later became ambassadors at major posts. But Bunker had no Washington mentor to whom he could personally relate during his time in Italy, as he had to Eddie Miller during his Buenos Aires assignment.

Foreign Service officers who worked with Bunker in Rome invariably contrast him with his successor, Clare Booth Luce. Looking back four decades later, they remembered Bunker as a nice gentleman, friendly and pleasant to work with, whose experience in business helped him successfully manage the complex operation of one of the largest U.S. overseas missions. He related well to everyone and no one disliked him. In their recollections, Bunker's opinions on Italian political developments were "steady, nothing sensational," or "not too sharp," and they generally agree that he (wisely) left political analysis largely to his staff. In the view of one old-timer, he was "a good, not outstanding" ambassador, the man who had been in Rome "just before Mrs. Luce."[12]

By contrast, they remembered Ambassador Luce as "sharp as a tack," "bright, brittle, decisive, a strong-minded person." Her outspoken comments sometimes got her in trouble, unlike Bunker who was scrupulous in avoiding anything untoward and displayed his customary sensitivity in his dealings with the Italians and with Washington. Ambassador Luce, these officers recalled, used her Washington connections to influence policy, notably in her persistent, high-level effort to bring about an active U.S. role in negotiating a Trieste settlement. Following the setback to de Gasperi's center coalition in the 1953 election, she famously urged the Eisenhower administration to encourage an "opening to the right" in Italian domestic politics, a new approach designed to bring the conservative Monarchist

Party into the Christian Democratic-led government. Bunker did not develop any important new initiatives during his tenure as Luce soon did. Much more reserved and cautious than she was, and, of course, much less glittering, he had accurately forecast that he would be the victim of invidious comparisons. "Surely you would not expect me to compete with that glamour," he warned his sister when rumors began to circulate that Luce might succeed him.[13]

The first major political event Bunker confronted was the local elections in Rome and Southern Italy, held in late May 1952. Although the threat the Communists and their allies posed was no longer considered the dangerous menace it had seemed before the Christian Democratic victory in the landmark 1948 parliamentary election, Bunker's embassy regarded these provincial and municipal contests as a test of confidence in de Gasperi's formula of liberal, mildly anti-Fascist democracy based on the parties of the center coalition. Many considered them a preview for the parliamentary election of 1953.[14]

The outcome was a setback for the center coalition. The Monarchist Party and the neo-Fascist Italian Social Movement (MSI), both with special appeal in the south, scored the most impressive advances. The Communist-Socialist bloc made lesser gains. The embassy took these results coolly; it forecast that the center coalition's now scant majority was unlikely to shrink further in the 1953 parliamentary election and might even increase slightly.[15] The historian H. Stuart Hughes later concluded that "The provincial elections . . . demonstrated that after seven years of rule de Gasperi's hold on the electorate was slipping."[16]

Despite his embassy's forecast, which in the event proved too optimistic, from that point until he left Italy two months before the June 1953 parliamentary vote, concern about its outcome strongly influenced Bunker's actions. Embassy messages repeatedly cited the parliamentary election in arguing for policies and programs that could improve the center coalition's prospects. Bunker personally appealed to senior Washington policymakers to take the election into account when making important decisions.[17] Under his control, and with his full approval, the CIA developed an expanded pre-election program of covert assistance to anti-Communist groups.[18]

This election-oriented approach was particularly evident in Bunker's handling of U.S. economic assistance. He took a major interest in the management of the program and was satisfied that under his direction the sprawling aid mission and the embassy's sizeable economic staff worked in close collaboration. His business experience helped him make the complex operations of the U.S. government in Italy what one of his deputies later admiringly termed a seamless web.[19] Confident that the aid program was well-managed and well-focused, Bunker wrote to the director of the Office of Western European affairs in the State Department that he considered inadequate the $80 million Fiscal Year 1953 (July 1952–June 1953) economic aid package that Washington agencies had been using for illustrative purposes. The figure should be between $110 and $130 million, he argued, because that amount was "cheap insurance for all that we have put in here and all that we have at stake in this crucial year."[20]

Bunker paid special attention to the off-shore procurement program, U.S. purchases from European producers of defense equipment and supplies for American and allied forces. In personal messages, he urged Secretary Acheson, Mutual Security Administrator Averell Harriman, Secretary of Defense Robert Lovett, and other senior administration officials to recognize the importance of buying more from Italian sources. He pointed out to his Washington audience that the program meant as many as 30,000 jobs in defense and allied industries, a major consideration in a country with two million unemployed. To show the Italians how significant he considered off-shore procurement, he often appeared at ceremonies related to the program. The embassy gave these events wide publicity. Bunker's messages to Washington seem to have had considerable impact there. Just before leaving Rome, he reported to the Italian defense minister that total off-shore procurement orders in Italy for Fiscal Year 1953 would reach new highs.[21]

Bunker recommended that in the pre-election period the United States not put too much pressure on the Italians to move forward with the planned buildup of their military forces, part of a NATO-wide expansion program. In his view, Washington should quietly urge the Italians to honor existing commitments but avoid calling on them to agree to further major undertakings. It had to be careful not to press the de Gasperi government to move more quickly than the Italian political situation permitted. It should also seriously consider limiting the size of U.S. civilian and military agencies in Italy so as to minimize the "overpowering ubiquity of Americans now in Europe engaged in defense operations."[22]

Bunker shared Washington's interest in resolving the Trieste problem in the pre-election period, or at least not exacerbating it. He played a major role in U.S. efforts to deal with this sensitive issue. The Italians were not reticent in pointing out that the status of Trieste would have an important bearing on the 1953 election. With this consideration no doubt in mind, U.S. policymakers resisted a British proposal to pressure de Gasperi to accept the partition of Trieste along the line that divided the territory into Anglo-American and Yugoslav zones of military administration. Washington knew that de Gasperi believed that this formula would go down badly with the Italian public and damage his political prospects. Despite Bunker's strong efforts, the Italian premier also rejected proposals more favorable to Italy that both the outgoing Democratic administration and its Republican successor subsequently put forward. De Gasperi bluntly told Bunker that if he acquiesced he would soon be out of office.

The Trieste problem thus remained unresolved when Bunker left Italy. It was finally settled in 1954 when his former deputy in Rome, Llewellyn Thompson, negotiated an agreement in London with British, Italian, and Yugoslav diplomats partitioning the territory between Italy and Yugoslavia, largely along the line that divided the zonal military administrations.[23] Bunker often maintained later that the groundwork he laid as ambassador paved the way for the eventual settlement of what had seemed an intractable problem during his time in Rome.

The United States was less willing to take de Gasperi's political concerns into account on the European Defense Community issue. Washington urged the Italians to ratify promptly the treaty Italy and other prospective participating countries had signed in May 1952. It held to this position despite the premier's fears that pressing the matter to a parliamentary vote could damage his coalition's election prospects. Bunker doubted that the Italians would complete the ratification process before the increasingly recalcitrant French did so. He reported that de Gasperi had told him several times that as long as there was no settlement of the Trieste issue, ratifying an arrangement that put Italian troops under foreign command would be difficult.[24] The Italians did not welcome the idea of losing control of their armed forces while Yugoslavia, their adversary on Trieste, retained full control of hers.

Despite Bunker's misgivings, Italy was second only to West Germany in moving the ratification process forward in early 1953. But, as he feared, the Italians never completed it. The process got caught up in election maneuvering. Under instructions from the State Department, Bunker made several unusually strong démarches to de Gasperi in an effort to resuscitate it, but was unsuccessful.[25] The Italians postponed ratification until after the election, and the subsequent fall of de Gasperi delayed it further. De Gasperi's successor as premier linked ratification to a Trieste settlement satisfactory to Italy. The French National Assembly ultimately took the Italians off the hook by rejecting the EDC in August 1954.

Bunker found Rome a demanding assignment personally. An ambassador's day is normally long and rugged, he recalled, but it was especially so in Italy. The huge U.S. economic assistance program and the presence in Naples of NATO's Southern Command, headed by an American admiral, imposed responsibilities on him that went well beyond those he shouldered in his "normal" diplomatic activity. Moreover, Italians took a long midday break, returned to their offices at five, and kept going until nine in the evening, and Bunker felt obliged to work a full American day and Italian hours on top of that. "Then you are either entertaining [at home] yourself or being entertained at receptions and dinners almost every day of the week," he complained mildly in a press interview later. "When I got back from Italy, I told my former colleagues in the business world 'if you want to know what hard work is you should go to work for the government.'"[26] He repeated this assessment throughout his diplomatic career, to the bemusement if not the outright disbelief of those who had remained in the private sector.

As he had in Argentina, Bunker traveled widely and made frequent speaking appearances throughout the country. At times he spoke in Italian. Starting from scratch, he began to study the language four hours a week soon after he arrived in Rome. He eventually reached a level of proficiency that allowed him to use it in short, set talks. Accent marks and other helpful hints to correct pronunciation cover the Italian texts of speeches available in his files. But he was never able to carry on a serious professional conversation in Italian with the country's leaders, and he recognized that this was a handicap.

Despite these minor problems, Bunker thoroughly enjoyed his second ambassadorship and was sorry to leave Rome as early as he did. Although he knew that Eisenhower's victory would lead to his early departure, he accepted the election returns in a graceful and philosophical way.[27] A few weeks later, George Weller suggested in the *Chicago Daily News* that Eisenhower would be making a mistake if he let Bunker go, and rumors soon circulated that the new administration would put him in charge of Latin American affairs at the State Department.[28] But nothing came of this. Nor did Eisenhower's secretary of state, John Foster Dulles, permit Bunker to remain in Rome to cover the Italian election, as he had requested. When Dulles visited Italy in late January 1953, he told Bunker that although it had originally been assumed that he would not be replaced until after the voting, the repeated postponement of the election had made the situation less certain.[29] In the event, Bunker departed two months before the balloting.

Before they left Rome in April 1953, de Gasperi hosted a dinner in the Bunkers' honor. In his valedictory toast, the premier urged Bunker to tell the American people that the Italians "have understood and share the principles and feeling which underlie the policy of cooperation into which the United States has put its tremendous resources and the enthusiasm of its youthful people." The ambassador, he said, had been "an authoritative and enthusiastic promoter of those policies in Italy."[30]

Bunker gave his own valedictory at a final meeting of his senior staff. He eloquently stressed his commitment to U.S. purposes in postwar Italy and his admiration for the men and women of the Foreign Service, people with whom he had worked in Rome. He concluded with a quote from Justice Oliver Wendell Holmes. Someone had asked Holmes what he considered the best service one could do for one's country and for oneself. He had replied, "To hammer out as compact and solid a piece of work as one can, to try to make it first rate, and to leave it unadvertised."[31]

It was a fair assessment of Bunker's accomplishments in his brief eleven months in Rome.

4
Red Cross President

Bunker remained a director of the National Sugar Refining Company during his assignments to Argentina and Italy. He sometimes spoke of returning to the sugar business following his ambassadorial assignments and presumably could have done so.[1] But his experiences in Buenos Aires and Rome had reinforced his interest in serving the country and he was determined to find another position in public life.

For the next few years, at least, diplomacy appeared out of the question. After two decades in the political wilderness, the Republicans were in no mood to offer a post to a man who was not only a registered Democrat but a friend—almost a protege—of Dean Acheson, their favorite whipping-boy. John Foster Dulles, the crusty, ambitious Republican lawyer and foreign policy specialist who succeeded him, had served in the Truman administration as Acheson's special assistant and chief U.S. negotiator of the peace treaty with Japan. Despite this recent experience in bipartisanship, he was not inclined to intervene on behalf of Bunker and other Democrats who wanted to continue their diplomatic careers. Although the press reported in May 1953 that the secretary's brother, Allen Dulles, the director of central intelligence, was considering making Bunker a special deputy at CIA, no more came of that story than of earlier speculation that he was to be given a post at the State Department. Only during its second term did the Eisenhower administration place a few Democrats in foreign affairs agencies, Bunker among them.

With positions elsewhere in the administration similarly off-limits to card-carrying Democrats, Bunker looked outside the federal government for ways to continue in public life. He found one in the leadership of the American Red Cross.

Since 1905, the American Red Cross had been headed by a prominent personage appointed by the president of the United States. In the early 1950s this was the wealthy New York banker and railroad executive E. Roland Harriman. After three years in the post, Harriman, who served as an unpaid volunteer, concluded that the Red Cross had become so large that it needed a full-time salaried chief executive officer resident at its Washington headquarters. At his initiative, the organization's by-laws were changed to provide for such a position, to be designated president. The unpaid White House appointee would henceforth be called chairman.

Bunker was in many ways a natural choice for the newly created position. He was a distinguished looking man who had successfully directed large organizations, enjoyed the respect of his peers, and had some degree of public recognition. His membership in the Democratic party was no bar. Although the Red Cross operated under a federal statute, the political affiliation of its head had never been a decisive consideration. Harriman, a Republican, had been appointed by a Democratic president and reappointed by a Republican one.

Bunker's friendship with Harriman, which dated back to their days as undergraduates in the Yale class of 1916, helped his candidacy. The two men moved in the same social circles, and although Bunker may not himself have made Harriman aware of his interest in further public service, the East Coast old boys' network would have told him about it. Harriman discussed Bunker's candidacy with President Eisenhower, who gave it his blessing. The Red Cross Board of Governors then elected Bunker president in mid-November on Harriman's nomination. He took over on January 1, 1954, a few months shy of his sixtieth birthday.

The job was an almost perfect fit for Bunker, probably as good a berth from virtually every viewpoint as any in public life to which he could reasonably have aspired under current political circumstances. It offered him an opportunity to direct a large, important, and universally recognized organization. It gave him high visibility and burnished his credentials as an outstanding public figure, not least at the White House, where he developed cordial relations with Eisenhower. The assignment also brought him to the favorable attention of groups until then unfamiliar with his record, such as veterans organizations and state governments. It gave him further international exposure and experience through contacts with foreign Red Cross organizations and the Geneva-based League of Red Cross Societies. Finally, the Red Cross presidency carried with it a substantial salary, an important consideration for Bunker. Harriman had been willing and able to serve without compensation. Bunker received $30,000 annually, much less than he had made at the National Sugar Refining Company but a generous sum in those days when cabinet secretaries were paid only $25,000 a year.

Bunker's salary sparked complaints from a few Red Cross old-timers, who considered it uncalled for. Harriman disagreed. "By accepting a salary of $30,000," he wrote one dissatisfied local chapter official, "Mr. Bunker becomes about the largest individual contributor to the Red Cross because had he decided to return to a business post he could have commanded a salary far in excess of that amount. . . . Whether we like it or not, it is becoming increasingly difficult to find a man with the proper stature who has the ability, time and wealth to spend all his energies directing the intricate machinery of the Red Cross without compensation."[2]

These complaints soon died away as Bunker took on the job. It was a big one. The Red Cross maintained a nationwide organization of more than 3,700 chapters covering every county in the United States. It employed 16,000 paid workers and could call on two million volunteers. Although it operated under congressional mandate, its funds came exclusively from voluntary contributions. The Red Cross used this money to assist individuals, families, and small businesses caught up in disaster. It cooperated closely with government agencies responsible for restoring damaged utilities and other public facilities. The largest portion of its budget and most of its paid national staff were devoted to providing an array of services for members of the armed forces, their families, and veterans.

From the start, Bunker insisted on getting an eye-witness view of areas hit by natural disasters and conferring on-the-spot with local officials and Red Cross volunteers about their activities. The year 1955, his second year in office, was particularly difficult for the Red Cross. Bunker described it as the worst year for disasters in the organization's seventy-five-year history.[3] Hurricanes and floods in the eastern states, a major flood in California, and several unusually destructive tornadoes elsewhere in the country led the Red Cross to provide over $27 million in relief to victims.

Bunker frequently visited the scene. A letter he sent his sister in late September 1955 catches the flavor of what he was doing: "Since seeing you I have been to Pennsylvania, where the destruction around Stroudsburg, East Stroudsburg and Scranton was terrific. Then I have been to the Port Jervis area in New York, the week before last in Rhode Island and Putnam [Connecticut] and the surrounding territory. Last week I went to Boston for the governor's conference and then to Springfield and the Western Massachusetts region. All in all it is going to be a big job and a long one."[4]

Reflecting the Cold War tensions of the time, one aspect of Bunker's job was the involvement of the Red Cross in civil defense preparations. Although civil defense was primarily a government responsibility, Bunker believed the Red Cross also had an important role. In the early 1950s, it had signed agreements with the Federal Civil Defense Administration spelling out operating details designed to ensure maximum coordination between the two organizations in what Bunker later called a "working partnership." Under his direction, the Red Cross stepped up its planning for its role in a national emergency. It took measures to ensure the operation of its national headquarters and area offices in the event of an enemy attack and developed an emergency protection system for its telecommunications network that would allow the organization to continue essential communications under catastrophic circumstances. Bunker also improved Red Cross liaison with other government organizations such as the Defense Department and the Office of Defense Mobilization. As he told delegates to the 1955 Red Cross national convention in Atlantic City: "The range of assistance required of us encompasses help in feeding, clothing, and sheltering displaced persons, training in first aid and home nursing, and participation to a larger degree in the essential blood program were we to face a war situation in this country. In any future conflict what the Red Cross does could well tip the balance of morale in our favor."[5]

Although the American Red Cross engaged in international activities such as disaster relief and blood programs with other national Red Cross organizations through the League of Red Cross Societies, these functions were sporadic and limited compared to its work in the United States. For a once and future diplomat like Bunker, they were valuable nonetheless. He particularly welcomed the opportunity to travel to the Soviet Union for the first and only time, in June 1956 as the guest of the Soviet Red Cross. He visited Moscow, Leningrad (St. Petersburg), Sochi on the Black Sea Coast, and Kiev in Ukraine and considered the trip a useful addition to his continuing education in foreign affairs. En route he called on the heads of the British and Finnish societies in London and Helsinki.

The Soviets treated him well. Bunker and his three American Red Cross colleagues were interviewed on Soviet television and went on VIP tours of the Kremlin in Moscow and the Hermitage in Leningrad. However, they did not meet any senior Soviet leaders despite the high-level contacts of the head of the Soviet Red Cross, Professor G. A. Miterev, who had served for seven years as Joseph Stalin's minister of health. Even on unscheduled stops caused by bad weather, Bunker found people hospitable and inquisitive about what was going on in the United States. But the trip was not always pleasant. Years later Bunker still recalled visiting a farmhouse on a collective near Kiev, the only family home he got to see, and finding a poster there of an American soldier bayoneting a Korean. "What about that poster," he asked Nicolai Tchikilenko, one of the Russians traveling with the party. "Oh," Tchikilenko had replied, "we must let bygones be bygones."[6]

Bunker's Soviet visit had one important result. In the eleven years since the end of World War II, the American Red Cross had sent hundreds of requests to its Soviet counterpart seeking information on behalf of persons living in the United States about relatives in the USSR with whom they had lost contact during the war. The Soviets never answered them. Bunker made an emotional appeal for responses, citing some particularly poignant cases. The Soviets listened to him politely, but made no promises. But within weeks of his visit the logjam broke. A torrent of replies began to flow from Moscow, so many in fact that it took months for the American Red Cross to track down all the inquiring families. This evidence of goodwill helped ensure a cordial welcome for Miterev and his associates when they came to the United States on a reciprocal visit some months later.

Bunker, no doubt recalling his inability to visit private houses in the USSR, insisted that Miterev come to his own home during the Russian's visit. Compared to their palatial ambassadorial residences in Buenos Aires and Rome, the house the Bunkers rented from a retired admiral on 30th Street in the Georgetown section of Washington must have seemed tiny to them. Bunker later described it as "one of these old houses that was sort of held together with baling wire and string," but said he had found it adequate and well-furnished.[7] The small size of the place surprised Professor Miterev. "Why Mr. Bunker," his host recalled him saying, "I thought you'd be living on a much grander scale." "Oh, I've always lived very modestly," Bunker lied.[8]

On his return from the Soviet Union in the summer of 1956, Bunker stopped in France and called privately on General Alfred M. Gruenther, the NATO commander. The purpose of this meeting became clear a few months later, when Bunker resigned as Red Cross president and Gruenther succeeded him.

Eisenhower, it seemed, had long wanted his close friend Al Gruenther to be available to him in Washington as an unofficial adviser. The general's term at NATO was drawing to a close, and the Red Cross national headquarters offered a convenient perch for him just a few blocks from the

White House. Eisenhower had assured Bunker before Bunker set out for Europe that an important diplomatic post would be his if he would step aside and make room for Gruenther. The general wanted to know more about the job before agreeing, hence the long unadvertised discussion with Bunker. Gruenther's knack for probing questions was legendary. When he was satisfied with Bunker's answers, the deal was done.[9]

Bunker's achievements at the Red Cross were widely hailed. The *New York Times* said editorially that "for three years the American Red Cross had been under the devoted and efficient management of one of the outstanding public servants of our time." It hoped that his leaving the Red Cross "cannot and will not be the end of Ellsworth Bunker's public career."[10] Eisenhower congratulated Bunker "upon the fine record of the organization under your able administration." Responding to Bunker's interest in "helping in some small way with the great and valiant work" in which the president was involved, Eisenhower wrote in his elliptical style: "May I say that I, too, look forward to our continued association, and that I am grateful for your willingness to be of further service to our government?"[11]

Soon afterwards the president kept his promise. He named Bunker ambassador to India, succeeding John Sherman Cooper.

5
In Nehru's India

The Eisenhower administration's first choice to be its ambassador in New Delhi had been James B. Conant, longtime president of Harvard and later ambassador to the Federal Republic of Germany. When Eisenhower learned from Secretary of State Dulles that Conant was reluctant to accept the assignment, he said he "would be perfectly glad to send Democrats to one or two diplomatic posts." Dulles suggested that Bunker might be good for India, and the president, who had already promised him an appointment, readily concurred.[1]

If Eisenhower wanted to throw a few bones to the opposition at a time when bipartisanship in foreign policy was in short supply, he could hardly have done better than to choose Bunker as his first Democratic diplomatic appointee. By 1956, Bunker had become a respected figure in public life and presided over an eminently nonpartisan, nationally recognized organization. His record in tough diplomatic assignments was widely lauded. Eisenhower and Dulles knew him well. His acquaintance with the secretary dated back to their Manhattan days, when Sullivan and Cromwell, Dulles's prestigious Wall Street law firm, represented the National Sugar Refining Company.

Bunker's conservative, patrician style and establishment associations no doubt appealed to both the president and Dulles. So, it seems likely, did the fact that Bunker, though an unabashed registered Democrat, was not active on the party's behalf nor closely associated with any of the prominent Democratic politicians of the day. He had not been publicly critical of the administration's foreign policies and did not hold views that significantly conflicted with them. For Eisenhower and Dulles, Bunker probably seemed more a public-spirited citizen who happened to be a Democrat than an opposition stalwart.

A brief stint as a member of the U.S. delegation to the 1956 session of the United Nations General Assembly further burnished Bunker's diplomatic credentials and helped prepare the way for his New Delhi appointment. However, the administration ran into unexpected difficulty when it sought, as custom required, to clear the appointment with the nominee's home state senators, Vermont Republicans George Aiken and Ralph Flanders. The problem was Aiken. The senator and Bunker had been on good terms for decades. Like many other Democrats, Bunker had voted for Aiken and even campaigned on his behalf. But the flinty old Vermonter had been angered by the active support Bunker's younger son Sam had given to the Democratic ticket in the recent presidential campaign.

Fortunately for Bunker, Senator Flanders and the Republican national committeeman from the state, Edward Janeway, weighed in strongly in favor of the nomination, and the recalcitrant Aiken was soon persuaded to go along. With his concurrence, the nomination was sent on November 17 to the Senate, which was then in recess. Bunker was sworn in as ambassador on December 7. After Congress reconvened, the Senate gave its approval by unanimous voice vote on January 25, 1957.

Recess appointments offend Senate sensibilities and are usually made only when there is an urgent need for the nominee to take office. The administration had put Bunker on a fast track not to hurry him out to India—where he arrived only in March—but to enable him to participate as ambassador in the landmark visit of Indian Prime Minister Jawaharlal Nehru to the United States in mid-December 1956. It was during this visit, which Nehru's biographer Sarvepalli Gopal has rightly said "initiated a new phase" in U.S.-Indian relations, that Bunker and the prime minister first met.[2] Bunker was present throughout Nehru's four-day stay, except for the fourteen hours when the Indian leader and Eisenhower were alone at the president's Gettysburg farm. Getting to know Nehru and making a good first impression on him in the setting of the visit were important advantages for Bunker in establishing a relationship that would be crucial to the success of his mission. Eisenhower did his part, readily agreeing to the State Department's recommendation that he take the opportunity the visit offered to heighten his new ambassador's standing in the eyes of the prime minister.

Bunker was briefly concerned about the effect New Delhi's heat and dust might have on Harriet. But once the State Department medical authorities gave her a clean bill of health he enthusiastically welcomed the assignment. Like his posting to Rome, his first exposure to European diplomacy, it would be a new experience for him. Before he came to New Delhi as ambassador, he had not set foot in India or any other Asian country. Nor is there any evidence that he had given much thought to that part of the world. His association with the broader Third World that Nehru's

India aspired to lead was similarly limited. Apart from his occasional, much overblown connections with Mexico and the Caribbean, he had had little to do with developing countries and the daunting problems they faced in their quest for economic progress, political stability, and international recognition.

This inexperience did not prevent him from becoming, in the view of generations of Indians and Americans knowledgeable about U.S.-Indian relations, one of the most highly regarded ambassadors Washington sent to New Delhi. His effectiveness did not rest on popular appeal to the Indian people or on a public identification with India, in the manner of Chester Bowles and John Kenneth Galbraith, probably the two best-known U.S. envoys to India. Rather, Bunker's skill lay in managing the ties between the two governments and in cultivating a relationship with Nehru that was more professional than personal. For his part, Bunker came to regard his posting to India as by far the most professionally and personally satisfying of his ambassadorial assignments. He developed an abiding interest in the country and continued to follow developments there with warm concern for the rest of his life.

As Bunker's five predecessors in New Delhi could attest, the job of American ambassador to India was no bed of roses.[3] In the near decade between India's winning its independence and Bunker's arrival there, U.S.-Indian relations had often been troubled, not so much by bilateral problems as by fundamental differences in the policies the two countries adopted to deal with the Cold War, the dominant feature of international affairs in those years. The Nehru government dismissed the American assessment that the principal danger to world peace stemmed from a thrust for global domination by a seemingly monolithic communist bloc led by the Soviet Union. It strongly opposed Washington's efforts to bolster the security of the "free world" by an array of multilateral and bilateral military pacts and considered these likely to increase, not reduce, the danger of a third world war. It called instead for nonalignment between the two rival power blocs and the creation of a "zone of peace" comprising Third World nations that followed India's nonaligned lead. In its view, this approach could help relieve world tensions and promote international good will. The recent experience of India's struggle for independence from a white imperial power heightened its opposition to Western colonialism and "neo-colonialism" and its sensitivity to real or alleged manifestations of racism.

Except, as some critics caustically noted, in places like Kashmir where its own interests were directly involved, India advocated peaceful resolution of international disputes. It was convinced that without peace the country would be unable to achieve the economic development required to alleviate its desperate poverty.

These basic differences had surfaced in U.S.-Indian disagreements over many contentious issues in the 1940s and 1950s, including the Korean War, the rise of the People's Republic of China, armed struggles in Vietnam and elsewhere in Southeast Asia, and, especially in Bunker's time, the stubborn refusal of the Portuguese to abandon their enclaves in India.[4]

But important as they were to U.S.-Indian relations, these difficulties were overshadowed by an issue of much greater and more immediate concern to Indian interests: the security relationship between the United States and Pakistan initiated in 1954. The Nehru government was unmoved by the American contention that this tie was an important element in "free world" efforts to contain Communist aggression. It recognized that the link between Pakistan and the United States and its allies would destroy the natural balance of power in South Asia and undermine Indian preeminence there. It believed, correctly, that in joining the Western camp Pakistan had been primarily moved not by anti-Communist fervor but by an interest in strengthening itself against India. Dismissing Eisenhower's offer of similar military assistance, the Indians scoffed at the president's pledge to act should Pakistan improperly use American-supplied arms against them. They turned increasingly to the Soviet Union for support, further complicating Indian relations with the United States.[5]

By the time Bunker presented his credentials to President Rajendra Prasad on March 4, 1957, U.S.-Indian relations had bottomed out, to use historian H. W. Brands's phrase, but were still far from smooth. Nehru's visit to the United States, one of many that foreign leaders made to Washington following Eisenhower's reelection, was important in turning the tide. The president had by then become more receptive to the nonaligned policies the prime minister had long advocated. His interest in better relations with India was strengthened by concern over the inroads the post-Stalin Soviet Union seemed to have made there and elsewhere in the Third World by adopting more flexible positions toward non-Communist developing countries and offering them generous economic assistance programs and trade agreements. Eisenhower and others in Washington were looking for ways to counter these evident Soviet gains, which they believed could dangerously undercut U.S. interests.

For his own reasons, Nehru shared Eisenhower's desire for stronger ties. If he had always rejected the notion that nonalignment implied equidistance between the Western and Communist blocs, he also recognized that it was not in India's interest to drift too close to either. The contrasting actions of the two global superpowers in the weeks just before his visit to Washington—Soviet military intervention in Hungary and U.S. opposition to the Anglo-French invasion of Suez—may have helped persuade the prime minister that India should follow a less pro-Soviet line than it had. India's need for American assistance for its ambitious Second Five Year Plan, launched in April 1956, also impelled him to seek more amicable relations with Washington.

Although they broke little new ground, Eisenhower and Nehru had candid, friendly exchanges that produced a better understanding of one another's policies and concerns as well as a higher personal regard. Their mutual esteem, reinforced by a frequent exchange of letters, was an important element in the improvement that took place in U.S.-Indian relations during the second Eisenhower administration, the period of Bunker's ambassadorship then about to begin.

American envoys to New Delhi in the 1950s faced special difficulties aside from the problems caused by the basic differences between U.S. and Indian policies. Although Eisenhower had eventually developed good working relations with Nehru, many influential Americans distrusted the Indians and the policies they followed at home (considered too leftist) and abroad (too pro-Soviet). Many Indians had comparable misgivings about America. This mutual disdain was heightened by misperceptions and misunderstandings resulting from cultural differences and the limited contact historically between the two peoples.[6] Americans and Indians seemed to have a peculiar ability to rub one another the wrong way, an unhappy quality some attributed to their shared tendency to be annoyingly self-righteous and preachy. Moreover, few senior American officials had any deep knowledge of India or its problems. The encounters they did have with Indians, often at contentious international conferences, were rarely of the sort from which warm and confident relations develop.

Practicing his diplomatic skills in this unpromising environment, an American ambassador needed to represent U.S. positions fairly and accurately while at the same time doing his best to avoid giving offense to touchy Indian interlocutors who disagreed with them. He had to formulate recommendations that took account of Indian policies and sensitivities yet did not make him look "soft" on India to Washington. If he believed, as most ambassadors to New Delhi have, that India merited U.S. support, he had to make that case in ways that convincingly reflected both American interests and Indian economic and political realities. His job was made more complicated by the conviction many Indians had held since Chester Bowles's ambassadorship in the early 1950s that the proper standard for judging an American chief of mission in New Delhi was his willingness to argue India's cause in high places in Washington and his effectiveness in that role.

Inevitably, the personality and demeanor of the ambassador were important in determining how successfully he could steer through these diplomatic and bureaucratic shoals. Bunker was particularly fortunate in this respect. Jagat Singh Mehta, a senior Indian foreign ministry official who later became foreign secretary, recalled that Bunker "commanded great respect in Government and in influential circles in India. . . . He was every inch patrician with dignity in dress and demeanor, never succumbing to populism or pretending to imitate [Indian ways]. . . . He was a good listener[,] showing immense patience but in the end persuasive to hammer [out] feasible compromises."[7]

These traits stood Bunker in good stead with Nehru. The prime minister generally considered Americans brash, clumsy, and self-centered people, an attitude commonly attributed to his education in upper-class Edwardian England and his leftist political leanings. Nehru had had difficult relations with at least two of Bunker's predecessors, Loy Henderson and George Allen. But it seems likely that in the patrician personality of Bunker the aristocratic, well-educated, worldly Indian leader recognized a fellow elitist quite different from earlier American ambassadors, a man with whom he could deal on a basis of mutual regard and trust.

It is difficult to overstate Nehru's importance and prestige on the Indian and international scenes in the mid-1950s. Prime minister since Indian independence, he held unchallenged sway over both the government and the ruling Congress party. As minister of external affairs, he was the principal architect of India's foreign policy and was intimately involved in managing its diplomacy. He also developed the main features of much of Indian domestic policy. In these areas, unlike foreign affairs, he sometimes encountered dogged opposition, mainly from those critical of his proposals for economic and social reform.

Nehru was recognized abroad as perhaps the most outstanding figure in the Third World, a major statesman who had become a force to be reckoned with in international affairs despite his country's limited economic and military strength. The growing willingness of both the Western and Communist blocs to abandon their opposition to the nonaligned, independent foreign policies that Nehru pursued and promoted elsewhere in the Third World had enhanced his standing. So had the diplomatic and peacekeeping roles India had played under his leadership in Korea, Indochina, and other areas of Cold War confrontation. Although Nehru's foreign (and domestic) policies had their detractors in the United States and elsewhere in the West, he was widely admired there, especially by liberals, for his efforts to bring about economic development and social equity in a democratic setting.

Bunker treated Nehru with great respect. But he was too levelheaded and self-confident to be overawed by him. He enjoyed good access to Nehru and furthered this by delivering personally the texts of messages Eisenhower sent the prime minister. He regarded this correspondence as an important way to strengthen U.S.-Indian relations and at times suggested specific topics Eisenhower could usefully raise. His calls on the prime minister were impersonal and related to diplomatic business. He did not use them to offer unsolicited advice on Indian domestic policies except when these were directly related to U.S. activities in India, such as economic assistance programs. In Bunker's view, such intrusive freewheeling, whether in private sessions with Nehru and other government officials or in public presentations to broader audiences, went beyond the range of activities appropriate for an American ambassador.

Bunker spelled out his assessment of Nehru most comprehensively in a Columbia University oral history interview recorded in 1979, eighteen years after he completed his New Delhi assignment:

Nehru was . . . the indispensable man. . . . I don't think there was anybody else in [India] who could have held the country together and enable it to coalesce as Mr. Nehru did, . . . not only because of his ability but because of the image he projected as a leader. . . . Like everybody, he had his defects. I think . . . that he perhaps was weaker on economics than he was on politics. I think he put too much emphasis on industrialization to the neglect of agriculture.[8]

On the other hand, . . . he was a very skillful politician, much more so than [his daughter Prime Minister Indira] Gandhi.[9] He had a much more mature and broader view of the problems of India. And of the world. And of India's relations with the rest of the world, and, I think steered India on a very skillful course during that period.

He was not the easiest man sometimes to deal with. . . . Malcolm MacDonald [British High Commissioner to India] . . . said when you went to see Mr. Nehru, you never knew which Mr. Nehru you were going to meet. Which was true in a way. He had his moods. . . . But I found him very responsive really. . . . So my relations with him . . . couldn't have been more satisfactory or more congenial, as far as I was concerned.

A few weeks after Nehru's visit, in January 1957, Eisenhower signed National Security Council (NSC) report 5701. The document stressed India's strategic significance to the United States and accepted its nonaligned foreign policy. It recognized that a strong, independent, non-Communist India would occasionally challenge U.S. programs and activities. Nonetheless, it concluded, such an India "would be a successful example of an alternative to Communism in an Asian context and would permit the gradual development of the means to enforce its external security interests against Communist Chinese expansion into South and Southeast Asia." The report called for expanded U.S. economic and technical assistance to help the Nehru government achieve the goals of the Indian Second Five Year Plan (1956–61), which it termed "the best vehicle for action to promote U.S. interests in an independent and stable India."[10]

Bunker was still in Washington when the president accepted NSC report 5701 but does not appear to have participated in drafting it. Once in India, he enthusiastically supported efforts to implement its recommendations and those spelled out in similar policy papers that followed it. During his four-year tenure, he worked to strengthen U.S.-Indian relations and persuade other policymakers that the United States had an important stake in India and the success of the Nehru government. For him, India was "key to the direction things will take in this part of the world."[11]

Bunker generally accepted India as he found it, or as the Nehru government was trying to make it. He reflected later that Nehru had put too much emphasis on the public sector and rapid industrialization at the expense of private enterprise and the expansion of agricultural production. But if he had similar misgivings while he was ambassador, they did not lessen his call for generous U.S. support for the Second Five Year Plan, which enunciated those priorities. The next few years would be critical ones for Indian economic development, he told Secretary Dulles when they met in

June 1957 as India was coming to grips with an unprecedented foreign exchange crunch that impaired its economic prospects. "If [development] proceeded well we could reasonably anticipate a prosperous, stable and democratic India. If it did not . . . , there was a strong probability of the accession to power of some kind of extremist government."[12] He held that the most likely beneficiary of such a scenario would be the Communists. The cost to the United States would be high, "even higher than the loss of China to the Free World."[13]

In embassy cables, personal letters to Eisenhower and Dulles, and persistent lobbying on Capitol Hill and elsewhere during his visits to Washington, Bunker enthusiastically supported a generous level of U.S. economic assistance. His approach was nonideological, as Eisenhower's had become when he adopted what Dennis Merrill has called "a tolerant attitude toward India's mixed economy."[14] "There are faults in India['s] organization of its development programs," Bunker acknowledged in August 1958 as the plan neared its halfway mark. But "these should not obscure the facts of [the programs'] success to date and the strengths inherent in India's resources and will to develop."[15] The important thing was to help India help itself, not to quarrel with it over what policies could best bring about economic and social progress. "Our views and those of India differ at a good many points," he wrote Dulles, "and as a result it is sometimes difficult to keep one's mind on the overriding objective of making it possible for India to stay on the right track and, through her example, to lead the rest of uncommitted Asia to do the same. But if we now render the assistance that we believe will enable India to maintain and consolidate her democratic institutions, I feel sure that future generations will look to your Administration as the architect of democracy and freedom in Asia."[16]

Unlike some other administration policymakers and many members of Congress, Bunker saw nothing wrong in the United States providing funds to Indian government-owned enterprises. The Indians, he said, were pragmatic in their approach to investments, and their use of the word "socialism" should not frighten Americans. Aid should be "flexible as between project and other types of aid and as between the public and private sectors: . . . we should not be doctrinaire about this," he urged the president, who agreed.[17]

Bunker's support for proposed loans to the public sector included enthusiastic backing for the most controversial of these, a massive outlay to help India build a fourth government-owned-and-operated steel mill.[18] Against strong opposition from the U.S. Atomic Energy Commission, he called for U.S. financing of an Indian nuclear power plant, also in the public sector. "If the United States stayed out of the public sector . . . , [it] would be left to the USSR to exploit, and the Indians would believe that we were trying to impose our system of free enterprise on India," he told the National Security Council in 1959.[19]

At the same time, Bunker wanted American business made aware of the continuing vitality of India's private sector and urged U.S. government agencies to do what they could to stimulate private American investment in the country. He welcomed the many official U.S. trade missions that visited India. And, as he had in Argentina, he used his background as a businessman to explain to Indians that the capitalism practiced in the post-war West was not the evil and unjust system many of them thought it was.

In calling for increased economic assistance, Bunker and his embassy frequently cited the growing volume of Soviet aid to India. These arguments reinforced Washington's concern over Moscow's Third World strategy and were at least partly designed to do so. An embassy officer close to Bunker has reflected that he "was not really disturbed by the close relations between the Soviet Union and India and, while he never said so officially, he thought that the Indian problem was too great to be the burden of one particular country. . . . If the Russians wanted to engage in a large-scale assistance program with India, so much the better."[20] Bunker publicly acknowledged that, in the short run, Soviet assistance could assist in achieving the U.S. objective of promoting Indian economic development. "But," he added, "the Soviets were looking fifteen or twenty years ahead. At that time it might be found that India would not have made sufficient progress and this [Soviet aid] would increase the country's vulnerability to its own Communist Party."[21]

Bunker argued that "[while] the economic soundness of a given project must continue to be the basic factor determining eligibility for U.S. aid, [it is also] necessary that the end result . . . make the Indian people conscious of the magnitude of U.S. assistance, both absolutely and in relation to the Soviet effort, and . . . identify its purpose with Indian interests."[22] Such projects should deliver a product or service the general public could easily understand. They needed to address a commonly recognized problem, or appeal to national pride. He saw a major role for the large U.S. Information Service program in publicizing aid. To make the assistance program more effective, Bunker asserted, assistance should be appropriated on a three-year cycle rather than for single years, as was then the practice.

Bunker had many important allies in his effort to increase economic assistance to India. Eisenhower strongly favored higher aid levels; in FY (fiscal year) 1957 he made expanded assistance to the Nehru government a top administration priority.[23] Softening his objection to Indian nonalignment, Dulles followed. India's cause was helped by the resignation in 1957 of Treasury Secretary George Humphrey, a free-enterprise advocate, and the strongly positive position C. Douglas Dillon adopted as under secretary of state. In the Democratic-controlled Congress, Senators John F. Kennedy of Massachusetts and Hubert H. Humphrey of Minnesota took the lead. They were joined by Representative Chester Bowles, elected to the House from Connecticut in 1958, five years after returning from India. It was Bowles who had first popularized the idea that the outcome of the competition between democratic India and Communist China in economic development would have a profound effect elsewhere in the Third World and hence on American interests.[24] The Eisenhower administration endorsed Bowles's argument and Bunker enthusiastically supported it. On the Republican side of the aisle, another former ambassador to New Delhi, Bunker's immediate predecessor Senator John Sherman Cooper of Kentucky, strongly championed India. Influential MIT professors Walt W. Rostow and Max Millikan provided a persuasive Cold War justification for greatly expanded U.S. assistance to the Third World, especially to India, which they regarded as a model aid recipient.[25]

By the end of Eisenhower's second term, direct U.S. development assistance to India had tripled, from $60 million in FY 1957 to $181 million in FY 1961. These funds supplemented assistance provided through the Export-Import Bank and multilateral financial institutions, such as the World Bank. The United States had also begun supplying India massive quantities of food grains under Public Law 480. In May 1960, the Eisenhower administration agreed to provide India sixteen million tons of wheat and a million tons of rice over a four-year period. Their total value was over $1.5 billion.

Bunker had aggressively campaigned for the agreement, by far the biggest the United States had ever made with any country under PL-480 and certainly one of the most important accomplishments of his New Delhi tenure. He argued that by providing grain on such a massive scale the United States would not only help India meet its food needs in the early 1960s; it would also make a major contribution to the Nehru government's own efforts to relieve the country's most pressing problem, the failure of agricultural production to keep pace with population growth. The rupee proceeds of the sale of the grain to Indian consumers were to be used to finance major expansion of agricultural development projects, greater U.S. technical assistance for agriculture, and other programs to raise food grain production. PL-480 proponents contended that the large outlay would allow the United States to exercise greater influence on Indian food and agricultural policies in the Third Five Year Plan (1961–66) then being formulated.

As Bunker put it, PL-480 "presents a unique opportunity for the United States to meld the different elements of land aid programs into an integrated and consequently more effective whole. By this planning in advance PL-480 rupees can become an instrument of policy rather than a mere bookkeeping problem."[26] He also held that the food aid would effectively counter Soviet propaganda and help the political prospects of the outspokenly pro-American minister for food and agriculture, S. K. Patil. Patil, Congress party boss of Bombay and one of Bunker's favorite Indian politicians, had first proposed the program.

To underscore the importance of the initiative, Eisenhower himself signed the PL-480 agreement amid great fanfare. Not surprisingly, the shipments of grain that followed became a major theme in U.S. public information programs in India. Bunker and his successors invariably made their way to the Bombay docks to see and be seen at the grain-unloading operation.

But for all the hype, the program failed to achieve its basic purpose. Instead of boosting food production and permitting the United States to exercise a beneficial influence on Indian policy, as Bunker and others had expected, the availability of American grain dissuaded the Indians from taking the self-help measures necessary to break the stagnation in agricultural output. They concluded that they could always rely on the United States for cheap food. Not until President Lyndon Johnson took personal charge of food policy later in the decade did Washington insist that the Indian government adopt the major policy reforms that led to the Green Revolution in food grain production.

Bunker also called for measures in the political and political-military areas that he believed could supplement expanded economic assistance in strengthening U.S.-Indian ties. Although he accepted the U.S. security relationship with Pakistan as a difficult fact of life,—it was, he rightly said, "the greatest single liability that the United States has in its relationship with India"—he tried to lessen its impact. In his first year in

New Delhi he urged Washington to reject Pakistani requests for arms specifically designed to counter India or larger than he judged Pakistan needed to meet its collective security obligations.[27] Later, when increasing tension between India and Communist China made the Nehru government more interested in acquiring American aircraft and missiles, he called on Washington to make them available. Like many other U.S. policymakers, Bunker saw in the collapse of the era of Sino-Indian good feeling an opportunity to enhance U.S. influence in India and reduce the importance to Indians of American support for Pakistan.

At a White House meeting in April 1960, Bunker stressed to Eisenhower the tension that recent U.S. supply to Pakistan of Sidewinder missiles and high-performance F-104 aircraft had caused in India. The Indians feared that the equipment would make their air force obsolete. Bunker suggested to the president that "this source of friction could be overcome if, when we give Pakistan more modern military equipment, we . . . also offer to sell similar equipment to India."[28]

Eisenhower responded favorably. But a month later, when the Indians asked for Sidewinders with Bunker's strong support, the president reversed himself and concurred with the State Department recommendation to deny the request. The department maintained that Pakistan, as a "wholehearted ally," deserved better treatment than nonaligned India.[29] This remained U.S. policy on the issue even after Washington began to ship large quantities of hardware to India following the outbreak of the 1962 Sino-Indian border war.[30]

Washington was more willing to sell India less sophisticated equipment it could use in confronting China. A few weeks before the Indians made their unsuccessful request for the Sidewinders, Defense Minister V. K. Krishna Menon asked Bunker for urgent delivery of twenty-nine Fairchild C-119 transport planes to help supply Indian forces along the Sino-Indian border. The ambassador cabled Washington recommending approval: it was "clearly in our interest to do everything possible to stiffen the Indian government's position vis-à-vis Communist China." The sale would also offer the United States an opportunity to establish closer relations with the Indian armed forces.[31] At Bunker's urging, the U.S. Air Force provided aircraft from its own stocks within a few days.

To Bunker's consternation, Krishna Menon took credit for the prompt delivery. People said he could not get anything out of the Americans, he told Bunker, and this showed that they were wrong. If Bunker reported this comment to Washington, it could only have struck a very sour note

there. Though Bunker himself was personally somewhat fond of the iras-
cible minister, Krishna Menon's frequent anti-American polemics kept
him high on the Eisenhower administration's blacklist. Washington was
reluctant to develop significant security relations with India while he
headed its defense establishment.[32]

During Bunker's tenure, and at all other times before and since,
the future of the disputed state of Kashmir was and has remained the
most important obstacle to improved relations between India and Pakistan. With varying degrees of enthusiasm and uniform lack of success,
successive U.S. administrations have tried to help resolve this persistent
problem. Eisenhower's administration, like Truman's, recognized that
settlement of the Kashmir dispute was important for the stability and economic progress of South Asia. In its view, the dispute sapped the ability
and willingness of the two countries to confront the threat of Communist aggression and subversion. Washington recognized that U.S. support
for U.N. resolutions calling for self-determination for Kashmir through
a U.N.-administered plebiscite remained a constant thorn in its relations
with New Delhi. Although the Nehru government had initially pledged to
give the people of Kashmir the right to decide their own future, it later took
the position that the state was a permanent part of India and the matter
settled.

Bunker quickly reached his own conclusions about the Kashmir problem. Six weeks after he arrived in New Delhi, he warned Washington that
"no solution based upon a U.N. plebiscite can be considered either constructive or realistic." Nehru and his government were convinced that a
plebiscite would jeopardize India's vital interests and stability. "I am not
yet prepared to say whether [their] conviction . . . is sound or not," he
cabled, "but I do believe it is what [they] deeply feel and that this fact con-
stitutes a reality which foreign governments have to face."[33] There is no
available evidence concerning Bunker's views on the terms of an eventual
Kashmir settlement. His focus was on process. Recalling his experience in
dealing with the Trieste dispute as ambassador to Italy, he recommended
that it might be best to let tempers cool, await the arrival of governments
able to agree to a settlement, and then undertake behind-the-scenes private and confidential negotiations. "In Trieste," he wrote, "neither side
[Italy or Yugoslavia] renounced its claim, but I believe the settlement is
now accepted as final and fair. Perhaps something similar may be indi-

cated here with possible approach to overall settlements of Indo-Pakistan problems."[34]

Bunker reiterated his call for freezing the Kashmir issue six months later when India angrily opposed a U.S.-British-sponsored draft resolution at the United Nations that called again for a plebiscite.[35] By that time, the State Department was considering a comprehensive package that would deal with three major problems between India and Pakistan: Kashmir, the division of the waters of the Indus river system, and the accelerating arms race. Bunker supported and helped refine this approach. He recommended that Washington make the package more attractive by offering increased economic assistance, but advised against reducing aid if India or Pakistan rejected the proposed initiative.

Eisenhower enthusiastically approved the package proposal, which included a personal role for him in launching the discussions. Although the Pakistanis accepted in principle the president's offer of friendly assistance to bring the Indian and Pakistan prime ministers together to consider the proposal, Nehru turned it down. Reasserting India's bilateral approach to Kashmir and other disputes with Pakistan, he held that no third party could intervene in a matter that the two governments ultimately had to settle themselves. He saw no hope that the weak regime then in power in Karachi would abandon what he considered the intransigent and hateful policy toward India that successive Pakistani governments had pursued since 1947.[36]

Bunker tried to put the best face on Nehru's rebuff. He hoped the Pakistanis (and presumably Eisenhower) would understand that it applied only to method, not to objective. "This is and has always looked to be a long-range matter," he suggested. Nehru should not be pressed and might be more willing to discuss the issues when he had seen the results of the Pakistan elections scheduled for later in the year and developments in the Indus Waters negotiations then being held under World Bank auspices.[37]

Despite these brave words, nothing further came of the Eisenhower initiative. The advent of a strong, stable Pakistan government under General Mohammad Ayub Khan following a military coup in September 1958 did not lead Nehru to change his view of the *bona fides* of the Pakistanis in seeking to settle the Kashmir problem and other controversial bilateral issues. However, the World Bank did succeed in negotiating a treaty that resolved the Indus Waters dispute. The United States contributed substantially to the funding of the new waterways and dams called for by the treaty, which was signed in 1960.

Bunker eventually concluded that it would be best to follow a step-by-step approach in seeking to improve Indo-Pakistan relations. "[T]he Kashmir dispute will probably be the last problem to be solved by this . . . process," he asserted at a high-level Washington briefing in August 1959.[38] When Eisenhower was about to visit India (and Pakistan) a few months later, Bunker wisely advised the president that any offer he made Nehru to assist in resolving the Kashmir problem would be premature. "The question is still too highly charged with emotion and deep-seated feeling on his part arising out of history."[39]

As many other Americans did in the 1950s (and afterwards), Bunker valued the Indian democratic system and believed that the United States had an important stake in its success. He held that Americans, as citizens of a country that had benefited so much from revolutionary political, economic, and social change, should sympathize with Indian aspirations to raise living standards, reduce the gap between rich and poor, and develop sound social institutions, all through democratic means. Though many years later he told an interviewer that India needed a more authoritarian system than was found in the West, he did not disclose this view during his posting as ambassador, if indeed he held it at that time.[40]

At the same time, Bunker believed that an ambassador should focus on state-to-state diplomacy. Unlike many diplomats assigned to India, he was not fascinated by the Indian political process. He came to know many Indian political leaders and became fairly friendly with a number of them, mostly senior figures of conservative views. But as he had elsewhere, he left political reporting and analysis largely to his staff and relied on them to keep him informed of important developments, especially those that influenced U.S. interests in India. If he had any views on controversial domestic political issues of the day, he was careful not to convey these to his Indian interlocutors.

Nonetheless, he was not above intervening in Indian politics when he thought that doing so was important for achieving American objectives in India. As noted, in arguing for massive PL-480 food grain shipments he contended that the program would strengthen the political standing of S. K. Patil, the ambitious, pro-American minister of food and agriculture. He also recommended that political considerations be taken into account when determining the location of U.S.-supported projects. He wanted greater attention paid to West Bengal, a politically volatile state in eastern India where the Communist Party of India (CPI) enjoyed considerable popular support. But the most far-reaching U.S. intervention into Indian domestic politics during Bunker's New Delhi tenure came in Kerala, a small state in the southwestern corner of the country where the CPI had formed a government following its victory in the 1957 state legislative assembly election.

The CPI's success marked the first time a Communist government had come to power anywhere in the world in a free and fair vote. As Dennis Kux has pointed out, the election results "rang alarm bells in Washington," where "preventing additional Keralas became an important argument for augmenting U.S. assistance to India."[41] The Eisenhower administration at first adopted a wait-and-see attitude toward the CPI state government, but soon became more hostile. Bunker's embassy concurred with Washington's approach and made recommendations for implementing it. Eventually, a clandestine Central Intelligence Agency operation was mounted to help dislodge the Communists from power. This apparently involved agency funding for political demonstrations, organized by the Congress party and other opposition groups, that were designed to create a law and order situation sufficiently chaotic to justify the central government's dismissal of the Kerala administration. Citing such internal turmoil, New Delhi forced the Communists out in 1959.

The CIA's role in Kerala did not surface until Daniel Patrick Moynihan, who was American ambassador to India in the early 1970s, briefly acknowledged it in his 1978 book, *A Dangerous Place*.[42] The disclosure caused an uproar in India, especially since Moynihan had fingered former prime minister Indira Gandhi as the recipient of the clandestine funds. Mrs. Gandhi, who as prime minister often denounced the CIA, had been president of the ruling Congress party when the Kerala Communists were ousted. She had aggressively called for their dismissal and persuaded the central government led by her father to accept her position.[43] She angrily termed Moynihan's allegation "malicious, motivated, and absolutely baseless," but he stood by it.[44]

In an oral history interview he gave soon after Moynihan's book was published, Bunker admitted his own involvement. He expressed no regrets about the operation. He contended that the CIA had provided financial assistance to the Congress party because the embassy had hard evidence that the Soviets were funding the local Communists, "as they have done everywhere, all over the world. . . . But as we have done elsewhere in the world," he went on, "we've come to the assistance of our friends when we knew and had evidence [of] what the Communists were doing, financially and in other ways."

Bunker said the decision to provide funds was made "in Washington. . . . But then I had leeways [*sic*] and discretion as to how it might be done and in what amounts." He recalled that S. K. Patil, not Mrs. Gandhi, had been the intermediary. The agency, he said, had had "very good and very close" relations with Indian intelligence and was able to get from them "pretty good evidence as to what was going on and in what amounts."[45]

Bunker often seemed to act more like a senior Foreign Service officer than a political appointee. But he disagreed with those in the service's old guard who held that an ambassador should confine himself to diplomatic representation and political reporting and pay minimal attention to activities such as public affairs and economic assistance that had become important in the conduct of U.S. foreign policy after World War II. Meeting with a great variety of Indians, many of them impressed and flattered by his courtesy and interest, Bunker worked hard if unobtrusively to publicize and explain U.S. policies and programs. In doing so, he displayed great stamina and endurance for a man in his mid-sixties; one of his staff aides recalled that he averaged twelve to fourteen hours a day on the job. His extensive travels, which he urged his staff to emulate, took him to every one of India's fifteen states. "We have traveled the length and breadth of [India]," he said shortly before completing his assignment, "from the Burma border to western-most Saurashtra, from the high Himalayas to as far as we could go without getting our feet wet."[46] His style in the many public speeches he gave on the road and in New Delhi was deliberate and unremarkable. Speaking in English—like all but a few ambassadors to India he did not learn Hindi—he tried to avoid confrontation and controversy. His texts tended to be rich in platitudes. This may have made them rather tiresome to American ears. But it was no drawback in a country where such cliches were accepted as the stuff of public discourse and much admired if they were delivered with the appearance of sincerity, as Bunker did so well.

Bunker did not regard his formal public appearances or his travels around the country as opportunities for the dramatic, eye-catching front-page photos many other American diplomats assigned to Third World countries have sought. He avoided crowd-pleasing gestures like hauling in fish nets or wading in rice paddies. The pictures of him that appeared in the Indian newspapers usually showed a distinguished gray-haired gentle-man in a well tailored, often three-piece suit, signing an agreement with an Indian counterpart or delivering a prepared text. He stuck to the same old-fashioned suit-and-tie style when he was in his embassy office. Not for him the bush shirts and sandals in vogue among many Westerners in India then and later.

As good ambassadors do, Bunker thought it important to cultivate the press. He recalled that when he first entered public life he had been warned to be shy of the media. "But the more I thought about it the more I came to believe that, if what we were trying as a nation to achieve in the world and what I was trying to do in carrying out our national purposes were going to succeed, it would be possible only if backed by an informed and enlightened public opinion . . . created . . . through a frank exchange of views with the press."[47] He held regular informal, off-the-record sessions with American journalists stationed in New Delhi. Bunker's press atta-ché Eugene Rosenfeld recalls that the ambassador saw them as two-way streets: opportunities for him to pick up information from the press as well as to make his own points to them.[48] Bunker was generally happy with the exchanges, and the journalists seemed to have been pleased, too. He met regularly with Indian journalists as well. These sessions were less fre-quent, more formal, largely on-the-record encounters. He supplemented them with occasional press conferences that he gave on special occasions or during his visits to big cities elsewhere in India.

The high point of Bunker's assignment came in December 1959, when President Eisenhower fulfilled a long-cherished desire to go to In-dia. The president made good use of the sensible advice Bunker gave him about the issues he might appropriately raise and what he should say about them.[49] Bunker deserves considerable credit for the success of the historic visit, the first an American president made to India.

When Eisenhower came to New Delhi, U.S.-Indian relations had argu-ably reached unprecedented levels of warmth. The president himself, then entering his final year in the White House, had won worldwide admiration as a man of peace who was sincerely seeking to relax Cold War tensions. In this atmosphere, the genial, fatherly Eisenhower evoked from the Indian people a response never seen before or since when foreign leaders have visited the country. The president came away rightly convinced that U.S.-Indian understanding had been further strengthened, especially by his long and candid conversations with Nehru, the culmination of years of mutual cultivation.[50] His impressions of India and other countries in the region he visited were reflected in his foreign assistance requests for 1961, which called for expanded aid to South Asia.[51]

Bunker's message to Washington about the importance of the trip to U.S.-Indian relations is worth quoting at length:

> The President's mission demonstrated convincingly and appropriately at this [Christmas] season what deep and responsible chords are struck by the message "Peace on earth, good will to men." While the emotional upsurge that took place will doubtless dissipate, there is some validity in [Indian Vice President Sarvepalli] Radhakrishnan's observation to me that the effect of the visit will be permanent. It is likely to be lasting, I believe, due to the fact that the visit has for India broken down the last of the psychological barriers (inherited ones and those created by postwar developments, particularly colonial issues, military facts, fear of economic imperialism) that have stood in the way of giving trust and confidence to the United States. The visit was a fitting climax [to events] that began in late 1956 with Hungary, Suez, and the Nehru visit to the United States. Its timing could not have been more perfect. Such results, it seems to me, have been most significantly reflected by Mr. Nehru himself, who has not only shared but certainly played a key role in shaping past images and changing attitudes.[52]

In later years, Bunker loved to talk about the visit. His recollections often focused on the monumental traffic jam on the airport road that almost made him late for the president's arrival. He would describe the experience with great relish.[53] But the ambassador's oral history accounts are far less compelling than the vivid narrative Harriet Bunker wrote much closer to the event:

> Normally . . . it's a 20 minute 8-mile drive to Palam [airport], but we allowed 1½ hours leaving the house at 3 o'clock for a 4:30 arrival. Less than halfway there we found ourselves in a complete traffic stoppage—we couldn't move an inch—6 lanes of cars, cycles, [horse cart] tongas, buses, bullocks, camels and pedestrians were jammed up in an impossible tangle. The few police were helpless and the minute hand was rushing on to 4:30. Ell naturally was frantic. His President arriving and he, the Ambassador, not there! Even motorcycles were stuck, so he did the only possible thing—got out and walked. . . . Every time

the traffic moved an inch Ell jumped into the nearest car and between times walked, until he got near the head of the traffic jam, where "two beautiful Indian girls" [apparently Bunker's description] in a Fiat mille cento gave him a final lift, squeezing through traffic and taking to the wrong side of the road, pushing bullock carts right and left, reaching the airport at 4:25!!!! ... I got there about 4:35 to find that the President's plane was a half hour late because some one in Afghanistan had made too long a speech—so we all made it—but what agony. The Prime Minister, by the way, was just behind me tearing his hair like all the rest of us.[54]

Harriet was much more of a correspondent than Ellsworth, and her letters provide impressions of India and their life there that he only got around to describing in much less detail years later in oral history interviews. Written with a nice irony, they convey the mingled sense of fascination and unease, hope and despair, a Western newcomer to India often experienced in those days.

"I can't believe that my eyes have seen sights such as we have seen of beauty, loveliness and peace, poverty, dirt, and disease, all in a few short days," she reported to her children soon after she and Ellsworth arrived by a slow moving KLM Constellation in what was for them "the unknown east."[55] Though it was a far cry from the ambassadorial palaces she had known in Buenos Aires and Rome, she soon came to like their house in a pleasant residential neighborhood of New Delhi. "The garden is lovely and the kitchen though crawling with cockroaches turns out good food, even though a bit monotonous. When we spray adequately everything tastes of DDT; when we don't you can hear the bugs."[56]

A visit with Ellsworth to the celebration of Diwali, a Hindu religious festival, at the palace of the maharajah of Mysore was a totally new experience for her. Harriet marveled at the atmosphere of archaic grandeur of the vast, bee-ridden guest house, the unchanging centuries-old court rituals, and the dazzling brilliance of the palace complex, illuminated for the ceremony. For Ellsworth, what was more memorable was the tiger hunt the maharajah arranged. When rather than tigers the party encountered a herd of ghaur, a large, ferocious variety of bison, the maharajah handed Bunker an elephant gun and commanded him to shoot. Bunker had never bagged anything bigger than a duck. But as he later recounted, he drew a bead through his spectacles on a nine-foot bull, downing him with a single shot.[57]

Bunker was also accredited to Nepal,[58] and like so many Americans who have worked or visited there, Harriet was greatly taken by the country, as was Bunker himself. She traveled with him by jeep to remote Himalayan valleys and met U.S. officials assigned to the economic assistance program and their wives. She was with him at the royal palace in Kathmandu when he presented his credentials—and unexpectedly found herself in the presence of the king. "I had to think fast. I decided not to bow or curtsey but just slowed my pace, remembered just in time to slip off my glove, and shook hands and smiled up into a very sweet, sad young face."[59]

Like everybody else, Harriet complained about the heat of New Delhi's interminable summers. "It is so hot now," she wrote Katherine Parsons at the end of April 1958, "that even with air-conditioning we drip when we dress for dinner. I'm sick of smearing melted lipstick on a beady wet face. . . . We can't eat out any more because of the dust storms."[60] She was biting in her criticism of the new embassy chancery, designed by the American architect Edward Durrell Stone and widely hailed as an aesthetic masterpiece. Its golden columns and the 27,000 ornamental gold-hemispheres pressed into filigreed concrete outer walls made it look to her like an overdressed woman in gold lamé. "What are we Americans coming to, all that cheap meretricious stuff . . . in this cultivated, gentle country."[61]

She thought a lot about the way India's poor lived. "Morning noon and night I keep wondering what on earth the British did all this time in India. No one even thought to put a chimney or even a hole in the roofs of the huts to let the smoke out, so all the women have desperate eye trouble from smoke irritation. They built railroads but didn't sink an artesian well or provide for any kind of clean drinking water. Astounding."[62] She resolved to do something about it, first to improve her servants' housing, then on a broader scale.

Soon after she came to India, Harriet wrote her children that all the rooms in the house were cleaned constantly by sweepers using brooms made of straw tied together with a four-inch handle, just long enough to grasp. The brooms were whisked back and forth from a squatting position, a backbreaking operation. To relieve the pain and give the servants a sense of dignity, she promoted a long-handled broom that they could use standing up. This stand-up broom became "her thing." It caught the imagination of Prime Minister Nehru, who sent a circular letter to the state chief ministers on the importance to human dignity of standing up while sweeping. Despite this high-level support and Harriet's energetic promotion of the idea, most Indian sweepers preferred the time-honored method. Old-timers still speak well of her good-hearted efforts, but the traditional short-handled broom remains in wide use.

Bunker left India in March 1961 well satisfied with the state of U.S.-Indian relations at the end of his four-year assignment. Bilateral ties, he rightly concluded, were stronger than they had ever been; there had been fluctuations during his years in India, but the trend was steadily upward. In a handwritten outline evidently prepared for briefing Washington audiences after he got home, he listed the factors that he thought had contributed: (a) the "compulsion of events," including the Chinese 1959 invasion of Tibet, clashes along the Sino-Indian border, the visit of President Eisenhower, and the advent in January 1961 of the new, pro-Indian Kennedy administration; (b) "hard work on both sides;" (c) U.S. willingness to take Nehru into its confidence; (d) American treatment of India as an equal; and (e) the helpful role of Nehru at the United Nations.[63]

He was widely lauded on his departure by political leaders and the press. A large group of officials, prominent citizens, and diplomats led by Morarji Desai, a future Indian prime minister who was then Nehru's finance minister, gathered at New Delhi's old Safdarjung Airport to see him off. Desai told Bunker that "nobody could have represented your government and country better than you or understood us more perfectly," lavish praise from a politician ordinarily cautious in his public statements.[64] Editorials in leading newspapers hailed him for having worked unobtrusively and amiably to explain India and the United States to one another. "It is no exaggeration to say," commented the *Indian Express*, "that his work has prepared the ground for the closer relationship to which both countries are looking forward."[65] The *Times of India* judged that "of all the ambassadors from anywhere in the world since India's independence, few if any had Bunker's personality and ability."[66] "Mr. Bunker can look back with some satisfaction that Indo-American relations are now excellent and most friendly," K. Rangaswami wrote in the *Hindu* of Madras. "[His] sympathetic understanding of India's policies on the one side and appreciation of India's development needs on the other have largely contributed to the present happy situation. . . . Mr. Bunker's method of functioning may well be said to have set a pattern for his successors."[67]

Perhaps the most sensitive Indian assessment of the Bunkers' ability to reach out to people and establish lasting personal bonds and goodwill for the United States was written by "Argus" in the *Eastern Economist* magazine:

> I cannot think that the United States has had, since independence, any more effective representative, and . . . I predict that it will not have Mr. Bunker's equal again. In a sense, this is because his view of diplomacy was as catholic as his outlook. As distinguished from most diplomats who have conceived of their purpose as striking the pockets of influence in particular areas, the Bunkers broadcast their seed with an almost complete indifference as to whether it bore immediate fruit. The picture of the American ambassador was also curiously many sided: to the businessman he appeared as a leading businessman with deep knowledge of the sugar industry as well as of banking. . . . To the diplomatic world he appeared much more as a practiced diplomat who had survived the Perón administration in Argentina, great difficulties in Italy, and, not the least of all, a fairly difficult initial period in the Indian Union. To the social worker and the press he appeared as a fine observer of events capable of detaching himself with amazing ease from the material interests of his country as distinguished from the larger moral purposes of democratic living in which India and the United States are necessarily involved. . . . [The Bunkers] were able to disengage themselves from their ambassadorial responsibilities and established a direct bond with the Indian people in which lasting personal friendship arose above both influence and the immediate objectives of Indo-American relations. I doubt if any ambassador in New Delhi has accomplished the broad and lasting sweep of goodwill that the Bunkers together have achieved.[68]

Bunker preserved the clipping carefully in his papers.

A rising young New York businessman, 1924. Before becoming a diplomat, Bunker was a leading figure in the sugar refining industry. (Bunker Family Collection)

Yale undergraduate, 1915. A member of the Yale Class of 1916, Bunker remained a loyal Eli throughout his life. (Bunker Family Collection)

The Bunker family in Vermont, 1935. Ellsworth and Harriet Bunker had three children: Ellen, John (right), and Sam (left). (Bunker Family Collection)

Heading for Buenos Aires, 1951. Bunker's first ambassadorial post was Argentina, then led by Juan and Evita Perón. (Moore McCormack Line Photo in Bunker Family Collection)

As American Red Cross President, receiving a donation from the Italian ambassador, 1955. As a recent U.S. ambassador to Buenos Aires and Rome, Bunker knew his way around Washington's diplomatic circuit, to the Red Cross's advantage.

At the White House with President Eisenhower, late 1950s. To give his foreign policy a bipartisan flavor, Eisenhower offered diplomatic assignments to a few Democrats, choosing Bunker as ambassador to India in 1956. (Dwight D. Eisenhower Library)

Inaugurating the new U.S. Embassy in New Delhi, 1959. Designed by Edward Durrell Stone, the embassy is an architectural gem. Prime Minister Nehru and Indira Gandhi participated in the ceremonies. (Bunker Family Collection)

With Harriet at their residence in New Delhi, late 1950s. The Bunkers were a popular couple in India, where the ambassador is still regarded as one of the best diplomats Washington ever sent to New Delhi. (Bunker Family Collection)

Greeting Eisenhower at New Delhi's Palam Airport, 1959. Ike's momentous visit to India was the high point in Bunker's four-year assignment there. On Eisenhower's left is Indian President Rajendra Prasad, on his right are Indira Gandhi, Vice President Sarvepalli Radhakrishnan, and Prime Minister Jawaharlal Nehru. (Dwight D. Eisenhower Library)

Promoting American wheat products in the Indian market, late 1950s. Bunker's background as a businessman was helpful to him in India. Dressed in white to Bunker's left is Morarji Desai, later India's prime minister. (National Archives)

Traveling on the ambassadorial plane, late 1950s. Bunker tried to see as much of India and Nepal as he could, but unlike some other ambassadors to South Asian countries, he never "went native." (Bunker Family Collection)

On his farm in Vermont, 1960. Bunker was never much of a countryman, as his rather gingerly relations with his cows suggest. (Bunker Family Collection)

6
Recharging the Battery

Bunker's willingness to serve a Republican administration did not blot his copybook with the Democrats when they returned to power following John F. Kennedy's election in November 1960. A few weeks after the election, Kennedy asked Bunker to become assistant secretary of state for inter-American affairs, the position Bunker's friend Edward Miller had held when the Democrats were last in office. Bunker turned down the offer. He was concerned about Harriet's health: she seemed tired when they returned from India and doctors later found her anemic. At sixty-six, Bunker also wanted time to "recharge the battery" before taking on anything new.[1] He said later that he avoided the assignment by telling the president-elect that he did not think it right to be the only man born in the nineteenth century serving on a team made up of much younger people. Word of Kennedy's offer circulated in the State Department and Bunker's decision to decline it disappointed those who remembered him there.

He was soon back at his house in Dummerston Center, where his Vermont neighbors warmly welcomed him. He was elected president of the Vermont Council on World Affairs. The state Democratic party asked him to become a member of its platform committee and a delegate to the party's state convention, offers he had to turn down because of other commitments. Many foreign policy organizations were eager to have him on their boards. He joined the Atlantic Council, chaired by Christian Herter, a former secretary of state, and became a charter member of the advisory council of the International Movement for Atlantic Union, a trustee of the Asia Foundation and International House, a director of Education in World Affairs, and a member of the executive committee of the United States National Commission for the United Nations Educational, Scientific, and Cultural Organization. He participated in an advisory group the Council on Foreign Relations established to consider what to do about China. ("Frankly," he wrote a friend, "I don't know the answers now.")[2] John D. Rockefeller III offered to make him president of the Asia

Society, and Eric Johnson wanted him to become head of the Center for Economic Growth. After serious consideration, he declined both of those prestigious positions.

Bunker happily updated his ties with his alma mater. He addressed the fellows and undergraduates of the university's Davenport College and members of the Yale Class of 1916. When the maharaja of Mysore, his festival of lights host and one of the few intellectuals among the Indian princes, expressed an interest in a position at an American university, Bunker persuaded A. Whitney Griswold, Yale's president, to give the former ruler a brief lectureship.

He maintained his interest in India in other ways as well. In a letter to Finance Minister Morarji Desai congratulating him for undertaking tough and unpopular fiscal policies, Bunker reported that since his return to the United States he had been busy giving talks about India "and finding a tremendous interest in developments there."[3] He was host in Dummerston to many of his old Indian friends and contacts and kept in touch with others such as S. K. Patil, still India's food and agriculture minister. Never shy about tapping well-connected Americans for favors, Patil urged Bunker to help work out an equitable arrangement for U.S. import of Indian sugar. Although he was concerned about possible conflict of interest problems (he was still a National Sugar Refining Company director), Bunker passed on some suggestions that he thought could strengthen India's case for a permanent U.S. import quota.[4]

He continued to argue for high levels of U.S. assistance to India and welcomed the decision of the Kennedy administration to go well beyond the generous grants and loans of the final Eisenhower years. He urged again that the United States align itself with the forces of change in India and elsewhere in the Third World. In an eloquent letter to a participant in a conference on international peace, he wrote:

> In a world where the winds of change are blowing so strongly, and where as Mr. Nehru has said this great change is taking place in the minds of men, we so often give the appearance of being against change. This impression is heightened by our preoccupation with what we consider the evils of communism. Rightly or wrongly—and I believe wrongly—in many of the uncommitted and unaligned countries, communism, because of its rapid material advances, is looked upon as a means of achieving economic independence more quickly than is possible under democratic institutions. It is for us to prove that progress

adequate to meet the wants and needs of the newly emerging nations can be made without loss of freedom.[5]

The theme of change and the way the United States could influence it was prominent in his reaction to the Nehru government's occupation of Goa and other Portuguese enclaves in December 1961. As ambassador, Bunker had tried to head off such action by suggesting that India purchase the territories. The occupation was unnecessary and stupid, he wrote to his sister, but "change is inevitable and if we cannot find the way, through the U.N. or otherwise[,] to peaceful change, it will come in some other way." The United States should "facilitate change and bring it about in an orderly and peaceful manner whenever possible[;] when it is not possible . . . let us back the U.N. in bringing about and maintaining order, and providing a period of tutelage until the people are able to govern themselves."[6]

A year later, Bunker joined with other former U.S. ambassadors to New Delhi in organizing a private American group to assist India during its disastrous border war with China. When Prime Minister Nehru died in 1964, Bunker delivered a eulogy at a memorial service for him at the National Cathedral. His tribute was platitudinous and almost trite, like so many of the speeches he had delivered to appreciative Indian audiences, and avoided personal recollections. In a way, the unemotional eulogy was an appropriate conclusion to the strong, mutually respectful, but impersonal relationship between Bunker and Nehru that had marked their years together in New Delhi.

Bunker's continuing connection with India, his role in foreign policy organizations, his contacts with Yale, and his limited business associations kept him active and involved. This was important for a man in his late sixties by no means ready to retire. But Bunker needed something more demanding after his exhilarating experience in India.

Harriet's deteriorating health limited his possibilities. In the fall of 1961 doctors at Columbia-Presbyterian Hospital in New York City found that she had a stomach ulcer. This ruled out his accepting another ambassadorship: he could have had a major one for the asking. It also made difficult his undertaking the grueling routine of a senior foreign policymaking position in Washington. Instead, he made himself available for special diplomatic assignments.

Over the next few years, Bunker's remarkable achievements in carrying out a series of important troubleshooting responsibilities involving major U.S. interests in different parts of the world gave him fresh prominence and redefined his reputation. He had been respected earlier as a gifted patrician-businessman who, despite his inexperience in diplomacy, had quickly and easily become one of the most effective American ambassadors of the 1950s. The fact that his three embassies had been on three different continents and had governments, leaders, political systems, and relations with the United States very unlike one another enhanced his credentials.

Bunker's subsequent special assignments to resolve confrontations between the Dutch and the Indonesians in West New Guinea (1962), the Egyptians and the Saudis in Yemen (1963), and warring factions in the Dominican Republic (1965–66) built on these credentials and added a major dimension to them. By the mid-1960s, he had come to be recognized as the most skillful and effective American negotiator of his day.

It will be useful to understand what Bunker considered important for diplomatic success. He spelled out these criteria on several occasions.[7]

Every negotiation was quite different, Bunker found, but there are certain elements successful ones have in common. He put the integrity of the negotiator at the head of his list.

> If a diplomat tries to serve his country by lying to a foreign government . . . he will have squandered his most valuable asset, which is the respect that a foreign government develops for the representative of another country. . . . When a diplomat becomes widely known . . . as being unreliable, as playing fast and loose with the truth, even if this is the result of lack of precision rather than sharp practice, that reputation will dog him not only in the country of his assignment but also in subsequent assignments in other countries. And . . . if a diplomat acquires the reputation of being honest, reliable, and fair . . . this will stand him in good stead in the places to which he may be assigned in the future.

In arguing his case, Bunker believed, the negotiator needs to recognize what is important and why, what is more important than something else, and what is desirable rather than important. He must also have empathy, a capacity to put himself in the shoes of the negotiator on the other side of the table, imagine how that opposite number would see the situation from his perspective, and construct in his own mind a hierarchy of priorities for the other side.

He also stressed the importance of creativity. If the results of a negotiation are to be lasting, Bunker said, they have to include benefits for both sides and a mutual advantage in concluding the transaction. "It is the task of the negotiator to maximize those elements which are of most importance to his side; even while allowing the other side—indeed, sometimes even urging the other side—to maximize those elements . . . that are of importance to [it]." In doing so, one side may give up immediate advantage for the sake of long-term advantage, even while the other side is more concerned with the immediate advantage because of certain requirements of its domestic political situation.

The negotiator needed a sense of realism. "It goes without saying that [he] must also be attuned to the interests and political realities of his own country. The best treaty will be of no value if it cannot command the support necessary for its ratification." He called for patience and perseverance, not easily come by, Bunker thought, in can-do America, where quick results were often demanded of those at the negotiating table.

He preferred privacy and seclusion. "Whenever negotiations are being conducted in the glare of public exposure . . . you can be sure that the real negotiations will take place somewhere behind closed doors. Why? Because negotiations involve the trading of something that is less valuable to one side for something that is more highly prized by the other. And that process of trading involves the discussion of various hypothetical possibilities which may appear preposterous if they are lifted out of their context, but assume meaning when they become whole."

Precision, Bunker said, was desirable in diplomacy in general and in negotiations in particular. "There may be times when calculated ambiguity is necessary in order to bring two very different points of view together or when matters of face rather than substance are at stake. But it is risky and the chickens hatched in such circumstances can come home to roost in a very disagreeable manner. . . . The less clarity and precision there is in an international document the more likely it is to be ignored by one or more of the signatories."

A final, more subtle point Bunker made had to do with the often disparate nature of the opposite side.

I have found it useful [when negotiating partners seemed obdurate] to imagine that we have 'hidden allies' on the other side whose hand it was my job to strengthen. . . . I talked to the other delegation as if they were reasonable, even if the position they were taking was not reasonable at all. [Actually], it doesn't really matter whether in bilateral negotiations the other delegation actually contains such hidden allies. The human brain and the human mind are extremely complex and the thought processes of other people can very well contain elements that are both conciliatory and unyielding, with one element simply predominating over the other. By adding weight on the side of the scales that favors reasonableness, one appeals to people on the other side who can see the advantages of a compromise—or, if there are no such people on the other side, one must hope that one's arguments will at least be reported to the home office of the other delegation, where there may be more reasonable people in charge.

Many of these principles will sound familiar to students of classic Western diplomatic practice. Bunker followed them in all of his troubleshooting assignments. They would first become evident when he tackled the dangerous dispute between The Netherlands and Indonesia over possession of West New Guinea.

7 The West New Guinea Negotiations

By the early 1960s, the long era of Western colonialism in South and Southeast Asia was almost over. All that remained of European rule were a few tiny Portuguese enclaves, a handful of small British territories and protectorates, and the western half of the huge, remote island of New Guinea. There the Dutch held on, a decade after they had been forced to recognize the rest of their vast East Indian island empire as the independent Republic of Indonesia.

West New Guinea—or Irian Barat, Irian Jaya, and West Papua, as the Indonesians have successively called it—was, and still is, a primitive, inhospitable, sparsely populated land about the size of California. Its indigenous population, estimated at the time at about 700,000, comprised various tribes of Papuans, a Melanesian race sharply different from the mainly Malay people of Indonesia. Most of them lived in isolation from one another in swampy, malarial lowlands and inaccessible valleys cut into the rugged mountain terrain. They spoke a variety of mutually unintelligible languages and remained largely ignorant of the changing world outside. Only a tiny minority were aware of the claims and counterclaims made by the Dutch and Indonesian governments in their long, bitter dispute over control of the area.

Before the Japanese drove them out in 1942, the Dutch had governed West New Guinea as part of the colony of the Netherlands East Indies. After the war, they tried to reestablish their rule throughout the colony, but were frustrated by a nationalist movement that had declared it independent when the Japanese surrendered. Unable to restore the prewar status quo by force, the Dutch sought to separate the outer parts of the archipelago from the central islands, which they recognized would have to be conceded to the newly established Indonesian republic. The nationalists frustrated this strategy everywhere but in West New Guinea.

When the Dutch and Indonesians agreed in December 1949 to transfer sovereignty elsewhere in the islands, a vaguely worded compromise provided that West New Guinea would remain under The Hague's control pending negotiations to be held within one year. Subsequent efforts to resolve the issue broke down. The Netherlands held that West New Guinea was ethnically, linguistically, and culturally distinct from Indonesia. Its backward inhabitants should not be forced to join a newly independent, war-shattered state that could not develop the territory's primitive economy for their benefit. Indonesia, for its part, claimed that the republic was the successor government to the Dutch throughout the former colony. It stated publicly that it would take into account the special nature of West New Guinea and gave assurances that it would eventually allow the Papuans free choice. But few observers believed that the Indonesians would leave West New Guinea once they had won control of the territory.

Behind these conflicting positions lay other considerations, many irrational and emotionally charged, that made West New Guinea a major issue in the political dynamics of both countries and complicated efforts to resolve the dispute. The Dutch claimed that the remote territory had considerable potential for economic development and European settlement. It could be a strategic bastion of the "free world" at a time when Communist influence was rising in Indonesia and elsewhere in Southeast Asia, especially Indochina. Moreover, they insisted, they had a moral responsibility to promote the welfare of the territory's Papuan natives. They professed confidence that under their influence the small Papuan elite would continue to favor political association with The Netherlands.

These arguments largely rationalized more fundamental forces that drove Dutch policy. The unexpected loss of their large and prosperous East Indian empire had come as a great psychological shock. It had ended Holland's centuries-old role as a leading imperial power and reduced it to little more than a minor northern European state. Suffering from what the Dutch scholar Arend Lijphart has called the trauma of de-colonization, the Dutch were determined to salvage West New Guinea from the disaster that had overtaken the rest of their empire and deny it to the Indonesian leaders who had ousted them.[1]

The Indonesians also regarded the issue in highly emotional terms. For them, "liberation" of West New Guinea would complete their great nationalist revolutionary struggle against the colonialists. They rejected The Hague's contention that the Papuans' ethnic and racial distinctiveness from the rest of the archipelago called for separate status. Moreover, they regarded continued Dutch control over the territory as a threat to their own security and integrity. Many Indonesians considered the quest for West New Guinea the ultimate test of patriotism.[2]

In Indonesia, as in The Netherlands, the dispute was deeply caught up in domestic politics. The campaign to liberate West New Guinea offered Indonesia's ambitious and increasingly irresponsible president, Sukarno, a made-to-order formula for reinforcing his association with the revolutionary mystique that was central to Indonesian political dynamics in the early years of independence. By giving prominence to the widely popular "liberation struggle," Sukarno solidified and united the disparate political and military forces that coexisted in fragile and uneasy entente under his leadership. The Indonesian military also saw political and professional benefit in the issue, and the powerful Communist Party of Indonesia (PKI), which backed Sukarno, promoted it as a way to strengthen anti-Western forces in the country and move it closer to Moscow.

By the mid-1950s, bilateral negotiations between the Dutch and the Indonesians had sputtered to an end amid a welter of mutual recriminations. A series of Indonesian initiatives to settle the issue at the United Nations also failed. Increasingly frustrated, Djakarta adopted a more aggressive stance, expropriating without compensation the extensive Dutch holdings in the country, expelling the sizable Dutch community and, in 1960, breaking diplomatic relations. It strengthened its armed forces with Soviet equipment and made a few, largely symbolic, attempts to infiltrate West New Guinea. Strident propaganda campaigns at home and abroad accompanied these bellicose activities. The approach was designed to create a crisis that would undermine Dutch resolve, call the issue to world attention, and convince influential governments that the dispute should be settled in Indonesia's favor.

Meanwhile, Dutch attitudes toward West New Guinea changed as the traumatic impact of the loss of empire diminished. Recognizing that in an increasingly anticolonialist world The Netherlands could not hope to retain the territory, the Dutch came to favor early Papuan self-determination and internationalization of the West New Guinea administration. The Hague stepped up its modernization programs and heightened efforts to develop a Papuan nationalism that would resist integration with Indonesia. The sorry domestic record of the Sukarno government and its antagonistic policies toward The Netherlands stiffened Dutch determination to head off an Indonesian takeover.

Fearing an Indonesian military attack on the island, The Hague reversed its decade-old policy of keeping the dispute out of the United Nations. At the 1961 session of the General Assembly, Foreign Minister Joseph Luns offered a fresh formula that called for the gradual transfer of governing responsibilities to an interim U.N. authority charged with preparing the Papuans for the early exercise of self-determination under stable conditions. The Sukarno government vehemently lobbied against the proposal which it saw, correctly, as a scheme to prolong Dutch rule. The Dutch withdrew this "Luns Plan" after it failed to win the necessary two-thirds majority.

In the decade following Dutch acknowledgement of Indonesian independence, the United States maintained a neutral position on the West New Guinea dispute. Although both contenders resented this policy, its negative impact was much greater in Djakarta, where it contributed significantly to the deterioration of U.S.-Indonesian relations. This downward spiral in bilateral ties became even more marked following disclosure of the Eisenhower administration's covert support for an ill-starred rebellion against the Sukarno government in 1958. With Sukarno increasingly relying on Moscow for military and economic assistance and on the PKI for political backing for his authoritarian system of "guided democracy," the Kennedy administration faced a grim situation in Indonesia when it took office in January 1961.

In his overall foreign policy approach, Kennedy gave high priority to working with nationalist, nonaligned, often Moscow-leaning Third World governments to contain Communist aggression and subversion. Despite this policy, and what many in his administration saw as an increasingly dangerous situation in Indonesia, he made only a few symbolic gestures to cultivate better ties with Djakarta in his first year in power. The new administration maintained the policy of neutrality on the West New Guinea dispute that it had inherited from Eisenhower. It moved only slowly toward the idea that U.S. interests would be best served by supporting Indonesia's claims to West New Guinea while finding face-saving measures to assuage the Dutch.

Although this policy shift also reflected personnel changes in the foreign affairs agencies involved in policymaking on Indonesia, it was primarily prompted by the administration's growing concern that the frustrated, increasingly procommunist Sukarno government would try to seize West New Guinea by force.[3] Washington worried, with good reason, that a "colonialist" war over West New Guinea would be disastrous to "free world" interests not only in Southeast Asia but elsewhere in the Third World.[4] The Indonesians would enjoy strong support from Communist powers and many nonaligned governments, the United States would be widely perceived as pro-Dutch, and the PKI would grow even stronger, perhaps to the point of seizing power. This nightmare scenario was particularly stark for an administration much more concerned with the Third World than Eisenhower's had been.

The professed willingness of the Dutch to give up West New Guinea (though not to the Indonesians) and the defeat of the Luns Plan gave Washington an opening to play a greater role in working out a peaceful settlement of the dispute. During his two 1961 visits to Washington, Sukarno had discussed the issue with Kennedy, whom he reportedly admired. Though the talks had been inconclusive, some American policymakers argued that once the West New Guinea issue was settled (on Indonesia's terms), Sukarno and the Indonesian military would turn away from the Communists and devote more energy to improving Indonesia's parlous economic situation, to the Cold War advantage of the United States. As the crisis quickened later in the year, Kennedy told the Indonesian president that his administration was willing to play whatever role the Indonesians and Dutch found useful. Warning Sukarno not to use force, he pointedly stated that "some definitive action which will result in the Dutch relinquishing their position in the territory, and give Indonesia a greatly enlarged opportunity to influence the territory's future, now seems a wholly realistic prospect."[5]

In January 1962 Washington urged the United Nations to play an active part in bringing about a settlement. It wished to limit its own role to coaxing the two contenders to the negotiating table. United Nations Secretary General U Thant readily concurred with this approach. But the Dutch and the Indonesians, deeply suspicious of one another, could not agree on the terms for such U.N.-sponsored talks. The Dutch were prepared for negotiations without preconditions. The Indonesians insisted that The Hague first acknowledge that the purpose of the talks was to set a date for transferring West New Guinea to them. They were willing to give the people of the territory some form of self-determination five years after transfer, a promise the Dutch considered inadequate. Understandably, the Dutch wanted to know the details of how Djakarta intended to satisfy the interests of the Papuans.[6]

While this deadlock continued, Washington let it be known that it would not object to West New Guinea's ultimately coming under Indonesian control if some form of interim U.N. administration first allowed a graceful exit for the Dutch, followed later by some method of self-determination. But despite strenuous efforts, including visits to Djakarta and The Hague by Attorney General Robert Kennedy, the president's brother, the United States was unable to persuade the Indonesians to drop their precondition for bilateral talks. The Dutch, for their part, remained ready to hold talks without conditions but also stressed the importance of their moral obligation to the Papuans.

To break the impasse, Washington proposed that both sides agree to meet secretly in the presence of a third party—in diplomatic terms, a moderator—in order to work out a mutually satisfactory agenda that would be the basis for subsequent formal negotiations under the aegis of the United Nations.[7] To help move the Dutch and Indonesians to accept this approach and get the talks started, the United States focused on the choice of a moderator. Although it had been reluctant to play a central role in the negotiations, Secretary Rusk told Luns during the Dutch foreign minister's visit to Washington in early March that the United States "would not refuse [such a role] because of our interest in seeing such talks undertaken."[8] The Indonesians, apparently persuaded by then that the Kennedy administration favored a settlement that would satisfy their aspirations, wanted an American with no direct affiliation with the United Nations to be appointed as moderator of whatever talks were agreed to. The Dutch, for the same reason, preferred U Thant or another U.N. representative in the role.

In a March 6 discussion, Secretary Rusk and Dutch Ambassador J. Herman van Roijen developed a list of ten nominees for the moderator's job, most of them drawn from the American foreign policy establishment. Rusk made it clear that he strongly preferred Ellsworth Bunker for the position. He told van Roijen that Bunker possessed all the skills necessary for a moderator: an incisive mind, a sense of calm under fire, an attention to detail, and an ability to focus on the positive.[9] On instructions from Washington, the U.S. ambassador to Indonesia, Howard Jones, underscored Rusk's preference to Sukarno.[10] Sukarno eventually came around, as did the Dutch, who were at first negative on Bunker and would have preferred an American more "Europeanist" in foreign policy orientation.[11]

Bunker did not hesitate to accept the assignment. He wrote to E. Roland Harriman, his former American Red Cross associate, that he had been persuaded to take it by the assurance (presumably from Rusk) that since both sides were quite near agreement it would not take long to get the matter settled.[12] While the short-term feature of the assignment must have been an attraction to him given his concerns about Harriet, he probably would have agreed even if no such prospect had been mentioned to him.[13] He was at loose ends, and an important challenge like the West New Guinea negotiations was just right for him in the spring of 1962.

As Rusk had reckoned, agreement on Bunker helped move Indonesia and The Netherlands toward the negotiating table the United States had set for them. But the two parties finally agreed to talk to one another in Bunker's presence only after a further delay caused by a Dutch decision to send naval reinforcements to its forces in West New Guinea following provocative Indonesian threats.

After prolonged skirmishing over a suitable site, what were termed preliminary bilateral talks began on March 20, 1962, at the Huntland Estate in Middleburg, Virginia, close to Washington, with Bunker acting as moderator representing U.N. Secretary General U Thant. Ambassador Van Roijen and Adam Malik, the Indonesian ambassador to Moscow, led their respective delegations. The stated purpose of the Middleburg talks was to prepare an agenda for formal negotiations at U.N. headquarters under U Thant's direct aegis. In the event, the talks went well beyond that goal and produced agreed terms for settlement of the dispute.

Although Bunker officially took part in the talks as a private American citizen whom U Thant had requested to play the role of third-party moderator, he acted primarily in Washington's interests. Neither he nor anyone else seriously pretended otherwise. Dutch and Indonesian agreement to his nomination reflected their tacit acceptance of this role. While the administration may have welcomed his U.N. connection as a way to enhance his authority and make the United Nations rather than the United States ultimately responsible for the settlement, the progress of the negotiations and the close contact Bunker maintained with officials in Washington as they moved along made it evident that he was a representative of the U.S. government.[14] The Kennedy administration believed that his role, and its own, was to assure the success of the talks along the lines that it preferred. The Indonesians concurred with this U.S. "take-charge attitude," as Terrence Markin, a scholar who studied the negotiations in great detail, has called it, because they believed the administration would press the Dutch to compromise. The Dutch recognized that they had no choice but to acquiesce since they knew they could not repel an Indonesian military attack on West New Guinea without U.S. support.[15] U Thant and his U.N. colleagues went along with the fiction that Bunker and his team worked for them and never interfered.

Middleburg was an ideal setting for the talks. Secluded and comfortable, it was an easy drive from Washington, where Bunker consulted government colleagues and the Dutch and Indonesians used the facilities of their embassies to communicate with their home governments. Even more important from Bunker's viewpoint was the opportunity it offered for informal, relaxed exchanges in which the Dutch and Indonesian participants could develop easier relations as they chatted over cocktails and fine dinners, swam in the pool, and strolled in the estate's handsome gardens. Probably with this in mind, Bunker had tried to keep the delegations small. The U.S. team was limited to himself and two fairly junior State Department officials.

One of the American participants in the negotiations recalled years later the charm of Huntland:

> We had morning and afternoon negotiating sessions. Cocktails around six followed by dinner and then digestifs after dinner. The social occasions were relaxed, nonprotocolaire affairs where all members could establish personal links. There was a tacit agreement that the social occasions would not be used for negotiations. However, from time to time after dinner when the Dutch or Indonesians wished to discuss a matter bilaterally, [the chiefs of their delegations] would sit in a corner and converse in Dutch.[16]

The task facing Bunker and his American associates in the Middleburg negotiations was difficult but fairly straightforward. For its own regional and global interests, the United States needed to broker a settlement that satisfied the Sukarno government's insistence that West New Guinea irrevocably become part of Indonesia. The settlement also had to assure the Dutch that the wishes of the Papuans would somehow be taken into account. The disputed territory could not be handed over to the Indonesians directly or right away. Aside from the strong possibility that the Dutch would reject such an arrangement as an unacceptable humiliation, it might well be regarded elsewhere as an abject capitulation to Indonesian threats. Yet too long a delay could lead Sukarno to launch a war that would pave the way for the Communist takeover of Indonesia Washington so feared. As Robert Komer, a senior National Security Council aide who played a major role in the development of U.S. West New Guinea policy, tersely put it: "The real object of the exercise is not a bit of colonial debris but Indonesia itself."[17]

By the time the Middleburg talks began, the Netherlands government had become well aware of the administration's fundamentally pro-Indonesian approach. At a White House meeting a few weeks earlier, Kennedy had urged Foreign Minister Luns to "take a broad view of the free world's position in Asia" and seek a peaceful settlement of the West New Guinea issue. The president stressed the danger of a Communist takeover of Indonesia and "the consequent disaster to the free-world position in Asia" if war broke out over the territory. He dismissed Luns's effort to equate the Dutch moral commitment to the Papuans with the American commitment to the people of West Berlin, where the Wall had been erected six months earlier, and made it clear that The Netherlands could expect no U.S. military assistance if the confrontation escalated.[18]

As the talks got under way, Bunker asked the delegates to discuss the issues informally rather than to read out formal prepared statements.[19] The Indonesians reiterated long-standing positions. The sole purpose of the talks was to determine how West New Guinea would be transferred to their control. Only that item and normalization of Netherlands-Indonesia relations (an attractive bait for Dutch business interests) could be on the agenda for the formal negotiations at the United Nations. The Dutch said they wished to leave West New Guinea. They were willing to discuss the possibility of its transfer to Indonesia, which they said would require some form of impartial interim administration. But they recognized, quite rightly, that acceptance of the single-minded Indonesian position regarding the agenda would represent preemptive capitulation. They would not agree to any formula for transfer of the territory to the Sukarno government unless this included satisfactory arrangements for the exercise of Papuan self-determination, and they were prepared to accept an interim U.N. administration for that purpose. The Indonesians rejected this because it might lead to a Papuan decision to remain separate. Not surprisingly, Dutch representatives were unimpressed by Indonesian assurances that the Papuans would be allowed to decide their future status freely *after* the Indonesians had taken control of West New Guinea.

Bunker tried to break the impasse by calling on the two sides to discuss the modalities of the transfer from a practical viewpoint, including the form and responsibilities of the interim administration. As good mediators do, he sought to minimize differences between them and emphasized small areas of consensus. But he was repeatedly frustrated, as were the Dutch, by Indonesian insistence that interim administrative arrangements and Papuan self-determination could be considered only at the later, formal talks, in the context of an agenda item providing for transfer of West New Guinea to Indonesia. The Dutch negotiators, for their part, would not discuss transfer as long as the Indonesians refused to address the modalities of an interim administration.

This stonewalling led Bunker to resort to another familiar negotiating device: he adjourned the talks to meet one-on-one with the delegation leaders. These private discussions also failed to advance the negotiations. Ambassador Malik implicitly threatened use of force unless the Dutch promptly accepted Indonesia's Middleburg agenda. He then requested a recess so that he could report to Sukarno and seek greater negotiating authority from the president, as Bunker had suggested to him. The preliminary talks were accordingly suspended just three days after they had begun. Apparently convinced by then that a more central U.S. role was required, Bunker gave the delegation a vaguely worded document that was more a basis for discussion than a formula for a settlement.[20]

Three days later, Djakarta announced that its delegation was withdrawing from the discussions. It was an unpromising start.

As Bunker recognized, the Indonesian decision to walk out was part of an unsubtle negotiating strategy designed to persuade the Kennedy administration to adopt a more explicitly pro-Indonesian position in the negotiations by exploiting its fear of war. The Indonesians quickly achieved this goal. In a letter to Sukarno the day they announced their withdrawal, Bunker pointedly noted that "the end result of interim arrangements should be the assumption of administrative authority by Indonesia, and I personally am persuaded that a continuation of the negotiations will produce this result."[21]

He went further in a discussion with van Roijen, telling the shocked Dutch ambassador that if war was to be avoided the transfer of administration to Indonesia had to take place *before* the Papuans exercised self-determination. An interim U.N. authority could administer West New Guinea between the departure of the Dutch and the arrival of the Indonesians, and a small U.N. technical mission would stay on afterwards to fulfill the U.N. role in the self-determination process. Although Bunker contended that this arrangement was a realistic compromise, van Roijen correctly forecast that it would be seen in The Hague as an abject surrender of West New Guinea to Indonesia. When he registered his own strong objection to a senior State Department official, van Roijen was disingenuously told that the idea was Bunker's own and had not been endorsed by the U.S. government.[22]

This dishonest façade collapsed a few days later when, with State Department support, Bunker formally proposed a formula along the same pro-Indonesian lines to representatives of the two countries. As spelled out in this "Bunker Plan," the United Nations would administer West New Guinea for a one- to two-year period. During the second year, Indonesian officials would replace U.N. administrators, but U.N. technical assistance personnel would remain in an advisory capacity to help in the self-determination process. The Indonesians, by then in control of the territory, were to carry out this process within a specified number of years, to be decided upon in negotiations.

The Kennedy administration mobilized its highest-ranking officials to promote this proposal. The president had earlier written to Sukarno urging that he send his delegation back to Middleburg. In separate personal letters, he called on him and on Dutch Prime Minister J. E. de Quay to accept the Bunker Plan as a basis for negotiations.[23] Secretary Rusk made similar approaches to the two foreign ministers. Bunker himself promoted the plan with senior Dutch and Indonesian representatives in Washington.

The main argument made in this coordinated effort was that the plan provided a way for the Dutch to fulfill their desire to leave West New Guinea under honorable circumstances while at the same time offering the Indonesians the certainty that they would gain control of the territory within no more than two years—that is, before the Papuans had the opportunity to express their political will. The Americans assured the Dutch that U.N. participation in the self-determination process would fulfill their commitments to the Papuan leadership and continued to stress the danger that an Indonesian-Dutch conflict would pose for Western interests in the broader Southeast Asian region. They told the Indonesians that the Bunker Plan gave "specific form to Indonesian willingness to carry out Dutch promises to the Papuans, and [its] implementation [would] provide the Indonesians with an opportunity to demonstrate to the world community that the Papuans, when able to obtain a full understanding of the Indonesian position, [would] opt to join Indonesia."[24] The Papuans themselves were not consulted about the Bunker Plan or other aspects of the negotiations.

A good deal of diplomatic maneuvering followed as both sides sought to modify the plan to their own advantage. Not surprisingly, the Indonesians were more receptive to Bunker's formulation, though Sukarno quickly conditioned his early, private acceptance of the plan "in principle" by rejecting the two-year interim period and reiterating his public pledge to liberate West New Guinea before the end of 1962. The Dutch understandably highlighted their unhappiness with the Bunker Plan's self-determination provisions and complained that in unveiling the plan without serious prior consultation the United States had confronted them with a fait accompli. They maintained that the plan reflected U.S. appeasement of Indonesia; in this Dutch view, Sukarno had successfully frightened the Americans with the threat of a Communist takeover. In his discussions with both sides, Bunker held that contentious issues such as the length and conditions of transitional arrangements could be dealt with in resumed talks, where the two delegations would have their day in court. The important thing was to agree to reenter negotiations on the basis of his plan.

Despite their serious misgivings, the Dutch seemed by mid-April to be moving toward acceptance of the Bunker Plan, including its transfer schedule, provided that the projected transfer was made conditional on their receiving adequate guarantees safeguarding the interests of the Papuans. Bunker was prepared to agree to van Roijen's proposed revised wording on this matter; it was in many ways similar to his own and could be interpreted to meet the contending parties' requirements. The Indonesians also seemed ready to go along, though they continued to reserve their position on the length of the transitional period. But then, to Bunker's exasperation, the Dutch hardened their stand. Aware that the Americans would at best take a neutral position when, and if, the talks resumed, they demanded further revisions in the plan to safeguard the rights of the Papuans. They were not satisfied with Bunker's assurance that these issues would be worked out in the negotiations. Meantime, they reinforced their armed forces in West New Guinea, to Washington's distress. Neither side was willing to return to the negotiating table.

A serious confrontation now developed between the Dutch and the Americans. It quickly escalated when Luns made a speech at a NATO foreign ministers' meeting in Athens in early May highly critical of U.S. policy, including Washington's refusal to allow Dutch reinforcements to land at American air bases in the Pacific on their way to West New Guinea. (Throughout the crisis, the Kennedy administration held that a buildup of

Dutch forces would only further inflame the situation.) Carefully briefed by Bunker, Secretary Rusk took on his Dutch counterpart at a meeting that President Kennedy predicted "would mark a crucial juncture" in the negotiating process.[25] The president instructed Rusk to "tell [Luns] plainly that if our mediation is to continue, it is imperative that the Dutch return promptly to the table. . . . Otherwise," Kennedy threatened, he found it difficult to see "any further useful purpose to be served by Bunker's good offices."

Rusk's subsequent strong expression of U.S. impatience with the Dutch attitude led Luns to modify his position somewhat. But it was not until two months later that The Netherlands agreed unequivocally to resume the negotiations. "And even then," as Christopher McMullen pointed out in his study of the negotiations, "it was only the continued pressure exerted by the U.S. government, the U.N. Secretary General, and Ambassador Bunker—as well as the deteriorating military situation in West New Guinea—that finally led the more intransigent members of the Dutch government to accept a peaceful solution to the dispute."[26]

Bunker mixed private and public diplomacy during these difficult months. Meeting in New York in late May, he and U Thant agreed to make the Bunker Plan public as a way to put further pressure on the recalcitrant Dutch. The Netherlands government, so the reasoning went, would be hard pressed to explain to world opinion why it continued to reject a reasonable proposal that accorded with the prevailing anticolonial views of the time. It is not clear whether the subsequent publication of the plan influenced the Dutch, who were informed about it in advance. But that same day Luns told the American ambassador to The Hague that the Netherlands government was willing to resume talks on the basis of the plan and, specifically, "that if proper assurances re self-determination are received, he could agree to Indonesian administration prior to a plebiscite (the exercise of self-determination)."[27] The Dutch made clear, however, that this did not mean that they had accepted the transfer of West New Guinea to Indonesia as a precondition for returning to the negotiations.

To Bunker's dismay, these private Dutch assurances were not enough for the Indonesians. Suspicious of Dutch motives and intentions, they wanted the Netherlands government to confirm its new and more forthcoming position to U Thant. When it did so, Indonesia again raised the ante and insisted that the Dutch spell out their decision in a public statement. In the meantime, they stepped up their military activities within

West New Guinea and, rejecting U.S. admonitions, seemed confident that such saber-rattling would improve the chances of a settlement on terms they could accept.

With both sides maneuvering to obtain maximum guarantees before either would definitively agree to resume talks, Bunker made another effort to enlist public opinion in support of his plan. He told media correspondents that the negotiating delays resulted from emotionalism that required each side to seek maximum assurances regarding the other's intentions before again sitting down to negotiate. But the Dutch and the Indonesians continued to bicker over the subtle meaning of words. Recognizing that he would have to involve himself more fully if the talks were to resume, Kennedy joined in Bunker's patient efforts to end the impasse. Their activities took on a further sense of urgency as the Indonesians passed word that if negotiations broke down they would declare war on The Netherlands.

Bunker's patient efforts eventually helped end the impasse. At the end of June, more than three months after the preliminary talks had convened and then quickly adjourned, the two sides agreed to resume discussions. The Dutch recognized that the procedures and timetable for change spelled out in the revised plan Bunker had offered them in early April were the best they could hope for in an evolving political-military situation increasingly favorable to the Indonesians. The Sukarno government, for its part, continued to have reservations about the timetable, but was prepared to go back to the negotiating table once it was persuaded that the Dutch had accepted the sequence of events that the Bunker Plan laid down.

The critical Dutch concession on the timing of the exercise of Papuan self-determination meant that the Sukarno government had achieved its primary objective in the talks—control over West New Guinea —though it would have to wait out a period of transitional U.N. administration before it actually took over the territory. Although the Papuans were to be allowed to decide their eventual relationship with Indonesia, the Indonesians could be reasonably certain of the outcome since they would control the territory when the referendum took place.

Yet the Indonesians remained dissatisfied with what the Bunker Plan gave them. They displayed no magnanimity in their diplomatic triumph. Between resumption of the Middleburg talks in mid-July and the successful conclusion of negotiations a month later, they tried almost without letup to bring about major changes in the plan, including revision of some of its fundamental elements. To strengthen their bargaining position, they stepped up provocative military moves and repeatedly threatened to walk out of the negotiating process and go to war. They did not really want to abandon diplomacy, their negotiators told Bunker and others, but the pressure of their impatient military for drastic action would be compelling unless concessions were promptly made. These tactics often triggered dangerous, even critical situations before an agreement was reached and signed on August 14. Until the very end, it was not certain whether the long negotiations would end in a peaceful settlement or in the Indonesian-Dutch war the Kennedy administration feared.

The Indonesians sometimes overplayed their hand. Their threat to pull Foreign Minister Subandrio out of the negotiations—widely regarded as a signal of their intention to launch an early large-scale invasion of West New Guinea if they did not have their way at the talks—led to a sharp warning by President Kennedy. In a conversation the State Department described as "friendly, but entirely frank and firm," the president emphasized to Subandrio that the world would not be able to understand if the Indonesians embarked upon the tortuous and unpredictable path of military action when Indonesia had secured its primary objective by diplomatic and peaceful means.[28] The Indonesians quickly retreated. Bunker later told Kennedy that the admonition was the turning point in the negotiations. "[It] came at a critical stage of our talks and in my opinion made the difference between success and failure."[29]

Nonetheless, the Indonesians were able to score substantial gains that made the agreement even more of a lopsided triumph for them. Kennedy, Rusk, and Bunker repeatedly called on them to be generous in victory, but were powerless to deliver that result given the disproportionate negotiating strength of the two sides and Djakarta's apparent willingness to resort to war. The administration's principal goal, in any event, was to bring about a settlement both sides could accept. It was prepared to go along with a substantial tilt to the original Bunker Plan if the Dutch were.

The Indonesians' main target was the transitional arrangement. On the first day of the resumed talks, Malik stunned Bunker and van Roijen by proposing that the provision for an interim U.N. administration be scrapped. Instead, the Dutch should turn over West New Guinea to Indonesia directly, as they had transferred sovereignty over the bulk of the Netherlands East Indies in 1949. Claiming that the situation on the ground had changed over the previous three months, when 2,000–3,000 Indonesian paratroops had infiltrated the territory, Foreign Minister Subandrio made a similar approach to Rusk. Neither the secretary nor Bunker gave the Indonesians any encouragement. They were not about to abandon the "two-bite" formula U.S. policymakers had so long considered key to their strategy of sparing the Dutch undue loss of face in their final retreat from the Indies. The Dutch were equally negative.

Failing to upset the interim arrangement itself, the Indonesians then sought to shorten it. They had continued to reserve their position on the one-to-two-year period Bunker had stipulated. Now they called for termination of U.N. administration by the end of 1962. This timing, which would have truncated the U.N. role to four or five months, was designed to redeem Sukarno's pledge to the Indonesian people that when the cock crowed on January 1, 1963, West New Guinea would be theirs. Traveling in Europe, an irate Rusk cabled Washington: "It seems absurd to me that Sukarno insists on transfer during 1962 simply because he has made a speech or two promising that this will happen. We don't let Khrushchev get away with such tactics. I feel strongly that the United States cannot press the Dutch to yield on this point without surrender[ing] our own integrity and self-respect."[30]

Despite Rusk's angry reaction, the Indonesians eventually succeeded in reducing the transitional period well below Bunker's proposed one-year minimum. They took over the territory on May 1, 1963, only seven months after Dutch colonial rule ended. In an arrangement they worked out privately with U Thant that at least partly redeemed Sukarno's pledge, the Indonesian flag (along with the UN's) was flown over the territory from December 31, 1962.

This so-called "flag incident" almost led to a collapse of the negotiations on the eve of their successful conclusion. U Thant had not informed the Dutch or the American negotiators about his backroom deal with the Indonesians. Sukarno's public disclosure of it a few weeks later understandably upset Washington and The Hague. Bunker proposed a compromise solution: the Dutch and U.N. flags would fly together through December 31, 1962, the Indonesian and U.N. flags after that. Sukarno at first rejected this ingenious idea and once again threatened war. Fortunately, American pressure—including an uncharacteristically harsh demarche by Bunker himself—eventually brought him to take a cooler view, though only after Bunker's compromise formula was further amended to provide for the lowering of the Dutch flag for a single day when the U.N. first took over and the raising of the Indonesian flag not on January 1, 1963, but on December 31, 1962. (It would thus already be flying when the cock crowed on the new year.) The incident was another example of Indonesian determination to maximize their gains, however humiliating this might be for the Dutch or galling for the Americans.

Another, if less important, Indonesian objective was to stack the provisions on self-determination so as to make even more certain that the process would be a meaningless exercise with a foregone conclusion. A great deal of wrangling resulted, but with the increasingly dispirited Dutch running out of bargaining chips and the Americans anxious not to disrupt the end game of the protracted negotiation on the threshold of success, here too the Sukarno government largely had its way. In the final agreement, the authority of the United Nations in the self-determination exercise was seriously circumscribed. The U.N. secretary general *in consultation with* the Indonesian government would determine the number of international experts who could remain in the territory to assist in the process. Although the Dutch had argued for a much earlier self-determination exercise, as had some Papuans, the reference to the local inhabitants took place only in 1969. This timing gave the Indonesians six years to ensure that the Papuans voted the right way.

When the United Nations conducted a series of consultations with groups of Papuan representatives at that time, they found that the Papuans unanimously chose to remain with Indonesia. Few outsiders were surprised, or cared. Once settled on the terms of the revised Bunker Plan, West New Guinea had become almost instant history, even in The Netherlands, and by the end of the 1960s had long been overshadowed by more pressing world problems.[31]

Bunker was widely acclaimed for his role in bringing the negotiations to a successful conclusion. A jubilant Subandrio said at the signing ceremony at the United Nations on August 14 that "without the personal qualities inherent to Ambassador Bunker, it would [have been] almost impossible to formulate an agreement within such a short period."[32] The Indonesian foreign minister, referring to his skill in handling difficult and delicate subjects, told Howard Jones, "You can be proud of Bunker."[33] Van Roijen no doubt shared the widespread Dutch sentiment that the settlement was an exceedingly bad deal for The Netherlands.[34] But he joined in the public praise and wrote Bunker privately: "We are fully aware of the fact that without your patience, perseverance and resourcefulness, combined with what our Indonesian friends called your 'Oriental tact,' we never would have achieved the final positive result which both parties so strongly desired." [35] President Kennedy wrote Bunker that his was "an outstanding example of personal diplomacy, of which our nation and the entire United Nations should be proud." [36]

U Thant wanted to make Bunker U.N. administrator for West New Guinea. Both the Dutch and Indonesians favored the nomination, Sukarno terming it "an ideal choice." [37] But Bunker turned down the offer; he appears to have concluded among other reasons that functioning in the primitive conditions of West New Guinea would be too physically demanding. American media reaction to the settlement was mixed, but Bunker's role in it was generally lauded. His hometown paper, the *Brattleboro Daily Recorder*, was understandably proud of his achievement, "the first time the United States can take the credit for terminating a war since President Theodore Roosevelt was the intermediary in ending the Russo-Japanese war of 1905." [38]

Although Bunker worked in close coordination with other American policymakers and advisers, the credit for the techniques and strategy that brought the negotiations to a successful outcome was deservedly his. As the foregoing narrative suggests, that had been no easy task. Discussing Bunker's role thirty years later, Terrence Markin correctly concluded that although outside events, such as Djakarta's military buildup and Washington's apprehension about PKI and Soviet inroads into Indonesia greatly influenced the talks, "the dispute had not become so ripe for settlement that anyone serving as moderator could have brought the parties to terms. The person who took on that responsibility had the formidable task of keeping the Indonesians hopeful that they could achieve their aims peacefully while at the same time giving the Dutch the hope that they could gain enough concessions to preserve their sense of national honor." [39]

One sees many aspects of Bunker's approach to the West New Guinea negotiating process in his other diplomatic efforts. They include his ability to come across to his fellow negotiators as someone fair and impartial, a man they could trust. His patience and understanding of others' viewpoints stood him in good stead in dealing with people as stubbornly proud as the Dutch and as emotionally vengeful as the Indonesians. They also helped him win the confidence of Dutch and Indonesian leaders and negotiators often far apart in temperament, outlook, negotiating techniques, and goals not only from their negotiating opponents but from their own colleagues as well.

Bunker's character and standing permitted him to function effectively in the highest circles of government, an important advantage for a negotiator. He dealt easily, more or less as an equal, with U Thant, de Quay, and Sukarno, and was able to maintain close working relations with Kennedy and Rusk. Always a team player, he could recognize when it was important to have the president and the secretary (or, in the U.N. context, the secretary-general) intervene in the negotiations. The good relations he enjoyed with them helped ensure an effective division of labor, and he felt no loss of face when they took part.

In his own sessions with the Dutch and Indonesians, Bunker employed several stratagems long recognized by successful negotiators. Fortunate in having a pleasant and isolated rural venue for the talks, an arrangement he had promoted and greatly valued, he used the Middleburg country house first as a useful setting for an informal exchange of views. Although he must have known that the Indonesians, fearful of Sukarno's reaction to any unguided brainstorming on their part, were in no position to engage fruitfully in such an exchange, he wisely saw the exercise as a confidence-building measure, or at least a way for the opposing delegations to develop easier relations.

When, almost inevitably in such a difficult negotiation, the two sides reached an impasse on the major issues, Bunker repeatedly sought to get them to focus on smaller details as the basis for discussion. A variant of this approach, which he employed when the talks were suspended, was to persuade them to agree "in principle," and thereafter to negotiate over detailed points. As he pursued these techniques and sought to keep sessions friendly and constructive, he sought to minimize differences between the two parties and maintained that substantial progress was being made. He resorted to ambiguities and rather loose interpretations of conflicting positions to make these upbeat, often tenuous claims. Then, as Markin found, "he slowly drew these points of consensus together in a series of written records of the discussions to convince the parties that the views they shared in common could be threaded together to form a final agreement."[40]

When deadlocks developed, or sessions became acrimonious, Bunker would quickly recess the talks, often going into private sessions afterwards with the individual delegations. If the parties seemed unlikely to develop proposals acceptable to the other side, he moved quickly and decisively to bring forward a plan of his own.

This exemplified what was probably the most prominent hallmark of Bunker's negotiating style. He used it again when he acted as a third party in negotiations to end the crises in Yemen and the Dominican Republic and in bilateral negotiations with the Panamanians over the Panama Canal. In the West New Guinea negotiations, as in the others, he was successful in making his proposal the focus for all subsequent discussion: once the Bunker Plan was introduced, both the Indonesians and the Dutch were compelled to deal with it to the exclusion of any other approach.

The way Bunker introduced the plan also typified the way he liked to operate. He confronted the Indonesians and the Dutch with the proposals early in the negotiations; he did so suddenly; and he provided little advance warning. As noted, this led the Dutch to complain that they had been handed a fait accompli. The technique had a certain shock value, no doubt further sharpening Dutch awareness of their limited options. Moreover, the plan laid down only the main elements for a settlement. Far from a definitive document, it proposed a basis for negotiations that could bring the two sides back to the table. The Dutch and the Indonesians soon recognized it as such.

In trying to win acceptance of his plan, Bunker used public diplomacy to good effect. He brought pressure on the recalcitrant negotiators, first by releasing the text of the plan, with U Thant's agreement, then in meeting with correspondents on a background basis to explain and promote its provisions. No novice at media relations, he had become quite adept at them during his business and earlier diplomatic careers.

For all his reputation for straightforwardness in his diplomatic dealings, Bunker was not entirely above advancing arguments he could not have fully accepted himself. His discussion about Papuan self-determination was an example. When he tried to refute van Roijen's accurate contention that the plan's self-determination formula amounted to a Dutch surrender by countering that the United Nations would play a role in Papuan free choice, he must have been aware that Indonesian control over a territory whose backward inhabitants they could easily manipulate was highly likely to make a limited U.N. presence there futile. Perhaps he could justify the argument, to himself at least, by regarding it as a sop, a rather shaky talking point the Netherlands government could use with its public (though he surely would have known that the Dutch were literally the last people on earth to expect Sukarno and his henchmen to permit a fair referendum). What seems most likely is that, like other Americans involved, Bunker saw his plan as the best the Dutch could be offered if war and its traumatic consequences for "free world" objectives in Southeast Asia were to be avoided. The Netherlands government would have to be prevailed upon to accept it. Beneath his always courteous exterior, he could be quite tough when the occasion demanded, as it did in these negotiations.

With Bunker as moderator of the bilateral negotiations, the United States achieved its principal objective—avoiding a war over West New Guinea that could have had disastrous consequences for Washington's interests in Southeast Asia and beyond. But Indonesia's acquisition of the territory did not lead to the promising changes in Sukarno's policies that some in the administration had forecast when they argued for a more engaged U.S. role. This disappointing outcome led to Bunker's further, brief involvement with Indonesian affairs in the spring of 1965, recounted in Chapter 9.

8

Brokering a Yemen Settlement

A military coup in a remote part of the Arab world triggered a political crisis that led President Kennedy to turn again to Bunker to play a major international negotiating role. On September 26, 1962, dissidents led by Colonel Abdullah Sallal overthrew the centuries-old monarchy of Yemen, a small, backward country in the southwestern corner of the Arabian Peninsula. Sallal proclaimed a Yemen Arab Republic (YAR) and announced a program of radical change in the country's archaic political, economic, and social structure. He received immediate support from Egyptian president Gamal Abdel Nasser, whose government had helped foment and plan the revolt. At Sallal's request, Nasser soon began supplying troops, technicians, and arms to bolster the new regime in a civil war that developed between the YAR and tribesmen loyal to the deposed ruling family.[1]

The launching of the Yemen republic had major implications for the power balance in the Middle East. Under the banner of Arab nationalism, Nasser had sought since the mid-1950s to mobilize radical forces, sweep from power the region's conservative governments, and end Western presence and influence. The ambitious, charismatic Egyptian president intensified his campaign following the costly setback he suffered when Syria seceded from his United Arab Republic in 1961.[2] He regarded the overthrow of the Yemeni monarchy and its replacement by a radical republican regime as a triumph of the revolutionary nationalist cause and an opportunity to recoup the losses in prestige and influence Syria's defection had cost him. For Nasser, the events in Yemen were an important step toward his goal of remolding and dominating the Arab world and controlling its lucrative petroleum resources.

The kingdom of Saudi Arabia, ruled by the conservative Saud dynasty, was an obstacle to Nasser's plans, and the Egyptians had launched a strenuous propaganda onslaught against its royal family. The Saudi leadership was understandably alarmed by Sallal's coup and Nasser's strong support for the new republican government on their vulnerable southern border.

Crown Prince Faisal, visiting the United States at the time, told President Kennedy and other American officials he was convinced that Nasser intended to use Yemen as a stepping stone to take over Saudi Arabia either directly or by proxy forces in the region.[3] Saudi concern was heightened by Yemen's irredentist claims to areas on the Saudi side of the undemarcated border between the two countries. The Saudis feared that the YAR might revive these dormant claims at Egyptian instigation to put pressure on the kingdom.

When the Egyptians began sending troops to shore up the YAR, the Saudi government responded by providing arms, ammunition, and cash to tribesmen who had rallied to the royalist cause. This Saudi intervention, in which the conservative government of King Hussein of Jordan played a brief and limited role, led to a further escalation in Egyptian military involvement. By November, estimates of Egyptian personnel in Yemen ranged up to 10,000 and Egyptian air force planes were bombing Saudi border towns they considered supply points for the royalist army.

The uprising and the events it triggered posed difficult problems for the United States. Its interests in Yemen itself were limited. It had scant regard for the despotic and discredited rule of the ousted royal family, and had the coup not led to the involvement of outside powers it would not have been particularly troubled. What *did* concern the Kennedy administration were the potential consequences the Saudi-Egyptian confrontation posed for its broader objectives in the Middle East.

Developing stronger U.S. relations with Nasser was one of the more important of these goals. Breaking with Eisenhower's preference for the status quo in the Third World, the administration had calculated that reaching out to radical governments such as Nasser's with greater political understanding and generous economic assistance could lead these regimes to loosen their ties with the Communist bloc and adopt more constructive foreign and domestic policies. It had already made some progress in strengthening relations with Egypt but now feared that Nasser's aggressive actions in Yemen could jeopardize these gains by compelling it to come to the Saudis' assistance.

Recognizing that the kingdom's vast oil resources and strategic location made it highly important for the United States, the administration had continued Washington's longstanding policy of friendship for the Saudis and support for their security. It worried that Saudi intervention in the Yemeni civil war could undermine Saudi Arabia's pro-American monarchy, with grave consequences for U.S. interests in the country and elsewhere in the Middle East. In its estimate, Saudi support for the Yemeni royalists was unpopular in the kingdom.[4] Involvement in Yemen was distracting Faisal, by then Saudi Arabia's de facto ruler, from the social and economic reforms the Kennedy administration believed were the best way to ward off a radical upheaval. Such involvement could lead to a further escalation of hostilities that would confront the United States with painful choices between its Egyptian and Saudi interests.

As the Yemeni struggle intensified, its Cold War dimensions heightened administration concerns. The Cuban missile crisis that October had raised the U.S.-Soviet confrontation to new and dangerous heights, and the hostilities in Yemen soon brought into play the rivalry between the two superpowers for influence in the Middle East. The Soviets warmly supported Nasser and followed his lead in recognizing and assisting the YAR.[5] This close association between Cairo and Moscow fueled U.S. fears that Soviet influence in Yemen would grow, especially if the civil war continued.

Washington had been cautious at first in responding to the events in Yemen. It spurned suggestions that it intervene on the side of the royalists and chose to wait until the situation clarified before making a decision about recognizing the republican regime. It urged other powers not to get involved and looked for ways to limit the conflict. It also sought to reassure the jittery Saudis. When he met Faisal soon after the coup, Kennedy reaffirmed U.S. commitment to Saudi security and territorial integrity.[6] Later, as Egyptian planes and warships struck at Saudi targets, Washington staged air and naval demonstrations to underscore its support.

Kennedy became deeply involved in Yemen policy. After considerable controversy within his administration, he decided in mid-November to put forward a package of proposals designed to bring about reciprocal disengagement by the contending parties.[7] Its key elements included "expeditious and phased" withdrawals of Egyptian forces from Yemen and of Saudi and Jordanian forces from Saudi territory bordering Yemen, and termination of Saudi and Jordanian support to the royalists. Kennedy also called for an Egyptian pledge to meet its obligations as the Saudis and Jordanians fulfilled theirs, and a public YAR affirmation that it would honor its international obligations, seek normal and friendly relations with its neighbors, and concentrate its attention on domestic affairs. Once these two statements were issued, the United States would recognize the YAR.

In a separate, balancing letter to Faisal, Kennedy reaffirmed U.S. commitments to Saudi Arabia.[8]

The package reflected the administration's appraisal of the current situation. Washington believed that the YAR controlled most of Yemen's territory and that Nasser was determined to keep the Sallal government in power. Saudi-supported efforts to dislodge the YAR would be futile and dangerous. Continued U.S. nonrecognition of the YAR could lead to greater Soviet influence in Yemen.[9] However, the prospect of diplomatic relations could be a useful bait to extract an Egyptian undertaking eventually to withdraw its forces and a YAR pledge to avoid provoking its neighbors.[10]

The administration also concluded that it could live with a continuing Egyptian military presence in Yemen. Nothing in its package precluded the Egyptians from stationing advisers in Yemen to train the YAR military. In fact, Washington feared that if the Egyptians did not play that role, the YAR would turn to the Soviets to do so.[11]

Both the Egyptian and YAR governments eventually issued the statements Kennedy had called for. United States recognition of the YAR promptly followed. But Faisal considered the package one-sided and would not accept it. His deep hostility toward Nasser stiffened his determination to force the Egyptians to leave Yemen, the primary aim of Saudi policy.[12] He believed that if the Saudis stopped helping the royalists, Nasser would quickly renege on his disengagement pledge. Parker T. Hart, the U.S. ambassador to Saudi Arabia, reported the crown prince as "convinced that Nasser is his implacable enemy and he sees a chance to strike back by an operation of attrition which will injure Nasser's prestige in Yemen, Egypt, and the Arab world in general."[13]

In January, Faisal offered a counterproposal calling for withdrawal of foreign forces from Yemen followed by an end to all external military assistance. The people of Yemen should decide their own future in a plebiscite supervised by an international commission.[14] Angered by the U.S. formula for recognition, the crown prince stepped up assistance to the royalists.

Washington recognized that Faisal's personal pride and honor were deeply involved and looked for ways to break the impasse. It offered the Saudis an enhanced package of security assistance and resorted to private diplomacy by enlisting a retired American oil company executive who was an old friend of Faisal to visit Saudi Arabia quietly and persuade the crown prince to disengage. When these ploys failed to budge Faisal, it considered making Kennedy's proposal more palatable to him by persuading Nasser to withdraw a few Egyptian military units when the Saudis suspended their assistance to the royalists.

Meanwhile, the administration tried to persuade U Thant, the United Nations secretary general, to play a more active role. Fearing that he would be tarred as a U.S. tool, Thant had resisted an earlier U.S. request to appoint a special envoy to negotiate a disengagement agreement. Washington was annoyed by Thant's attitude and told him in late January that "as an earnest of U.S. support" it was willing to have an American undertake the mission if he wished. The man it had in mind was Ellsworth Bunker.[15]

After Bunker had completed the West New Guinea negotiations, he had become a special consultant to Secretary Rusk, an appointment that kept him available for further troubleshooting tasks. The idea of his playing the role of U.N. special representative on Yemen seems to have come from George McGhee, the under secretary of state for political affairs. Rusk enthusiastically endorsed McGhee's suggestion. The secretary said that Bunker would be "three times better" than other possible candidates whose names had been mentioned for the sensitive mission.[16]

Both Rusk and McGhee admired Bunker for resolving the West New Guinea crisis, and the secretary, at the time head of the Rockefeller Foundation, had also witnessed his performance as ambassador to India during a visit in the late 1950s. Neither they nor any other U.S. officials seem to have been concerned that Bunker would be a newcomer to the problems of the Middle East and had never met its leaders. Even the State Department's prominent Arabist contingent appeared to recognize that the task called for a senior figure who had demonstrated skill in gaining the confidence of suspicious, tough-minded, prickly antagonists, not a regional specialist. Bunker had those credentials. He also enjoyed the president's trust and gratitude for his New Guinea success, an important advantage given Kennedy's personal involvement. Ambassador Hart has recalled that the president "saw [Bunker] as a seasoned troubleshooter who could command respect and retain friendliness while administering necessary doses of advice."[17]

Although the two men were on good terms—another consequence of the West New Guinea negotiations—U Thant would not accept Bunker as his representative. According to Robert Komer, the senior National Security Council staffer dealing with Yemen policy, "our effort to sell Bunker to the secretary general as mediator . . . struck the rock of U Thant's reluctance to seem a U.S. stooge."[18] Thant eventually chose Ralph Bunche, the U.N. under secretary for special political affairs. Bunche was also an American, but his position as a senior U.N. official protected the secretary general from charges that he was unduly bending the United Nations to U.S. policy imperatives in dealing with the Yemeni crisis.

U Thant's decision to look elsewhere did not keep Bunker out of the Yemen loop for long. A few weeks later, as the situation on the ground continued to deteriorate, President Kennedy personally presided over the most comprehensive review of U.S. Yemen policy since the September coup. A key decision reached at this White House session was to send a special presidential emissary to Saudi Arabia with a letter from Kennedy to Faisal. The envoy was to be more than a mere messenger. He was instructed "to reassure Faisal of U.S. interest in Saudi Arabia; convince him of the importance of disengaging from Yemen; and explain to him how we think this can be done without loss of face."[19] U.S. policymakers had addressed these issues repeatedly for over three months, without success. Kennedy and his advisers believed that a presidential letter hand-carried by a senior emissary who could speak to the crown prince with authority and urgency would make the administration's arguments more forceful and persuasive, though the president himself was pessimistic about Faisal's reaction. Bunker was the obvious choice for the job, and Kennedy met him at the White House on March 1 to give him his marching orders.

These instructed Bunker to stress to Faisal, once again, that the only way to bring about Egyptian troop withdrawal from Yemen was by suspending Saudi support for the royalist cause.[20] When the Saudis did so, the United States would press for the departure of Egyptian troops. The administration was confident that a formula could be found to link the Saudi and Egyptian obligations that would be consistent with the crown prince's honor. Bunker was to warn Faisal that the United States was unwilling to allow the Saudis to provide a haven from which the royalists could operate against a government that Washington recognized, and to tell him that enhanced U.S. military backing would be conditional on Saudi disengagement. Bunker's instructions also called on him to reiterate the importance of Faisal's focusing on his modernization and reform program, which the United States would continue to support.

Bunker took six weeks to persuade the Saudis and the Egyptians to reach a disengagement settlement. At first he was billed as Kennedy's special envoy to Crown Prince Faisal. When U Thant and Faisal were unable to find a mutually acceptable basis for Bunche's proposed visit, Bunker took the lead in persuading the president to change his own role to full-fledged mediator. Bunche eventually went to Cairo and Sanaa, the Yemeni capital, but his discussions were limited to fact-finding.

During his negotiations Bunker visited the Middle East three times. On his first two trips he met only Saudi leaders. He had planned to go directly from Saudi Arabia to Cairo following his second visit to the kingdom, but to Washington's (and Bunker's) consternation Nasser postponed the negotiations. Following a rescheduled trip to Egypt, Bunker returned to Saudi Arabia, then went back to Cairo, where he clinched the settlement. He never visited Yemen and met no Yemeni leaders, royalist or republican. He operated exclusively at the summit: Faisal and Nasser were his negotiating partners at all formal sessions. The resident American ambassador always accompanied Bunker to these meetings.

In the course of this shuttle diplomacy, Bunker went to New York several times for consultations with U Thant, Bunche, and other U.N. officials. The administration disingenuously maintained that his activities supported the U.N. effort and took place under U.N. auspices. As Adlai Stevenson, the U.S. permanent representative at the United Nations, complained to Rusk: "We assured U Thant that [when he made his first trip] Ellsworth Bunker was essentially concerned with our bilateral relations with Saudi Arabia and we wanted the United Nations to do the main job. However, Bunker was in fact instructed to present to Faisal a concrete and detailed disengagement proposal, which he did with his usual skill and effectiveness. . . . We are [now] endeavoring to negotiate a whole disengagement process ourselves under a supposed umbrella which U Thant has in fact never offered us."[21]

Bunker kept the secretary general informed of his progress and repeatedly urged Faisal and Thant to find a way for Bunche to visit Saudi Arabia.[22] He told Nasser and Faisal that Washington expected the United Nations to monitor whatever settlement he worked out. But, as Stevenson wrote, Bunker's mission was an exercise in American diplomacy, and he took negotiating positions developed within the U.S. government without reference to the United Nations.

The White House and the State Department effectively coordinated the guidance Bunker received. Ambassadors John Badeau in Cairo and Parker Hart in Jidda planned strategy with him and at times spoke out in the negotiations. He developed strong relations with both envoys and made good use of their considerable experience in the Arab world.[23]

Despite Washington's high-level interest, Bunker enjoyed considerable latitude at the negotiating table. Talcott Seelye, a senior State Department officer who assisted him throughout the negotiations, recalled that before each session, Bunker, Hart or Badeau, and Seelye himself would meet to develop tactics and talking points. In these exercises, they were largely on their own, though bound of course by the broad policy framework and terms of reference Washington had developed.[24] In this setting, Bunker and his colleagues independently formulated several proposals and negotiating strategies that helped bring the talks to a successful conclusion.

Bunker was delighted both personally and professionally with the assignment. After the West New Guinea experience, he was ready to take on another tough negotiating job. He hoped that the negotiations would not keep him away from Harriet for too long. By then she was very ill. When her stomach pains persisted in the fall of 1962, a more thorough examination revealed that she had cancer. After surgery at Columbia-Presbyterian Hospital in New York City Harriet was flown to São Paulo, where she and Ellsworth had built a small house on the grounds of the home of her daughter Ellen and Ellen's husband, Fernando Gentil, an oncologist and surgeon. She remained bed-ridden there under Dr. Gentil's care throughout the Yemen negotiations.

As the negotiations lengthened, Bunker grew increasingly restive and anxious to be with Harriet. During the early months of her recuperation he frequently visited her in São Paulo, and special arrangements were made for him to communicate with her and Gentil through the American consulate general there. At one point, when Harriet's condition worsened, there was some talk about his leaving the negotiations. Fortunately, she rallied sufficiently for him to carry on.

Bunker faced daunting problems as he undertook the negotiating process. Neither Nasser nor Faisal believed the other would fulfill his promise to disengage. As noted, Faisal was convinced that Nasser was determined to overthrow the House of Saud in his quest for power and was using Yemen as a stepping stone to that goal. He wanted to make Nasser bleed in Yemen to undercut his prestige and authority in the Arab world. His mistrust for the Egyptian president led him to insist that Saudi aid to the royalists cease only after all Egyptian troops had been withdrawn from Yemen. He believed that the YAR would collapse once the Egyptian expeditionary force had left, and wanted a deadline set for its withdrawal.

Nasser found these conditions unacceptable, as Faisal must have known he would. The Egyptian president's overriding objective was to safeguard the YAR regime. He was confident that once the Saudis stopped helping the royalists the civil war would quickly end. He was prepared to remove the bulk of his armed forces from Yemen when that happened and not before. He could not believe that Faisal would honor an undertaking to cut off the flow of Saudi arms and money and feared that if the crown prince unexpectedly did so, the Saudis would resume their assistance once the Egyptians were on their way out.

At the same time, Nasser wished to end Egyptian participation in the civil war if he could do so on acceptable terms. Yemen was costing Egypt much more in money and lives than he had anticipated. But he had invested too much to pull out his troops without either a victory or a negotiated settlement that kept the YAR in power. In the meantime, the situation seemed to be going well for him on the battleground. His forces had launched a major offensive and were making good progress in cleaning out centers of royalist resistance. So he was in no hurry to reach an agreement to disengage.

Faisal, for his part, could not have felt easy about the prospect of a prolonged proxy war in Yemen despite the steep preconditions for disengagement that he set out. The Saudis had been shaken by Egyptian attacks on their territory and evidence of major Egyptian efforts to subvert the Saudi state. Coups in Syria and Iraq that brought pro-Nasser regimes to power heightened their sense of vulnerability. Although some of Faisal's advisors suggested that France could provide the security the Saudis required, and he apparently considered engaging mercenaries, the crown prince recognized that the best hope for the Saudi monarchy's survival remained American political and military support. He seemed prepared to do what he could consistent with his honor and prestige to ensure that it continued. This was an important asset for Bunker.

The personal rapport he established with Faisal also helped Bunker. Ambassador Hart recorded later that "Bunker, with his courtly dignity and innate kindness, obviously pleased Faisal."[25] Hart concluded that Bunker's ability to develop good relations with Faisal was "for lack of a better phrase . . . [one] patrician recognizing another. This kept the discussions calm, reasonable and to the point."[26] Bilateral ties with the United States and personal style were less significant advantages in Bunker's dealings with Nasser, who depended far less than Faisal did on American support and was not particularly impressed by gentlemanly behavior.

Bunker came to the negotiations with a carefully developed eight-point disengagement program. This remained his basic negotiating document throughout his talks with Faisal and Nasser.[27] Its main provisions were Saudi agreement to suspend support of the Yemeni royalists, Egyptian agreement to begin withdrawal of troops when the Saudis suspended their assistance, and the consent of both governments to the stationing of neutral observers on the Saudi-Yemeni border and at YAR harbors and airports to certify that these undertakings were carried out. Other important terms included Egyptian implementation of its pledge to fully remove its troops from Yemen and Saudi banning of royalist use of its territory to attack the YAR. Egypt was to "encourage" the Sallal government to concentrate on domestic affairs and avoid provoking its neighbors. The United States undertook to provide increased security support to the Saudis to ward off Egyptian attacks. (For obvious reasons, this provision was not revealed to the Egyptians until the negotiations were successfully concluded.)

Both Parker Hart and Christopher McMullen, a U.S. Foreign Service officer, have examined the progress of Bunker's negotiations in great detail. This study will accordingly focus on Bunker's handling of several major problems in the negotiating process.

Perhaps the foremost of these was Faisal's attitude toward the United States. As he began his discussions, Bunker recognized the importance of overcoming the crown prince's resentment about Washington's recent Yemen policy and restoring his confidence in U.S. commitment to Saudi security. He needed to persuade Faisal that the United States wished to help him, but could do so only if the Saudis stopped assisting the royalists' effort to overthrow the YAR, a government Washington recognized. In the process, he had to take account of Faisal's sensitivities to negotiating ploys the prince might consider pressure tactics or undue interference in Saudi domestic affairs.

Bunker's success in developing a relaxed, unhurried atmosphere in the discussions greatly assisted in persuading Faisal that the United States was a faithful partner. As Ambassador Hart had found, Faisal valued warm, personal dialogue and came to accept Bunker's sometimes unwelcome advice as the candid expression of a well-meaning friend. Bunker's approach —we want to help you, please don't make a problem for us—seemed to go over well with Faisal, especially after the prince had had ample opportunity to reiterate his resentments about American perceptions and policies.

The personal messages Kennedy sent the prince helped. At times Bunker edited and embroidered them to make them more convincing. The authority Washington had given him to offer Faisal an impressive security assistance package strengthened his arguments. This package included stationing a squadron of U.S. F-100 fighters and other supporting aircraft in the kingdom (later termed Operation Hard Surface), assisting the Saudis to develop an adequate air defense system, and expediting the training of Saudi Air Force and air defense personnel. The Saudis would receive the package only when they ended their support for the royalists.

As Bunker pursued his efforts, Faisal softened his insistence that he would stop assisting the royalists only after Egyptian troops had been withdrawn. He told Bunker at their second meeting that he was prepared to accept suspension of aid in principle if he received assurance that Egyptian forces would indeed leave Yemen.

This was an important breakthrough for Bunker. By agreeing to a position of parallelism between Egyptian troop withdrawal and suspension of Saudi aid, Faisal gave him the crucial opening he needed to develop a negotiating process. With this Saudi concession in hand, Bunker could then try to persuade Faisal to accept the main lines of the U.S. proposals for disengagement. Once he had made substantial progress with the Saudis he could approach Nasser reasonably confident of reaching a final settlement. This strategy determined the sequence of his shuttle diplomacy.

The negotiating process that Faisal's concession made possible was not an easy one. The crown prince immediately complicated it further by unveiling a list of conditions for the cutoff of Saudi aid. Some of these were stipulations about the way the Egyptians were to withdraw, such as his demand for an immediate end to all Egyptian military activity within Yemen and the regrouping of their forces under the supervision of neutral observers as they prepared to leave the country. More far-reaching was Faisal's insistence that the Egyptians withdraw all these forces from the country by an agreed date.

Recognizing that Nasser would not accept most of Faisal's demands, Bunker at first temporized. He disingenuously held that he was not authorized to act as a mediator. He would be glad, so he told Faisal, to pass the proposals on to the U.N. secretary general; they were not his business to handle. This was technically correct, though, as Stevenson had pointedly noted, Bunker's status had not deterred him from presenting the U.S. eight-point proposal to the Saudis.

When Bunker returned to Saudi Arabia later wearing his mediator's hat, he argued that most of Faisal's points regarding the modalities of Egyptian withdrawal would take too much time to negotiate. They were in any event unnecessary since they dealt with issues that would automatically be carried out once the Egyptians began to leave. Faisal disagreed but was willing to compromise. He was prepared to concede, for example, that the withdrawing Egyptians could defend themselves if the royalists attacked them. Eager to move the negotiations along, Bunker warned him that distinguishing between offensive and defensive operations would be difficult and time-consuming. He reinforced his argument with an oral message from Kennedy in which the president told Faisal that his proposals "could not, in our judgement, be successfully negotiated, certainly not within the short time we feel remains in which to avert a broadening of the conflict."[28]

Kennedy's message also cited the worsening security situation the Saudis faced in Yemen, elsewhere in the Middle East, and within the kingdom itself. A good example of Bunker's use in the negotiating process of the president's concern, the message exemplified the "scare tactics" the U.S. side sometimes employed with the Saudis to bring an early end to the crisis. Bits and pieces of Faisal's demands about troop withdrawals were worked into the final agreement but did not significantly change Bunker's original formulation.

Bunker used different tactics in dealing with Faisal's demand for the withdrawal of all Egyptian troops by a fixed deadline. He stressed to the crown prince that Nasser would be under great pressure to complete the pullout once he had agreed to withdraw. He and Kennedy asserted that the president himself would press Nasser to remove his troops from Yemen in phases and expeditiously (without defining those words).

Bunker used this "trust us" approach most explicitly when he met the prince on his third and final visit to Saudi Arabia immediately after talking with Nasser in Cairo. He had come away from Egypt convinced that Nasser would never agree to a withdrawal timetable or deadline. The Egyptian president envisioned a gradual drawdown of his forces and their replacement by YAR troops. As noted, Nasser's primary interest in Yemen was to safeguard YAR rule. That imperative would determine the pace of the possibly lengthy withdrawal operation. Under these circumstances, talk about timetables was fruitless, as Bunker soon learned when Nasser rebuffed his efforts to raise the issue.

Although Nasser's acceptance of some kind of vague timetable would have made it easier for Bunker to win over the Saudis, the United States could live with the Egyptian position. Its fundamental objective was to end the Egyptian-Saudi military confrontation. As a State Department document put it, "with the cessation of Saudi Arabian government arms shipments and the gradual withdrawal of [Egyptian] military forces, the main thrust of royalist resistance will probably be lessened and the tribes, who on the whole are without clear-cut loyalties, are likely opportunistically to accommodate themselves within the [republican] central government within the limits of traditional tribal independence."[29] Washington could therefore accept a drawn-out withdrawal of most Egyptian forces, with some remaining as "military advisors" to the YAR army.

It believed that such an arrangement would also benefit the Saudis. They would be rid of a costly and unpopular war, and the subsequent stationing of an American fighter squadron on their territory would enhance their security. Under these favorable circumstances, Faisal could again focus on reform and modernization, the progressive programs that Washington thought necessary to preserve the Saud dynasty in a changing and threatening Middle East.

With these considerations in mind, Bunker presented the case against a deadline to a perturbed and unhappy Faisal. He reported that Nasser had been reluctant to indicate a time frame for withdrawal and told the prince that if he insisted on a time limit, it would have to be long enough to ensure that the Egyptians could comply with it. Such a timetable would probably be longer than the situation required because Nasser would want to protect himself against unanticipated contingencies. Bunker declared that in light of Nasser's attitude Faisal should rely on President Kennedy's interest in prompt disengagement and his concern for the prince's honor and dignity. Such presidential involvement would be more effective insurance for the Saudis than setting an unrealistic schedule.

Eventually, Faisal accepted an agreement that said nothing about a withdrawal deadline. Bunker recalled that as he did so the crown prince told him: "I don't trust Nasser but I trust you, Ambassador Bunker, and that is why I go along with the agreement."[30]

But Bunker would probably have failed to bring the crown prince around if he had not persuaded Nasser to make what could be represented to Faisal as a significant Egyptian concession on another important issue: how the timing of Egyptian withdrawal and Saudi aid termination would relate to one another.

This matter had been a major obstacle to a settlement. In a meeting shortly before Bunker began his mission, an exasperated Dean Rusk told the Saudi ambassador: "The issue confronting us is not one of policy, but of timing and arrangement. We face a dilemma in which both sides demand that the other disengage first."[31] The eight-point plan that Bunker presented to Faisal during his first Saudi visit called for "an agreement by [Egypt] to begin withdrawal of its troops simultaneously with suspension of aid to the royalists by the Saudi Arabian Government."[32]

But simultaneity could be interpreted in different ways. Early in the negotiations, Bunker had suggested that Egyptian withdrawal should begin as soon as observers stationed on the Saudi-Yemeni border had verified that Saudi aid to the royalists had stopped. Yet U.S. officials had for months spoken about the need for at least a token withdrawal of Egyptian forces at the same time as the Saudis halted assistance, and on his first visit to Saudi Arabia Bunker recognized that this would be necessary to bring about Saudi concurrence. Accordingly, the message he brought from Kennedy as he began his second Saudi round urged Faisal to "let Ambassador Bunker try to work out with Nasser an arrangement whereby, on a date to be mutually agreed, you will suspend aid to the royalists at the same time the UAR will begin its withdrawal by moving a unit out of Yemen."[33]

When he did so on the second day of his round with Nasser, Bunker stressed the importance of at least a token simultaneous withdrawal. Without it, the Saudis would refuse to disengage. As suspicious of Faisal's good faith as Faisal was of his, Nasser remained adamant. He maintained that no withdrawal could take place until there was actual evidence of the cessation of Saudi aid and Egyptian forces had had an opportunity to clean up pockets of tribal resistance the Saudis had sustained. When Bunker argued that the Egyptians could withdraw at least one battalion from their 30,000-man force without imperiling YAR security, Nasser consulted his senior military aide and said he was prepared to remove a battalion, not concurrently with the Saudis' action but within fifteen days of it. Only after prolonged further negotiations could he persuade Nasser to withdraw one or two companies when the Saudis cut off their aid.

Bunker used unusual negotiating tactics to win Nasser's acceptance of immediate token withdrawal. As McMullen described it:

Having failed to convince Nasser on this point after two tough negotiating rounds, Bunker apparently decided to leave out the principle of simultaneity . . . from the revised set of 'proposals,' and to argue for this in his oral discussions with Nasser. In effect, Bunker was presenting the Egyptian President with a 'proposal' which was less than the official American mediating position [and was] clearly at odds with the principle of simultaneity which the envoy had earlier presented to Faisal as the basis for disengagement. This unorthodox tactic had the psychological advantage of making Bunker's argument for simultaneity appear to be a personal appeal for reasonableness, rather than a formal proposal which was obviously backed by the U.S. government in addition to being required by Faisal.[34]

Even so, Nasser gave in only as the meeting was ending. Bunker remarked at that point that he would be meeting Faisal the following day. "If you really want to make it probable that I will not return to bother you again," he told Nasser, "just give me a company or so on the day Faisal begins to cease his support."[35] It was in this less than formal negotiating environment that Nasser agreed to Bunker's personal appeal.

Aside from these key issues, Bunker had to deal with many other problems relating to his eight-point negotiating brief that needed resolution before the Egyptians and Saudis could reach a settlement. These included establishing a demilitarized zone along the Saudi-Yemeni border, the role and positioning of impartial observers, ending the Egyptian-Saudi propaganda war, removing members of the Yemeni royal family from border areas, and halting Egyptian air attacks on Saudi territory. At times Bunker used somewhat unorthodox negotiating tactics in successfully achieving agreement on these delicate issues. For example, the proposals he presented for Nasser's consideration were neither the positions he had been able to wring out of Faisal in the course of his two earlier visits to Saudi Arabia nor those of the United States government. Instead, they were concessions Bunker believed he could eventually obtain from Faisal that would also seem reasonable to Nasser.

Bunker worked on these issues at the same time as he negotiated more basic ones. His progress on them probably helped encourage the Saudis and Egyptians to move forward on the others. Resolution of many of these lesser matters involved time-consuming haggling over words and nuances to satisfy the political requirements and, especially for Faisal, the honor of the contenders. Bunker was skillful in such exercises, vexing as they often were. He could master small details and find phraseology acceptable to both sides. He was always patient with them, even when they argued over virtually meaningless distinctions (such as whether to call for "expeditious" withdrawal or withdrawal "as soon as possible"). As good third-party mediators do, he sometimes left it to one party to originate wording on matters important to it but less significant to the other side.

A final issue was the problem of the YAR's obligations under the agreement. As noted, Bunker had not negotiated with the Yemenis. He counted on Nasser to persuade Sallal to accept the settlement. At Bunker's request, Nasser won Sallal's formal agreement to desist from further inflammatory speeches against Yemen's neighbors and to live at peace with them. The undertaking was not included in the Egyptian-Saudi agreement, however. Faisal, who still refused to recognize the YAR, insisted that it be a bilateral matter between the United States and Egypt.

Both the Saudis and the Egyptians preferred to treat their compromise settlement in a low-key manner. Neither side wanted to expose itself to propaganda charges that it had suffered a setback, and the Saudis had never publicly acknowledged that they were involved in the Yemeni civil war. Thus there was no public signing of the agreement, which Bunker nailed down on April 10, 1963, when the Saudis agreed to the text he had worked out with Nasser in Cairo the day before. He handled this final negotiation through diplomatic channels and did not need to return to Saudi Arabia for the purpose. The Egyptian and Saudi radios reported the agreement soon afterwards. U Thant formally announced it on April 30.

But Bunker's impressive achievement proved ephemeral. It was undermined by further foot-dragging at the United Nations.

The settlement Bunker negotiated stipulated that Egypt and Saudi Arabia would cooperate "with the U.N. representative, or some other mutually acceptable mediator, in reaching agreement on the process and verification of disengagement."[36] On his return from the Middle East, Bunker briefed Thant and Bunche and urged the secretary general to send a special representative to the region to implement the agreement. But Thant proved as diffident in shaping an appropriate post-settlement U.N. role as he had been in brokering a resolution earlier. Ignoring U.S. pleas for the early stationing of observers as called for in Bunker's formula, he readily accepted the Soviet contention that the Security Council must approve the agreement before the United Nations could send personnel to the field. The council did not do so until June 10, two months after Bunker had completed his work.[37] Peacekeeping troops arrived on the Yemen-Saudi border only on July 4.

By that time a good deal of momentum had been lost. The small peacekeeping force, operating on a tight budget and spread much too thinly over difficult territory, could not prevent the royalists from continuing their cross-border activity nor stop Egyptian bombing of Saudi facilities. For months U.N. headquarters barred the force from contact with the royalists, who in any event had not been parties to the accord and did not consider themselves bound by it. Nor did the Egyptians begin to reduce their military presence as they had agreed to do. In the weeks immediately after they signed the agreement, they sent fresh contingents to replace departing units. Whether the Saudis ever fully suspended their aid to the royalists is less clear, though the level of their assistance did decline in the short term. The simultaneous disengagement thus never occurred.

Bunker blamed the delay in implementing the agreement for its ultimate failure. In his view, the Soviets were responsible for this.[38] Carl von Horn, the Swedish general who headed the ill-starred U.N. mission in Yemen in 1963, also came to this conclusion. He wrote later that disengagement might have worked had there been "a swift and impressive assembly of an international force whose appearance would have made an impact."[39] But the chance was missed, and both sides had time for unhelpful second thoughts.

Some analysts question, however, whether Nasser really intended to begin a phased withdrawal of his combat troops from Yemen or, if he did, whether he had not soon changed his mind when he found that his appraisal of the military situation following the successful Egyptian military offensive against the royalists in February–March 1963 had proved overly optimistic, thus making a pullout too hazardous from Cairo's viewpoint.

The discredited agreement, and the contingent of United Nations peacekeepers sent to implement it, remained in place for a year and a half. In September 1964, the Saudis, frustrated by continuing Egyptian military activity and the ineffectiveness of the United Nations, announced they would no longer help fund the mission. By then some 60,000 Egyptian troops were in Yemen. Egyptian forces remained in the country until 1967, when the situation created by the Six-Day War led Nasser to withdraw them. The civil war continued for another three years. The Yemenis then worked out a power-sharing agreement that brought several royalist representatives into the republican government and allowed royalists to remain in control (under republican veneer) of areas they had held earlier. Saudi Arabia recognized the YAR two months later.

Despite the quick breakdown of the agreement, the Kennedy administration was right in seeking to resolve the Yemeni conflict. The dangers to U.S. Middle East interests were too great for Washington to stand aside, especially when the United Nations was reluctant to become involved. Although hostilities continued, the U.S. negotiating effort helped Washington achieve important objectives. Ground fighting, which had earlier spilled over onto Saudi soil, was thereafter confined to Yemen and did not escalate into a serious Egyptian-Saudi confrontation. Saudi stability was preserved and American oil interests safeguarded. The stationing of a U.S. Air Force fighter squadron in Saudi Arabia that Washington had made conditional on the signing of an agreement contributed to these welcome developments. The United States was able to maintain satisfactory relations with both Cairo and Riyadh. And the Soviets were unable to achieve paramount influence in Yemen.

Bunker believed the U.S. effort had been worth the try. He always maintained he had been right in persuading Kennedy that Washington needed to play a mediating role, not merely sit on its hands, or wring them, while the United Nations dawdled. Despite the unhappy denouement of his negotiations, he emerged from the Yemen talks with his credentials as a top-ranking American troubleshooter further burnished. To White House satisfaction, and with minimal Washington guidance, he had carried out his high-wire negotiating act with imagination and persistence at a time when such shuttle diplomacy was not the standard negotiating technique that it subsequently became. His success made him even more of a target for major negotiating assignments. These would come next in the Johnson administration.

9
Troubleshooting in the Dominican Republic and Elsewhere

A few months after the Yemeni negotiations ended, John F. Kennedy planned to show his regard for Bunker's diplomatic achievements with a flair that reflected the style of his administration. In February 1963, he had changed the format for awarding the Medal of Freedom, the highest civilian honor a president could bestow in peacetime. The medal, until then given only sporadically, would be presented at a special annual ceremony recognizing and rewarding "those who contribute significantly to the quality of American life." Kennedy placed Bunker in the first group of recipients, an impressive selection of twenty-nine Americans and two foreigners that included such well-known personalities as Thornton Wilder, Pablo Casals, Marian Anderson, Jean Monnet, and, no doubt to Bunker's great satisfaction, Bob Kiphuth, the legendary swimming coach and director of athletics at Yale.

By the time the awards were presented in early December at a White House ceremony, Kennedy was dead. His posthumous addition by President Lyndon Johnson to the group of medal winners helped give the event great prominence and poignancy. Bunker was among eight winners who received "special distinction." His citation read: "Citizen and diplomat, he has brought integrity, patience, and compassionate understanding of other men and nations in the service of the Republic under three presidents." When Johnson visited Vietnam four years later, he presented a second Medal of Freedom to Bunker, by then ambassador in Saigon. Bunker was the first person to be awarded the medal twice.

When he received the award, Bunker had been working for a year on a long-range strategic study of Brazil that Secretary Rusk had asked him to undertake. His efforts, which included a long visit to Brazil to confer with prominent Brazilians and U.S. officials, eventually came to naught.

The main purpose of the study was to develop U.S. policy toward the left-wing regime of President João B. M. Goulart, which was causing problems for Washington. The project was nearing completion when the overthrow of Goulart in a military coup made it largely irrelevant. It was never disseminated.[1]

In January 1964, President Johnson named Bunker ambassador to the Organization of American States (OAS). Although this job carries a prestigious title, its incumbents ordinarily play less influential roles than do U.S. ambassadors to the United Nations and NATO. It is less powerful a position than that of the assistant secretary for inter-American affairs, the job that Bunker had turned down when Kennedy offered it to him three years earlier. Although Bunker's prestige gave his views greater weight than most of his predecessors', he did not play a significant role in the day-to-day conduct of relations with Latin America.

As things turned out, however, Bunker spent a substantial part of his two-and-a-half year OAS tenure engaged in sensitive troubleshooting assignments of the kind he had carried out with such skill in dealing with the West New Guinea and Yemen crises. Two of these assignments involved OAS matters, in Panama and the Dominican Republic. The third concerned a major challenge to U.S. interests by Indonesian President Sukarno.

Bunker had just taken over as OAS ambassador when rioting sparked by Panamanian opposition to the continued American presence in the Canal Zone led to a bloody confrontation between the protesters and U.S. troops. The Panamanian government quickly broke diplomatic relations with Washington. Asserting that Panama had been the victim of an unprovoked American attack against its territory and civilian population, it appealed to the OAS for help.

From January to early April Bunker vigorously defended the U.S. position against these charges. In consultation with a specially appointed OAS committee, he tried to work out an understanding with the Panamanians to defuse the crisis. He eventually succeeded in doing so through some adroit, quiet diplomacy, much of it conducted with his Panamanian opposite number at one of his favorite Washington haunts, the exclusive F Street Club, a few blocks from OAS headquarters. Years later he recalled what had happened there:

We [American and Panamanian negotiators] came up with a good many drafts of a resolution aimed to restore relations and get negotiations going, but none of them was satisfactory to one side or the other. Finally, I said to Miguel Moreno, who was the Panamanian ambassador to the OAS at the time, I think the only way we can get this thing worked out, Miguel, is for you and me to get together by ourselves away from all this and see if we can't come up with something. So, actually, we came over here to the F Street Club and carried on our talks here between meals. . . . And we did come up finally with a resolution, a proposal that was accepted by both sides.[2]

The Bunker-Moreno agreement won quick approval from Johnson and Panamanian president Roberto Chiari. The brief document provided for the resumption of U.S.-Panamanian diplomatic relations but was deliberately vague concerning negotiations for a new Panama Canal treaty, a major Panamanian demand. As Washington wished, it did not include a U.S. commitment to negotiate a new treaty. But it did state in language that satisfied the Panamanians that special ambassadors would be appointed "with sufficient powers to seek the prompt elimination of the causes of conflict between the two countries, without limits or preconditions." Their objective would be to reach "a just and fair agreement."[3]

Soon afterwards, President Johnson appointed Texas businessman Robert Anderson, who had been secretary of the treasury in the Eisenhower administration, as special ambassador for negotiations on the status of the Canal. These negotiations continued intermittently for a decade and a half. Bunker did not deal with the issue again until the early 1970s, when President Richard Nixon named him to succeed Anderson. The final settlement, reached in 1979 during the Carter administration, was his last major diplomatic achievement.[4]

Bunker's difficult early months at the OAS were made much worse by personal tragedy. In early March, as the cancer metastasized to her lungs, Harriet's doctors decided that she should be moved from São Paulo, where she had been staying with her daughter Ellen and her family, to the Columbia-Presbyterian Hospital in New York City. Ellsworth went to Brazil to help with these arrangements. He and other family members accepted the advice of his oncologist son-in-law, Fernando Gentil, who recommended against special chemotherapy treatment to keep Harriet alive. Mercifully, she suffered little pain during her six weeks at Columbia-Presbyterian. With Ellsworth and their three children around her, she died peacefully there on April 18, 1964, at the age of sixty-five.

In its obituary, the *New York Times* recalled Harriet's introduction of the long-handled broom in New Delhi and spoke of Prime Minister Nehru's praise for her initiative.[5] President Johnson wrote Bunker: "The courage which both your wife and you have shown in these last months has been known to all of us in the government, and your own readiness to take on arduous public service in this hard time has added to the debt your country owes you."[6]

Following funeral services for Harriet at St. Michael's Episcopal Church in Brattleboro and her burial at a cemetery not far from the family's Dummerston home, Bunker returned to his OAS job. He seems to have borne his grief as well as one can at the end of a long, very happy marriage. Ellen Bunker Gentil recalled that he had shown great emotion only twice—when Harriet was moved from Brazil and when the family brought her body home to Vermont. She thought that he tried to overcome his sorrow by keeping busy in Washington.

There were few important developments at the OAS that could keep him closely occupied, however. The year between the U.S.-Panama agreement in April 1964 and the U.S. intervention in the Dominican Republic in April 1965 was a fairly quiet time for the organization. Bunker's policymaking role in such OAS matters as the imposition of hemispheric sanctions against Castro's Cuba was in any event limited. The ordinary activities of the organization did not pose a serious challenge to a man of his talent, experience, and energy.[7]

Rootless after Harriet's death, Bunker found comfort in the companionship of an old acquaintance from his years in India, Carol Laise. Before he undertook his special Dominican assignment in June 1965, it was evident that their friendship was blossoming into romance.

Carol Laise was a senior Foreign Service officer in the State Department's Bureau of Near Eastern and South Asian Affairs. A vibrant, attractive, blonde in her late forties, she had worked for Bunker at the embassy in New Delhi, where she was a first secretary in the political section. She was born in 1917, the year after Bunker graduated from Yale, and joined the department's Bureau of International Organization Affairs after wartime service in the London office of the U.N. Relief and Rehabilitation Administration. Like many other civil service officers, she entered the Foreign Service in 1955 when the Eisenhower administration integrated the Foreign and Civil Service components of the department.

The following year Laise was assigned to New Delhi, her first overseas diplomatic post. Many Indians considered her the most effective officer in the mission's large political section. Jagat Mehta, a senior Indian foreign service officer at the time, has recalled that "even as a first secretary she had extensive and influential reach. . . . There was no one in Delhi of any consequence with whom she was not on friendly terms."[8] Bunker shared this high regard. He and Harriet liked Laise personally and considered her a friend as well as a colleague.

The Foreign Service in those days remained very much a man's world that was only gradually coming to recognize that women officers could be effective in senior positions. There was a kind of unwritten understanding that a limited number of important jobs should be open to women. Laise's success in New Delhi made her a prime candidate to compete for these when she returned to the department following a training assignment at the prestigious National War College. Personable, ambitious, and a hard task master, she displayed in Foggy Bottom a talent for moving things through the foreign affairs bureaucracy, and being seen to do so, rather than for conceptualizing innovative policies. She supplemented her professional abilities with abundant feminine charm. As director of the department's South Asia office Laise won the favorable attention of Secretary Rusk and other senior officials for her part in shaping U.S. relations with India and Pakistan during and after their 1965 war. By then she was recognized as one of the most capable women in the upper ranks of the Foreign Service. Like most such women officers in those days, she had never married.

Bunker's OAS duties and his romance with Laise were interrupted in March 1965 when President Johnson sent him on a highly important mission to Indonesia. U.S. relations with the Sukarno government were rapidly deteriorating, and the administration needed a fresh and objective reading of the potentially dangerous situation. It sought a trustworthy assessment of the authoritarian and reckless Indonesian president's thinking about the direction of bilateral ties and sound advice concerning the appropriate size and nature of the U.S. diplomatic mission in Djakarta. The Indonesians had attacked or seized several American government buildings and private businesses and were harassing the thirty-strong Peace Corps and other elements of the large mission. They seemed likely to step up such anti-American activity.

Many senior officials in Washington had concluded that they could no longer rely on the longtime American ambassador to Indonesia, Howard Jones, whose strategy of advancing U.S. interests by cultivating close personal relations with Sukarno had clearly failed. Bunker's successful handling of the West New Guinea crisis made him uniquely qualified for the job, and when Under Secretary of State George Ball recommended him, Johnson quickly concurred.[9]

When Bunker took on the mission, which he accepted without hesitation, Sukarno's policies were not only damaging U.S. interests in Indonesia. They also had serious implications for American goals elsewhere in Southeast Asia. Washington rightly feared that the United States had emerged as Sukarno's major foreign enemy and target despite its recent role in resolving the West New Guinea crisis to Indonesia's advantage. It was troubled by his growing collaboration with the Communist Party (PKI) at home and the People's Republic of China abroad and his efforts to assume leadership of anti-imperialist, anticolonialist "new emerging forces" in the Third World. It was especially concerned by Sukarno's vow to destroy Malaysia, a newly established pro-Western amalgam of former British territories bordering Indonesia with which the United States had friendly relations. George Ball used stark words in proposing the Bunker mission to Johnson: "Our relations with Indonesia are on the brink of falling apart."

Bunker arrived in Djakarta on March 31, 1965, by special aircraft. Over the next fifteen days, he had four substantive meetings and a couple of luncheons with Sukarno. One of the luncheons, a typical Sukarno production, famously included Bunker's (and Sukarno's) dancing with beautiful Indonesian girls the president had brought along for his own and his foreign guests' pleasure. Accompanied by Ambassador Jones and sometimes by other American officials, Bunker also had separate meetings with other senior Indonesian civilian and military officials and several foreign ambassadors. Aside from occasions when his subordinates chimed in at his bidding to agree with him (like trained seals, Bunker observed), Sukarno did almost all the talking for the Indonesian side at sessions in which he participated.

Bunker repeatedly told the Indonesians that President Johnson was concerned by recent trends in bilateral relations. Washington wished to get a better understanding of Indonesian attitudes and make certain that Indonesian leaders understood its views. The United States wanted friendly and constructive relations with Indonesia, like itself a country created by anticolonial revolution. It needed to learn whether the Indonesians held similar views, as that would determine what kind of ties the two countries would have over the next few years (and, by implication, the size and nature of the presence the United States should maintain in Indonesia). If the Indonesians reciprocated this U.S. desire, it was up to them to establish the basic norms that would permit such relations.

Bunker said that the United States had tried to avoid letting its disagreement with Indonesian policies toward other countries in the region affect bilateral ties. Differences between the two countries on foreign policy issues need not poison relations since they reflected divergent approaches rather than conflicts over ultimate objectives. He told Sukarno that the United States was not working against him and, specifically mentioning the Central Intelligence Agency (CIA), assured him on President Johnson's behalf that no U.S. government agency was seeking overtly or covertly to overthrow him.

The administration was bewildered, Bunker said, by Sukarno's labeling Washington its principal enemy. It believed that Indonesia should play an important role in international affairs. Peaceful settlements with their neighbors would enhance the Indonesians' ability to do so. Discussing U.S. activities in Indonesia, Bunker said Washington did not wish to impose irritants in bilateral relations and would close out programs the Indonesian government did not want.[10]

Although Sukarno and his colleagues asserted that they too wanted good U.S.-Indonesian ties and seemed tacitly to agree that no insurmountable obstacles stood in the way of achieving them, they repeatedly told Bunker that they could not divorce bilateral dealings from what they regarded as hostile U.S. positions on Malaysia. Sukarno was vehement in making a basic change in Washington's Malaysia policy a price for improved bilateral relations. (Bunker refused to be drawn into the substance of the Malaysian issue. He confined himself to reasserting Washington's position that it was not directly involved in the dispute and would welcome Asian powers' resolving the problem by any peaceful means acceptable to those concerned.) The Indonesians asserted that better future ties would also depend on changes to their liking in U.S. policies toward Vietnam, China, Korea, and other countries in what Sukarno called "the Afro-Asian world."

Bunker was generally restrained in responding to Sukarno's onslaughts. But he allowed David Cuthell, a State Department official who accompanied him, to take a harsher line. When Sukarno stated that the Johnson administration should have known that Indonesia would resent U.S. recognition of Malaysia, Cuthell observed that the Indonesians supported regimes that the United States bitterly opposed, such as North Korea and North Vietnam. When Sukarno asked how relations between the Indonesian and American people could be improved, Cuthell queried in reply how Sukarno would react if Washington requested him publicly to criticize Ho Chi Minh and defend the United States. Bunker recognized that there was a time and place for such tough, even nasty retorts in negotiations, but he rarely made them himself.

After the first two meetings with Sukarno, Bunker reported that Washington's primary interest in bilateral relations was gradually getting through to the Indonesians. "My visit is not going to result in dramatic change in Indonesian policies," he warned, "but I think it important by [the] time I leave [that] the Indo[nesian]s have it clearly in mind that in our view [the] ball is in their court." [11]

At Sukarno's urging, Bunker broke off his discussions in Djakarta to attend the opening of the People's Consultative Congress, the Indonesian national assembly, in Bandung. He had misgivings about going to the hill town, where the first Afro-Asian summit had convened a decade earlier. North Korean President Kim Il Sung would be on the platform and Sukarno seemed likely to deliver another one of his shrill anti-imperialist diatribes. But Sukarno was insistent, and Bunker made the trip.

Sukarno's speech proved even more provocative than he had expected. The president angrily declared that capitalism should be wiped out, again resolved to destroy Malaysia, and delivered attacks on the United States that Embassy Djakarta reported were "specific, extensive, and virulent." [12] "Do we have to sit here and listen to this crap?," Bunker recalled asking Ambassador Jones when Sukarno's outbursts were translated for them. [13] When Jones told him he had sat through worse, and none of the other Western diplomats rose to leave, he decided to stick it out. He came away more convinced than before that Sukarno had singled out the United States as Indonesia's greatest enemy.

The visit to Bandung provided further drama. Like so many other Americans in Indonesia in those days, Bunker found himself the target of an anti-American mob. "I was confronted at the entrance to my hotel by a thousand or more students shouting 'to hell with Bunker'," he recalled. He remained characteristically calm during the episode, drinking a beer as he watched the hostile students from a window of his hotel. Indonesian army units eventually dispersed the demonstrators. [14]

Apparently unfazed by his Bandung experiences, Bunker returned to Djakarta for further discussions and negotiations. Meeting again with Sukarno, he emphasized with Washington's prior approval that his mission was "not a last-ditch operation but rather an element [of] continuing dialogue." He said he had hoped to report to President Johnson that the Indonesian leader agreed that their two countries should regard one another with friendship and respect, but added that after hearing his Bandung speech he wondered if Indonesia preferred to treat the United States as an enemy. Discussing official U.S. activities in Indonesia, Bunker regretted that programs designed to increase understanding had become irritants between the two countries. But he also expressed the hope that the United States could retain a nucleus around which new cooperative programs could be built if the Indonesians desired them. Sukarno, for his part, again focused largely on the Malaysia issue, castigating U.S. policy and demanding that Washington support Djakarta's position. He reiterated that until the United States "pull[ed] out [this] one big nail," bilateral relations would not improve.[15]

Despite the basic disagreements this discussion again disclosed, the joint statement Bunker and Sukarno agreed to on April 14 proved remarkably amicable. The two governments recognized that "friendly relations between Indonesia and the United States are of the greatest importance to the people of both countries" and that foreign policy differences "should not be allowed to affect unduly the general pattern of friendship which has existed for so many years between them." The differing U.S. and Indonesian positions on Malaysia were spelled out in separate paragraphs, but without the rancor that Sukarno had expressed earlier. The two sides agreed that U.S. assistance programs should be reviewed and revised on a continuing basis to assure that they met the desires of both governments. Peace Corps activities would be phased out, but Bunker persuaded Sukarno to agree to continue the program of U.S. technical assistance to Indonesian universities.[16]

Returning to Washington, Bunker briefed Johnson and submitted a long report of his findings and recommendations. He was pessimistic about short-term prospects for improved bilateral relations. Although Sukarno blamed U.S. policy on the Malaysia issue for worsening ties, in Bunker's view the fundamental problem was his ambition to lead Afro-Asian countries in a struggle against "the forces of neo-colonialism and imperialism" headed by Washington.

Bunker found that as the symbol of Indonesian unity and independence,

Sukarno remained the country's dominant, virtually unchallenged leader. Despite unsatisfactory bilateral relations, Washington should keep trying to work with him to the extent possible and maintain a dialogue between him and President Johnson. But Bunker also urged that the United States play for long-term stakes by keeping quiet lines open to other forces in Indonesia, particularly the military. In the meantime, it should reduce its visibility, remove vulnerable Americans from isolated regions, and maintain a skeleton U.S. Agency for International Development (USAID) staff to continue small and popular assistance projects.[17]

Bunker had done the best he could under extremely trying circumstances. Handling his assignment in his customary professional and conscientious way, he gave Washington what it needed: an objective evaluation of the difficult, worsening situation in Indonesia and realistic recommendations about the policies the United States should pursue toward the Sukarno government. His judgments on future U.S. government activity and the need to further reduce the American presence in Indonesia were especially important. They led to a drastic cutback in the size of the U.S. diplomatic mission, from several hundred at the time of Bunker's mission to only thirty-five six months later.

Although the joint communiqué Bunker negotiated with Sukarno seemed, as Ambassador Jones reported, "a considerable victory and a testimony to Bunker's negotiating skills," no one, not even the ordinarily optimistic Jones, thought it represented a turning point in U.S.-Indonesian relations.[18] Effecting such a major change in Sukarno's policies toward the United States in what would have been a "mission impossible" had not been the purpose of Johnson's sending Bunker to Djakarta. Edward E. Masters, who as political counselor at Embassy Djakarta accompanied Bunker on many of his calls, believes that "Bunker realized from the outset that there was no possibility of turning Sukarno away from his anti-U.S., anti-imperialist, pro–Communist bloc rhetoric and policies."[19] Both Masters and Deputy Chief of Mission Frank Underhill (though not Jones) agreed with that early assessment. Bunker's mission proved that it was correct.

Johnson approved Bunker's recommendations when the two men met at the White House on April 26. The recommendations shaped U.S. policy for the next six months, as bilateral ties continued to deteriorate and the evacuation of Americans proceeded. Then, in late September and early October, an abortive Communist-led coup attempt followed by a successful countercoup spearheaded by the army suddenly and radically transformed the Indonesian scene. Mass executions decimated the PKI, and Sukarno, who had connived with the Communists in the coup attempt, was eventually driven from power. The new government, which would rule Indonesia for the next three and a half decades under General Suharto's leadership, was very much more to Washington's liking. The cutback in mission staff that Bunker recommended had sharply reduced the danger to Americans during the violent upheavals.

In late October 1965, as these dramatic developments played out, National Security Advisor McGeorge Bundy wrote President Johnson: "Events since the . . . abortive coup are so far a striking vindication of U.S. policy towards [Indonesia]. . . . More specifically, they are a vindication of last spring's Bunker report." [20] Bundy's tribute was widely shared as Washington moved to build the constructive relationship with Indonesia that Bunker had recognized could never develop while Sukarno held power.

By then, Bunker was probably too busy with fresh responsibilities to savor praise. He had been back in Washington only a week or so when President Johnson announced on April 28, 1965, that at his orders a force of 400 marines had just landed at Santo Domingo, the capital of the Dominican Republic, to protect the lives of U.S. citizens endangered by political violence. Johnson was not candid in justifying the dramatic, hastily decided action. The primary reason for the intervention was Washington's fear, heightened by panicky reports from Ambassador W. Tapley Bennett, that the political upheaval that had broken out in Santo Domingo four days earlier could lead to a Communist takeover of the republic. The major problems the intervention caused took fourteen months to resolve.

The landing of the Marines was the latest in a long series of events that traumatized and polarized the Caribbean island republic following the assassination in 1961 of Rafael Trujillo, its corrupt and brutal longtime dictator. A parade of short-lived regimes followed. Of these, only the government of the left-of-center reformer Juan Bosch was democratically elected, in December 1962. The Dominican armed forces ousted Bosch when he had been in office only seven months, and he fled to Puerto Rico. Four days before the U.S. intervention, the unpopular rightist triumvirate that had replaced him collapsed in the face of an armed uprising launched by dissident army officers. This pro-Bosch coup was supported by politicians of Bosch's own party (the Partido Revolucionario Dominicano, PRD) as well as more radical groups, including the country's three Communist parties. Most of the Dominican military joined conservative civilian political elements to oppose them. The advances the pro-Bosch forces were making in the bitter and bloody confrontation between the two armed rivals in the streets of Santo Domingo set the stage for Johnson's action.

Washington's involvement in Dominican affairs was nothing new. For decades successive administrations viewed the republic and other Caribbean territories primarily in terms of U.S. security and pursued policies designed to prevent them from falling prey to European powers. This interventionist approach included an eight-year military occupation of the republic, from 1916 to 1924. More recently, especially after Fidel Castro seized power in neighboring Cuba in 1959, Washington focused its attention on perceived Communist threats. Fearful of the politically disastrous specter of a "second Cuba" in the republic in the turmoil following Trujillo's death, the Kennedy and Johnson administrations used political influence and economic assistance to help the Dominicans try to build a stable, more prosperous, preferably democratic nation on the wreckage of three decades of Trujillo misrule. U.S. officials became deeply enmeshed in the politics of the country. They kept an especially wary eye on its known Communists and the much larger number of Dominicans they suspected were "Castroites" or potential Communist dupes.

Johnson's intervention, the first U.S. military occupation of a Caribbean country since the marines withdrew from Nicaragua in 1933, quickly triggered major controversy. Many Latin American governments, including some friendly to the United States, considered the action an unwelcome return of Yankee imperialism. Latin public opinion largely shared this view, and reaction elsewhere in the Third World was also mainly negative. The Soviets, for their part, tried to make Cold War capital of the intervention but avoided direct confrontation with Washington. In the United States, the strong opposition to Johnson's action was spearheaded by troubled liberals who had a few months earlier enthusiastically supported the president for reelection against his seemingly more bellicose Republican challenger, Barry Goldwater. The administration's vulnerability to attacks at home and abroad was heightened by its often inconsistent and clumsy efforts to explain and implement its Dominican policy.[21]

The controversy the intervention provoked at a time of increasing preoccupation with Vietnam soon led the administration to look urgently for ways to extricate itself from the island without endangering U.S. national interests or the president's domestic political standing. It eventually found in Ellsworth Bunker the shrewdness and patience that would enable diplomacy to succeed.

Bunker was not part of the inner circle of officials to whom Johnson turned when the Dominican crisis erupted. No record is available of his immediate reaction to the president's decision, though he told an interviewer years later that he believed that Ambassador Bennett had overestimated the Communist element in the uprising and misled Johnson.[22] In another interview, he commented that it would have been wiser to have informed the OAS before moving the marines, but doubted the United States could then have quickly got the two-thirds vote in the OAS Council required for approving the intervention.[23] In fact, Johnson and Rusk had decided quite deliberately not to inform the OAS for that reason.

Although he had not participated in the initial decision, Bunker's OAS assignment, his membership on a special task force that Bundy chaired, and his strong standing with Johnson and other senior officials gave him an important and highly visible role in formulating and implementing Dominican Republic policy following the armed intervention. His immediate task was to deal with the sensitive situation in the OAS Council, where ambassadors of member states met in almost continual session for a week after the marines landed. Washington's deliberate bypassing of the organization and its flouting of its noninterventionist commitments under the OAS charter incensed many Latin governments, and their representatives angrily condemned the United States. But once U.S. troops were well established on the ground the administration sought to repair the damage by encouraging the slighted body to play a major part in resolving the crisis.

Bunker tried to calm the atmosphere, head off calls for condemnation of the intervention and demands for an immediate U.S. withdrawal, and promote constructive OAS approaches that the administration could accept.[24] He succeeded in winning approval for a proposal to transform the U.S. military presence, by then some 23,000 troops, into an OAS-directed Inter-American Peace Force (IAPF). Quickly set up under the command of a Brazilian general with a U.S. lieutenant general as deputy, the force eventually comprised contingents from seven OAS countries. U.S. troops drawn mainly from the original occupying force were by far its largest national group. Except for the Brazilians, the other six contingents amounted to little more than window-dressing.

Washington also backed OAS calls for a cease-fire between the two sides, welcomed OAS Secretary General José Mora's mission to the embattled republic, and sponsored the formation of a five-nation OAS Special Committee whose mandate was to do "everything possible to get the reestablishment of peace and normal conditions" there. Bunker was not appointed to the committee; at that point the administration preferred a less visible role for itself at the OAS on the issue. Nor did he take part in unilateral U.S. efforts to resolve the crisis. A team that included senior representatives of the White House, the State Department, and the Pentagon undertook the most important of these. Led by Bundy and Deputy Secretary of Defense Cyrus Vance, the high-powered group tried through negotiations with the rival factions to place in power a provisional government headed by António Guzmán, a moderate leader of Bosch's PRD. Like the OAS missions, the Bundy-Vance team and other envoys Johnson sent to the Caribbean failed to bring about a settlement.[25]

With diplomatic efforts deadlocked and the contending parties as intransigent and bellicose as ever, the administration concluded that a new approach was needed. It successfully urged the OAS to appoint yet another mission, this time an Ad Hoc Committee comprising three ambassadors. Abandoning the low-profile approach that had led it to pass up participation in the OAS Special Committee, it made Bunker available for this latest panel. Two of his OAS colleagues joined him—Ilmar Penna Marinho of Brazil and Ramón de Clairmont Dueñas of El Salvador. Their arrival in Santo Domingo on June 3 was a major turning point in the crisis.

Events demonstrated that Bunker was almost ideally qualified to take the lead in negotiating a Dominican settlement. Patient and imperturbable, he was able to persuade the president and others in Washington that his careful, unhurried style was the best way to deal with highly complex issues. He brought to the negotiations common sense and a fresh and open mind free from the ideological rigidity that handicapped many of his senior U.S. colleagues. Rarely discouraged during the lengthy course of the negotiations, he did not let his frustration interfere with an almost indefatigable determination to reach a settlement.

Bunker related remarkably well to the Dominicans, including some of those most suspicious of U.S. motives and intentions. As Harry Shlaudeman, his principal deputy in Santo Domingo, has pointed out, it would be hard to imagine anyone more unlike the Dominicans than Ellsworth

Bunker. The *New York Times* caught some of this flavor in describing Bunker's contacts with the pro-Bosch forces: "Attired in a well-cut suit with high starched collar and Panama hat, the imperturbable Mr. Bunker seemed in startling contrast to the sweating, bearded rebels in fatigues he dealt with."[26] He was at first angrily attacked by the pro-Bosch press, which invented a string of mildly obscene epithets to describe him. (A particular Bunker favorite was "the male duck of wheeler dealers," which may have lost something in translation from the Spanish "*el pato macho de manganeo.*") But the force of his personality, his physical courage, and his impressive presence as a distinguished, white-haired elder statesman soon led Dominicans of all political persuasions to treat Bunker and his proposals with unusual respect.

Bunker became in practice if not in title the chairman of the Ad Hoc Committee. Although he was careful to consult with his colleagues, the committee's achievements were largely his doing. The Brazilian and Salvadoran ambassadors deferred to him not only because he represented the most powerful and immediately concerned of the three participating countries. Like the Dominicans, they were impressed by his personality, diplomatic skill, experience, and hard work. His OAS hat was a major asset. He could operate not only as a U.S. emissary but also as the representative of a hemispheric organization charged with carrying out its formal mandate.[27]

But Bunker would not have been able to play either his OAS or his U.S. role as effectively as he did if he had not enjoyed President Johnson's strong support. After the failure of the administration's earlier Dominican initiatives, Johnson was prepared to give Bunker unusually wide authority and latitude. He made it clear from the beginning of the Ad Hoc Committee's effort that Bunker was his personal representative.

As the Ad Hoc Committee developed and implemented its strategy for resolving the crisis, the president's confidence in Bunker grew. Aware that he had Johnson's backing and easy access to the White House, other government officials tended to defer to his judgment. As Shlaudeman has recalled, "Ellsworth didn't throw his weight around; he didn't have to."[28] The exchange of cables on the negotiations is remarkable in that it was dominated not by instructions from Washington, as usually happens when major U.S. political and security interests are at stake, but by Bunker's own assessments, intentions, and recommendations.

The committee interpreted its imprecise mandate broadly and under Bunker's leadership established a role for itself basically independent of its OAS parent body.[29] It did not submit its plans to the OAS Council nor seek policy guidance from it. Some delegates charged that the OAS had improperly abdicated its responsibilities to a U.S.-dominated committee. But for various political reasons, most Latin governments preferred to distance themselves from the committee's efforts and accepted its role. With Johnson's confidence and virtual freedom from the OAS, Bunker had unusual advantages as he undertook his difficult assignment.

He built on these assets by his operating style. Housed in the Hotel Embajador, a down-at-the-heels tourist establishment in downtown Santo Domingo, Bunker and his small staff worked essentially as an independent mini-embassy. They preferred not to rely on the large U.S. mission headed by Ambassador Bennett and did almost everything on their own. Their tight organization acted quickly and efficiently to devise strategy, deal with day-to-day developments, and keep Washington informed. Shlaudeman drafted most of the many crisp cables the group sent to the White House and the State Department. Captioned "From Bunker," who supplemented them with personal phone calls, they received prompt, high-level attention, often from President Johnson himself.

Bunker also developed independent relations with American media representatives who covered the Dominican crisis. His successful effort to establish some sense of comity in U.S. government relations with the media in Santo Domingo contributed significantly to his overall performance. The news people had concluded earlier that Johnson and his representatives were lying to them about Dominican developments and had some vivid evidence of this.[30] By ending excessive official secrecy and misleading statements, Bunker restored the government's integrity and the media's confidence in what it was told. When he completed his Dominican assignment, the media representatives gave him a dinner marked by good fellowship and not a little hilarity, especially on the part of those who shared Bunker's fondness for off-color jokes.[31]

The Hotel Embajador was a strange place to work. Following Johnson's ill-advised telecast offer to evacuate any foreign national who wanted to leave the Dominican Republic, all seven hundred or so Chinese in the country, most of them rural restaurateurs, promptly set off for the hotel expecting that they would be taken out of the country from there. Before the offer was rescinded, one group did in fact reach Puerto Rico, never to be seen again. The remaining Chinese were eventually ejected from the hotel, but not before they had practiced their cooking skills in their rooms and imparted to the Embajador a distinctive odor that lingered for months.

But nothing bothered Bunker, Shlaudeman recalled, except waiting for the check in the hotel restaurant. Invariably the waiter would assure him "*ya viene*," a phrase that must have reminded him of the "just now coming" he had no doubt heard many times during his years in India. When the check did not come, Bunker would get up and stalk out with one or more waiters running after him. It was for him a rare display of impatience.

Bunker continued his courtship of Carol Laise from the "Hotel Ya Viene," as he came to call it. He obviously had a great time pursuing the romance, phoning her almost every night, ordering flowers, and making dinner reservations for his next trip to Washington. When he traveled between Washington and Santo Domingo, he carried with him a set of framed photos of Carol that he placed in his bedroom. He had evidently recovered from the loss of Harriet and was, Shlaudeman remembered, "full of beans."[32]

As it began its yearlong labors, the Ad Hoc Committee had two major, closely related objectives. The first was to establish a single, stable, popularly accepted administration to replace the two rival claimants. These competing regimes were organized as the Government for National Reconstruction (GNR), led by the rightist General António Imbert Barrera, and the pro-Bosch constitutionalist government—so called because it favored a return to the 1963 constitution enacted during Bosch's presidency—headed by Colonel Francisco Caamaño. The GNR was supported by military commanders who had no personal loyalty to Imbert. The constitutionalist camp was a melange of PRD politicians, pro-Caamaño military, and a variety of Marxists, opportunists, and armed adventurers.

The second objective was to end the conflict and eventually rebuild the armed forces, reintegrating under a formula that would place under greater civilian political control the small number of army units that had joined the constitutionalists and the "loyalist" majority faction associated with the GNR. Recent bloodshed had worsened the mutually antagonistic attitudes of the two military groups. As Bunker soon learned, the unwillingness of both to entertain any compromise that would allow their rivals to hold positions of power following a settlement made resolution of this military problem even more difficult to reach than an acceptable political arrangement.

When the Ad Hoc Committee reached Santo Domingo the political and military situations were stalemated and the country was a shambles.[33] Neither side would negotiate with the other nor offer any meaningful concessions. The economy, weak to begin with, had been badly disrupted. Schools and universities were closed, most newspapers had shut down, and the treasury was bankrupt. The city of Santo Domingo was a tinderbox. The constitutionalists controlled most of its central area. A cordon of IAPF troops separated them from "loyalist" forces on the outskirts of the city. These IAPF units isolated the constitutionalists from other parts of the country, where their cause enjoyed considerable support. Exchanges of gunfire frequently raised the level of tension between the IAPF and the constitutionalists, who charged that the force was pro-rightist and demanded its immediate withdrawal. Using the committee's authority over the IAPF, Bunker spent much time trying to defuse these dangerous firefights.

Bunker arrived in Santo Domingo without any clear instructions apart from a general understanding that he was to prevent the Dominican Republic from falling to "Castro-Communism." As a result, he often made decisions on his own.

The Ad Hoc Committee first sought out Dominican opinion—what Bunker called "pulse-taking." The contenders refused to speak to one another but were willing to talk to committee members. During their first week on the island Bunker and his colleagues met the rival factions' senior leaders and scores of politicians, businessmen, clergy, intellectuals, rural and youth activists, and other influential figures. These soundings typified Bunker's preference for talking to as many people as possible in his negotiations. They soon led the committee to conclude that it could not follow traditional methods of mediation. It needed instead to make its own proposals and negotiate them separately with the two sides.

Bunker soon called for early elections as the central element of a settlement. "I am convinced after intensive investigation on the scene" he cabled Rusk, "that a political formula which would meet our requirements [and] be acceptable to . . . key elements in the Dominican body politic . . . is virtually impossible to achieve. . . . The only way to break the present political impasse here and restore a measure of harmony is to let the people decide for themselves through free and open elections supervised by the OAS and the formation in the meantime of a provisional government of technicians who, governing under an institutional act with strong OAS support, could take the country to elections."[34] Bunker thought his formula would attract broad popular support in the republic and win international acceptance. In its reply the following day, Washington substantially agreed with his ideas, though its assumption seemed to be that a period of up to two years would be necessary before the balloting.[35]

The idea of early elections had been in the Santo Domingo air before the committee arrived. The GNR had in fact proposed elections under OAS supervision, but with the unacceptable condition that it remain in office during the election period. Shlaudeman, who had reached Santo Domingo before Bunker did, recommended early elections in a memorandum he gave the ambassador when he arrived.

Bunker's embrace of the concept transformed the peace process. Previous efforts had concentrated on establishing a new government, permanent or provisional. This had led to haggling over intractable issues and had not worked. Now, as Shlaudeman recalled, "the idea was . . . to shift the primary focus to an electoral solution which we thought would tend to defuse the other problems, as well as to attract wide public support."[36]

Bunker concluded that his ideas would be badly received by political leaders but might win popular backing if properly packaged and explained. He had been pessimistic about prospective constitutionalist reaction when he first put his plan to Washington. A few days later, an outbreak of severe fighting involving heavy casualties between the IAPF and their forces deepened constitutionalist misgivings about OAS and U.S. intentions. The rightists, for their part, had eagerly expected the Johnson administration to crush the "communist-dominated" constitutionalists and were disappointed when it chose instead to seek a negotiated settlement.

Bunker's expectation that factional and popular reactions were likely to differ led the committee to publicize its proposals in two separate documents. It gave the contending leaders a paper, "Proposals of the Ad Hoc Committee for a Solution of the Dominican Crisis,"[37] that asserted that the best way to satisfy the country's yearning for peace and normal democratic institutional life was to hold fair elections. The paper called for voting for national and municipal offices no earlier than six months but no later than nine months in the future. The OAS would cooperate in ensuring that these elections reflected the will of the Dominican people. During the electoral process, the IAPF, "reduced to the number strictly necessary to carry out its mission," would assist the Dominican authorities to maintain order.

In the meantime, a broadly representative provisional government under a single (unspecified) leader would be installed following Ad Hoc Committee exchanges with political groups and community leaders. The regime would govern under an institutional act—a temporary constitution—that would ensure broad civil liberties but skirt controversial matters. A constituent assembly convoked within six months of the elected government coming to power would draft a permanent constitution. To deal with the military conflict, the committee called for the grant of full amnesty to those willing to lay down their arms, return of the regular armed forces to their barracks, and the disarming of irregular forces on both sides. It avoided the sensitive issues of the restructuring of the armed forces and their subordination to civilian authority, important U.S. goals.[38]

In a second, widely distributed broadside, "Declaration to the Dominican People," the committee deliberately went over the heads of the leaders to appeal for public support. It explained its mission ("not intervention, but rather conciliation"), described its efforts to sound out public opinion, expressed confidence that despite the political impasse "there is a solution that all democratic men and women of good will can support," and outlined the basic elements of such a settlement. The declaration ended on a stirring note: "The Dominican people long for peace and freedom. This is the hour of decision."[39]

The Ad Hoc Committee's proposals did not deal with a formidable list of matters. In addition to fundamental military issues, these included the nature, leadership, and composition of the caretaker government; the details of the act under which it would rule; the way elections would be held and their results guaranteed; the IAPF's role and length of stay; and provisions for ending political terrorism, protecting human rights, and controlling the Communists. As Bunker recognized, these matters could be settled through compromises reached in extensive negotiations within the framework the committee's initiative had provided. The continuing enmity between the two sides and Bunker's own enterprise, forcefulness, and negotiating style made the committee the focal point in the negotiating process.

The initial reaction of both sides was mixed. As negotiations slowly proceeded, the constitutionalists objected to several of the committee's more important proposals, especially the military provisions. Imbert, who had other problems with them, reiterated that his government could act as a transitional regime, which he was now prepared to broaden. But both sides agreed that the committee's framework offered a basis for further bargaining.

Faced with this expected opposition, Bunker played his cards with skill and patience despite occasional outbursts from Washington for quicker progress.[40] He recognized that he had to narrow controversial issues to their essentials and propose revised formulations amplifying the committee's initial framework that Dominican and world opinion, and, of course, the Johnson administration, would consider reasonable. He held a strong hand. The presence of the IAPF and the determination of the OAS and the United States to keep it there despite calls from both sides for its prompt removal ruled out a military victory for either and brought home to all but the most intransigent the inevitability of an eventual compromise settlement. Widespread popular desire for peace and normalcy helped. To strengthen it, Bunker arranged to have U.S. helicopters shower 70,000 copies of the committee's declaration over the countryside. He also helped develop extensive propaganda efforts that Washington readily funded.

Imbert's heavy dependence on the United States for money to keep his government operating was another asset for Bunker. (He had no similar help in his dealings with the constitutionalists, whom Washington did not subsidize.) So was dissension within both camps. The committee put lines out to many groups and individual Dominicans; its strategy was to isolate the intransigents and exert its influence on the more responsible political leaders to persuade them to accept a reasonable compromise. The Dominicans' awareness that the negotiating process would culminate in an internationally supervised election also encouraged forward movement. Many on both sides thought they could win and, with Bunker's encouragement, decided to take a chance in a fair ballot. Those who were dubious about an electoral approach found opposing it awkward. Moreover, the GNR had already called for early elections (with itself remaining in office) and it could not now easily reject them. And for the constitutionalists, thoroughly stalemated and squeezed firmly into their narrow zone, early elections offered the prospect of winning at the ballot box what they recognized they could not win in battle.

The most important early advance was the selection of a candidate to head the provisional government. The committee had made the nomination a top priority and Bunker considered it the key to resolving other important problems. The choice of Héctor Garcia Godoy for the position was very much his doing. A businessman, diplomat, and charter member of the Dominican establishment who had served as foreign minister in the Bosch government, Garcia Godoy was highly regarded by a broad range of

Dominican leaders. He had ties to Joaquin Balaguer, the emerging power on the right who had been Trujillo's figurehead president and then briefly led the government after the dictator's assassination. He also had links with Bosch and the constitutionalists and with the business community. Moreover, unlike other potential candidates, Garcia Godoy wanted the job and was prepared to take it on whatever terms were offered.

Bunker recommended Garcia Godoy to Washington as an effective, moderate, reliable friend of the United States. To Dominicans, he stressed Garcia Godoy's experience, integrity, domestic and international stature, impartiality, and broad acceptability.[41] Bunker and Garcia Godoy would have their differences and the Dominican's tendency either to vacillate or act impetuously sometimes troubled the steady and patient American ambassador. But Bunker never regretted his decision to sponsor him.

The Johnson administration readily accepted Garcia Godoy, who was already well regarded in Washington. The Dominican factions proved more of a problem. The radical left, including the Communists, stoutly opposed him, but Bunker's extensive lobbying helped Garcia Godoy win the support of other factions in the constitutionalist camp. Although Imbert held out against him, the rightist leaders in the armed forces found him reasonable, liked his ties with Balaguer, and consented to the appointment.[42]

As it pursued its discussions with a broad range of Dominican leaders in late June and July, the Ad Hoc Committee gradually began to make progress, though never fast enough for Washington. Bunker tried to develop a new, revised package that incorporated proposals from both sides and met the Johnson administration's objectives. Among these, safeguarding the country from Communism remained foremost. A dispute over the text of an interim constitution was resolved by an adroit formula Bunker worked out that reconciled the conflicting views of the two parties by drawing from two previous constitutions and dropping controversial provisions from each. He allayed misgivings about the timing of elections by persuading the two sides to accept a six-month political truce followed by three months of campaigning. They agreed that the newly elected government would convoke a convention to draft a permanent constitution within four months of its taking office and that the IAPF should remain in the country through the elections.

The committee, now assisted by Garcia Godoy, persuaded the GNR and

the constitutionalists to come to an understanding on the critical problems of the demilitarization of the constitutionalist zone, the disarma-
ment of civilians there, the integration of the zone with the rest of the
city of Santo Domingo, and the reintegration of constitutionalist forces
into their former regular army units. This progress was achieved only after
highly contentious negotiations. Even then all sides understood that effective compliance would depend on Garcia Godoy's success in bringing the
armed forces under control.[43]

As the negotiations dragged on, Bunker tried to allay Washington's concerns. He cabled in late August: "I am aware of [the administration's] feeling of exasperation and frustration . . . at delays caused by the constant
maneuvering for advantage by both [sides] and by the childish refusal of
each . . . to deal with or even recognize the existence of the other. This is a
feeling fully shared by myself and my colleagues. However, given the mandate under which we are operating, I see no alternative to continuing along
the course we have set, combining patience with pressure and persuasion
to achieve our objectives."[44]

The provisions that the two sides had accepted were wrapped in a settlement package, an Act of Reconciliation, that the committee drafted. The
revised text, which retained the committee's original basic approach, was
signed on August 31. Imbert refused to accept the package despite Bunker's lengthy efforts to persuade him to make a graceful exit. He remained
a stumbling block to the bitter end, insisting he would neither sign the act
nor resign.[45] Only the threat of U.S. financial pressure and Johnson's public admonition, made at Bunker's request, finally led him to step down.
The GNR secretary of defense and the chiefs of the three armed services
then signed on behalf of the rightist regime. Their approval paved the way
for the installation of Garcia Godoy as head of the provisional government on September 3. He had been unwilling to take over until all of the
contending factions signed the agreement.

Despite the constitutionalists' earlier concern that the Ad Hoc Committee was stacked against them, the political compromises Bunker brokered
seem if anything to have tilted toward the liberal, democratic settlement
the moderate majority among them favored. The constitutionalists were
pleased with the relatively lenient arrangements for the treatment of the
Communists and the decision to keep the OAS Human Rights Commission in the country during the election period. (With Bunker's support,
the commission had moved to deter atrocities and terrorism, largely the
work of the rightists.) Moderate constitutionalists, happy with the selec-

tion of Garcia Godoy as provisional president, noted with satisfaction that even before his September 3 inauguration he had become an important force for a reasonable compromise settlement, as Bunker had foreseen and planned. They were also gratified by the provision that all parties holding principles compatible with representative democracy could participate in the elections. This meant that Bosch and his PRD party could run, with a good chance of winning. In an insightful study, Jerome Slater has noted that by midsummer "the most bitter Dominican criticism of the United States and the OAS was coming from the right rather than the left, with Bunker and the Ad Hoc Committee accused of being pro-constitutionalist, if not pro-Communist!"[46]

With the installation of Garcia Godoy, the Dominican political terrain changed. But although the locus of authority shifted from the Ad Hoc Committee to the provisional government, Bunker remained a pivotal figure. The enormous political stake the Johnson administration had in a settlement and the president's personal confidence that Bunker was best positioned to arrange one ensured that the administration would want him to continue to play a major part in Dominican affairs. Dominican recognition of the overwhelming power of the United States, the high regard Garcia Godoy and many other Dominican leaders had for Bunker, and, not unimportant, Bunker's control over the troops of the IAPF also ensured that he would remain a force to be reckoned with.

His role changed somewhat, however. Garcia Godoy, not the Ad Hoc Committee, now took most of the initiatives and made the final decisions. Bunker kept in very close contact with Garcia Godoy, acting primarily as his adviser and as an intermediary and conciliator between the president and other major Dominican civilian and military leaders. Bunker accepted his new role easily and enthusiastically, and carried it out with his customary energy and dedication.[47]

Bunker's overriding goal during the provisional government period was to advance the political process he had initiated with the signing of the Act of Reconciliation so that the projected elections could be held on schedule, a popularly chosen government installed, and the IAPF withdrawn. He recognized that this would require Garcia Godoy to take tough but conciliatory measures to strengthen the authority of the provisional government. With this in mind he sought to head off or defuse confrontational situations, especially those arising between Garcia Godoy and the regular military. He feared, rightly, that these could lead either to Garcia Godoy's overthrow or his resignation. In Bunker's view, Garcia Godoy's departure would seriously jeopardize if not destroy the prospect of an early settlement, and he was determined to do all he could to keep him in office. If Garcia Godoy needed Bunker and the IAPF to enforce his major decisions and have his way with other Dominican military and civilian leaders, Bunker needed Garcia Godoy even more.

Unlike many others in the Johnson administration, Bunker held that Garcia Godoy should be given as much responsibility and authority as possible compatible with U.S. national interests. He believed that this would make the provisional government more effective. He did not want the government to become a puppet of the United States, a role Garcia Godoy would have rejected. He dealt with Garcia Godoy in a respectful and candid manner, and though sometimes frustrated beneath his celebrated unflappability, never used intimidating tactics or lost his patience. He made it clear that he wanted to work with Garcia Godoy, not direct his steps. Bunker often urged Garcia Godoy to adopt more cautious approaches than the president preferred in handling the seemingly endless crises his government faced. But when Garcia Godoy stuck to a position, Bunker accepted it.

As Garcia Godoy selected members of his government, Washington became concerned about the role suspected Communists could play in the new Dominican political dispensation. Bunker was relaxed and understanding when the president chose a broad-based ministry that included important leftist elements. Administration officials such as Ambassador Bennett and Thomas Mann, who as assistant secretary for inter-American affairs and later under secretary was the key State Department officer dealing with the crisis, were more fearful than Bunker was about the danger that Communists posed to the Garcia Godoy government. They were also more prepared than he was to identify Juan Bosch and his associates with them.

Bunker believed that the Communist threat had long been blown out of all proportions and was always skeptical concerning warnings about Communists and Communism in the Dominican Republic. He trusted Garcia Godoy, although he believed that some of his appointments were unnecessarily provocative to the rightists. Nonetheless he recognized that the president needed to construct a government broad enough to win the support of moderate Dominican opinion and at least the acquiescence of the constitutionalists. He stressed to Garcia Godoy the importance of a balanced approach in dealing with the conflicting interests of the rival Dominican factions. This would help ensure his survival and enhance his effectiveness.

For Bunker, the first two months of the provisional government, September and October, were the most difficult period he confronted in his year in Santo Domingo. Shlaudeman has recalled, "This was the only time during the entire exercise when Ellsworth's characteristic optimism flagged. He (and I) thought this whole ramshackle edifice [the Garcia Godoy government] might well collapse at any minute."[48] Many in Washington looked askance at what Garcia Godoy and Bunker were trying to do. Some seemed to suspect that Bunker was moving too far in the direction of the Communists.

Bunker's dismay is easy to understand. Garcia Godoy faced enormous obstacles. His most immediate problem was to end the continuing division of the country into two armed camps by implementing the tortuously negotiated program to integrate the constitutionalist zone in central Santo Domingo with the rest of the city and country. This proved exceedingly difficult. Convinced that the well-equipped regular forces were determined to destroy them, the constitutionalists were in no hurry to agree to the relocation of their military units outside the city or to collect and turn over to the new provisional government the arms the civilians in their zone had obtained during the uprising.

Garcia Godoy recognized that eliminating the constitutionalist zone was an essential first step in restoring normal conditions. Bunker reported: "He has sought to accomplish this without violence or repression, moving cautiously and maintaining a conciliatory attitude toward the rebels so as to avoid renewed conflict. Progress has been slow and the failure of the Provisional Government to take hold in a more authoritative fashion has been disappointing."[49] Yet Bunker also found that the president's methods had reduced constitutionalist animosity and agreed with his practice of avoiding abrupt moves that could cause them to shift back to belligerence before their zone was integrated.

Bunker played a major role in bringing about this integration, especially in helping devise an acceptable plan for relocating constitutionalist military units in a camp on the outskirts of Santo Domingo. Despite many challenges, especially opposition to the relocation proposal from hard-core leftists in the constitutionalist ranks, the zone was eventually dismantled and the whole country came at least nominally under the provisional government.

Aside from frustrating Washington and at times taxing even Bunker's patience, Garcia Godoy's way of dealing with the constitutionalist zone problem also worsened his difficult relations with the regular military. They increasingly suspected that he favored the constitutionalists and considered his unwillingness to move more rapidly and forcefully to eliminate the zone evidence of his leftist leanings. They found further proof in the substantial representation Garcia Godoy gave in his cabinet to the constitutionalists, his removal of the national police from armed forces' control, and his willingness to allow the return to the republic during the period of political truce of their old nemesis, Juan Bosch.

The regular military were also highly displeased by Garcia Godoy's role in the forced departure from the country of General Elias Wessin y Wessin. As head of the autonomous Armed Forces Training Center at San Isidro outside Santo Domingo, Wessin had been probably the most powerful of the rightist military leaders before his "transfer" to the post of Dominican consul general in Miami. And they were especially outraged when Garcia Godoy announced on September 28 a plan to reintegrate into the regular armed forces the constitutionalist officers and men who had served in them before joining the uprising. To most regular officers, this was intolerable despite the reintegration provision included in the Act of Reconciliation. Garcia Godoy, for his part, mistrusted the military as much as they did him. Suspecting, with good reason, that they were trying to subvert his government, he looked for ways to exert his authority over them. He was convinced that he would only be able to do so when the men who had led the armed forces against the constitutionalist uprising were no longer in command.

Bunker also wanted the military depoliticized, but he favored a more measured approach. In early September he had used the IAPF to expel Wessin, whom the force had thwarted as he moved his tanks toward the capital in an apparent coup attempt. The Ad Hoc Committee, the Garcia Godoy government, and IAPF officers had worked closely together in the sensitive expulsion operation which had climaxed with an IAPF "honor guard" escorting Wessin to a U.S. military aircraft that took him out of the country.

Bunker urged Garcia Godoy not to tackle other military leaders before completing the dismantling of the constitutionalist zone. Much more than the president, he saw the military as a valuable asset for the Dominican Republic. "Defective as it may be," he told him in late October, "the military establishment must be held together to prevent a Communist takeover. Leaders of the armed forces must therefore have the respect and support of the officer corps. Any new armed forces' chiefs that might be appointed would have to meet these qualifications."[50] He reported to Washington the same day: "Garcia Godoy must convince the military he is not intent on turning the country over to the constitutionalists, while the armed force must give evidence that they support the provisional government and mean to meet their obligations under the Institutional Act."[51]

Bunker frequently met leaders from both sides to defuse the confrontation and lessen the growing violence that again threatened to tear the country apart. As rumors of coups intensified, he warned that any attempt to overthrow the Garcia Godoy government would be in clear defiance of OAS efforts to restore democracy in the Dominican Republic. This threat probably helped dissuade the regular military from supporting a short-lived coup attempt led by rightist civilians in the provincial city of Santiago soon afterwards.

But this respite was quickly shattered when regular troops who had been attached to the GNR attacked a smaller group of armed former constitutionalists in a bloody firefight in the city that ended only when IAPF units reached the scene. This outbreak proved too much for Garcia Godoy. Rejecting Bunker's gradualist approach, which called for the dismissal of military officers junior to the chiefs, he decided to assign the leaders of *both* the regular and the constitutional forces to posts abroad. He quickly ran into a stone wall when the defense minister and the three service chiefs refused to quit and instead tried to force Garcia Godoy's own resignation.

Bunker then took the lead in efforts to end the confrontation. Mc-George Bundy's comments to President Johnson at the time are again worth quoting: "This looks to me like one of those desperate situations in which Spanish honor and common sense may be in headlong collision. There is no one in the world who can do more to head off such a collision than Bunker, and he has been repeatedly told that we trust his judgement. Thus at the moment all I can do is give you this warning as a pleasant addition to the troubles of the day. I do not think there is anything specific we can or should do from here."[52]

Bunker's many cables reporting the Ad Hoc Committee's activities over the two months needed to resolve this crisis provide a detailed account of a master diplomat in action.[53] Quickly convinced that a settlement required the prompt departure of Caamaño, he carefully orchestrated an effort to persuade the constitutionalist colonel to accept the post of Dominican military attaché in London. Bunker's offer of security guarantees for the constitutionalists left behind in the republic significantly helped bring about Caamaño's eventual exit following three difficult weeks of negotiations. So did the two men's personal relations. Bunker had carefully cultivated the recalcitrant colonel, with useful results: according to Bunker, Caamaño said that he regarded the ambassador as a surrogate father.

With Caamaño headed for England, Bunker turned his attention to Commodore Francisco Javier Rivera Caminero, a naval officer who had become minister of defense. He too eventually decided to leave, for an attaché posting in Washington, under a complicated arrangement Bunker developed to help him save face. He was replaced by a more moderate and accommodating figure. Garcia Godoy himself then agreed to compromise, undertaking to leave the armed forces chiefs in place "as long as [they] adjust their conduct to complete obedience to [the] government and to absolute impartiality during the course of the forthcoming electoral campaign."[54] But faced not long afterwards by a crippling strike by workers demanding the removal of the unpopular army and air force chiefs, he used the loophole this wording offered and assigned the two commanders to powerless jobs in the Defense Ministry.

Bunker went along with this move. By that time he too had become convinced that a clean sweep of the chiefs was required. To force them out, he had been prepared to use the IAPF, or, if the countries that contributed forces to it were unwilling, U.S. military units alone. Washington authorized this action if it proved necessary. Bunker also asked that U.S. naval forces be moved closer to Dominican shores to convince the commanders to quit. But he balanced this effective use of force in diplomacy by persuading Garcia Godoy to remove a sizeable number of leftists from the government, thereby making it easier for the chiefs to acquiesce. Garcia Godoy sacrificed wider military reform as a concession to the armed forces.

The attitude of the Brazilian commander of the IAPF, General Hugo Panasco Alvim, further complicated Bunker's life. Alvim outspokenly favored the rightist military. When they seized the Santo Domingo radio station in angry retaliation for Garcia Godoy's attempt to dismiss the armed forces chiefs, he refused to act on a committee request to evict them, and publicly stated that the IAPF would never attack units of the regular army. Bunker reported to Washington that "our difficulties with Alvim stem from his simplistic and distorted view of the Dominican situation in general. He apparently believes the rightist propaganda line that Garcia Godoy is, at best, a dupe of 'the communists,' among whom all constitutionalists are included. According to this school, the president's action in replacing the chiefs is part of an overall scheme to destroy the armed forces."[55]

Bunker became fed up with Alvim's attitude and was probably aware that in his worse moments Alvim alleged that Bunker too was a communist. Bunker knew Brazilian President Humberto Castelo Branco, and during a visit to Rio de Janeiro for a meeting of OAS foreign ministers persuaded him to curtail the general's assignment.[56] Alvim was replaced by a moderate, less senior Brazilian army officer with whom Bunker worked well. As part of the bargain, Bunker to his regret lost the services of Lt. General Bruce Palmer, the commander of U.S. forces in the Dominican Republic who acted as Alvim's deputy.[57]

Despite its condemnation by Juan Bosch, who objected to the ousted chiefs' continued presence at the defense ministry, the settlement of the military leadership issue significantly calmed the political waters and set the stage for the election campaign that began a few days later. The three months of intensive canvassing and the balloting that followed on June 1 went off remarkably well. Held under the sharp eye of dozens of OAS and other observers, including a large number of prominent American liberals, the poll was widely judged to have been free and fair.

To the surprise of many who thought Bosch likely to win, the victor was Joaquin Balaguer, the conservative candidate. He received 57 percent of the vote to Bosch's 37. (The rest went to splinter group candidates.) Bunker had seen confidential polling data indicating that Balaguer would win easily and was pleased when the results confirmed these. The *New York Times* reported on the eve of the election that while Balaguer was a marginal favorite among most U.S. officials, there was also "a clear determination among them not only to accept whoever wins but to give the winner as much support as possible."[58] Some Dominicans alleged that the vote had been rigged (though not on U.S. instructions) and claimed that improper pressures had been brought to bear on voters in rural areas. But these charges were not substantiated. Bosch and his supporters accepted the result, as did other liberals and radicals in the republic and elsewhere in Latin America.

Bunker's role was widely hailed, even by Bosch, the disappointed former president. In a conversation with Vice President Hubert Humphrey, who came to Santo Domingo for Balaguer's inauguration in early July, Bosch warmly expressed his admiration for Bunker and described himself as "Bunker's chief of public relations" in the Dominican Republic. Bunker received similar plaudits from Balaguer and other Dominican leaders.[59]

Lyndon Johnson was as effusive as the Dominicans. Bunker had removed a major foreign policy millstone from his neck. At a White House press conference a few weeks after the Dominican election the president was unstinting in his praise for a man who had by then become his favorite American diplomat: "Bunker belongs not only to the United States but to the hemisphere. He has rendered great service to both. Wise in the ways of statecraft, unvacillating in his faith in the democratic process, tenacious in the pursuit of fair solutions, firm and patient in the face of adversity, respected by all for his integrity and impartiality, he has brought high honor to himself and the Organization of American States."[60]

The Johnson administration's decision to send armed forces to the Dominican Republic was prompted by an exaggerated estimate of a Communist threat to the country. The unilateral intervention had a negative impact elsewhere. It weakened the authority and prestige of the OAS, sparked anti-U.S. sentiment among the Latins, and contributed to disillusionment with Johnson's foreign policy in the United States just as he was expanding the American role in Vietnam. These adverse consequences persisted despite the absorption of the U.S. military force into the IAPF and the role of the OAS Ad Hoc Committee in resolving the crisis.

Supporters of the action correctly point out that the intervention had positive results for the Dominican Republic itself and U.S. objectives there even though the concerns that led Johnson to order it seem unwarranted in retrospect. As Professor Samuel Huntington argued a few years after Bunker completed his mission and the IAPF had departed: "Whether or not there was a threat of communist takeover on the island, we were able to go in, restore order, negotiate a truce among conflicting parties, hold reasonably honest elections which the right man won, withdraw our troops, and promote a very considerable amount of social and economic reform."[61]

Bunker would certainly have agreed with Huntington's positive assessment. Although he did not believe the intervention prevented another

Cuba—in his view the Communist strength in the Dominican Republic had been overestimated—he thought it possible that Castro might have tried over time to increase Communist influence there. In any event, he was satisfied that the policies he developed and persuaded Washington to accept made possible the sequence of events Huntington spelled out, and was pleased with what he had accomplished.

Despite the controversial nature of U.S. Dominican policy, Bunker had few detractors. Even those who took a much less positive view than he did about the outcome of the military intervention gave him high marks for his sure-footed, patient diplomacy, especially his selection of Garcia Godoy. Given the complex nature of the Dominican issue and the way the Johnson administration developed foreign policy, it is very difficult to identify any significant missteps Bunker made in bringing his mission to a successful conclusion.

The Dominican Republic was probably Bunker's finest diplomatic hour. But the greatly enhanced prestige he now enjoyed at the White House had unintended consequences. General Bruce Palmer had seen this coming. He told Bunker when they were still together in Santo Domingo that the two of them had performed so well that they would both end up in Vietnam.[62] Palmer was assigned there in March 1967 to command the Second Field Force Vietnam, a U.S. Army corps headquarters. Although Bunker received other assignments following his success in the Caribbean, he too went to Vietnam, as ambassador, just two months after the general arrived.

10
To Center Stage in Vietnam

After seeing in the new Balaguer government, Bunker returned only briefly to his regular duties as ambassador to the OAS. In October 1966, President Johnson gave him another appointment, this time as ambassador-at-large. The position allowed him to carry out with a more formal title the troubleshooting missions that had by then become his well-recognized specialty. Bunker seems to have been unaware of the appointment in advance. He wrote to the president: "The news reached me at my home in Vermont and came as a wonderful and most gratifying surprise."[1]

Bunker's first task was to undertake at the president's request a study of Israel's water problems and the possibility of relieving them by desalinization of sea water in a U.S.-supplied nuclear-powered plant. He visited Israel in December and January to discuss the issue with Prime Minister Levi Eshkol and other officials. But the project eventually faded away, the victim of technical uncertainties and the steep costs involved in implementing it.

The only real benefit Bunker got from his negotiations in Israel was his purchase of a diamond wedding ring for Carol at a Tel Aviv jewelry store his Israeli counterpart recommended. It presaged a highly unusual event, the marriage of two ambassadors. In September, Johnson had named Carol ambassador to Nepal. Before she left Washington for Kathmandu in December, she and Bunker quietly decided to marry.

Carol's assignment as ambassador probably hastened their decision. The appointment had been widely expected. As she crisply recalled: "The White House took the initiative because Lyndon Johnson wanted to increase the number of women ambassadors and no nonsense about it. Since [Nepal] was in my area [of responsibility], it was thought that it would be a good place to send me."[2]

To underscore the importance the president and his administration attached to placing women in senior diplomatic positions, Vice President Humphrey and Secretary of State Rusk both participated in Carol's

swearing-in ceremony. Their presence was more than symbolic, however. Humphrey and Rusk knew Carol well and valued her professional com-
sia with the vice president only a few
I worked closely with her during the

ne as no surprise to their friends and
ker has recalled that she had hoped
been happily married and had liked
a surprise to many who had followed
ship was the timing of the wedding,
ring a visit by Bunker to Kathmandu

ly to a few friends and relatives. The
n Sam, then head of the Ford Foun-
man. They also got word to Lyndon
ly delighted that two of his ambassa-
ed in a congratulatory letter that the
to take place between two American

n what was happening were Carol's
arnes Jr., and his wife Betsey. Barnes
plans to him soon after he welcomed
," she told him, "I've got a bombshell
al moment of panic. He did not know his
new ambassador well and wondered uneasily what might have triggered
her impending outburst. Carol quickly cleared up the mystery. "I'm getting married to Ellsworth Bunker," she announced, "and I want you and
Betsey to take charge of all the arrangements. But don't tell anybody." Her
marching orders to him included three main tasks—find a minister, organize a wedding reception, and arrange a honeymoon trip. "And keep it all
secret," she reiterated.

Fortuitously, Betsey Barnes's father, Rev. H. Norman Sibley, a retired
Presbyterian minister, was planning to visit Kathmandu for the Christmas
holidays. He performed the ceremony on January 3, 1967 at an improvised
altar in an upstairs sitting room of Carol's ambassadorial residence.

Soon afterwards, unsuspecting Nepalese and members of the diplomatic corps arrived at the residence for a reception. They had been told in
their invitations that the gathering was in honor of former ambassador to
Nepal Ellsworth Bunker. Carol and Ellsworth greeted them, giving no clue

that anything unusual was going on. Some time afterwards, Carol called for attention. The Barneses recall the scene: "She formally presented Ellsworth as a distinguished guest, evoked his ties to Nepal and then, almost as an afterthought, introduced him as her husband." There was a second or so of complete surprise, then the guests broke into cheers.[5]

Ellsworth and Carol spent their honeymoon in Nepal, traveling initially by jeep to Tiger Tops, the plush, renowned safari hotel in the country's jungle region. After five days of this luxurious life, when they explored the jungle by elephant and jeep, they switched to roughing it, camping with young Peace Corps volunteers. "The first night," Bunker reported to his daughter, "we spent in a little village and our room was a little lean-to about 6 by 10 with a dirt floor, two cots and sleeping bags, with not even a nail to hang clothes on. But we had what was probably the biggest bathroom in the world with the highest ceiling—a cane field with the stars overhead."[6] They cooked curried goat over open fires. Then it was back to their ambassadorial duties.

But, for Ellsworth, with a new twist. He had no intention of living ten thousand miles away from his new wife, and persuaded the State Department to let him operate out of Kathmandu rather than Washington, the customary base for ambassadors-at-large. This unusual arrangement seemed to work well for the few weeks it was in operation. Although Kathmandu airport was well off the beaten track, the intermittent assignments an ambassador-at-large carried out in those days did not require instant access to major jet routes. In later years, as he continued his diplomatic career well into his eighties, Bunker would speak wistfully of a blissful retirement as a pampered, carefree ambassadorial spouse. Early 1967 in Kathmandu was the closest he ever got to that idealized existence.

Nepal's capital was certainly a very pleasant place to live, especially in the winter months when Bunker first took up residence. Like so many Americans who lived or traveled there, he was fond of the country and the Nepalese people. He was still well remembered from the late 1950s, when he was accredited to both India and Nepal, the last U.S. ambassador to play that dual role. Returning as resident ambassador-at-large, and classified by the Nepalese government as a "distinguished visitor without rank," he added panache to the diplomatic community. Carol worked hard at her job and developed warm relations with many Nepalese, from the king and queen on down. They all seemed to enjoy having Ellsworth in Kathmandu. The small official American contingent was also pleased to have him there, Carol for obvious reasons, her staff because he was an amiable and undemanding gentleman whose distracting presence kept their hard-charging ambassador from overworking them.

In early March Bunker was in Brazil on his way back from an OAS meeting in Buenos Aires when he got word from Secretary Rusk that the president was planning to appoint him ambassador to Vietnam. The assignment would be the most difficult and controversial he had so far tackled in his quarter century in diplomacy. Catapulting him to the center stage of U.S. foreign policy, it kept him in Saigon for six years, first under Johnson, then, after January 1969, in the administration of Richard M. Nixon. By the time he left the embassy on his seventy-ninth birthday in May 1973, four months after the Paris Agreements had ended the American military role in Vietnam, Bunker had become an internationally renowned figure.

The policies the Johnson and Nixon administrations adopted during his long Saigon assignment embittered and divided the nation. Bunker at times advocated more aggressive positions to achieve U.S. objectives than Washington was willing to take, and was correctly counted as a "hawk" on the war. But he was comfortable with the changing approaches Johnson and Nixon followed and loyally implemented them.

When the North Vietnamese Army overran South Vietnam in 1975, he did not accept the widespread judgment that those policies had failed. Nor did he ever express any regrets about his Vietnam role. He would have disagreed with those who said later that he ought to have declined Johnson's call. In this view, which some of those who worked most closely and admiringly with him share, Bunker's place in history would have been far more impressive had his diplomatic career climaxed with the Dominican triumph and not included the long and controversial mission in Vietnam that followed.

This is a valid argument. It is one of the ironies of American diplomatic history that for all the skill Bunker demonstrated in an array of difficult assignments, he is now remembered more for the role he played in the Vietnam debacle than for any of his achievements over his long career as an ambassador and troubleshooter.

Johnson had turned to Bunker to replace Ambassador Henry Cabot Lodge, the prominent Massachusetts Republican who had been

Richard Nixon's vice-presidential running mate in 1960. By late 1966 Lodge was eager to leave Saigon both for personal and professional reasons.[7] According to his biographer Anne E. Blair, he had objected to what he concluded were Johnson's policy of seeking to win in Vietnam through conventional military methods, with American troops carrying the main burden. As Philip Habib, who was political counselor in Lodge's embassy, told Blair, "He may also have 'had enough' of the beleaguered post in which he had served thirty months in all."[8]

An imperious, demanding, self-important man whom many would contrast unfavorably with Bunker as ambassador to Vietnam, Lodge held the position twice in the early and mid-1960s, both times under Democratic presidents. He is best remembered in these two Vietnamese assignments for the role he played in the coup that led to the ouster and assassination of President Ngo Dinh Diem in the final weeks of the Kennedy administration. The only professional politician ever appointed to the position, he had lent a bipartisan color to Vietnam policy that Kennedy and Johnson both found useful.

Lodge's desire to leave Vietnam was paralleled by an interest on the part of several Johnson advisers in having him replaced by someone who could better manage U.S. programs there and deal more effectively with the Vietnamese.[9] Moreover, despite his objections to Johnson's evolving Vietnam policy, which he did not voice publicly, Lodge was so closely identified with the president's position that the bipartisanship that his appointment represented had diminished as a political asset. And by early 1967 the president was having more difficulty on Vietnam with Democrats than with Republicans, further reducing the usefulness of a prominent GOP leader as ambassador in Saigon.

Several well-known names came into play as possible replacements for Lodge. Prominent among them were McGeorge Bundy, by then president of the Ford Foundation; Clark M. Clifford, a Washington lawyer and close friend of Johnson's who had been special counsel to President Truman; and even Secretary of Defense Robert McNamara. For a time, General William Westmoreland seemed the front-runner. With the title of chief of the Military Assistance Command, Vietnam (MACV), Westmoreland had been in charge of American forces in the country since 1964. His backers, who included McNamara and General Earle Wheeler, chairman of the Joint Chiefs of Staff, argued in favor of his continuing in military command while taking on the ambassadorial duties. They likened the arrangement to General Douglas MacArthur's role in occupied Japan.

The State Department strongly objected. In a memorandum spelling out why it thought the idea unwise, Under Secretary of State Nicholas Katzenbach argued that what was needed was not an army general but an outstanding civilian with "extraordinary political sensitivity in order to operate effectively during the coming period of intense Vietnamese political activity and factionalism." Someone, he said, like Ellsworth Bunker.[10] Two weeks later, McGeorge Bundy also called on the president to appoint Bunker. Bunker, Bundy wrote, "has the precise combination of strength and sensitivity that Saigon now needs." Like Katzenbach, Bundy focused on the evolving Vietnamese political scene and the problems it would pose for the United States: "The spotlight on Saigon politics will be very intense in the next twelve months, and Bunker would be the ideal man to play the U.S. hand."[11]

Johnson initially decided to combine the conflicting recommendations he received. In a letter he wrote Rusk a few days after hearing from Bundy, he stated that "the best solution is to give General Westmoreland the overall task of Ambassador while maintaining his military command." But reflecting the views he had received from Bunker's supporters, the president added: "The bringing to life within the next six months of constitutional government in Saigon is as important to us as the course of military events in the field. . . . [T]here is one American above any other who is qualified to guide this process," he concluded, and that was Ellsworth Bunker. Johnson instructed Rusk to ask Bunker if he was willing to serve as ambassador-at-large in Saigon, "assuming responsibility for our political policy under Westmoreland's general direction."[12]

Rusk never had to carry out these instructions. He quickly talked Johnson out of the bizarre, unwise, and probably unworkable arrangement. Soon afterwards the president called Bunker to the White House and asked him to be ambassador to Vietnam in his own right.[13]

Johnson later wrote (and told Bunker at the time) that the decision to send him to Saigon reflected his satisfaction with the ambassador's handling of the Dominican crisis.[14] Walt Rostow, who as Bundy's successor as the president's assistant for national security was involved in the selection process, recalled that Johnson admired Bunker as "a man of total integrity, totally disinterested, with extraordinary diplomatic gifts." According to Rostow, the president thought that "for an austere Vermont gentleman, Bunker had a particular genius for people from underdeveloped countries!"[15]

From the administration's viewpoint, Bunker's appointment offered many diplomatic and political advantages. He had proven his ability to get along well with sensitive foreign leaders of all descriptions. His recent success in dealing with the difficult and recalcitrant Dominican warring factions suggested that he was well qualified to handle the often troublesome and unpredictable military officers and politicians who would preside over the Republic of Vietnam during his ambassadorship. Bunker had also demonstrated in his Dominican role an ability to collaborate effectively with the U.S. military, a vital asset for an American envoy to Saigon. As a distinguished ambassador and diplomatic troubleshooter who had worked successfully for Democratic and Republican presidents alike, he was admired and respected on Capitol Hill, an important advantage at a time when opposition was mounting against administration Vietnam policy, especially in the Senate Foreign Relations Committee. His status as a senior statesman of sterling character who knew his way around the corridors of power also gave him high standing in the foreign policy establishment and among foreign affairs commentators in the media, where skepticism about Johnson's approach to Vietnam was also on the rise.

Unlike either of his two immediate predecessors as ambassador to Saigon, the Republican politician Lodge and General Maxwell Taylor, a recent chairman of the Joint Chiefs of Staff, Bunker did not have an important political or military constituency. He was an archetypal patriot with no policy axe to grind, and Johnson could confidently expect that he would work loyally with the administration as it faced the uncertainties of the Vietnam War. Although Bunker had not previously dealt directly with the Vietnam issue, nor put his views about it on record, the president would have reasonably concluded in the winter of 1966–67 that a man of his background and experience would accept without significant demur the main thrust of the administration's Vietnam policy.[16]

At the time of his appointment, Bunker was almost seventy-three. If Johnson had any concerns about the ability of a man in his mid-seventies to lead a massive diplomatic mission dealing with crucial issues on a round-the-clock basis in a steamy, polluted, war-torn country, he did not allow them to deter him. Unlike the White House staffers who had dismissed Bunker as a candidate for assistant secretary of state for inter-American affairs a couple of months earlier because they thought it "probably unfair to ask him to assume [such a] burden at his age,"[17] the president did not consider the assignment too heavy a responsibility for an elderly man. He told Rusk that he was aware that Bunker would be making a sacrifice, but recalled that Henry Stimson had been the same age when he returned to government in 1940 to become for five years Franklin D. Roosevelt's secretary of war. Bunker's vigor in carrying out his mission in the Dominican Republic probably helped persuade the president that his age was nothing to worry seriously about. To someone of Johnson's cast of mind, the ambassador's recent marriage might also have suggested that the old man was still going strong. In any event, no one, certainly neither Johnson nor Bunker himself, expected that Bunker would remain in Saigon until 1973, four years after the war had driven the president from office.

Bunker had some doubts about the assignment. He was reluctant to abandon the comfortable arrangement he had worked out as an ambassador-at-large based in Kathmandu. Much more important, he did not want to leave his new bride for a full-time posting to a distant embassy that could keep them separated for years. But there was never any doubt what his decision would be. It was one thing to pass up an assistant secretary's job in the Kennedy administration State Department in 1961. It was quite another to turn down a direct request from Johnson to take on the crucial Saigon assignment. The ambassadorship was an offer he could not refuse.

Johnson made the offer to Bunker at a private meeting in the White House Oval Office, where the president could bring his formidable powers of persuasion to bear had Bunker sought to resist. The deal was swiftly done. Johnson later wrote a warm letter to Carol. He said that he had hesitated a long time before asking Bunker to assume a duty that would often separate the two, but had finally chosen him "because I regard him, as you do, as one of the wisest men America has produced in our time."[18] Carol no doubt welcomed the message, though she was surely shrewd enough to recognize that Johnson's claim to have hesitated on connubial grounds was at best exaggerated. But she was as aware as Ellsworth was of the significance of the offer, and like him she knew when the call of duty had to be answered.

Johnson announced the Bunker appointment in a highly publicized speech he gave on the Vietnam War on March 15 to the Tennessee legislature, at a session marking the 200th anniversary of the birth of Andrew Jackson. In his address, which the historian William Conrad Gibbons later described as "probably the most definitive and strident defense of U.S. policy in Vietnam of his entire Presidency,"[19] Johnson gave a lengthy justification of the bombing of North Vietnam, repeated his willingness to end the war if the other side would show the same willingness, and in a phrase that made the headlines, expressed his firm determination to "stay the course."[20] Veteran *New York Times* correspondent James Reston, who accompanied him to Nashville, wrote after hearing the speech that "President Johnson looks more and more like a man who has decided to go for military victory in Vietnam, and thinks he can make it."[21]

Toward the end of his lengthy address, the president disclosed that he had "drafted" Bunker to replace Ambassador Lodge, thus associating the selection of his new envoy with the administration's determination to do everything necessary to attain U.S. objectives in Vietnam. He described Bunker as "able and devoted, full of wisdom and experience acquired on five continents over many years." The president also announced the appointment as Bunker's deputy of Eugene Locke, a Texas friend then ambassador to Pakistan. National Security Council staffer Robert Komer, who had become the White House official responsible for overseeing programs to pacify the Vietnamese countryside, was to go to Saigon to head up the effort at that end. Additional highly regarded military personnel were to be assigned to General Westmoreland's staff. "So you can be confident," the president said, "that in the months ahead we shall have the ablest, the wisest, the most tenacious and the most experienced team that the United States of America can mount."

The unusual setting for the president's announcement of his new diplomatic team was reportedly prompted by word that columnist Joseph Alsop was about to leak Bunker's appointment. Johnson's decision to bring the new group with him to Guam later that week for a major conference on Vietnam may also have influenced the timing. Almost all the high-ranking U.S. civilian and military officials who dealt with the issue were to attend, together with the leaders of the South Vietnamese government.

The surprise appointment was well received. Press accounts stressed Bunker's long experience, renowned patience, and, above all, his talent as a negotiator, a skill the commentators thought important both in dealing with political infighting in Saigon and with possible future contacts between the South Vietnamese government and the Communist National Liberation Front. Although almost all stories mentioned Bunker's advanced age, they expressed confidence that, as with Ambassador Averell Harriman, another prominent senior citizen in the thick of the diplomatic fray, this would not impede his ability to carry out his demanding assignment. Opponents of the war were seemingly as pleased as Johnson's supporters in hailing the decision. Columnist Walter Lippmann, one of the most vociferous of the president's critics, called Bunker the best possible choice. Lippmann warned, however, that "the appointment . . . might turn out to be another of those diversionary actions which have so often accompanied and covered up an escalation of the war."[22]

Bunker's participation as ambassador-designate at the top-level conference that met on Guam March 20–21 was his first full introduction to the complexities of the Vietnam issue and the senior officials dealing with it. When the meeting took place, the massive intervention of U.S. combat troops in South Vietnam to counter Vietcong guerrillas and regular North Vietnamese Army units was entering its third year. American armed forces in the country totaled almost 400,000. That number was due to rise to 470,000 by the end of 1967, and General Westmoreland was asking for more in 1968. An escalating bombing campaign against targets in North Vietnam and large-scale search-and-destroy operations against Communist forces and base areas in the South had accompanied the troop buildup.

Although this huge U.S. military presence and the substantial economic assistance that accompanied it had shored up the faltering South Vietnamese government and armed forces, the situation on the ground seemed stalemated. Skeptics both within and outside the administration questioned the effectiveness of both the air and land campaigns in permanently hampering the Communist war effort. President Johnson had in late February made a decision to increase the use of force, including stepped-up efforts to inhibit North Vietnamese use of infiltration routes in Laos, though not to the extent Westmoreland and the Joint Chiefs of Staff recommended.

Despite claims by proponents of greater force, there was no indication that the war would soon end. The political and military objectives of the opposing sides seemed irreconcilable, and neither was prepared to accept a meaningful compromise. As his Nashville speech suggested, the president still thought the United States could win the war militarily. For Washington, which regarded the hostilities primarily as the consequence of aggression by the North rather than as a guerrilla insurgency, this meant forcing the North Vietnamese regime in Hanoi to abandon its long effort to impose Communism on all of Vietnam and accept a negotiated settlement in which the people of the South could determine their own fate. For their part, the tough and patient leaders in Hanoi were confident that over time they could wear down the Americans, just as they had prevailed over the French in 1954. They had consistently rebuffed the Johnson administration's intermittent initiatives to persuade them to enter talks designed to produce a settlement.

As a new boy on Johnson's Vietnam team, Bunker mostly listened at Guam. Bui Diem, Vietnam's insightful ambassador to Washington who also participated in the conference, gives a good description of the image his new American counterpart projected in the bilateral sessions: "Ellsworth Bunker sat at the table without saying much. A thin old man, but erect and obviously energetic, he stretched his long neck at us as if he wanted to size up at a glance all these Vietnamese faces. There was an air of impenetrability about him, a shield of dignity that marked him instantly as an aristocrat. . . . None of us suspected that we had in Bunker a dedicated friend whose aloof manner belied his warm heart." [23]

At the conference, Bunker consulted Ambassador Lodge and, as Bui Diem noticed, took the opportunity to make some preliminary assessments of the two Vietnamese leaders he would soon deal with in Saigon: General Nguyen Van Thieu, the head of state, and Air Vice-Marshal Nguyen Cao Ky, the prime minister. Thieu and Ky had led South Vietnam in an uneasy tandem since 1965 following yet another of the country's military coups. At the time of the conference the flamboyant and mercurial Ky, only thirty-seven, was responsible for the day-to-day operations of the government. This gave him a much more powerful role than his reserved and cautious forty-four-year-old colleague. Watching Johnson in action with them, Bunker got an even better sense of the importance the president attached to speedy progress on a new, democratic constitution for Vietnam, to be followed by free and fair elections.

As Johnson saw it, such political advance would help relieve mounting criticism at home that his administration was senselessly backing an unworthy authoritarian regime of military men in what it avowed was the cause of self-determination. Efforts to develop an elected, constitutional government would soon be topmost on Bunker's agenda. As noted, his admirers expected that his near-legendary skill as a negotiator between rival political factions would help bring that process to a successful conclusion. That is why they had recommended him to Johnson for the Saigon job.

At the conference Bunker heard for the first time, firsthand, General Westmoreland's basically sanguine assessment of the military situation in Vietnam. Reviewing the MACV commander's briefing, which they found contributed to the "unrealistic military euphoria" that pervaded the Guam discussions, the authors of the *Pentagon Papers* accurately reported: "Recent American successes reinforced the belief that [the United States] had hit upon the key to winning—despite continued large scale infiltration. Westmoreland and others on his staff believed we were again flirting with the elusive 'crossover point' when enemy total strength would begin to decline, battle, diseases and desertion losses would exceed gains."[24] It was not the last overly optimistic account of military progress and prospects for early success that Bunker would hear from Westmoreland and his successors at MACV.

The Senate Foreign Relations Committee unanimously confirmed Bunker following his return from Guam.[25] The full Senate followed suit the next day. In the committee's confirmation hearing, members led by its Democratic chairman, J. William Fulbright of Arkansas, were lavish in their praise of Bunker and treated him with respect and admiration. Opponents of the administration's Vietnam policy such as Fulbright and Democratic Senator Wayne Morse of Oregon joined their more hawkish colleagues in agreeing, in the words of Claiborne Pell, a Rhode Island Democrat, that they were "delighted at this appointment and [could] not think of a better man for a most difficult job."[26] ". . . [T]hose of us who are against the war owe you exactly the same cooperation that those who are for the war do," said Senator Morse.[27]

But for all the warm appreciation the senators expressed for Bunker's character and qualifications, the hearings inevitably had a hard edge. Fulbright and Morse used them to belabor current Vietnam policy and what they considered its failures. Though they were careful to exclude Bunker from their criticism, they asked him some tough questions. Airing again his well-known position that the purposes of the war remained unclear, Fulbright queried Bunker about the administration's definition of self-determination. The senator said he had been dissatisfied with Ambassador Maxwell Taylor's testimony on the point. It had seemed to him to suggest that the administration was insisting that South Vietnam choose a constitutional system similar to that of the United States. He got Bunker to agree that self-determination meant a free choice. "I hope you are speaking what the government really believes, an absolutely free choice," Fulbright concluded. "That is hopeful."[28]

In the time-honored way ambassadorial nominees try to deflect senatorial questioners, Bunker said in reply to other difficult queries that he could provide meaningful answers only after spending some time in Saigon. His high standing with committee members allowed him to get by with this response. He replied graciously to the senators' expression of hope that once he had completed his on-the-job training he would tell the committee more about administration policy, embassy operations, and future directions the situation in Vietnam might take. In the meantime, as John Sherman Cooper, the Kentucky Republican who had been Bunker's predecessor in New Delhi, said in expressing what seemed to be the committee's view: "I feel sure that he will advise the President and . . . recommend to him any changes with respect to Vietnamese policy that he felt were proper and . . . in the interests of our country."[29]

The serious if largely nonconfrontational hearing had one light note. Toward the end of the session, Fulbright commented that Bunker had recently been fortunate in acquiring a very distinguished wife who was also herself an ambassador. He wondered if there was any precedent for having a man and wife as American ambassadors to important countries. "I do not think there is, Senator," Bunker replied, "but I may say that it was not the easiest of my negotiations."[30]

The president's offer to Bunker of a plane to visit occasionally with Carol provoked the only recorded criticism of the appointment on Capitol Hill. Republican representative H. R. Gross of Iowa had a sharp exchange with Secretary McNamara about the arrangement, later known at the embassies in Saigon and Kathmandu as "mating flights."[31] Gross said it was disgraceful for the U.S. government to facilitate the travel of "this seventy-two-year old bridegroom to further his romance." Angered by the outburst, McNamara replied: "We are not short of pilots and planes, and we can surely allow the use of a plane to transfer Ambassador Bunker once in a while out of the combat environment in which he will be working twenty hours a day, seven days a week, to visit his family. We do it for others, and we should certainly do it for him."[32]

Stopping briefly en route in Kathmandu to visit Carol, Bunker reached Saigon on April 25, only hours after Lodge had left, to begin the longest assignment by far of any American ambassador there. He was the next-to-last of the career diplomats and civilian and military political appointees to preside over the varying fortunes of the United States in the Republic of Vietnam. Two years after Bunker completed his assignment in 1973, Graham Martin, the Foreign Service officer who was his sole successor in Saigon, fled the embassy by helicopter as North Vietnamese troops moved into what the victorious Communists soon renamed Ho Chi Minh City.

Bunker approached his assignment with a profound sense of mission. In the first of the weekly telegrams he sent Johnson from Saigon, he spoke of his and his staff's "dedication to the great effort in which we are engaged here, an awareness of its vital importance and a determination that we shall succeed."[33] For all his imperturbably calm exterior and legendary coolness under fire, he was from the beginning of his ambassadorship a passionate true believer in the importance of preventing South Vietnam from falling to Communism. Although he recognized, as Johnson did at the time, that spectacular progress and easy solutions were not in prospect, he was convinced that the policies the administration was pursuing were fundamentally sound. He believed, correctly, that the president had sent him to Saigon to get a job done—to help Johnson win the war and ensure the security and independence of South Vietnam. As he saw it, his assignment was to implement existing policies with determination and efficiency, not to recommend major changes in them.

Bunker's confidence in Johnson's policies was bolstered by his strong conviction that the administration and its predecessors had been correct when they determined that U.S. national interests required the containment of Communism at the borders of South Vietnam. Like many other supporters of military intervention, he held that were South Vietnam to succumb to Communism other Southeast Asian countries would follow. After the fall of South Vietnam in 1975, he claimed that this domino theory had been vindicated by the subsequent Communist seizure of Laos and Cambodia. If other countries in the region had not been overwhelmed by the Communists, it was because U.S. intervention in South Vietnam had bought them time. He endorsed the contentious claim that military intervention was fully justified by the obligations the United States had undertaken as a member of the Southeast Asia Treaty Organization (SEATO) and its commitments to the United Nations. He also argued that intervention was morally right because it accorded with long-standing American support for self-determination.[34]

All of these rationales for intervention reflected the conventional hawkish wisdom of the time. But unlike many who subscribed to it but later changed their positions, Bunker kept the faith. Though he ruefully conceded after South Vietnam fell to the Communists that the American people did not have the staying power to support the waging of an unconventional and unfamiliar struggle over a prolonged period, he did not let that concern deter him when he was ambassador. During that time he remained confident that the war was winnable. Indeed, he left Vietnam following the signing of the Paris peace agreement convinced that it had been won. He blamed South Vietnam's collapse two years later on America's failure to honor President Nixon's commitment to come to its assistance should the North Vietnamese violate the agreement, as they did in launching their successful offensive in 1975.

As American involvement in the war grew, the sprawling U.S. mission in Saigon had become a very special place. Its staff reflected in size, rank, and quality the top priority the Johnson administration gave to Vietnam. The State Department, U.S. Information Agency (USIA), U.S. Agency for International Development (USAID), CIA, and other U.S. government agency officers who staffed the mission during Bunker's ambassadorship included some of the best people their organizations could find.

The mission had a broad mandate to recruit the officers it wanted.[35] Despite the hardships involved, especially the requirement to leave their families behind, ambitious, fast-rising "comers" were attracted to Vietnam because it was important, highly visible, and, for professionals, often fascinating. It was "where the action was" and assignments there could bring career rewards. A good number who were less eager to serve in Saigon went without protest because they considered it their duty at a time when other Americans were being drafted into the military and sent to Vietnam. Not surprisingly, many Saigon mission officers later moved on to important positions in other overseas posts and Washington. Bunker devoted considerable time to recruiting senior officers, not hesitating to go to the secretary of state to get the ones he sought.

Like his predecessors, Bunker wanted the large and complex Saigon mission he headed to be a highly activist organization. In his view, its officers needed to be deeply involved both in extensively reporting developments in Vietnam and in significantly shaping them. He directed the operation through the Mission Council, a group of a dozen or so civilian and military agency heads and embassy section chiefs that met weekly under his chairmanship. The title of the body, a grander version of the conventional "country team" of senior officers at other U.S. diplomatic establishments, mirrored the importance and scope of the Saigon mission and the professional standing of the council's members, who included two four-star generals. Bunker was in unquestioned command as he presided over it. William Colby, who worked under Bunker for three years as head of the rural pacification program and later became director of central intelligence, recalled: "With his air of distinction and formality, he was invariably mild and soft in manner, but he exuded the authority of his office and made it clear that he would brook no lack of discipline."[36]

This aura of authority was heightened by Bunker's colleagues' awareness that he had President Johnson's ear as well as his confidence. They knew that before he went to Saigon, Bunker and Johnson had agreed that he would submit directly to the president a weekly assessment of developments in Vietnam, thus assuring him regular White House access. Bunker's ability to lead was also heightened by his impressive physical presence, as it had been throughout his diplomatic career and earlier. An account in the *New York Times*, published as he prepared to go to Vietnam, said he had "the air of having bathed every day of his life in cold spring water."[37] Although his colleagues ran large programs, and many of them had egos to match, they readily accepted his leadership. Bunker gave them considerable scope, but insisted, with less than total success, that they work as part of a combined effort. He was careful about consulting them on important policy and organizational issues and never sought to go around them. But the final decisions and judgments were his.

In the Mission Council, weekly briefings, and less formal settings, Bunker developed warm relations with the senior officers who directed U.S. military operations in Vietnam. He considered them and the troops they commanded courageous, patriotic men fighting a difficult war that was unfamiliar to American experience. He was highly satisfied with the way he and his civilian staff were able to work in close cooperation with General Westmoreland, his deputy and successor General Creighton Abrams, and other brass. Westmoreland and Abrams accepted from the outset that as ambassador he was in charge, Bunker recalled. "I never had any problem with Westmoreland or Abrams or anyone else [in the military]. Westmoreland and Abrams never took any major step without consulting me first."[38] "They made it very clear to their own organizations that no action was to be taken before I was informed of it. And that was . . . followed out to the letter."[39]

Bunker respected Westmoreland and often praised him in his messages to Johnson. But he regretted that the general did not have more imagination and stronger intellectual qualities.[40] When Johnson moved Westmoreland to the Pentagon in early 1968 amid charges that the general had failed to foresee the Communists' Tet offensive, Bunker seemed to have been as disagreeably surprised as Westmoreland himself. Writing to Carol, he found the move a typical Johnson maneuver: ". . . gives Westy a promotion [to Army chief of staff], and doesn't let him down, thumbs his nose at Westy's critics, but gets rid of criticism of Westy which was becoming politically embarrassing."[41]

He was glad that General Abrams got the expected nod to take over. He found the looser, brainier "Abe" a more effective and congenial colleague. Abrams had arrived in Vietnam a month after Bunker, and until he succeeded Westmoreland in June 1968 had special responsibility for improving the quality of the Vietnamese armed forces. From the beginning of his ambassadorship, Bunker gave this objective the highest priority, and the two men saw eye-to-eye on its importance in the successful waging of the war. Abrams's biographer Lewis Sorley wrote later, "Abrams and Bunker from the start formed a close relationship, one based on shared values and a shared objective: preparing the South Vietnamese to defend themselves before American forces were withdrawn."[42] They kept one another fully informed of what they were doing and thinking, and there is no available evidence of any significant differences of view between them over the five years they worked together in Saigon. On issues of military strategy and tactics, Bunker was almost invariably willing to defer to Abrams's judgment, as he had accepted Westmoreland's. He later termed Abrams an extraordinarily able soldier and said the general had become one of his real heroes. An honorary pallbearer at Abrams's military funeral in 1974 after he died of cancer while serving as Army chief of staff, Bunker was given the honor of handing the general's folded flag to his widow following the ceremony at Arlington National Cemetery.

Westmoreland and Abrams admired Bunker and valued the backing he gave them. Westmoreland wrote later: "My military colleagues and I gained a staunch supporter in Ellsworth Bunker. Although his military experience was limited to artillery ROTC at Yale University sixty years before, he understood the application of power. The only way we were going to work ourselves out of a job in South Vietnam, he recognized, was to put more pressure on the enemy."[43] Sorley, noting the "tremendous rapport and professional respect" Bunker and Abrams had for one another, commented that "Bunker had the qualities Creighton Abrams admired most, integrity, fortitude, loyalty, dedication, selflessness, and wit."[44] *Los Angeles Times* correspondent George McArthur has recalled seeing vivid evidence of the general's high regard for the ambassador: "I was in Abrams's office when one of his secret phones rang. He went to a distant corner of the office to take the call. I noticed that the notoriously slouchy Abrams snapped to attention when he picked up the phone and remained at attention throughout the call. It was Bunker calling, of course, and Abrams just naturally came to attention whenever he talked to him."[45]

As he had at his previous embassies, Bunker delegated considerable authority to his deputy. Because of the size and importance of the Saigon mission, the second in command carried the unusual title of deputy ambassador rather than minister or minister-counselor.

Bunker had three deputies during his long assignment. The first, Eugene Locke, was the only one drawn from outside the Foreign Service. He came to Saigon less than a year after Johnson had appointed him ambassador to Pakistan, his first diplomatic posting. Bunker developed high regard for the wealthy, well-connected Dallas lawyer and politician in the nine months they worked together and was sorry to lose him when he left in January 1968 to run for governor of Texas. He recorded that Locke had done an outstanding job. As Locke reached Dallas to begin his campaign, Bunker drafted a humorous message of support for his fellow Eli: "At meeting this morning, Mission Council voted unanimously for Locke. All rooting for you. Long Yale cheer for Locke. Breck-ek-coax-coax-coax. . . . Yale, Yale, Locke, Locke."[46] Texas voters were less enthusiastic, and Locke lost the race.

Bunker carefully considered several senior candidates to replace him. He eventually chose Samuel D. Berger, a career foreign service officer who had been ambassador to Korea in the early 1960s and was then serving as a deputy assistant secretary of state in the Bureau of Far Eastern Affairs.

Sam Berger was by any measure an unusual figure in the U.S. Foreign Service of the postwar decades. The son of immigrant Jewish parents, he had come into the service from the labor union movement and never forgot it. Over the years, he became a skilled, experienced Far East hand who could be counted on to deal effectively with difficult situations and people.

Bunker and Berger were cut from very different cloth. Keyes Beech of the *Chicago Daily News* accurately wrote: "It was difficult to conceive of a more unlikely team than the tall, aristocratic Bunker and the short, squat, hard-faced Berger. Yet they complemented one another perfectly."[47] The two men quickly developed unusually close personal and professional relations, with the scrappy and irreverent Berger becoming a true alter ego to his patrician boss. Bunker later described Berger as the best deputy he ever had. All seven of the deputies with whom Bunker worked in his five ambassadorial assignments subsequently became ambassadors themselves or had been ambassadors earlier, so this was no mean compliment.[48]

The last of Bunker's deputies was Charles Whitehouse, a career officer who had served earlier in Vietnam and elsewhere in Indochina. A tall, distinguished white-haired man who ranked with Bunker himself as Hollywood central casting's model of an American ambassador, Whitehouse was number two at Saigon during the final year of Bunker's assignment and saw the ambassador off in May 1973. His experience in posts in provincial Vietnam was an important asset for him as deputy ambassador. Understandably, he did not at that late stage in Bunker's Saigon years come to have the strong ties with the ambassador that Berger had developed during his much longer posting. After he completed his assignment in Saigon following Bunker's departure, Whitehouse became, successively, ambassador to Laos and Thailand.

Under Bunker's direction, the mission staff put in very long hours. A six-and-a-half or seven-day work week was the norm. The twelve-hour time difference between Saigon and Washington made their ordeal worse. Phone calls and "night-action" cables from the White House and the State Department frequently interrupted the sleep of embassy staff—and Bunker himself. They were then expected to work their normal day. One officer remembered that under those stressful circumstances the embassy took on a hothouse atmosphere as the staff poured out reports and struggled to meet Washington's urgent, never-ending demands.[49] Another recalled: "The place was a crazy sort of operation. The political section was in competition with the wire services. They shot off cables and threw themselves into their work. They had no family there so they had nothing else to do."[50] Bunker's secretary Eva Kim, who has held many high-level, demanding positions in Washington and abroad, said she never worked so hard in her life.[51]

Bunker joined in these intense labors, displaying the stamina and steadfastness of a much younger man. Of the three major issues the mission faced in his early months there, he took the development of constitutional government as his own. He allotted pacification to Robert Komer and the strengthening and restructuring of the Vietnamese armed forces to Westmoreland and Locke.

Confronting enormous demands on his time and attention, Bunker paced himself and left many of the details to his staff. Some of them recall that they tried to shield him from overwork. He also sought to take in stride Washington's constant calls for action. Johnson and his advisors wanted everything done at once, so Bunker in his unruffled way went about assigning priorities to their anxious demands based on his own judgment of the relative importance and urgency of the messages. He called on his senior staff to reflect on the problems they faced in a calm and detached atmosphere, in effect to emulate him. Few of them were able or willing to do so.

Bunker's formal meetings with Vietnamese were largely limited to Thieu, Ky, and a few other high-ranking government officials, senior military officers, and political leaders. His role as ambassador obliged him to appear at many diplomatic functions and other events that chiefs of mission were expected to attend. He hosted many such affairs himself at his heavily fortified residence, an unprepossessing house at the end of a quiet dead-end street next to a cemetery, which he contrasted unfavorably with the impressive buildings he had lived in at Buenos Aires, Rome, and New Delhi. He provided hospitality there to many house guests: senior officials from Washington, members of Congress, media people, old Yale friends, even the Anglican bishop of Singapore. It could be a chore. "Joe Alsop arrives tomorrow and will be staying here for two days [when he moves to a hotel]," he advised Carol. "But having put up Henry Brandon [of the *Times* of London] for more than a week, I felt I could do no less for Joe; no more, for two days of his pontificating is about all I can take."[52] (In the event, Alsop would not be bound by the ambassador's plans for his early departure. In a letter to Carol the following week, Bunker reported that "Like the Man Who Came to Dinner . . . Alsop has decided he likes it here and has stayed on.")[53] Carol shared his unhappiness with the situation. "As far as I can see," she wrote to Bunker's sister Katherine Parsons soon after he arrived in Saigon, "Ellsworth seems to be running a full time hotel with wholly inadequate facilities."[54]

The required hospitality included a good number of lunches and dinners (as well as beds) for visiting American VIPs who came to Saigon in seemingly endless numbers to observe the progress of the war and to be seen to have done so. Bunker protested to Washington about the flood of high-level U.S. officials. When he found that no fewer than 138 such visitors were scheduled to come to Vietnam during a three-week period in January 1968, he sent a message to Rusk and McNamara calling for the establishment in Washington of a "State/Defense Visitors Bureau" to control the flow of trips of marginal value and urgency. The two secretaries took no action on the proposal.[55]

Bunker got little enjoyment from entertaining American visitors, Vietnamese leaders, or his diplomatic colleagues. He often complained to Carol that in her absence he preferred to dine alone. It was for Bunker a lonely life. He found some pleasant distraction in reading books Carol sent him and playing doubles tennis. He often took on opponents much younger than himself. One of them has recalled that "our dilemma [was] not to hit the ball too far beyond Ellsworth's reach, yet not too close for fear of being accused of coddling him. A real delicate balance."[56]

In the midst of all his preoccupations, he tried hard to ensure prompt delivery of Yale football films for screening at his residence by the Yale Club of Vietnam, which he had founded. (Some who watched the films remarked that in a way they were like the Vietnam War. They always showed big Yale plays, but in the end Yale lost.) He also got relief and, judging from his frequent mention of sermons in his letters to Carol, a good measure of intellectual and spiritual satisfaction from attending Anglican Sunday morning services or listening to the Protestant Hour on Armed Forces Radio when he was too busy for church. His frequent—and unclassified—letters to her also included candid accounts of political developments, personalities, and policy decisions. These messages would have caused considerable distress to his embassy's security officers had they known their contents. He and Carol supplemented their letters with messages that she sent with varying success via a ham radio operated by Father Moran, a Jesuit priest who ran several schools outside Kathmandu. But these long-distance contacts were a poor substitute for her presence, and he wrote longingly to her about plans for her to come to Vietnam, his efforts to visit her in Nepal, and projected rendezvous in Hong Kong and Bangkok. But there is no evidence that either of them considered the possibility of Carol's leaving her embassy and joining him permanently in Saigon.

Security requirements intensified his loneliness. A contingent of marines lived at his residence and kept careful watch when he traveled through the streets of Saigon in a deliberately unobtrusive but heavily armored Plymouth. Any trip outside the city was a major logistical exercise; Eva Kim recalls that he tried to schedule an out-of-town journey once a month, but he was so zealously guarded during these forays that their value was limited. Impromptu visits almost anywhere were out of the question. Even dining out could be difficult and embarrassing. Bunker recalled a night when he and Carol found themselves the only guests other than his ever-present guards at a large and popular Saigon Chinese restaurant. Ordinary customers had been turned away for security reasons.

But difficult as life in Saigon was for Bunker, its oppressiveness could not change the warm personality that lay beneath his cool and proper official persona. With his close staff and friends, he would exhibit the same dry wit and quiet camaraderie that had charmed so many in the past. Embassy veterans still recall the small acts of courtesy and thoughtfulness he displayed despite his heavy responsibilities. As always, he would regale his associates with stories of his student days at Yale and his experiences in the sugar business in Latin America, no doubt telling them with ever greater exaggeration as the years passed. He continued to enjoy telling off-color stories. Barry Zorthian, who worked closely with him as the embassy's minister for public affairs, remembered Bunker telling him: "You know, the Communist press in India claimed that my marriage to Carol and posting in Nepal was simply one of convenience; I was really there to keep an eye on the Chinese. There was no element of love in the union." The ambassador had closed with a chuckle and a twinkle in his eye, "Little did they know."[57]

Bunker was confident that he could effectively relate to the Vietnamese despite his unfamiliarity with the country and its political culture. Earlier in his diplomatic career he had successfully bridged wide cultural gaps in his dealings with Asians, Arabs, and Latin Americans. Many of them had hailed him for his ability to establish rapport and confidence. He often asserted that what was important was a sympathetic approach, an open mind, a desire to understand the other person's point of view, and an ability to listen. After he left the embassy, he told an interviewer that winning the trust of the Vietnamese government had been his most important accomplishment in his Saigon years. "I think they had confidence in my integrity and trustworthiness, and consequently I think I had more influence with [President] Thieu and the GVN [Government of Vietnam] than . . . any other ambassador who had been there."[58]

Bunker found the role of a major GVN ally a thankless one. He considered the Vietnamese an engaging people and came to like and admire them. But he also soon discovered that dealing with them could be difficult. Like other Americans, he concluded that their historical experience made the Vietnamese constantly sensitive to pressure from outside and determined to persevere on their own terms. Recognizing this, he wisely tried to avoid the heavy-handed approach that was too often the hallmark of U.S. diplomats and Washington-based officials in their dealings with client states. He believed, correctly, that only when the Vietnamese acted for their own reasons could real progress be made. Strong American unilateral measures were necessary from time to time but only after the groundwork had been properly laid in the minds of those the United States wished to influence.

What he needed to do in Vietnam, Bunker believed, was to walk a thin line between partnership with the Vietnamese and U.S. manipulation of their fate. He preferred to err on the side of partnership. But as the record of his six years in Saigon makes clear, this sensible attitude did not deter him from making both far-reaching and highly specific political, economic, and security demands on the Vietnamese when he (or Washington) found it necessary.

Although he had no real evidence to support this view, Bunker held that democratic institutions could find fertile soil in Vietnam despite its authoritarian traditions and parochial loyalties. But he faulted critics of the war who set what he correctly considered unrealistically high standards of democracy for the country. He also rejected the allegation some of these critics made that the United States was forcing on the Vietnamese a political system alien to their nature in order to justify retroactively America's imposing an anti-Communist war on them.

In his first months in Saigon, Bunker directed much of his and his mission's attention to South Vietnamese domestic politics. At Guam, Johnson had stressed the great importance he attached to the 1967 presidential, senate, and national assembly elections and his hope that they would usher in a stable, constitutional government the United States could effectively work with and support. The installation after free and fair races of a popularly chosen Vietnamese executive and legislature determined to fight the war could also lessen growing criticism of U.S. intervention at home. Bunker shared Washington's assessment of the high stakes involved and was well aware of the role the administration expected him to play in moving South Vietnam's political evolution in the right direction.

The United States, Bunker believed, needed to exert its influence to keep the electoral process fair and ensure that election maneuvering did not interfere with the war effort. He did not favor American intervention to bring about an outcome to Washington's taste, and scorned the notion that he ran Vietnam, or could have done so, from his embassy office. Many Americans and Vietnamese subscribed to this exaggerated assessment of the ambassador's role. Vietnamese called him the "blue-eyed sorcerer" in deference to his supposedly occult powers. Bunker was happier with his other Saigon nickname, "Mr. Refrigerator," which he preferred to consider a compliment to his Yankee reserve.

Chief of State Thieu and Prime Minister Ky both wanted to become president, and Bunker's focus on the elections brought him into close, sensitive contact with them and other powerful military officers and civilian politicians caught up in what was for Vietnam a novel experience. During the run-up to the June 30 deadline for filing nominations, the most important U.S. concern about the elections was the impact they could have on the unity of the military and its ability to prosecute the war. Washington, and Bunker, worried that the military would fracture if both Thieu and Ky contested. As Bunker put it, "The stability which we have had for the past two years has rested on a degree of military unity which is fragile and now already subject to very heavy strain. If the military breaks on political grounds, we fear that they will not be able to perform their vital fighting and pacification roles. . . . We also fear," he added ominously, "that the losing faction in the political struggle will be sorely tempted to try to redress the balance with the military resources at their disposal." He warned that "this raises the specter of coups and countercoups that plagued Vietnam for so long after [President Ngo Dinh] Diem was overthrown."[59] (To Bunker's evident relief, one of the ringleaders of the coup that ousted Diem, General Duong Van Minh, known as "Big Minh," then in exile in Bangkok, was barred from contesting.)[60]

Ky was the first formally to declare his candidacy. According to Ky, "The army had indicated to me privately [in early 1967] that they wanted me to run for president under the new constitution and I had agreed to do so."[61] As Thieu vacillated, maneuvered, and eventually announced that he would contest, Bunker worried that the potentially destructive rivalry between the two men put at unacceptable risk both the prestige of the United States and its investment in Vietnam of men and money. He hoped that Ky and Thieu would reach an amicable arrangement and in many separate meetings and at least one joint one with them urged them do so. He also encouraged the efforts of intermediaries such as Ambassador Bui Diem to bring about a settlement. For Bunker, the ideal solution would have been for the armed forces to adopt an apolitical role, with both Ky and Thieu running for president as leaders of competing groupings that included important civilian politicians. This was highly unrealistic given the views of the senior commanders of the Vietnamese armed forces at the time. Bunker himself recognized that there was too much at stake to make his approach possible, and questioned whether the unity of the military could be maintained if both men became candidates. Meanwhile, Washington grew increasingly edgy. In an "Eyes Only" message that typified administration concern, Rusk warned Bunker that "we really must get the Ky-Thieu situation clarified in a way that maintains military solidarity," and passed to him the president's apprehensions on that score.[62]

As the Thieu-Ky struggle continued, Bunker feared that Ky was using his powerful position as prime minister to build up support through blatant use of government funds, police pressure, selective press censorship, and other unfair tactics. He spoke sharply to Ky about this. He wrote urgently to Washington about the importance of taking measures to ensure that the election was honest—and seen by Americans and Vietnamese to have been so.

Although General Westmoreland later recalled that the ambassador and other members of the U.S. mission aside from himself privately supported Ky, Bunker appears to have maintained a neutral position between the two contenders.[63] The interventions that he made or considered making seem to have been prompted by assessments that Ky was likely to win. They were designed to make the prime minister's eventual election more palatable both in Vietnam and at home. In a message to Rusk, he described Ky as "on balance, the best available candidate, though not exactly a prize package."[64] Bui Diem, who favored Ky, has written that "After the war I asked Ellsworth Bunker about the American stance in the election. He told me that personally he felt more comfortable with Thieu . . . but that Ky would have been quite acceptable. There was, he said, no American attempt to influence events one way or the other."[65]

Bunker's limited early regard for Ky soon dissipated. He came to judge the air vice-marshal a vain and impetuous man who relished his "jet-jockey image" and was glib and insincere in private discussions. He concluded that the older Thieu was by far the more qualified of the two, superior to Ky in intelligence and insight despite his limited education. He found Thieu steadier and more focused, more honest and straightforward. For his part, Ky seems to have reciprocated Bunker's disdain. In his autobiography, he damned Bunker with faint praise (he "was not a bad fellow") and alleged that the ambassador ("poor Bunker") was trying to impose American standards of life on people he did not understand.[66]

Maintaining unity, and fearing that two uniformed candidates would open the way for a civilian president, a caucus of forty-eight top-ranking military commanders eventually chose Thieu as the more senior of the two contenders to be their presidential candidate.[67] Ky agreed to become Thieu's vice-presidential running mate provided he received substantial power over appointments to the new government, a condition Thieu and the other generals apparently met, at least briefly.

When Ky forecast earlier that the contest for the nomination was like a western movie and would come out all right in the end, Bunker expressed the hope to Washington that "the happy ending . . . will not be preceded by the gun play which is a normal part of every western."[68] Now he was able to observe that "the Vietnamese [had] dealt with the problem entirely by themselves and in so doing displayed . . . an encouraging degree of maturity."[69] "I am more than ever persuaded," he told Washington, "that our approach to the problem was the right one, i.e. to exert continuing but careful pressure on the principals, but to bring them in the end to work out their own solution."[70]

But Bunker also worried about the enormous advantage incumbency gave the military slate over civilian candidates. Concerned about post-election military-civilian relations, he told Thieu and Ky that if elected they should broaden the composition of their government by appointing strong civilians. This would lessen suspicion that their victory merely perpetuated military rule and generate greater sympathy for Vietnam in the United States.

His apprehensions about reaction at home to a contest that pitted deep-pocketed military incumbents against less well-funded civilian challengers figured significantly in his thinking about the presidential election. He worried that American correspondents would highlight this disparity and other evidence of unfairness and brand the contest a travesty.

By then, Bunker had developed a strong disdain and distrust for most American reporters stationed in Vietnam. His bitter and sustained anger toward them became a highly emotional matter that seemed anomalous in a composed man ordinarily temperate in his views and in his expression of them. He considered a majority of American journalists in Vietnam highly irresponsible, ready to report every rumor however implausible without bothering to check the facts. Reiterating a favorite complaint of at best questionable validity, he cabled Johnson: "It is a strange thing that in a country which is engaging in its first real experiment in democracy and under wartime conditions, [the American media] seem to be expecting standards which have not yet been achieved in countries far more mature politically, even in the United States. Nevertheless, it is typical of the cynical and skeptical attitude of a large part of the press here."[71] He was especially disturbed by the *New York Times*'s coverage, which he called "extremely biased and prejudiced."[72]

Bunker tried to encourage a more balanced view by hosting a series of small dinners for the press where he could share with correspondents his assessment of Vietnamese developments and stimulate what he said was more reflective reporting and less knee-jerk sensationalism. But, as Barry Zorthian, who arranged the sessions, has recalled, the atmosphere was formal and the journalists learned nothing that they could not have found elsewhere. The ambassador, Zorthian asserted, was rarely candid with the media, except on occasion with the few whose reporting he valued.[73]

In a long report he sent to Washington in mid-January 1968, when he had dealt unsatisfactorily with the press for nine months, Bunker wrote:

> We have sought to present the true dimensions of the conflict in Vietnam to American and world opinion as objectively and fairly as we can, but we have had to do this through a press which . . . has been unusually skeptical and cynical. One experienced journalist gave an explanation for this which may have some validity, i.e. that there is a generation gap here in that many of the young reporters have never seen nor experienced war before and consequently suffer from an emotional trauma which results in subjective reporting. However that may be, the result of all of this is that there tend to be two separate and only partially connected realities: the view of Vietnam as we see it here in Vietnam and the view that is being presented to American and world public opinion. . . . I think we have made some, though limited progress, in dealing with [the problem].[74]

It seems not to have occurred to Bunker that the fault might lie as much or more with the way the embassy and MACV dealt with events as with journalists' coverage of them. There were indeed two separate and only partially connected realities in Vietnam. But Bunker had no basis for his wholesale condemnation of reporters for allegedly distorting their copy because of cynicism, "emotional trauma," or their imposition on the Vietnamese of impossibly high political standards. Many of the reporters he was most critical of, such as R. W. Apple of the *New York Times*, enjoyed excellent reputations. When Bunker first leveled his accusations against the journalists, most of them had probably spent more time in Vietnam than he had. Nor were American reporters in Vietnam necessarily doves, as Bunker seemed to suggest. As Richard Harwood of the *Washington Post* put it a few months after Bunker arrived in Saigon: "It [was] not only 'doves' among the correspondents who have lost faith in the ability of the Americans to salvage their $25-billion-a-year enterprise in Vietnam" and were reporting that the war was going badly.[75]

Bunker continued to hold his unjustifiably negative view of much of the American media throughout his Saigon tenure. By contrast, he had high regard for the reporting in the *Economist* of London. He found some Americans he considered exceptions. Robert Shaplen of the *New Yorker*, Keyes Beech of the *Chicago Sun-Times*, and Robert Kaiser of the *Washington Post* were among the few whose coverage he believed accurate and thoughtful.[76]

Bunker and the mission followed the election campaign with painstaking care. Bunker did not hesitate to make many suggestions to Thieu, Ky, and others about what they should do to ensure a fair contest. He persuaded President Johnson and senior visiting American officials to make similar calls for an honest race.[77] Urging the disappointed (and hence potentially dangerous) Ky to take a full part in the race, he flatteringly compared the prime minister's willingness to accept the vice-presidential position with Johnson's agreeing to become Kennedy's running mate in 1960. When Ky reportedly stated that if the election produced unacceptable results a military coup would follow, Bunker warned him not to make such comments. As the hard-fought contest neared its end, he professed to be generally satisfied with the campaign arrangements that the exercise of American influence had helped bring about. He was especially pleased with the lifting of press censorship and the provision in the election rules that gave all candidates access to television and radio. He had urged both.

The Thieu-Ky ticket won, as Bunker hoped and expected. "We thought [their winning] would be the most effective [way of] carrying on the war and carrying the country along," he recalled.[78] He agreed with a visiting high-level American observer group led by Henry Cabot Lodge that the elections were properly conducted and fair. Despite wartime conditions, some 83 percent of the registered voters cast ballots. (Seventy percent of those eligible to vote had registered.) Some irregularities were reported, but in Bunker's widely shared view these did not significantly change the outcome. Ky, who as prime minister controlled the election machinery, agreed with this assessment. He cited as evidence the low (34 percent) vote he and Thieu had received.[79] This limited plurality was somewhat less than the 35 to 45 percent Bunker had predicted earlier in what he admitted was "a horseback opinion."[80]

Bunker attributed the Thieu-Ky victory to their being better known, backing for them *en bloc* by various important ethnic and religious groups, fear of change, Vietnamese voters' tendency to stay out of trouble by doing what they thought the authorities wanted, and splitting of the opposition ballots among ten civilian slates. Self-styled peace candidate Truong Dinh Dzu, a controversial lawyer, led the most successful of these, receiving 17.2 percent of the total votes cast. Bunker was not pleased with Dzu's good showing, which seemed to have surprised him and the embassy: "Dzu put the peace issue forward in the rawest and most uncomplicated form. To the unsophisticated and the war weary, this probably had a powerful appeal."[81]

Bunker hailed the election as an important step toward government by law and the civilianization of Vietnam's regime. He acknowledged that the new government faced many problems. "The Viet Cong are still here, even though their claim to represent the people of South Vietnam is much reduced. Corruption and authoritarian attitudes are still embedded in the government and the society. Thieu-Ky will still have to prove . . . that the election was not merely a device to legalize their regime, that the new government is not merely 'more of the same.' It will take time to shake out the new institutions. The Thieu-Ky relationship will have to be worked out."[82]

But he was characteristically optimistic in reporting many reasons for encouragement: "The way is at least open for the building of a broad political base for the new government. A real dialogue with a real loyal opposition in the new legislature now appears possible. . . . More important, the way is more open for peace. Peace has been openly discussed in a free election campaign. The new government has the popular mandate and the prestige which only an election could give it; hopefully these facts will bring Hanoi nearer to abandoning its aggression in favor of negotiations."[83]

Future events would prove many of these hopes unwarranted.

Bunker ranked the pacification program with the establishment of stable, constitutional government. He considered both as important as the conventional military effort in winning the war. Soon after he arrived in Saigon, he agreed to Washington's proposal to transfer responsibility for pacification to General Westmoreland at MACV. This change reflected the situation on the ground: more military officers were engaged in this "other war" than AID, State, and USIS civilians.

Nonetheless, as Johnson had announced in Nashville, Robert Komer, a civilian, came to Saigon from the National Security Council staff to head the program, formally called Civil Operations and Revolutionary Development Support, or CORDS. A former CIA official, Komer was called "the Blowtorch" or "Blowtorch Bob." He proved an aggressive, abrasive, egotistical operator who soon established a reputation for knocking heads together—civilian and military, American and Vietnamese—in his eagerness to move the pacification program forward. Bunker respected Komer's professional ability and drive. But like many others he was put off by his pushiness and his penchant for personal aggrandizement and self-promotion. The ambassador was amused when Komer put a four-star license plate on his military vehicle, to the consternation of both the generals and the military police at MACV. He was not amused when the Blowtorch sent to Washington without his prior knowledge a message recommending the dismissal of the Saigon AID director. Ambitious for promotion, Komer sought the deputy ambassador's job when Locke left. Bunker never considered him for the position—he would have been a disaster—and deftly spurned his evident but unspoken interest without impairing their important working relations.

Bunker believed that pacification needed to be invigorated, speeded up, and given greater emphasis. Though he generally accepted Komer's views and did not interfere in the day-to-day management of the program, he became deeply involved. Pacification moved forward rather slowly in 1967 despite Komer's dynamism, but Bunker seemed satisfied. He lauded Komer for making American weight felt much more than it had been in the GVN planning efforts. Nonetheless, he told Johnson, "Because pacification is at best a gradual . . . process"[84] he did not expect the program to bring about a dramatic increase in the number of Vietnamese living in secure areas. MACV's hamlet evaluation system that measured this was in any event a faulty yardstick, and even Bunker thought the statistics it produced more valuable for the trends they indicated than for their claimed precision.

He vigorously supported the controversial Phoenix program for identifying and eliminating the Vietcong infrastructure and strongly defended it later against charges that it had been a program designed to assassinate Communist agents and sympathizers. He told an interviewer in 1980: "It was not an assassination program. People were killed when they resisted arrest, yes, of course. But the great majority of those people were not executed. There were casualties, of course, because there was resistance, but it was an important program."[85]

Looking ahead to the new year Bunker was more optimistic. He cabled Johnson that 1968 would see much greater progress, approvingly quoting to the president Komer's optimistic comments to the press: we're up from a crawl to a walk—next year perhaps a trot. In Bunker's view, a further substantial cut in the already declining Vietcong population base would create even more serious VC recruiting problems and make war much more of a battle against the North Vietnamese Army.

Bunker did not try to become directly involved in the military effort. He recognized the limits of his military experience and left combat operations to more qualified hands. Initially, he was satisfied with General Westmoreland's "attrition" strategy of primarily relying on American might to seek out the enemy far away from population centers, break his hold over his base areas, and push his units deep into the jungles and hills. He later enthusiastically supported General Abrams's different, "clear and hold" approach, which focused on providing security for South Vietnamese hamlets and villages and made greater use of Saigon's armed forces. In retrospect, he judged it superior to the attrition policy. Difficult as it was for an ambassador to move about in safety, he tried to see some of the war for himself. Though he was distressed by the destruction inflicted by American forces, most of which he considered unavoidable, his observations in the field seem to have strengthened his conviction that the war had to be brought to a successful conclusion. If it was not, all of the sacrifices and suffering he found would be meaningless.

From the time he arrived in Saigon Bunker argued, as Westmoreland did, that choking off infiltration from the north was the crux of the military problem. He confidently forecast that if the administration permitted the South Vietnamese army to intervene in Laos and cut the Ho Chi Minh Trail, the Communist forces would shrivel into irrelevance and the war would be reduced to a police problem. Otherwise, the war would go on at great cost for years. In Bunker's view, the American people would not give the administration time to fight such a protracted conflict.

Senior American military commanders in the field had made similar calls for invading Laos for some time. As the official who drafted the record of the June 1967 Saigon meeting in which Bunker argued this case with Defense Secretary McNamara dryly noted, "[Westmoreland] was fortunate in having such a staunch ally in his battle for expanded operations in the sanctuaries as well as the moral support for a more intensive war effort."[86] When the administration rejected this Bunker-Westmoreland proposal, Bunker was not impressed by the reasons Washington offered. These included assertions that intervention would violate the 1962 Geneva Accords on Laos, cause problems with the Chinese, and require more troops than were then available. He considered the decision a major strategic mistake.

But Bunker did not favor early intervention into Cambodia, a major North Vietnamese–Vietcong sanctuary. In December 1967 he persuaded President Thieu to drop a proposal that would have permitted South Vietnamese forces to cross the Cambodian border in "hot pursuit" of enemy forces and briefly remain there. But as his future recommendations would indicate, this did not mean that Bunker ruled out intervention over the longer run. In a message the following month that foreshadowed developments in the year just beginning, he wrote: "[The enemy will be forced] to place greater reliance on sanctuaries in Cambodia and Laos. Should a political decision be made to do so, we will be prepared to neutralize the enemy's base areas across the Cambodian borders by limited objective ground attacks"[87]

Military developments figured importantly in the ninety-six long messages Bunker cabled directly to the president, weekly when Johnson was in the White House, less frequently after Nixon took over in January 1973. The messages, a distillation of material the various sections of the mission sent to the ambassador's office, were collated by an embassy officer before Bunker put his own imprint on them. Although other senior officers in the mission eventually came to regard the messages as rather routine, Bunker always considered them a highly important channel to Washington. This seems to have been a sound judgment. According to David M. Barrett, an historian of the Vietnam War, "[National Security Adviser] Walt Rostow was convinced that nothing shaped Johnson's perception of actual conditions in Vietnam more than Ellsworth Bunker's weekly cables to the president."[88]

Bunker spent much time on the messages, and they clearly evidence his mark and style. This is especially true of the tightly written opening summaries in which Bunker gave the president an assessment of the main developments in Vietnam over the period and told him what he and his staff were doing about them.

The messages were given very limited distribution in Washington and were even more tightly held at the mission. They were published in 1990 with only minor deletions, mostly to protect sources and methods.[89] The series provides a useful running account of Bunker's actions and views over his long ambassadorship, or at least a good compilation of what he thought it was important for the White House to know as it focused on Vietnam. Taken as a whole, the messages project what Bunker himself called his essential optimism about Vietnam developments. A staff aide who worked with him on them has recalled that the ambassador told him it was important that this series of cables have a sanguine tone.[90] Such a tone does seem to come out more distinctly in the presidential messages than it does in contemporaneous embassy cables, including those drafted by Bunker himself. But this may also reflect Bunker's practice of using the cables to the White House for longer range analyses in which his optimistic approach was more likely to come to the fore.

The messages to the president also convey Bunker's conviction that the policies and programs the administration pursued over the years were correct. More fundamentally, they reflect his understanding of his job as ambassador. This was to carry out the president's policy, to make it work, to show that it was working, and to defend it against attack. The president was his chief, and *The President*. Bunker considered it his duty to do all he could to carry out his instructions, have them succeed, and make the president look good.

11
Tet and Afterwards

In the year-end evaluation he sent to President Johnson on January 13, 1968, Bunker was optimistic about the military situation: "In the field of military operations the bringing into proper balance of the ratio of combat to support troops in the U.S. forces and the steady improvement of the Vietnamese armed forces, together with the contribution of our free world allies, resulted in increasingly effective action against the enemy. He has been thwarted in his attempts at penetration south of the DMZ, his bases increasingly neutralized, and he has been steadily pushed back toward the Laotian and Cambodian borders. . . . Since January 1967 losses have been inflicted on the enemy at a rate which exceeds his input of personnel." Moreover, Bunker assured the president, "The atmosphere in which the war is being fought has slowly changed for the better, as a result of the elections, the establishment of stable government, the steady if slow progress in pacification, and the Communist failure on the battlefield. . . . Our policies have been prudent and sound, our actions have been careful and considered. We have built a foundation on which, I believe, we can build the structure of success."[1]

This upbeat assessment was similar to many Bunker had sent to Washington earlier. His report on the military situation was based on doubtful evidence. Like other analyses he prepared about the progress of the war, it largely reflected the outlook and conclusions of MACV (Military Assistance Command, Vietnam), which Bunker seems to have accepted without serious question.[2]

Johnson had summoned Bunker and Westmoreland to the United States two months earlier, in November, and they had presented similarly optimistic analyses in public appearances and closed-door briefings. The Bunker-Westmoreland visit, like Vice President Humphrey's attendance at the Thieu-Ky inaugural ceremony a fortnight earlier, was primarily designed to promote American public and congressional support for the war.[3] The theme of this "progress report" was that the war was going well, much better than the home front seemed to recognize, and had certainly not reached anything approaching the stalemate that American correspondents in Saigon had described in their reports.

Expanding on this theme in an address to the Overseas Press Club in New York, Bunker claimed that the United States had come a long way toward fulfilling its objectives in Vietnam. He reported favorably on the military situation ("today, the initiative is ours"), progress in the pacification program, and advances the South Vietnamese had made toward viable representative government.[4] In a joint appearance with Westmoreland on NBC's "Meet the Press" that got front-page treatment in the *New York Times* and elsewhere, Bunker declared that "we are making steady, not spectacular, progress. We are at the point now not only of being able to continue, but to accelerate the rate of progress."[5] He had taken a similar position the previous day at an executive session of the Senate Foreign Relations Committee, where he was again listened to with respect despite the strong misgivings many of its members continued to have about the administration's Vietnam policy.[6]

Although Bunker did not seek personal publicity nor particularly relish a public affairs role, the "experienced diplomat known for Vermont understatement," as Hedrick Smith described him in the *New York Times*, proved an effective spokesman for the administration's position. Pollster Lou Harris credited the widely reported assessments the ambassador and the general presented with having helped spark a resurgence in public support for Johnson's handling of the war. Walt Rostow, pleased and impressed, suggested to Bunker that he and Westmoreland appear regularly on television from Saigon.[7] But while some critics of administration policy accepted the Bunker-Westmoreland assessment of the current situation, they pointedly questioned the assumptions on which their optimistic forecasts of the future were based. Crucial among these assumptions were improvements in 1968 and beyond in the performance of the Vietnamese government and armed forces and North Vietnamese inability during that time to send and support a larger army in the South than they currently maintained. Skeptics also doubted the Bunker-Westmoreland assessment that the Soviet Union and China would sit still while the Communists in South Vietnam faded away before the military might of the United States and its Saigon ally.

The rosy outlook Bunker and Westmoreland tried to project in their November visit badly undermined their credibility when the Vietcong

launched a major offensive two months later. Violating a Tet holiday cease-
fire, the Communists on January 31 attacked thirty-five of South Vietnam's
forty-four provincial capitals and sixty-four of its 242 district headquarters. Their objectives, home to most of the country's urban population,
included Saigon and four of the country's five other major cities.

The night before the offensive began, Bunker had been at a party two
young embassy officers hosted to celebrate the lunar new year and "the
light at the end of the tunnel."[8] A few hours later, a squad of Communist
commandos blew a hole in the outer wall of the embassy compound in the
heart of Saigon. Killing five American soldiers, they entered the grounds of
the new chancery building that Bunker had inaugurated with much fanfare
the previous October in the presence of President Thieu and Vice President Humphrey. (He had cabled Johnson at the time that the chancery was
"as you intended it would be, . . . a fitting symbol of our determination
to stay the course in Vietnam.")[9] The commandos launched several rocket
grenades at the chancery, causing minor damage. Allan Wendt, the embassy duty officer, locked himself in the code room. He recalled that he
and the other Americans inside the building were convinced the Vietcong
would break in and murder them. The attackers were never able to enter,
however, and in the ensuing six hours all of them were killed or captured
in fierce fighting. The embassy building was declared secure at 9:15 A.M.,
about six and a half hours after the first call for help.[10]

As the attack got under way, Bunker's residence also came under Vietcong fire. His Marine guards awoke him and, without giving him time
to dress, hurried him off in an armored personnel carrier to a safe house
maintained by the embassy security officer. From there, Bunker, still in his
bathrobe, was soon in direct contact with embassy officers at the chancery
compound and with General Westmoreland to get firsthand accounts of
what was happening. At dawn, the Marines poured tear gas into his house
to flush out any Vietcong who might have slipped in during the night.
When the gas cleared he returned, dressed, and went to the chancery. Photos taken at the time, which soon appeared on front pages everywhere,
show him in his customary carefully pressed light seersucker suit somberly
inspecting the damaged, corpse-strewn compound. Then he went to his
third-floor office, sent off a reassuring cable to Carol in Kathmandu, and
tried to assess what had happened.

By any reasonable military standard, the offensive failed. The Vietcong
were soon driven from the urban areas they had seized. They held out only
in the ancient capital of Hue in northern South Vietnam, where they mur-

dered over three thousand Vietnamese and foreigners before South Vietnamese Army (ARVN) and U.S. Marine units dislodged them after a month of fighting. The Vietcong could not induce any large-scale defections from the Vietnamese military and police, many of whom fought well against them. Nor, contrary to their hopes and expectations, could they persuade significant numbers of Vietnamese civilians to rally to their side. By the end of the offensive, the hitherto hidden Vietcong cadres operating in South Vietnam had suffered massive losses, by U.S. count more than half the men they had committed to the offensive. In many areas they had been shattered and dispersed. Allied military casualties were less than a tenth as great.

Bunker was concerned, with good reason, that despite the massive defeat the Communists had suffered, Tet could seriously weaken support for the administration's Vietnam policy in the United States by further heightening public distrust of its claims of steady progress. His actions on the eve of the offensive provided powerful ammunition to critics of the policy. Although he had sent at least one message cautioning Washington that the Vietcong might violate the Tet cease-fire, and Westmoreland had sent many more warnings about the possibility of Communist attacks around that time, neither had prepared the administration or the American public for an assault of the magnitude of the offensive the Communists unleashed on January 31.

During the month of January, the weekly cables Bunker sent Washington had been generally reassuring about the military situation. Just two weeks before the attacks, he even recommended that wives be permitted to return to Saigon for the Tet holiday. Some did. On the eve of Tet, he had urged his sister and brother-in-law, then vacationing in Nepal, to visit him in early February with Carol. His optimistic forecasts of steady military progress during 1968 included no suggestion that the Vietcong were capable of launching an assault throughout South Vietnam a week later, let alone a warning that the Communists intended to mount one. He appears to have agreed with Westmoreland's assessment that the Communists would launch a major offensive in the north around Khesanh, a mountain bastion they had been besieging for weeks, not an onslaught all over the country.

Given his past experience with them, Bunker expected that American correspondents stationed in Vietnam would file especially damaging stories. He could not have been surprised when the media's initial coverage, expressed in cataclysmic tones, was in direct disregard of the briefing he had held for them at the embassy the second afternoon of the attack. By that time, sufficient reports had been received to make clear the extent of the Communists' losses, but the media paid little heed. In Bunker's view, which was widely shared by supporters of the war and many others, their subsequent coverage was a powerful factor in making Tet a major propaganda victory for the Communists. It strengthened his own strong conviction, which he was careful not to express publicly, that most American correspondents in Vietnam were biased, irresponsible, and self-serving.[11]

While Bunker accused the Vietnam-based American media of irresponsibly helping make Tet a major turning point in attitudes at home toward the war, he had no regrets about what he had himself done, or failed to do. He would not concede that he, or Westmoreland, had been remiss in not preparing the administration and the public for the shock of Tet. Ignoring his failure to report the possibility of a countrywide offensive by the Communists, he claimed later that the attack itself had not been a surprise, only its timing: "There never had been an attack on Tet and it was generally assumed that the Tet truce would be observed."[12] He was unapologetic about the optimistic reports and statements he had made in the months before Tet. They were vindicated, he maintained, by the success of the American and South Vietnamese forces in absorbing the losses the surprise offensive had inflicted and quickly regaining the battlefield initiative.

Bunker was soon caught up in the debate within the administration over post-Tet policy. During the two months between Tet and Johnson's March 31 announcement of a partial bombing halt, the president and Secretary Rusk frequently requested his views of proposed policy initiatives and his assessment of the likely reaction of the Thieu government and the South Vietnamese public to them. But he was not asked to return to Washington for consultations with the president and other senior officials until after the basic decisions had been made and announced. Nor was he fully aware of the crucial policy battles that raged at the White House in February and March, not surprisingly given Johnson's chronic preference for playing important cards close to his chest. In any event, Bunker's reputation for backing such hard-line options as Vietnamese intervention into Laos and his well-known optimism about prospects in Vietnam under current policy could hardly have encouraged those who sought a major change in approach to look to him as a potential ally.

Like other hard-liners, Bunker favored the concept of negotiations with Hanoi only if these would lead to a settlement that assured that South Vietnam did not fall to the Communists. He saw the negotiations as a means to confirm victory, not a process to work out a compromise peace. The promising circumstances he believed were developing on the political and military fronts in South Vietnam reinforced his conclusion that the administration need not offer significant concessions for such talks, particularly not in response to the pressures and passions of antiwar elements whose attitudes and tactics he viewed with distrust bordering on contempt. If it did so it would be giving Hanoi unnecessary advantage at a time the tide was turning against the Communists on the battlefield and they were consequently getting more interested in coming to the negotiating table. "Our objective," he cabled on March 1, "should be to take measures which will encourage the North Vietnamese leadership to seek negotiations on an acceptable basis in recognition of our determination to continue on our present course until they do."[13]

The impact of negotiations on the South Vietnamese leadership and public and the consequences this would have for future U.S. policy particularly troubled him. American willingness to enter negotiations, if billed as a major concession to the Communists, could impair the morale and cohesiveness of the Thieu government as it struggled to recover from the Tet offensive, he argued. It would sharply reduce South Vietnamese determination to stay the course. He reported that in the post-Tet atmosphere talks between Washington and Hanoi had become even more suspect in Saigon. In his view, this meant that "continuing close consultation with the GVN [Government of Vietnam] and the latter's inclusion at an early stage in any negotiations with Hanoi assume an even greater importance now."[14] He believed that a few more months could make all the difference in restoring Saigon's confidence. "Time," he concluded, "should work to the U.S. advantage in terms of Vietnamese receptivity to further negotiation initiatives, whereas too early a move might have an extremely negative effect and undo much that we and the GVN have been able to accomplish since the Tet attacks."[15]

With these considerations in mind, he opposed proposals that called for the cessation of all offensive activity against North Vietnamese territory. He thought that Hanoi would respond to such a total bombing halt not by reciprocating with a real step toward peace but by seeking to give the impression that it had taken such a step. He was more amenable to the proposal for a bombing halt covering only part of North Vietnam. The Thieu government would be more prepared to accept such a halt, he reported, especially if the cessation followed an announcement of an increase in U.S.

military support to the South Vietnamese. But he cautioned that such a position needed to be presented carefully to Saigon with due regard for South Vietnamese apprehension that it could foreshadow the United States abandoning Vietnam to Communism.

If Bunker opposed the doves on the bombing halt—and the call many of them voiced for significant changes in the fundamental goals of U.S. policy in Vietnam—he did not fully embrace the recommendation General Westmoreland and Joint Chiefs of Staff Chairman Earle Wheeler made soon after Tet for the deployment in Vietnam of 206,000 more American troops during 1968. In his analysis of this issue, Bunker wrote that it was important to maintain a careful balance between a further U.S. military buildup and the modernization of the Vietnamese armed forces. He was concerned that too big an expansion of the U.S. military presence would offer the Vietnamese "an escape route from their responsibility."[16] It could also lead the United States to play the role of colonial power. He favored only a limited buildup. The dispatch of the balance of the troops Westmoreland proposed should be reexamined in light of the situation in the summer.

Bunker's reaction reflected his confidence in the fighting ability of the South Vietnamese army once it received better equipment and training. He highlighted this faith in his reports to the president, which frequently featured accounts of improved ARVN performance. He gave high priority to greater U.S. support for the ARVN, and resented what he called the myth in the minds of the American public that they were not carrying their load. But he also cautioned that Washington not demand that the Vietnamese do more than their limited human resources would reasonably allow. This could lead them to throw up their hands, leaving the United States to carry the burden.

What some called the battle for the heart and mind of the president on Vietnam policy climaxed on March 31. In a broadcast that evening best remembered for his declaration that he would not seek another presidential term, Johnson announced that he was restricting U.S. air strikes on North Vietnam to the area below the twentieth parallel. This spared 90 percent of North Vietnamese territory, including Hanoi and the major seaport of Haiphong. The president also authorized the opening of negotiations whenever the Communists were ready for them.

Like all but a handful of Johnson's closest confidants, Bunker was taken by complete surprise by the president's decision not to run again. It was already the morning of April 1 when he sat down with members of the Mission Council to listen to the historic message. He wrote Carol soon after the bombshell burst: "A more stunned, incredible, unbelieving group, including myself, I have never seen." He had high praise for the speech, which he regarded as the best Johnson had ever given. It had all the ingredients Bunker valued: "Reasonable, conciliatory, yet making it clear that we have promises to keep and we mean to keep them." It was, he said, a "testament of commitment and faith" that "plac[ed] principle and patriotism above self."[17] He sent the president a highly flattering message: "While I am deeply grieved by your decision not to accept another term, as all must be who have had the privilege of serving you, I have only unbounded admiration for the motives which impelled you to an action unparalleled in our history."[18]

Bunker moved quickly to deal with the political fallout of the speech in Vietnam. He told Thieu that the new policies Johnson had announced did not represent a departure from the administration's basic position on Vietnam. Johnson's decision not to run again would give him a freer hand to pursue these new policies. Thieu forecast that there would be much speculation among Vietnamese about whether Johnson's statement did in fact signal a significant change in U.S. policy and what effect the statement would have on American public opinion. But Bunker was pleased to find that he had taken the speech in stride: "[Thieu] was constructive, did not appear to be alarmed by the most unexpected turn of events, and was more puzzled than worried."[19]

Bunker was further gratified when Thieu remained calm in the days that followed. But he urgently advised Washington of the "utmost importance that we not only keep [the GVN] informed but that we consult, so that they have a sense of participation. We need not tell them everything, but as much as we can, and form is also very important. There must not be the appearance of unilateral action or unilateral statements. . . . I am confident," he concluded, "we can take them along and minimize their problems if we are sensitive to the requirements here."[20]

Reviewing the period soon after Johnson's speech in a letter to Carol he sent a few days after cabling this admonition to Washington, Bunker wrote: "It was a week . . . pervaded by an atmosphere of apprehension and doubt about our intention on the part of the Vietnamese. Whether we would take unilateral decisions or actions without adequate prior consultation, and I must confess that I shared their apprehension and have tried to impress on Washington this is a sure way to destroy their morale and much that we have so painfully built up. It has been a highly sensitive situation when we have several times been walking on a knife's edge and had it not been for Thieu's calmness and common sense, we could have been in considerable trouble."[21]

By then, relations between the Vietnamese president and the American ambassador had come a long way since their first encounter on Guam a year earlier. During Bunker's early months in Saigon, their exchanges had focused on domestic politics in the run-up to the elections. Then and later, Bunker tried in his dealings with Thieu and his colleagues to find a middle ground between doing too much and not being sufficiently forceful. It was not easy. Resident American officials were involved in all phases of Vietnam's public life, and the administration expected them to use their leverage to produce results.

Although Bunker often reminded Washington and his own mission to be careful in selecting areas where American influence and persuasion could be most usefully applied, even he sometimes lost sight of the pervasiveness of U.S. involvement in Vietnam. Cabling the president in September 1967, he seemed unconscious of the irony of his message: "We have developed within the Mission a suggested government program which I shall present to General Thieu . . . designed to make clear to the people that the government is theirs, dedicated to the promotion of their welfare and to the resolution of their problems."[22] According to Hubert Humphrey, even Thieu's inaugural address had been largely written by the American embassy.[23]

Bunker recognized that the mission would have greater difficulties dealing with the new, elected government than it had had with the military regime. "We shall have to be more sensitive to Vietnamese pride and sensitivities and apply pressure and leverage in more subtle ways," he advised Johnson in early October.[24] We could live with this sensitivity, he said later, if it stayed within reasonable bounds, "for it represents a healthy spirit of developing nationalism and independence."[25]

As the lengthy electoral process came to an end on October 22 with balloting for the lower house of the Vietnamese legislature, Bunker's discussions with Thieu shifted to a broader menu of issues. These included reorganization of the civil administration, such as steps to lessen corruption, and economic stabilization. Supplementing the efforts of other senior officials on his mission council, he also discussed major initiatives in the pacification program and ideas for the reorganization and improvement of the Vietnamese armed forces. He continued to keep Thieu regularly abreast of Washington's efforts to find a basis for a peace settlement with the Communists and to elicit his views on that sensitive subject. His report to Thieu of his visit to the United States in November 1967 was characteristically optimistic, but he also used it to impress on the Vietnamese president the strong sense he found at home of the importance of the GVN moving swiftly to deal with the many problems it faced.

The Tet offensive significantly added to the urgency and scope of Bunker's calls to Thieu to mobilize resources and provide leadership. Bunker led the way in the mission's efforts to impel the Vietnamese to come to grips with the enormous economic and social difficulties Tet had created. Carol, who came down from Kathmandu soon after Tet, found him exhausted by the unremitting work in curfew-bound Saigon. "It [Tet] has meant being on the job 24 hours out of 24 hours," he reported to Rostow.[26] But he was as cool and unflappable as ever as he sought to persuade Thieu and his colleagues to give a new political lead that would rally the Vietnamese people behind the government. He offered them a host of ideas and generous material assistance to help get things back on the right track. In another back-channel message to Rostow, he wrote that "if we can get the GVN activated, which we intend to exert every effort to do, with our support I think we can turn the recent events into a psychological plus as well [as a massive military victory]."[27]

Bunker soon became convinced that his prodding was paying off. He reported that despite continuing shortcomings in Vietnamese government performance, the GVN had come to show more drive and effectiveness than at any time since he had taken charge of the embassy. He gave a good deal of the credit to Thieu, filling his messages to Washington and letters to Carol with praise for the Vietnamese president's accomplishments. "Because of his temperament," he told Johnson in mid-March, Thieu "does not give the picture of the dynamic, charismatic leader we might think of as ideal. But he has shown increasingly a desire to take hold of the reins."[28] He wrote Carol a week later: "Thieu seems to be gaining confidence and so is taking decisions and actions more quickly and on a wide range of matters."[29] "I must confess," he cabled Washington in early April, "I am more impressed each time I talk with Thieu. He is thinking hard and fairly clearly about his problems. . . . He is making tough decisions, despite his reputation for indecisiveness. . . . He has political sense, is tough-minded and realistic."[30]

Thieu seems to have reciprocated Bunker's sentiments. According to Nguyen Tien Hung, who worked closely with the president, "Thieu respected Bunker because of his age . . . and experience [and] knew he was a man of integrity. Although he realized that Bunker had no power and 'was only a messenger,' he held him in high personal regard."[31] Bui Diem, who dealt frequently with both men, found that Thieu and Bunker were quite close. The president, he wrote, regarded Bunker "with more trust than he ever had for any of the other ambassadors with whom he had dealt." But Bui Diem questioned whether Bunker's "elegant and understated manner" was an effective way to coax favorable decisions from the indecisive and guarded president.[32]

Traveling with Thieu in the Vietnamese countryside, Bunker was taken —probably in both senses of that word—by the president's rolling up his trousers and jumping into a rice paddy, to rousing cheers from assembled farmers.[33] He hailed Thieu's choice as prime minister of the veteran politician Tran Van Huong, whom he had defeated in the presidential race, as a move on his part to establish a true military-civilian partnership. It was clear, Bunker reported to Johnson in June, that Thieu had chosen to become a constitutional president rather than act as the representative and leader of a small group of generals.[34] "Thieu . . . keeps his cool and his sense of humor," he confided to Carol later in the year, "and I continue to be impressed with his political sense."[35] "He is acting less and less like a general and more and more like a politician and is becoming a very good one."[36] "The Thieu-Huong alliance," he told Johnson in October, "has resulted in a government which is more popular, more effective, and more stable than any since the early years of the Diem regime."[37]

Peace efforts became a more important subject in the Bunker-Thieu dialogue following the opening of talks in Paris on May 10, 1968, between the North Vietnamese and an American delegation headed by Averell Harriman. The talks were still being arranged when Bunker returned to the United States for a brief round of consultations in mid-April. His visit to Washington began on a strong note of irony. Parts of the city were still under curfew following riots touched off by the assassination of Martin Luther King. The State Department had consequently vetoed

Bunker's request for a room at his favorite downtown hotel and reserved quarters for him at one in a more secure area. "It's just like Vietnam," the returning ambassador quipped to a department officer who met him at Andrews Air Force Base. He repeated the comment to Johnson when they met with other senior officials for discussions at Camp David the next day. Bunker recalled that the president was not as amused as he was. "Who slipped up on that?," he had asked. "I told them to put Ellsworth in the White House." "I guess that ought to be secure," Bunker allowed.[38]

At Camp David, Bunker again stressed to the president and other senior officials the importance of dealing sensitively with the GVN on negotiations. He continued to hold that from Saigon's standpoint it was not a good time for such talks. "In three or four months they'll be stronger." He reiterated that the GVN feared that a coalition with the NLF (National Liberation Front), widely regarded in Saigon as the possible outcome of a negotiated settlement, would lead to a Communist takeover as had happened in Czechoslovakia. Asked why the Thieu government should feel such concern about the NLF if it was getting stronger as he had said, Bunker replied that the GVN was not afraid of the NLF militarily, just politically. "They are fearful that if they take [the NLF] into their bosom, they'll end up running the show."[39] Bunker urged the administration not to appear too eager to pursue the peace talks. He also feared that the North was taking advantage of the reduced bombing to build up its forces in South Vietnam.

When Hanoi insisted that the talks convene at a site such as Warsaw or Phnom Penh, which would imply that Washington was knuckling under to the Communists, Bunker helped persuade Johnson to reject the proposal despite the president's earlier pledge to go anywhere, any time, in the cause of peace. Returning to Saigon as the two sides continued to haggle over an acceptable meeting place, he laid out his position succinctly in a back-channel message to Rostow:

What is most needed is a continuation of the present U.S. attitude of firmness and patience combined with an announced willingness to meet with the other side on reasonable terms. I see no need for dramatic or hasty actions to demonstrate our reasonableness and the genuineness of our intentions. On the other hand, I believe that we should make known in accurate but non-polemical terms the military advantage which Hanoi is taking of this prolonged period of haggling in order to reinforce Communist elements in the South through the infiltration of unprecedented quantities of men and supplies. In another week or so, we may be forced to indicate to Hanoi that, in the absence of progress on talks, we shall have to reexamine our bombing restriction policy. This may jar loose a decision on their side, but we should be serious in issuing this warning, and not do it as bluff.[40]

When the talks ultimately began in Paris, Bunker continued to take a tough line. He strongly opposed full cessation of the bombing of the North without major concessions by Hanoi, including a substantial reduction in North Vietnamese movement into the South and an end to attacks on Saigon. He dismissed the Soviet argument that the United States must cease all bombing to save face for Hanoi as "a shell game which Asians play against innocent Occidentals when it suits their purpose."[41] At the same time, he set up a series of weekly meetings between a South Vietnamese team headed by Thieu and a U.S. mission delegation under his own leadership to explore various aspects of a possible peace settlement. The meetings were also designed to keep the Vietnamese leadership informed of developments in Paris and influence them to compromise on various points in what might become fast-moving negotiations. Bunker hoped that the sessions would help limit GVN concern that Washington would use the talks to undercut them.

Not that he had many meaningful developments on the Paris talks to report to Thieu and his colleagues. The discussions soon reached an impasse. The U.S. side continued to call for the withdrawal of North Vietnamese forces from South Vietnam. The Communists, rejecting this demand, insisted that the Saigon regime be revamped to include representatives of the Communist-dominated National Liberation Front of South Vietnam.[42] They used the formal sessions at the Hotel Majestic as a propaganda forum. Informal meetings between the leaders of the two delegations were eventually arranged, but they too made no headway.

Despite the lack of progress in Paris, Bunker and his staff were kept busy answering a seemingly endless barrage of cables requesting embassy comments on the latest moves and prospective developments in the stalled negotiations. He was often awakened in the middle of the night to provide replies. Sometimes he drafted these in bed, handing the longhand texts to a staff aide who took them back to the embassy code room for transmission to Washington. On one such occasion, he had no sooner fallen asleep again when the nightly rocketing began to get uncomfortably close. Following standard operating procedure, his Marine guards hustled him down into "Ellsworth's Bunker," a specially sand-bagged wine-cellar-like room where he whiled away the hours of shelling by reading books that Carol had sent him.

In his letters to her, Bunker grumbled about "egg-sucking messages from Washington's professional worriers." He also complained about Saigon diplomatic life. In one message that vividly highlighted how tiresome it had become for him, he told Carol that the foreign minister's three-hour black-tie dinner honoring the departing Canadian ambassador was "one of those dreadful stag affairs, a literal pain in the neck, for the nerve [which had been bothering him] did flare up again, the result . . . of having to face again the dead sparrow with his glazed eye looking up at me from the soup, and all the other Vietnamese food I find hard to take, plus the effort of trying to carry on a conversation through language barriers."[43]

Occasional holidays with Carol in Kathmandu and elsewhere provided welcome relief—a wonderful sense of freedom Bunker called it. "Returning from the heavenly kingdom in Nepal with all its beauty and serenity to this tragic land where killing goes on day after day . . . makes me realize more than ever, if that were possible, what the heavenly time spent with you means."[44] But those escapes made it even harder for him to buckle down again to his almost nonstop embassy duties, which now included reading tedious telegrams coming at him from both Washington and the American delegation in Paris.

In his own messages, he tried in particular to convey to Washington Thieu's concern that once South Vietnamese representatives were included in the talks, the way these were structured would have profound implications for the GVN's legitimacy and international image. On the eve of the opening of the Paris sessions, he had warned the White House that "it is apparent that as we enter preliminary talks [with Hanoi] our problems [with Saigon] will revolve particularly around the role of the National Liberation Front, both in negotiations and in the eventual political settlement."[45] Hanoi continued to insist that the NLF be represented in any substantive negotiations following these preliminary discussions, and Washington had devised a deliberately imprecise "our side/your side" formula to accommodate both the NLF and Saigon when, and if, such "serious" talks took place. This formula provided for two-sided negotiations in which Washington and Hanoi could each organize its side as it wished. The Thieu government and the NLF would both be able to participate, the government on one side, the NLF on the other. In the U.S. view, the arrangement had the advantage of depriving the NLF of the distinct status

Hanoi demanded for it. Such status would have suggested that the NLF enjoyed sovereign power. Although Thieu's government would also not have separate status, unlike the NLF it was a functioning government with recognized international standing. Washington considered the GVN's being subsumed on one undifferentiated side an acceptable trade-off needed to get the expanded talks started.

Although Bunker supported the "our side/your side" formula, and had helped persuade Thieu to accept it, he was nervous about the way Saigon viewed it. In his reporting, he asserted that within the formula the GVN would insist that it be accepted as a spokesman for "our side" to whom Hanoi must listen and talk. He believed that the South Vietnamese had accepted the formula only because the United States had convinced them it was the only way to bring them into negotiations with Hanoi.

He became increasingly sensitive to proposed moves on Washington's part that he thought would increase Saigon's anxieties about the talks. He expressed these concerns forcefully in a message to Under Secretary of State Nicholas Katzenbach in early July:

> We are both thoroughly in agreement on the importance of finding a negotiated settlement to the war but I fear (I hope I am wrong) that in our desire to get there quickly, we may allow all that we have worked to achieve here, step by painful step, in the way of a stable, effective, democratic, constitutional government and a stable settlement in Southeast Asia to be undermined. . . . If [the views of the GVN leadership on the basic issues involved in the negotiations] are not sufficiently taken into account in developing our negotiating stance in Paris, we may find that we are negotiating from a position of weakness in Vietnam which does not now exist, but which could become a fact if we are not careful.[46]

As the spring and summer months of 1968 ground on without any breakthrough toward peace, Bunker cast a baleful eye on the struggle within his Democratic Party for the succession to Johnson. Caught up in what he considered an effort to win the war, he had no sympathy with either of the two declared "peace" candidates, Senator Eugene McCarthy of Minnesota or Senator Robert Kennedy of New York. Bunker had been a strong admirer of President John Kennedy. This may have contributed to the special animus he developed toward Robert, whom he regarded as an opportunist who had turned against the war when he found public opinion veering in that direction.[47] He was appalled later by the disturbances outside the Democratic convention hall in Chicago, and expressed the same contempt for the long-haired student protesters as he did for journalists who denigrated the war. He contrasted both unfavorably with the young Americans in uniform he knew in Vietnam.

Bunker had been relieved when Hubert Humphrey entered the race. But as the campaign continued, the vice president's penchant for erring in his description of Vietnam policy often troubled him. "Someone ought to make a study of the threat to international relations posed by compulsive talking," he complained to Carol.[48] It seemed to Bunker a few weeks before the election that the campaign had turned up little in the way of high-level debate. "On Vietnam, Hubert seems to have gotten so tangled up in his own words that I am not sure he himself knows what he means. And Nixon, true to form, seems to be working both sides of the street."[49] Bunker appears to have kept to himself how he finally voted that November.

Meanwhile, he continued to focus on key issues within Vietnam. The pacification program had been badly disrupted by the Tet offensive and for some time it became little more than a relief and recovery effort. Resumption of the long-term drive to achieve territorial security, which Bunker described as the backbone of any effective pacification program, was hampered in his view by the post-Tet defensive mindset of the Vietnamese armed forces and their U.S. advisers. They recovered only slowly from the shock of the offensive. A longer-term problem was the inadequacy of the GVN apparatus responsible for operating the program. Under Bunker's direction, Komer developed proposals for improving the management of the pacification effort and persuaded the Vietnamese to accept them. The mission estimated in mid-October that despite the program's shortcomings and fresh Communist offensives in May–June and August–September, the proportion of the population under government control had slowly and steadily increased though it was still not fully back to the pre-Tet level. (Like all such statistics, these figures are open to question.) Bunker looked forward to further improvement on the ground during the Accelerated Pacification Campaign the GVN planned to pursue with U.S. support in the final months of 1968 and early 1969.[50]

As he pushed the pacification program, Bunker continued to urge Thieu and his colleagues to do more to mobilize Vietnam's human resources for the war effort. Yet he was reasonably satisfied with GVN performance. "While many weaknesses and shortcomings remain in the effort to effect total mobilization," he reported in October, "when one considers what has been achieved [in mobilizing over a million men] from a manpower pool representing two-thirds of a population of 17 million, the magnitude of the accomplishment is impressive."[51] He was pleased with what he considered the improved performance of the ARVN, especially the Vietnamese army's role in halting the Communists' August–September offensive—their third, weakest, and last in 1968. In that operation, he reported with considerable satisfaction, the Vietnamese had borne a greater share of the fighting than in any previous Communist drive and killed twice as many of the enemy as U.S. forces had.

The problem of corruption also had high priority on his agenda. Bunker applauded Prime Minister Huong's anticorruption drive, which he believed had definitely reduced corruption levels. He recognized that Huong still had a long way to go, however. While he continued to urge the Vietnamese to do more, and the mission tried to help them do it, Bunker was realistic about the problem. He recognized that corruption was endemic to Asian societies like Vietnam.[52] Americans might deplore this and do what they could to improve matters, but they should not try to judge the Vietnamese by U.S. standards.

Bunker's persistently hawkish views—his conviction that the Communists were not sincerely interested in a negotiated settlement, his opposition to a complete bombing halt pending conclusive evidence that they were, his call for greater efforts to interdict Communist infiltration through Laos, and his confidence that the war could still be won and South Vietnam made secure against the Communist threat—made him a natural ally of such civilian and military hard-liners in the Johnson administration as Dean Rusk, Walt Rostow, and the Joint Chiefs of Staff. They also put him on a collision course with the new secretary of defense, Clark Clifford. Clifford, who had replaced McNamara at the end of February 1968, had himself been a Vietnam hawk. But in the winter of 1967–68 he had concluded that the United States could not win in Vietnam. His views were influential in bringing about the changes in policy the president had announced on March 31.

Clifford and Bunker's first face-to-face clash came in July when Clifford made his initial visit to Vietnam as defense secretary. He had been less than impressed by the performance of the GVN and its armed forces and found little basis for Bunker's enthusiastic support of the Vietnamese president. He became convinced that under Thieu's leadership the GVN did not really want the war to end—"not while they were protected by over 500,000 American troops and a 'golden flow of money.'"[53]

Not surprisingly, Clifford found that Bunker was shocked at his bluntness in warning the Vietnamese leaders that in the absence of visible progress the American public would simply not support the war effort much longer, and in telling them that if the Johnson administration could not achieve a settlement in Paris it would expect the South Vietnamese gradually to take over the war. He concluded that "our gentle and dignified Ambassador" had not been as tough and candid as he should have been in putting these home truths to Thieu and his colleagues. According to Clifford, Bunker vehemently opposed his suggestion to push for an end to the war in the remaining six months of the Johnson administration. In his view, the ambassador considered it heresy to suggest that Saigon should bend a little to help get meaningful negotiations started.[54]

The Bunker-Clifford confrontation then shifted to Honolulu, where the two men joined Johnson, Thieu, and a small number of senior U.S. and Vietnamese officials for a summit conference on the war. In a private meeting, Clifford reiterated to the president his contention that the war could not be won and that the Thieu government did not want it to end. He urged Johnson to tell Thieu that the administration was going to make an all-out effort to settle the war in the next six months. He later wrote in his autobiography that Johnson had told him that he had been impressed with these points and had raised all of them in a private session he had with Thieu. Bunker's account differs. In a letter to Carol soon after the Honolulu conference, he mentioned that the president did not accept Clifford's recommendation that he (Johnson) tell Thieu it was essential to reach a settlement within the six months he remained in the White House. Bunker reported his version of the Honolulu summit to her with considerable satisfaction:

> The Vietnamese were very pleased, I think, at the way things went. They received the assurance they wanted to hear from the President that we would not run out on them and at the same time had a full review of the Paris talks and possible negotiations, assurance they would play a principal role in them and a survey of some of the alternatives they had. In this Thieu showed a flexibility which pleased our people. I was also pleased because the President took the line I hoped he would and which I had recommended, making it clear that while he hoped a settlement

would be possible, it would have to be the right kind, and if this were not possible, he wanted to leave the situation in shape for his successor to handle.[55]

Bunker went on to praise the way Thieu had handled himself publicly, most notably in his dealings with the aggressive correspondents who covered the White House.

As his words suggest, and as Clifford ruefully conceded, Bunker returned to Saigon satisfied. So, he reported to the president, had Thieu, another clear indication that Clifford had not brought Johnson around.[56] Since the Honolulu conference had failed to resolve the conflict among Johnson's advisors over Vietnam policy, Clifford was correct in concluding that "in the delicate balance within the Administration over how to deal with Saigon, the decisive vote went to the man on the ground, Ellsworth Bunker."[57]

Over the next months, Bunker used this position to discourage Johnson from breaking the Paris deadlock by offering a total bombing halt unless, as he had consistently urged, the Communists undertook to match the halt with military restraint. He feared that an inadequately compensated bombing halt would be seen as a reflection of administration weakness resulting from political turmoil at home. In his view, the U.S. position where it really mattered in the negotiations—on the battlefield—was "strong and becoming stronger."[58]

He was critical of Averell Harriman, the head of the U.S. delegation in Paris. He worried that Harriman, sensing that the end of his long career might be at hand should Nixon win in November, had become extremely eager for a settlement. "So am I," he wrote Carol in a comment that caught the flavor of his thinking, "and so I think are most all Vietnamese, but not at the expense of the blood, sweat, tears and treasure we have committed here to principles we believe in, which I believe are in our own interests in this part of the world."[59] He was concerned, too, about the impact of the American presidential race: "Now that the campaign is getting underway, we shall have any number of willing hands telling us how to settle the war and negotiate the peace."[60]

By early October, with the U.S. presidential election only a month away, there seemed scant prospect of progress at the stalled Paris peace talks, let alone of a settlement of the Vietnam conflict. Washington continued to reject the familiar North Vietnamese demands—an unconditional end to American bombing of the North, the withdrawal of U.S. forces from South Vietnam, and the replacement of the Thieu government by a coalition that included the National Liberation Front. Although there were major differences on Vietnam within the Johnson administration, the American position as it had evolved since Johnson's March 31 speech was that if the United States stopped the remaining bombing, "prompt and serious" talks with the Communist side would have to follow. "Serious" was defined as including Saigon's participation in the talks. Hanoi would also have to provide assurances that in the event of a complete bombing halt it would deescalate the conflict. For Washington, this meant that the Communists would cease their violations of the demilitarized zone between North and South Vietnam and avoid significant attacks against major Southern cities. Bunker fully subscribed to this position.

During the second week of October, the Communists moved away from their hard and, to the Johnson administration, unacceptable line. At a private session on October 11, they asked Ambassador Harriman and his deputy, Cyrus Vance, whether the United States would call a bombing halt if it had a clear answer regarding Saigon's participation in the next stage of talks. With the concurrence of Bunker and General Abrams, who both predictably concluded that North Vietnam's shift reflected its military weakness, Washington reacted quickly and favorably. Efforts were soon under way to hammer out an agreement with Hanoi on the precise timing of the bombing halt and the beginning of the expanded, "serious" talks that were promptly to follow. These U.S.–North Vietnam negotiations also dealt with the structure of the talks—how the Thieu government delegation and one representing the National Liberation Front were to be fitted in and described. Agreement was also needed on the form of Hanoi's undertaking to deescalate the conflict in the DMZ and around the cities. This had to avoid wording that could be labeled a "condition" for the halt, which was unacceptable to the Communists. Washington instructed Bunker to inform Thieu of these developments and to make certain that the South Vietnamese were prepared to concur should the United States reach agreement with Hanoi.

Bunker's lengthy, intensive effort to persuade Saigon to take part in expanded negotiations on terms that conformed with the agreement Washington reached with Hanoi later in October ranks among the most daunting and frustrating exercises in his diplomatic career. The Thieu government's concern about the implications of the negotiations for U.S.

steadfastness was heightened by the projected presence of the National Liberation Front on the Communist side of the negotiating table under the "our side/your side" formula Washington had developed. It feared that this arrangement would be perceived, not least in South Vietnam itself, as giving the NLF equal status with the legitimate government of the Republic of Vietnam in the contest for sovereignty over the South.

This problem alone would have made Bunker's efforts difficult. They were further complicated by the impending American presidential election. For the Johnson administration, this timing lent tremendous urgency to reaching agreement on halting the bombing of North Vietnam and initiating expanded talks. For the president, such an agreement represented a last chance to bring about a significant advance toward a Vietnam settlement while he was still in control of U.S. policy. For partisan Democrats such as Averell Harriman and Clark Clifford, agreement meant a boost for Hubert Humphrey as he sought to overcome Richard Nixon's narrowing lead in the White House race. Bunker was not alone in surmising that Hanoi had chosen a time just before a closely contested election for negotiating an agreement to move forward in order to maximize its bargaining power with the administration.

Saigon saw the connection between the Paris talks and the election quite differently. It was to the Thieu government's advantage to delay until Washington no longer felt the pressure of the election deadline and Hanoi could no longer benefit from this. But even more important, Thieu and his colleagues reckoned that their interests would best be served if the hawkish Nixon and not the increasingly dovish Humphrey were elected president on November 5. They no doubt recognized that if a bombing halt and the launching of expanded, "serious" talks could be brought off before then, Humphrey would have a better chance of winning. Nixon and other senior figures in his campaign used a prominent Washington Republican insider, Anna Chennault, as an intermediary to bring Thieu to this judgment.[61]

Thieu initially agreed without reservations to the American negotiating position when Bunker met him on October 13. "After all," Bunker quoted the president as stating after he had assured him that Washington was prepared to resume the bombing if the North Vietnamese violated the Demilitarized Zone or attacked the main cities, "the problem is not to stop the bombing but to stop the war, and we must try this path to see if they [Hanoi] are serious. . . . I thought this a statesman's view," Bunker commented in his report.[62] But after consulting his colleagues, the South

Vietnamese president quickly retreated. The main objections he raised revolved around the NLF's role at the expanded conference, which he demanded be redefined in ways the American negotiators recognized would be unacceptable to Hanoi. As his discussions with Bunker wore on, he added new conditions. More time was needed for Saigon to get a delegation to Paris; Hanoi had to guarantee in advance that it would deal directly with the Thieu government's delegates at the talks; the South Vietnamese National Security Council's approval was required; the South Vietnam Assembly needed to vote on the matter—the list of alleged problems kept growing. Thieu and his colleagues complicated the negotiations by making unhelpful public statements and leaking sensitive information. Although at one point agreement seemed at hand, the breakthrough Washington anxiously sought continued to elude Bunker.

Bunker's pre-election efforts climaxed with a marathon series of meetings totaling some nine hours on the night and early morning of October 31–November 1 (Saigon time). He cabled Washington in exasperation afterwards: "It turned out to be a sterile exercise, with the GVN generally throwing up obstacles to agreement faster than we could remove them."[63] He had again failed, he reported, to persuade Thieu to accept an agreed position that could be embodied in the text of a joint U.S.–South Vietnamese announcement of the bombing halt and the expanded talks that would follow. Johnson announced the bombing halt unilaterally a few hours later and noted that representatives of the government of South Vietnam were free to participate in the new round of negotiations.

A couple of days later, Thieu ended all possibility that South Vietnam would agree before the election to join the Paris talks by announcing his government's negative position in an emotional speech in the National Assembly. In the address, which the *New York Times* reported was received with wild enthusiasm, the president asserted that Hanoi had failed to meet three conditions. The most important of these was that the North Vietnamese delegates appear alone at the bargaining table and not bring along the NLF as a separate delegation.[64] Shamefully, Thieu refused to see Bunker before he gave this address even though the ambassador was seeking to deliver a letter to him from President Johnson.

Johnson and his inner circle of Vietnam policy advisers had monitored Bunker's negotiations with the South Vietnamese with mounting concern. The president and the more hawkish of the other senior American officials, such as Dean Rusk and Walt Rostow, were satisfied with Bunker's performance in these sessions. Clark Clifford was not. Nor was Averell

Harriman, who with Cyrus Vance had succeeded in working out an agreement with the North Vietnamese in Paris while Bunker was failing with Thieu in Saigon. Clifford, whose differences with Bunker on Vietnam had by then become even more pronounced, believed that Bunker, misled by an excessive regard for the South Vietnamese president, "misread Thieu at every step of the way" and was overly optimistic in his assessments of South Vietnamese positions. He held that Bunker was not sufficiently forceful in his effort to bring Thieu around nor sufficiently committed to that goal.[65] Averell Harriman's biographer, Rudy Abramson, has written that Harriman believed Bunker was committed to a military solution in Vietnam and considered him among the most rigid of the U.S. officials involved. According to Abramson, Harriman blamed Bunker for Thieu's refusal to take part in the talks as the election slipped away.[66]

A careful reading of the voluminous files reporting the negotiations that are now available at the Lyndon B. Johnson Presidential Library, the National Archives, and elsewhere does not offer evidence to justify such harsh appraisals. At several points in the negotiations Bunker was, no doubt, more confident that agreement could be reached with Thieu than subsequent developments warranted. On two occasions, he urged that Thieu be given more time, reasonable requests under ordinary negotiating circumstances that went down badly with a secretary of defense and a chief negotiator driven by a desire to install Hubert Humphrey in the White House. Bunker did not share Clifford's and Harriman's political partisanship and the sense of urgency this produced. Negotiating under a deadline that the opponent is aware of was for him a prescription for trouble.

Read as a whole, the messages indicate that Bunker carried out what proved to be an impossible assignment resolutely and with an energetic tenacity unusual in a man of seventy-four. Hopeful that he could achieve a breakthrough, he followed his instructions carefully, arguing the American case with the patience, resourcefulness, and skillful attention to detail for which he had become well known. He presented tough U.S. positions to Thieu in unvarnished terms.[67] Despite the exasperating antics of the South Vietnamese and the hot breath of Washington on his neck, he remained courteous and cool.

It is hard to see how any other envoy could have done better under the circumstances unless the administration had been prepared to threaten to withdraw from Vietnam if Thieu did not give in. Johnson would not do this, though Clifford and Harriman, who were eager to terminate U.S. involvement, might well have pushed for such an approach had they thought the president would have considered it. Commenting afterwards in a letter to Sam Berger, William Bundy, who as assistant secretary of state for Far Eastern affairs was a key player at the Washington end of the negotiations, wrote: "For my money, I regard the case as one of two great men [Bunker and Harriman] seeing the situation from different angles. For my own part, I think Ellsworth and you have been right in essence in everything you have done, and resourceful and wise in your execution of it beyond all measure of praise. Whether we really lost any golden opportunities I leave to history, but I would start extremely doubtful. Nor, in the nature of the transition and a new atmosphere, do I believe it had nearly as serious an effect on American attitudes and public support as we certainly feared at many points along the way."[68]

The effort to persuade the South Vietnamese to take part in the talks continued, somewhat anticlimactically, following Richard Nixon's narrow victory in the presidential poll. Thieu finally agreed to do so on November 27, after further lengthy negotiations with Bunker and other embassy representatives about the structure of the talks and, perhaps more important, a strong message from Nixon, by then president-elect. But not until late January, following further weeks of haggling over the shape of the table where the four parties would sit under the "our side/your side" formula, did a South Vietnamese delegation finally take part in the Paris talks. By then, Johnson had left the White House.

Bunker analyzed Thieu's delay in his last formal report to Johnson, sent from Saigon on January 16. At that point, he probably knew little if anything of Anna Chennault's role. After reiterating his familiar theme about the importance to the Saigon government of public recognition of its exclusive sovereignty over South Vietnam, he wrote that "Thieu's recoil from [the our side/your side] formula at the moment of truth in October sprang from these basic factors: his inability adequately to prepare public opinion; his normal reluctance to bite the bullet; and his hope that with a new U.S. administration coming in he could postpone or perhaps evade entirely the bombing halt and the confrontation with the NLF it implied." Security considerations, which at first made it difficult for Thieu to share the U.S. plan with his colleagues and bring them around, had compounded the problem. Bunker concluded: "In retrospect . . . the time lost between October 31 and November 27, when the GVN took the decision to go to Paris, could only have been avoided by loosening up on security; and since that might have jeopardized the chances to come to an agreement with the North Vietnamese. . . . the delay was inevitable."[69]

Bunker added to his assessment some thoughts that reflected his most fundamental concerns about U.S.–South Vietnamese relations: "At the root of our problems with them over issues in negotiations is the basic matter of mutual trust and mutual objectives. Whatever the reason, the events of late October and November left many Vietnamese leaders, Thieu included, with doubts as to our ultimate intentions. . . . [What] is troubling the Vietnamese . . . is the question of where we are trying to lead them. Given these fears, they are hesitant to make concessions which would not trouble them if they were really confident that our ultimate objective remains an independent, non-Communist South Vietnam free to work out its own destiny without outside interference."

"The way in which we do and say things," he concluded in speaking of the administration about to take office, "will be as important as what we do and say. The Vietnamese basically like and trust Americans and believe that we share mutual objectives and interests." He was confident, he said, "that with the right approach it will be possible for us to bring them along with us in the necessary atmosphere of mutual trust."[70]

It was Bunker's job, as he saw it throughout his Saigon assignment, to do everything he could to help create that atmosphere.

I2

Vietnamization Has Succeeded

After announcing his cabinet and other senior appointees, including Henry A. Kissinger as national security adviser, Richard Nixon phoned Bunker in Saigon early in the new year to ask him to stay on as ambassador. William P. Rogers, Nixon's designee as secretary of state, recalled that he recommended the reappointment to the president-elect because he considered Bunker the best candidate available. Nixon, he said, readily concurred. According to Rogers, there was no sense in the Nixon camp that an incoming administration that said it had new ideas on Vietnam needed a fresh face at the crucial Saigon mission.[1] William Bundy has correctly observed that retaining Bunker and other senior members of the U.S. diplomatic-military team in Saigon was intended as a signal of continuity in the conduct of the war.[2] The *Washington Post* praised the decision in an editorial: "To have replaced Mr. Bunker at this point . . . would have seriously shaken Saigon, where Mr. Bunker, a tireless and talented man, has ably discharged his primary mission, as he has conceived it, of keeping the present Saigon Government upright, and preserving the far-from sturdy political structure which the United States has labored so long to patch together."[3]

Bunker with pleasure promptly cabled the text of the editorial to his sister in Hartford. But he accepted the president-elect's decision with mixed emotions. He had not expected to stay on if Nixon won and was pleased that the new administration wanted him.[4] He was performing what he considered the ultimate duty of his life and would not have given his job up for any other, particularly when, as he believed, prospects in Vietnam had become more promising. But he also fervently wished to be with Carol and did not hesitate to say so. They had considered the possibility of his reappointment when she visited him in Saigon for the Christmas holidays and "were both determined on one thing, and that is that we do not want to go on living two thousand miles apart."[5] He reported his conversation with Nixon to Carol without enthusiasm.[6] After they had talked together further in Kathmandu, he informed Washington that the two of them "were prepared to fall in line with any overriding national interests or the interests of the [Foreign] Service."[7]

Bunker's role changed under the new administration. It was not a question of his personal or professional standing. Although he had known Nixon only slightly before the 1968 election and never developed the same warm relations with him as he had with Johnson, he quickly earned the president's (and Kissinger's) trust and respect. What was different was the new administration's increasing focus on Kissinger's secret negotiations with Hanoi. Anthony Lake has argued:

> [Bunker's] views from Saigon probably carried greater weight in the Tet and immediate post-Tet period in the Johnson administration than they did in the period when Nixon launched the new strategy and Kissinger was implementing it in secret negotiations. . . . When the point of the war was mostly programmatic—pacification, etc. etc.—then the ambassador's . . . coordinating [role] . . . pushing the programs, helping conduct a war effort in its civilian as well as military dimensions, was extremely important. As it became more and more an issue of the negotiations and the [related] military strategy, the role of the embassy became less important.[8]

But if this was the view from Washington, Bunker's activities and the continued sense of fulfillment he got from them strongly suggest that he did not think that he and his embassy had been downgraded. While he recognized that the negotiations were crucial, he held, correctly, that the situation on the ground in South Vietnam was critical to their outcome. He believed that the operation he led continued to play a key role in influencing that situation. In any event, he had no more difficulty in adjusting to the changes in style and substance the new administration brought to Vietnam policy than he had in handling the twists and turns in Johnson's approach. If he wanted to leave Saigon before the end of the six-year stint he eventually spent there, it was for personal, not professional reasons.[9]

Bunker warmly supported the administration's moves to strengthen the Vietnamese military forces and replace American troops with them. As his messages and other comments about the real and potential competence of the Vietnam armed forces made clear, he was a strong believer in Vietnamization well before Nixon's secretary of defense, Melvin Laird, gave it that name in 1969. He recalled later that President Johnson had spoken favorably of such a policy as early as January 1967, during the White House session at which he offered Bunker the Saigon assignment.[10] Bunker's own advocacy of Vietnamization was doubtless well known to the new administration. It is difficult, however, to weigh his influence in leading Nixon to adopt the policy and make it a central feature in the administration's strategy for ending U.S. participation in the war.

Nixon had told Bunker in Washington in April 1969 that he wanted to begin bringing American troops home that year. The ambassador was present with Thieu and other U.S. and Vietnamese leaders on Midway island in June when Nixon announced that 25,000 troops would initially be repatriated. Soon afterwards, with Bunker's enthusiastic support, the administration stated that the primary mission of U.S. forces in Vietnam was to improve the capability of South Vietnamese troops and prepare them to take over. Nixon formally spelled out this Vietnamization strategy in a November 3 address. Over the next three years, the program of withdrawing U.S. troops, coupled with upgrading and extending the responsibility of the Vietnamese armed forces, went forward at an irregular pace determined by military requirements, American domestic political pressures, and budgetary considerations. By the time of the peace accords in January 1973, only some 25,000 U.S. military personnel remained in South Vietnam.

While he welcomed Vietnamization, Bunker counseled caution in its implementation. The congenital impatience of Americans, he feared, could be the Achilles heel of the strategy. A few weeks after the Midway conference, he advised Nixon that "the crucial factor . . . is the rate at which [Vietnamization] takes place." He warned that if U.S. troop reductions outpaced the Vietnamese leaders' belief in their ability to take over, "it could destroy their self confidence and all that we have built up here step by painful step."[11] The following month he cabled Washington, "Depending on how it is carried out, Vietnamization can . . . spur the GVN [Government of Vietnam] and RVNAF [Republic of Vietnam Armed Forces] to greater self-reliance and better performance. On the other [hand], it could result in the destruction and loss of all that we have achieved here."[12]

Bunker believed that success in pacification was critical in making Vietnamization possible. The challenge of Vietnamization was to convert a guerrilla war into a conventional one. In his view, pacification and Vietnamization went hand in hand, the first to defeat the Vietcong, the second to prepare the ARVN (Army of the Republic of Vietnam) for the conventional defense of South Vietnam against North Vietnamese regulars. As local forces broke the Communists' hold over the villages and assumed the burden of mobile security in and around populated areas, the ARVN could effectively replace American combat units in the task of keeping the North Vietnamese Army's main force divisions tied up in fighting near or beyond the border. He was confident that this challenge could be met.

As Vietnamization moved forward, Bunker expressed satisfaction with the way both the Vietnam government and his own were handling it. An observation he cabled Washington in March 1970 typifies both his optimistic assessment and his formula for success: "Vietnamization of the war is proceeding with no major hitches encountered or looming on the horizon. Assuming that we provide the ARVN the kind of combat support—air, artillery, helicopters, logistics—that has been so critical to American success against the enemy, I continue to feel that the RVNAF can steadily assume a greater responsibility for the war regardless of enemy intentions."[13] He credited Thieu for the absence of any U.S.-Vietnamese confrontation over the pace of American troop withdrawals and cited with satisfaction the Vietnamese president's effort to depict Vietnamization "not as something forced on South Vietnam but as springing from its own initiative, as a matter of national dignity, of obligation, and as an opportunity—provided its friends will help the country in making the necessary adjustments."[14]

In Bunker's view, destruction of North Vietnam's capability by the ARVN and the gradually departing Americans was vital to the success of the linked Vietnamization and pacification programs during Vietnamization's initial months. He strongly supported General Abrams's tactic in late 1968 and 1969 of aggressive small-unit operations and B-52 raids on Communist troop concentrations scattered throughout the South. This kept the enemy away from populated areas, reduced injury to civilians, lowered American casualties, opened up new areas for pacification, and prepared the ground for the South Vietnamese to take over the war.

He also backed Abrams's request for authority to direct air strikes against Communist troop concentrations, logistic lines, and ammunition dumps in areas of Cambodia close to the Vietnamese border. According to U.S. intelligence, this was the location of the Central Office of South Vietnam (COSVN) headquarters that directed North Vietnamese military operations in much of South Vietnam. Bunker had long favored attacking Communist supply routes in the neighboring Indochinese countries and was not troubled by the possible illegality or immorality of intervention into what he termed "supposedly" neutral Cambodia. Hanoi had violated Cambodia's neutral status to pursue its ambitions in South Vietnam, and there was no justification for its forces enjoying sanctuary across the Cambodian frontier. As he put it in an "Eyes Only" cable to Secretary Rogers following a comprehensive briefing by Abrams, "I realize fully the political implications of such a strike. . . . If [Cambodia's long-time neutralist ruler Prince Norodom] Sihanouk complains, our rejoinder must be that COSVN is located on his territory and has been for years. He has done nothing about it although his forces in the area are fully aware of COSVN's presence."[15]

Bunker saw the proposed air attacks as justified retaliation for recent Communist shelling of Saigon and other South Vietnamese cities and also urged the resumption of the bombing of North Vietnam.[16] Nixon authorized B-52 attacks on Cambodia, the secret bombings that continued for fourteen months, but did not resume raids on the North, probably because he feared that they would disrupt the Paris talks and further fuel domestic opposition to the war.

Bunker shed no tears when Sihanouk was overthrown in March 1970 in a parliamentary coup that brought to power Lon Nol, Cambodia's rightist prime minister. Bunker had little regard for Sihanouk's leadership and had for years discouraged moves to improve relations with him. Like Washington, he at first adopted a wait-and-see attitude toward Lon Nol.[17] As instructed, he warned Thieu on March 28 not to send ARVN units across the border in support of the new, initially neutralist government as its rag-tag forces battled against the Communists.[18] But the imperiled Lon Nol soon abandoned his neutral position and appealed for outside help. When Bunker was awakened at 3 A.M. on April 23 by a top-secret, "Eyes Only" message from the White House that asked him and General Abrams to assess the advisability of U.S. military intervention, he predictably joined Abrams in recommending combined American and South Vietnamese operations across the border.[19]

Nixon, who faced conflicting views within his administration on how to respond to the Cambodian crisis, announced the joint incursion in a dramatic and emotional broadcast on April 30, best recalled for his outlandish claim that failure to intervene would reduce the United States to the status of a "pitiful helpless giant." Public clamor against the controversial move soon led him to limit it to a two-month operation extending only twenty-one miles into Cambodian territory. American troops and the bulk of the ARVN forces that had gone in with them were withdrawn by June 30.

Estimates of the military effectiveness of the operation have varied. Earlier claims of major success in disrupting Communist supplies and offensive capabilities were scaled down over time. At home, the Cambodian incursion produced widespread demonstrations and disorders on college campuses and elsewhere, culminating in the death of four students at Kent State University in Ohio. The move significantly intensified congressional and public opposition to the administration's Vietnam policy. Within the administration itself, it led to the resignations of several important NSC (National Security Council) officials, including Anthony Lake and William Watts, who objected to the decision to intervene.[20]

Bunker was typically upbeat about the outcome of the incursion. At the time and later, he stressed in his reporting the boost it had given to the ARVN. In his view, widely shared, South Vietnamese forces had performed well in the operation. Their morale, always an important factor for him, had risen as a result. But like other Americans at the embassy in Saigon, he was shocked and surprised by the tremendous uproar the incursion triggered at home. He could see no ground for protest over the intervention, let alone for the impassioned strikes and marches that swept American colleges and cities. He could only deplore the violence and what he considered the irrationality that followed the incursion.

It was not that Bunker was unaware of antiwar sentiment. American doves—politicians, academics, media stars, and others—regularly visited Saigon and were outspoken in telling him and his staff that the war was hopeless and immoral and had lost all domestic political support. But he had scant regard for these critics, or for the Saigon press corps, which his chief of staff Charles Hill piquantly recalled, "was a Greek chorus constantly intoning this theme to us."[21] Fully convinced that Nixon's policies were correct, Bunker did not appreciate the emotional resonance the critics' positions had at home nor how quickly an escalation of the war could heighten this. On his periodic visits to the United States on consultation or leave he had greater access to the American media's presentation of the story. But it is not likely that he engaged in many sustained, serious discussions with opponents of administration policy. Sessions with his Vermont neighbors Senator George Aiken and Professor John Kenneth Galbraith, both fully capable of giving him an earful, were probably among the few opportunities he had to meet informally with critics of the war whom he respected.

The public outcry in no way weakened his support for the operation. He held steadfastly to the view that the United States had paid dearly for its toleration of Communist violation of Cambodian neutrality over the years. If anything, Washington had delayed too long in countering it. Unlike many others, he remained convinced both that the incursion had been the right move and that it had brought lasting benefit to the U.S. cause in Indochina.

With General Abrams, Bunker also strongly advocated the early 1971 ARVN incursion into the Laos panhandle. The operation, code-named Lam Son 719, was designed to cut off the flow of North Vietnamese troops and supplies down the web of roads and paths that made up the Ho Chi Minh Trail. Although Abrams developed the concept and detailed plan of this search-and-destroy operation, Congress's prohibition against the employment in Laos of U.S. combat troops or advisors meant that the ARVN was responsible for establishing its specific objectives and achieving them. Lam Son 719 benefited from major U.S. air support, including helicopters, but the ground operations were entirely in ARVN hands and became the largest and most ambitious offensive ever carried out by South Vietnamese forces. The attack into Laotian territory was approved by Nixon and had the support of most of his key advisers, though some appear to have been cajoled or deceived by the president and the operation's advocates into agreeing to it.[22]

Bunker had favored an incursion into the Laos panhandle as early as June 1967, soon after he came to Vietnam. His warm support for Lam Son 719 demonstrated the importance he consistently placed on interdicting enemy movements down the Ho Chi Minh Trail. It also reflected his strong faith in the judgment of General Abrams and his military colleagues and his own well-known confidence in the growing prowess of the ARVN. This regard was now higher than ever. As he cabled Nixon in January 1971, he was convinced that the overthrow of Sihanouk and the subsequent U.S.-GVN cross-border operation in Cambodia had provided an "exceptionally beneficial impetus" to both Vietnamization and pacification. He assured the president: "The [South] Vietnamese have seen that the relatively rapid withdrawal of our troops has brought no military defeats, but rather improved performance by their own forces. The early apprehension has now given place to a sense of satisfaction that they are approaching the point where they can go it alone."[23]

Although Bunker went on to caution that the South Vietnamese recognized, as he did, that the ARVN would still need training assistance, materiel, and air support, he concluded that "they enter 1971 with a kind of confidence that will stand them in good stead over the coming year."[24] As Hanoi made a major effort to strengthen its supply system overland through the Laos panhandle to replace the loss of land and sea routes through Cambodia, he was persuaded that the enhanced ARVN, proven on the Cambodian battlefield, could effectively carry out on its own a large-scale operation that would critically curtail the flow of North Vietnamese men and materiel southward and blunt an expected Communist thrust into South Vietnam later in the year.

Launched on February 8, 1971, Lam Son 719 soon ran into deep trouble. With inadequate numbers and handicapped by the absence of American advisers and air controllers, the invading South Vietnamese troops suffered heavy losses at the hands of forewarned and reinforced North Vietnamese units, which put up fierce resistance to their advance. Badly rattled, Thieu ordered them to halt when they were less than halfway to their objective, the Laotian town of Tchepone, a supply center on the Ho Chi Minh Trail. They eventually reached what was left of Tchepone on March 6, weeks after their target date for its capture. Three days later, Thieu decided to end the operation on the advice of his commanders (and contrary to the urging of General Abrams, who wanted the ARVN forces reinforced). The difficult withdrawal that followed had some of the characteristics of a rout. The most publicized of these in the American press were the efforts of fleeing ARVN troops to cling to the skids of U.S. helicopters in their desperate bid to get away. The last column of the bloodied ARVN forces engaged in Lam Son 719 reached South Vietnamese soil on March 23.

By most contemporary and later accounts, Lam Son 719 was a major setback for the ARVN that exposed its limitations in planning and executing complicated military operations and highlighted Thieu's lack of resolve in critical situations. The U.S. side also came in for a share of the blame. Some observers scored Washington for agreeing to the incursion without adequately questioning its feasibility and criticized the U.S. military for hurrying the Vietnamese into the operation and then supporting them inadequately. There was a great deal of finger-pointing all around.[25]

As the operation staggered toward its inglorious conclusion, Bunker tried to cast it in a positive light. He claimed that it had achieved most of what had been hoped for. He saw Lam Son as a significant step forward for Vietnamization. "Lam Son 719 has been a political plus in the confidence it has created in the ability of the ARVN and pride in its accomplishment," he reported. "There has been satisfaction in the fact that fighting has taken place outside the borders of South Vietnam and that while the ARVN has had heavy losses it has inflicted far heavier casualties on the enemy."[26] Thieu had told him, he said, that as a result of the experience gained in Lam Son 719, the ARVN had improved its organization and command and would benefit in future operations from the knowledge it had gained of NVA (North Vietnamese Army) combat tactics and methods of fighting.[27]

As seemed invariably the case when American or South Vietnamese forces stepped up offensive operations, Bunker had no regrets about his support for Lam Son 719, at least not at the time. But years later, in 1983, he declared that "1971 was too late for Lam Son since we were unable to make any contribution to it and the job was too big for the ARVN."[28] In 1971, he likened the intervention into Laos to the repulse of the Communist attacks during Tet in 1968. In his view, both had been military successes in the field that were seen as defeats in the United States.

Bunker unfairly took the American media to task, as he had at Tet: "The propaganda of Hanoi is supplemented by the reports of the American press," he wrote Carol with some emotion soon after Lam Son 719 had concluded.[29] "Sometimes," he told a conference of U.S. commanders in Vietnam, "they seem to have a vested interest in failure."[30] Inaccurate and biased reporting was as responsible for the psychological setback that Lam Son 719 had produced at home as it had been for a similar outcome after Tet three years earlier. He told Thieu that to offset such a defeatist reaction in South Vietnam, "we should do everything we can to attest to the victories our forces have gained, and counter the major propaganda campaign being mounted by North Vietnam."[31]

Although Bunker was unusually critical of Thieu for his unwillingness to fire corrupt and inefficient senior officers involved in the battle, Lam Son 719 did not shake his confidence that the president was the best available leader for South Vietnam despite his shortcomings. Bunker spoke harshly both to the Vietnamese and to Washington about the Thieu government's corruption. He warned Thieu that corruption was not only Vietnam's problem: "The inability of the GVN to do anything about high level corruption is sharply affecting my ability—the American ability—to help you. The problem is thus a problem of Vietnamese-American relations."[32]

"Corruption is a cancer," he wrote Nixon in January 1971, "which will, unless checked, sap the strength of [Vietnamese] society."[33] He complained that despite American prodding, Thieu was often indecisive and hesitant in moving military officers and civilian officials who had proven incompetent and corrupt. Sometimes he even promoted them. "Looking ahead to the time when the South Vietnamese will be on their own," he had written in the final paragraph of an August 1970 message to Nixon, "I think the problem will be less a military one than [one concerning] the moral fiber of the country. The ability of the government to eliminate corruption, the special privileges held by the few, inequalities in the distribution of sacrifices and benefits, and [the need] to create a condition of reasonable social justice can well be the determining factor[s] in the struggle with the communists."[34]

He also scored Thieu for his inept handling of the press and political opposition and for his inability to develop a cohesive and broad-based political organization. He assigned some of the blame for this organizational failing to the endemic disunity that he found characteristic of Vietnamese politics. Bunker acknowledged having had to speak to Thieu about the president's occasional impatience with constitutional restraints. He also took the Saigon government to task for its permissiveness, if not its complicity, regarding the sale of narcotics to American troops, a major problem for U.S. military commanders in the conduct of the war.

But Bunker's concern about these issues, and his reporting of them, was overshadowed by a steady flow from him and the mission of favorable assessments of developments in Thieu's South Vietnam. Advances in the twin programs of Vietnamization and pacification, the impressive land reform program that Bunker had strongly urged on Thieu, and the substantial improvement, with massive American assistance, in the Vietnamese economy headed the list of encouraging news. Backing up these assessments was a flood of statistical and anecdotal evidence of progress in many areas: enhanced ARVN capacity, improved rural security, more Vietcong defections, the holding of village elections, distribution of land to the landless, and increasing agricultural productivity all figured prominently. Bunker reveled in reporting to Washington about the pacification and new wealth of areas long off-limits to supporters of the government, about South Vietnamese farmers replacing their bicycles with motor scooters, and about vegetables finding their way to urban markets on reopened roads and waterways that the Communists had long made impassable. As he settled into a steady, mutually confident relationship with Thieu in the Nixon-Kissinger years, his messages presented a picture of sustained if uneven advance toward stability, security, and a measure of prosperity for South Vietnam.

Some on the embassy staff differed sharply with his assessments, especially officers in the political section but others, mostly younger officers, as well. Their negative views about Vietnam's prospects were shared by many

American correspondents, with whom they regularly compared notes. This pattern, senior officials taking an optimistic view of developments, more junior ones and media representatives more skeptical, was not uncommon throughout the war.

Bunker's critics in the embassy did not accuse him of deliberate dishonesty. Nonetheless, misleading and excessively sanguine reporting and analysis was one of the persistent weaknesses of his leadership of the Saigon mission. He was too optimistic in his analysis of Thieu's government, the Vietnamese military, and the capability of the two to resist the Communists once U.S. armed forces had left the country. He and senior mission officials who shared and reinforced his views downplayed, preferred not to notice, or were ignorant of many negative aspects of the Vietnamese scene.

James Nach, a political officer who was one of the leading dissidents in the embassy, thought that Bunker's mindset unduly influenced his perceptions. "It was how he viewed things. Bunker and other senior officers were unable to comprehend what was happening. . . . He had that particular mindset because he wanted [the U.S. effort in Vietnam] to work so much. He wanted South Vietnam not to be overrun by Communists. It was as if a computer was screening out information that was not in accord with desired results, whether it was the families of well-placed GVN officials dealing out drugs to GIS or the terrible losses the ARVN was taking." [35]

Although these critics tended to dwell too heavily on the repressive and corrupt features of South Vietnam's political and economic system, they are right in maintaining that Bunker did not encourage his well-staffed embassy to look too hard at the dark side of Vietnamese political and social life or to report their discouraging findings vigorously to Washington. He did not share the enthusiasm many of his younger officers had for digging up evidence of corruption and other shortcomings in South Vietnam or in following up such findings with effective efforts to remedy those defects.

But Bunker's preference for hopeful optimism stemmed from many factors aside from an ardent wish that Communists not win the battle for South Vietnam. He had an important personal stake in the success of U.S. policy, which he had helped fashion and strongly supported. He did not want to call what he would have termed "undue" attention to the shortcomings of that policy on the ground in Vietnam.

Bunker's sanguine approach mirrored the attitude of many senior U.S. diplomats at embassies in client states during the Cold War. Like him, they tended to exaggerate the accomplishments of their host governments unless the situation had so deteriorated that regime change became advisable. In Vietnam, where American interest in the success of the local government was unusually high, this proclivity to report the glass half full rather than half empty was especially pronounced. It was bolstered by a powerful U.S. concern for stability. Only a few years earlier, South Vietnam had been the victim of repeated military coups. Thieu's government had broken that pattern, and it was easy enough to accept that without him the situation could revert to the chaotic conditions of those times. So why highlight the president's shortcomings when a successor regime could well be weaker and less helpful to U.S. interests?

Bunker's own style and circumstances contributed to his "clientitis." By most accounts, he was rarely inclined to press and probe for information that might have seriously disturbed the rosy scenarios he drew for the White House and others. He met socially and professionally from time to time with leaders of the anticommunist political opposition, and they passed to him their critical assessments of Thieu and his government. But he ordinarily showed little curiosity about Vietnam. Moreover, his ability to get around personally and find out more about the country to the limited extent he might have wanted to was inhibited by security considerations. These confined him to American and Vietnamese government installations and a few other highly guarded places. They ruled out the kind of contact active ambassadors seek in less dangerous environments.

On the military side, Bunker consistently relied on the ordinarily upbeat judgments of General Abrams and his senior military colleagues at MACV (Military Assistance Command, Vietnam). His disinclination to challenge them may have been heightened by what seems to have been his rather romantic view of U.S. fighting men, whom he contrasted favorably with the civilian youths he thought were degrading American society at home. He only dimly recognized that many of the ills he excoriated among long-haired young people in the United States also infected the GI's he lauded in Vietnam.

But above and beyond these considerations was Bunker's definition of his mission as United States ambassador to the Republic of Vietnam. As noted earlier (Chapter 10), he strongly believed that he was in Vietnam to carry out the president's policies and make them work. In undertaking his mission, he reserved his energy, time, and powers of concentration for the overriding objective of those policies—reaching a settlement in Vietnam that preserved the South from Communist conquest. He was convinced that to achieve that goal he had to develop and maintain a close working relationship with Thieu. He saw no alternative leader whom the United States could trust to help it attain its objectives in Vietnam. Given this attitude, it is not surprising that he tried to avoid making Thieu look bad to the extent he could.

Bunker's warm and supportive relations with Thieu came under considerable strain soon after Lam Son 719, however. The problem was the conduct of the 1971 Vietnamese presidential election in which Thieu sought a second term. Its outcome—not the fact that Thieu won but how he won—represented a serious setback to Bunker's efforts to promote stronger political institutions in South Vietnam and win greater sympathy and support at home for the administration's policies there.

Well before the October balloting, Bunker had written forcefully to Washington about the importance of the presidential election and the simultaneous races for the lower house of the Vietnamese national assembly. "It is basic to U.S. interests in South Vietnam," he bluntly warned in a message in early January, "that the 1971 elections should contribute to government stability."[36] Only Thieu's reelection, he argued, could ensure this stability; neither of the president's potential challengers, Vice President Nguyen Cao Ky or retired General Duong Van Minh, had what was needed.

Bunker had had few good things to say about Ky in his four years of dealing with him, and had watched with satisfaction the dwindling away of his political power over that time. He saw Ky's possible candidacy largely as a spoiling operation against Thieu. General Minh had been the titular leader of the group of army officers who in 1963 overthrew President Diem. He had soon been forced out by his military colleagues and exiled to Bangkok. Bunker considered him politically naive and indecisive, a poor administrator who projected himself as a "peace candidate" eager to end the war by a negotiated settlement. If Minh won in 1971, Bunker forecast, "excessive compromises with the Communists and weak and inefficient government would almost certainly set the stage for a military coup."[37]

Bunker spelled out the implications of his conclusion that the incumbent president was indispensable: "[A] principal objective of U.S. policy in Vietnam over the next ten months should be the reelection of President Thieu and the election to the Lower House of deputies who would support both Thieu's own election efforts and Thieu's policies." To achieve these objectives, Bunker recommended that the United States not publicly intervene in the electoral process but "covertly take certain actions [to] strengthen the electoral chances [of Thieu and his supporters]." [38] The precise actions to be taken, he said, would require careful study.

Bunker had recommended, understandably, that his message be shown in Washington only to Kissinger and a few other senior officials. (In Saigon, it was not seen by embassy political officers who would be responsible for reporting the election campaign.) In April, the State Department advised the embassy that U.S. interest in a fair election should be well advertised. It called the embassy's attention to the strong belief expressed in some quarters, which it did not identify, that "the U.S. Government or at least the U.S. mission in Vietnam prefers the reelection of President Thieu, will support him, and will do little or nothing [to] discourage his rigging of the election." [39] The embassy was soon stressing its neutrality. It issued guidelines to U.S. government personnel in Vietnam to avoid taking sides and Bunker gave a public address in which he stated that the United States did not support any candidate.

While the CIA station in Saigon evidently carried on pro-Thieu covert activities as he had recommended, [40] Bunker did what he could to make the contest appear free and fair. He personally met the leading political players to talk about the electoral process and urge them to behave. When Kissinger visited Saigon in June, Bunker arranged for him to confer with Ky and Minh, in an obvious effort to project an image of U.S. neutrality. When Bunker told Thieu that same month that reports the embassy had received made it clear to him that the GVN was operating the electoral machinery unfairly, the president angrily condemned his opponents for spreading slanderous stories about him. But Bunker did not publicize his dissatisfaction with Thieu, and William Bundy was right in concluding that "to South Vietnamese accustomed to studying him, the way [Bunker] went on dealing calmly and confidently with Thieu carried its own unmistakable message" — that the Americans were supporting the Vietnamese president. [41]

Thieu was in any event widely expected to win. In Bunker's view, the success of the pacification and land reform programs and the general prosperity of the rural areas all helped him. But despite his apparently strong position, Thieu appeared bent on making the contest a two-man race, himself versus Minh, with Ky excluded. He probably reckoned that this would further strengthen his chances of winning the big majority that he wanted. Controversial legislation recently enacted ostensibly to avoid the large number of contenders who had entered the 1967 race required that a candidate obtain a substantial number of endorsements from elected members of the National Assembly or provincial councilmen in order to qualify. To freeze Ky out, Thieu tried to mop up for himself all the available endorsements except the number Minh needed to become eligible. Since Minh repeatedly said that he would withdraw if he thought the contest would not be fair, Thieu's move against Ky and the fixing of the contest that implied meant that the election might turn out to be a one-man race.

Such an election was a nightmare scenario from the administration's — and Bunker's — point of view. It would make a mockery of their claim that democracy was taking root in South Vietnam. American opponents of the war, recently incensed by the publication of the *Pentagon Papers*, would cite it as further evidence of a failed policy of support for an authoritarian, repressive regime. Moreover, Thieu's uncontested election and the way it was brought about could also cause worrisome threats to the political stability of Vietnam.

Despite Thieu's effort to sidetrack him, Ky declared his candidacy. As the vice president struggled to find endorsements, Bunker tried hard to persuade Thieu to drop his blocking maneuvers. He found the president's tactics both stupid and contrary to the spirit of the Vietnamese election law and wrote to Carol about clashing with Thieu in a disagreeable encounter: "I pointed out to [Thieu] that he would overreach himself and destroy himself in the process, that in the present mood of Congress and public opinion, he would make it impossible for us to continue our economic and military aid."[42] The president denied any wrongdoing.

Minh announced his candidacy soon afterwards but stressed that he might later withdraw. Bunker's impression, which was shared by many other foreign observers, was that Minh was designing a scenario that would let him pull out should he conclude that he could not win. Bunker was also convinced that Minh would gladly contest if the Americans would assure him of victory. In fact, both Minh and Ky recognized the stake the Nixon administration had in an election that could be billed as free and honest, and reckoned that their best course was to have the United States pressure Thieu to play fair.

As expected, Ky was unable to obtain the necessary endorsements. Minh, also as expected, had no difficulty in getting them. The fate of the election now depended on him. Bunker was away in the United States for consultations on the secret Paris negotiations, so Minh sought a meeting with Deputy Ambassador Sam Berger, chargé d'affaires in the ambassador's absence. In a long and difficult session, he passed to Berger what he claimed was documentary evidence of Thieu's plan to rig the election, called on the United States to do something to stop this, and remained uncommitted in the face of Berger's urging that he remain a candidate.[43] Soon afterwards, Bunker weighed in with a message from his farm in Vermont to strengthen Berger's plea, asking Minh to refrain from any action that would compromise his candidacy until they could meet on the ambassador's return from the United States the following week.

When he got back to Saigon, Bunker went at once to see Minh. He was accompanied by Richard S. Thompson, an embassy political officer who knew Minh well. After some preliminaries with Minh and one of his lieutenants inside Minh's orchid-covered house, Thompson and Minh's aide were sent outside to the patio. In the private session indoors, Bunker again encouraged Minh to stay in the race. According to Bunker, he asked the general if he had the financial resources needed to wage a successful campaign. Bunker denied subsequent allegations some close to Minh soon made that he had offered Minh $3 million to remain a candidate and that Minh had refused.[44] Bunker conceded, however, that his query about campaign funds might have led Minh's people to conclude that the United States was prepared to put up a large amount of cash to head off a one-man race by Thieu. In a 1999 interview, Thompson told the author that he believed Bunker had offered Minh funds, probably as campaign expenses.[45]

The day after his meeting with Bunker, Minh withdrew. The general claimed that he had pulled out because the election could not be fairly conducted. Bunker was convinced that the real reason was that he believed he could not win unless the Americans intervened in his favor. Minh had in fact suggested earlier to Kissinger and other American officials that the large number of U.S. advisers stationed in Vietnam should be mobilized to monitor the election campaign and the balloting.

The drama of the opposition candidacies still had a few acts to go. The Supreme Court overturned its earlier decision and qualified Ky, but the vice president, disregarding Bunker's plea, then withdrew on grounds that the election would be rigged. According to Ky, Bunker offered to find financing for his campaign.[46] Embassy staff discussed getting the election postponed or the rules changed, and Bunker told Ky that if he withdrew, the election might have to be put off. (Far from persuading Ky to stay in the election, Bunker's suggestion of a postponement was probably a factor in encouraging him to withdraw.) Bunker himself would have preferred postponement, but the White House pulled him back from that position and he made no effort to dissuade Thieu from proceeding.

Minh's decision thus set the stage for the uncontested race the United States had so strongly wanted to avoid and, in Bunker's view, could have been avoided. "If all the individuals concerned—Thieu, Minh and Ky—had had a little more patriotism and less concern with face and pride, a contested election reasonably well run could have been held," he told Carol.[47] "What a missed opportunity for Thieu, who by setting the country on the path of democracy had the chance to become a great man in the history of Vietnam."[48]

Thieu confidently characterized the anticlimactic, now meaningless, election as a referendum on his performance as president. The day before the balloting, Kissinger told Bunker that the badly flawed election would not undermine U.S. support for Thieu. "We have concluded," Kissinger wrote, "that we must keep on our present course. Thieu remains the essential ingredient in the game plan described to you by Haig." He said that Washington was relying heavily on Bunker's leadership in "insuring that there is no maneuvering which might have the effect of encouraging attempts to replace Thieu [and] keeping the most rigid discipline within the U.S. Country Team on this subject." Dwelling on the second point in a way rarely used in discussing embassy staffing, Kissinger told Bunker: "Because of the overriding importance of political stability between now and the turn of the year, the president wishes you to know that he is prepared to support you fully in relieving immediately any member of the Country Team who [sic] you might consider not to be fully supportive of this policy."[49]

Bunker replied that he entirely agreed that Thieu was essential and assured the president that he intended to "maintain discipline within the Country Team and to hold the line here."[50]

When the balloting took place on October 3, Thieu received over 90 percent of the vote. A surprisingly large 78.7 percent of the registered voters went to the polls. As expected, antiwar forces in the United States derided the outcome. They called the election a charade and maintained that the United States had enough influence in Vietnam to have prevented Thieu from turning it into such a farce. The political instability that the embassy had worried about did not materialize, however.[51]

Looking back in 1979 at his experiences, Bunker described his inability to persuade Minh and Ky to contest the election as one of his greatest failures in Vietnam.[52] But in a letter he sent to Carol when it became clear that Thieu would be the sole candidate, he reiterated a theme he had struck before when confronted by political disappointments in his dealings with Vietnamese and other Third World leaders: "I think we need not be too surprised by these developments. We tend to expect too much from under-developed countries, especially where we are heavily involved. We per-suade them to adopt our kind of democratic forms and when they don't function as we think they should, we feel frustrated and rejected." He found a silver lining. "Here at least the Constitution has given them the means for peaceful change and one hears no serious talk of a coup. The military in a short space of four years seems to have become apolitical and wants to steer clear of politics. Nor can we continually arrange things for them in ways that seem best for us. They will have to make their own mis-takes and sort things out for themselves."[53] He took a similar line in his message to Kissinger immediately after the election.[54]

Representative Lester Wolff of New York did not share Bunker's philo-sophical approach. In a September 15 letter, the antiwar Democrat urged President Nixon to fire him. "His weak-kneed approach in representing the U.S. position in Saigon has brought on the farcical election. . . . Ambas-sador Bunker seems to be more concerned with coddling President Thieu than with impressing upon him the seriousness with which the United States regarded the issue of free elections." The State Department sprang to Bunker's defense. The congressman was told that "President Nixon re-cently said that the Ambassador 'has attempted, in every way possible, to get people into the race so that there would be a contested election.' The fact that such an election did not take place cannot, in any sense, be con-sidered a reflection upon the Ambassador's abilities or intentions."[55]

The Nixon administration followed two parallel tracks in its Viet-nam policy. It moved forward with the Vietnamization and pacification programs designed to bring U.S. troops home, turn over responsibility for South Vietnam's defense to the strengthened forces of the ARVN, and as-sure an increasing measure of security to the South Vietnamese popula-tion. At the same time, it sought through secret negotiations to reach an agreement with Hanoi that would lead to a cease-fire, final withdrawal of remaining U.S. forces, release of U.S. prisoners of war, and a settlement between the contending South Vietnamese parties on the political future of the South.

From the time Bunker first became involved in Vietnam policy in 1967, he had been a staunch advocate of Vietnamization and pacification and played an important part in their design and implementation. His role in the secret negotiations was far less central. He did not participate directly in the negotiations with Hanoi representatives that took place intermittently over much of the first Nixon administration. Such a role would have been inappropriate for him as ambassador to Saigon. But he was kept informed about their progress—more than can be said about almost any other American officials aside from those directly involved—and was able in a limited and sporadic way to influence their direction.

The secret discussions began in the summer of 1969 when Kissinger met in Paris with senior Hanoi official Xuan Thuy. By then the "serious," publicized, four-power negotiations that Bunker had worked so hard to persuade Saigon to attend had been going on fitfully for five months. Like the talks in 1968 between the Johnson administration and the North Vietnamese, they had made no progress. Two major differences divided the negotiators. The Communists continued to insist on Thieu's resignation and the virtual dismantling of the Saigon government. They also demanded the withdrawal of all U.S. troops from South Vietnam and were not prepared to discuss the pullback of North Vietnamese armed forces from the South. The U.S.–South Vietnam position called for the eventual total withdrawal of both U.S. and North Vietnamese troops, to be completed at the same time. The United States was already in the process of pulling out 25,000 men, as announced at the Nixon-Thieu meeting at Midway in May.

The talks continued intermittently into 1970 under the leadership of Kissinger and a more senior Hanoi official, politburo member Le Duc Tho, but were suspended when both sides became preoccupied with the fighting in Laos. When they resumed in May 1971, Kissinger used them to table important modifications in the American position. These included the setting of a date for total U.S. withdrawal without a parallel pullout of North Vietnamese forces, provided Hanoi forswore further infiltration of its troops into other Indochinese countries. This went further than the ambiguous hint of possible U.S. acceptance of a continued North Vietnamese presence in the South that Nixon had included in a speech in October 1970.[56] The Kissinger proposals also included a cease-fire throughout Indochina when withdrawals began, guarantees for the future neutral status of Laos and Cambodia, and the settling of the political future of South Vietnam by the South Vietnamese themselves.

But Hanoi continued to insist that Thieu must go, and in the run-up to the 1971 presidential election in the South even suggested that the United States should arrange to get rid of him. When it became clear in August following Minh's withdrawal that Thieu would be reelected, the North Vietnamese broke off the talks. Commenting to Kissinger at the time, Bunker cabled that he had feared that the political situation in the South would lead Hanoi to dig in its heels. "I think they must calculate that Thieu has weakened his position both domestically and abroad, hope that this may become increasingly evident over time, and so are inclined to wait."[57]

In a January 1972 broadcast, Nixon shocked the American public and the world when he revealed for the first time that secret meetings had taken place (twelve by then). He made a new offer, linking the withdrawal of U.S. forces to the release of all prisoners and not to the simultaneous pullout of North Vietnamese troops. He proposed to carry out that total withdrawal within six months of an agreement and the beginning of a ceasefire. Nixon also offered to provide a major reconstruction program for all of Indochina, including North Vietnam, once the war was over. Kissinger had made a similar offer earlier in his private conversations with the North Vietnamese.

Hanoi's launching of a major assault on South Vietnam in the spring of 1972—its Easter Offensive—ruled out any significant progress in the private talks until the military and political outcome of the North Vietnamese attack became clear. The North Vietnamese leadership almost certainly saw the assault primarily as a move that would affect the negotiations sharply in their favor. If Hanoi "inflicted a crushing defeat on the Saigon government army, they could prove the failure of Vietnamization and convince the United States that an agreement on their terms was the only way out."[58]

The Easter Offensive was a defining event in Bunker's Saigon assignment. He believed that it would bring to a moment of resolution the struggles of the past decade. It was for him a critical test for the policies he had recommended and pursued during his five years in the country.

By the time the offensive took place, approximately 500,000 U.S. troops had left Vietnam, along with much of their enormous firepower and support facilities. Of the 70,000 who remained, only 6,000 were combat troops. If the South Vietnamese armed forces were able to turn back Hanoi's all-out drive in the absence of any significant U.S. combat presence on the ground, that would conclusively demonstrate that Vietnamization and pacification had placed the South in a position to defend itself with the aid and support it could reasonably expect from its American ally in a postwar situation. To put it more succinctly, it would mean that the war had been won, as Bunker and the Nixon administration defined winning. Bunker was confident that the ARVN was prepared for the onslaught, which was widely expected to be Hanoi's strongest and most sustained of the war. He forecast that the South Vietnamese forces would give a good account of themselves in the fighting and, with help from U.S. air power, succeed in containing Hanoi's drive.

The Communists struck in three successive waves, committing 120,000 regular NVA troops and thousands of Vietcong guerrillas in a conventional military operation. They staged their most powerful attack against Quang Tri, South Vietnam's northernmost province bordering on the Demilitarized Zone. This three-pronged pincer operation, which included large numbers of Soviet-supplied tanks, artillery, and rockets, led, on May 1, to the fall of the province's capital. In the south, near the Cambodian border northwest of Saigon, the North Vietnamese forces fought a prolonged, bitter battle for An Loc, the capital of Binh Long province, against determined ARVN defenders, whom they encircled for weeks inside the devastated town. The Communists' third wave struck in the central highlands, where they besieged the town of Kontum.

Bunker was visiting Carol in Kathmandu when the offensive began. Hurrying back to Saigon, he remained in frequent touch with Abrams throughout the battle. As their deputies prepared highly classified joint weekly assessments of the progress of the struggle, for clearance by Bunker and Abrams and onward transmission to Washington, Bunker quietly wrote out his own private reports for Carol. They add a valuable personal touch to the official assessments.

His April 7 letter, the first he sent to her following his return to Vietnam, provided a succinct reading of the military and political scene a week after Hanoi struck:

> The situation here is difficult and likely to remain so for a long time, but no different than I had expected. This is bound to be a year of testing for the Vietnamese and for Vietnamization. Hanoi will try to prove that Vietnamization is a failure and that it won't work. They will hope to influence our elections and . . . bring about the collapse of the Saigon government and to influence the negotiations in Paris. Their grand plan is quite clear, to capture Quang Tri and Hue in Military Region One

[in the north], to capture Kontum in the central highlands, to occupy Tay Ninh and Binh Long provinces in Military Region Three, to try to conduct scare attacks in Saigon and then probably to call for a cease-fire and coalition government. But . . . I am not pessimistic. I do not believe they can do this. I think they will eventually be turned back by the combination of the Vietnamese ground forces and our combined air forces, but it may be quite a long process.

As the bloody battles continued along the northern coast, the highlands, and, most dramatically, around An Loc, where Bunker praised the 5,000 men in the town for holding out "in an extraordinary display of heroism and guts," he wrote Carol that Vietnamese forces when well led had fought well. "There have been failures and weak spots but many units have fought heroically. Their [South Vietnamese] air force has performed brilliantly."[59]

He and Abrams met Thieu to discuss shortcomings in command. He reported to Carol that Thieu "took some drastic and much needed action in replacing some of the generals who had turned in inept or lackluster performances, including two of the corps commanders." But the difficulty, he found, "is that in the kind of Mandarin tradition that still persists in this society, the man at the top often is not given the bad news that he needs to know until he is overtaken by events. This has happened to a degree with Thieu and I think he was taken aback when [Abrams] and I laid it all out very clearly to him."[60] He said that Thieu had eventually reacted well, met his commanders, took decisions, and was positive about what had to be done.

At the same time, Bunker welcomed the Vietnamese president's decision to step up mobilization of manpower and joked to Carol that with the draft now extended to age forty-three even his barber would be called up, to the ambassador's mock distress. He also saw in the offensive an opportunity to persuade Thieu to take measures against corruption, which he thought would have a stimulating effect on morale. "But I am not optimistic about this," he said in a letter to Kathmandu, "for I have been trying to do this for years with little success."[61]

The tide of battle eventually turned Saigon's way. On May 8 Nixon announced his decision to counter the offensive by mining North Vietnam's key Haiphong harbor and (for the first time since 1968) bombing targets throughout the North. In the South, massive attacks by B-52 bombers smashed the Communist besiegers of An Loc and Kontum and devastated North Vietnamese army concentrations elsewhere. By the end of June,

Hanoi had lost 400 of its tanks and an estimated 48,000 of their men had been killed or wounded. When the offensive was finally defeated in September with their retreat from Quang Tri, the Communists had suffered more than 100,000 casualties, perhaps 40,000 of them killed (one-fifth of the attacking force), and had lost more than half their tanks and heavy artillery.

Like everyone else, Bunker recognized that the Easter offensive could not have been stopped without the use of U.S. air power. But he approvingly quoted General Abrams's reported comment that it was equally true that even ten times the air power the United States had used would not have held the Communists back if the ARVN had refused to stand and fight.

As the battle entered its second month, Bunker mentioned to Carol that Dean Rusk had written him on the occasion of the fifth anniversary of his becoming ambassador to Vietnam. The secretary, he reported, had told him that much had been accomplished in those years. "It is true," he wrote her, "that a great deal has been achieved, . . . but it is being put to the test, and all the burden in the ground war is being carried by the Vietnamese. It remains to be seen," he continued, "if the system in the South, with its freedom, relative economic prosperity and high living standards but with moral shortcomings of corruption and inequality of sacrifice, has the stamina and will to stand up to the rough, highly disciplined, rigidly controlled northerners."[62]

At the end of the offensive, he was convinced that the test had been passed.

Meanwhile, negotiations continued. A session held in May, when the Communists believed they were on the verge of military victory, reached a complete impasse most noteworthy for the arrogance of the Hanoi representatives. A few days later, Nixon, announcing his decision to mine Haiphong harbor and bomb throughout the North, disclosed the latest U.S. negotiating position. He now called for a standstill cease-fire (making more explicit the concession that North Vietnamese forces need not withdraw), release of prisoners, and total American withdrawal within four months, the shortest deadline for a pullout ever offered. As in earlier American proposals, a political settlement would be left to the South Vietnamese parties themselves, to be worked out following the cease-fire and withdrawal.

Productive rounds of secret talks resumed in July and August, when it had become clear to Hanoi that its hopes for a decisive military victory in the South had been dashed. In these talks, two major issues remained unresolved. Hanoi was unwilling to agree to a cease-fire before negotiations began among the South Vietnamese on the country's political future. It also adamantly opposed the Thieu government's remaining in power while these negotiations took place. But in further talks in September that followed the final defeat of the North's offensive, the Hanoi representatives expressed a new willingness to make concessions on these key issues and other divisive problems. This set the stage for a climactic four days of negotiations the following month, leading to a breakthrough on October 12, when a text was finally hammered out exactly four years after the breakthrough that led to a bombing halt in the last months of the Johnson administration.

The October draft represented a major retreat from the positions the North Vietnamese had persistently held since the United States became involved in the war. The draft's overarching approach was to differentiate between military and political issues, a concept Kissinger had first proposed before he joined the Nixon administration. On the military side, the agreement provided for a cease-fire followed by the total withdrawal within sixty days of all U.S. and other allied troops from South Vietnam. The return of prisoners of war was to be completed when the last remaining American forces were withdrawn. There was no provision for the simultaneous withdrawal of North Vietnamese troops from the South, a demand the U.S. had long since abandoned. (Kissinger argued that the ban on the introduction of replacement troops into the South and other provisions of the agreement would lead to the eventual atrophying of the North's forces there.) The United States and North Vietnam were allowed to provide arms to the South Vietnamese parties, but only to replace those already supplied.

On the political side, the Hanoi negotiators finally agreed that Thieu and his government could remain in place. The Saigon government and the Vietcong Provisional Revolutionary Government (PRG) were enjoined to respect the cease-fire in place and to settle all contentious matters through negotiations. A joint GVN-PRG body and an international commission were to be set up to supervise the truce. Saigon and the PRG were to hold consultations to set up a Council of National Reconciliation and Concord, a three-sided body (Saigon, the PRG, and a group of neutrals chosen by each) whose carefully circumscribed powers did not include governmental authority. Elections to decide the political future of the country were to be held under international supervision. Other provisions included undertakings to respect the neutrality of Cambodia and Laos and U.S. economic assistance to the Indochinese countries, including North Vietnam.

Although its defeat in the Easter Offensive obviously influenced Hanoi's thinking, the most crucial element in its decision to adopt a more compromising position was almost certainly its perception of the evolving U.S. presidential election campaign. This factor explains the sudden change in the North Vietnamese negotiating position in September and, even more, in October. So long as there was a chance, in Hanoi's view, of a victory by Democratic candidate George McGovern, North Vietnam had every incentive to wait out the election. The positions McGovern took on the Vietnam issue in his campaign met Hanoi's military and political demands. However, by late summer it had become clear even as far away as Hanoi that by all polling and other indices Nixon was headed for a landslide victory in the November voting.

This led the North Vietnamese to fundamentally recalculate their position. They now figured, mistakenly, that Nixon and Kissinger would be eager to reach a settlement before the election in order to expand the president's margin and make his victory even more certain. According to this calculation, the American side would be prepared to be more flexible in its negotiating position. Conversely, the North Vietnamese may also have reckoned that a Nixon reelected for four more years, with no need ever to face another election, would become even tougher in his dealings with them. They were fully familiar with his willingness to take punishing action against them and may well have concluded that it would be best to come to an agreement before they had to deal with an uninhibited postelection Nixon who would owe them nothing.

Thieu had been kept generally informed about the progress of the talks. He is said to have been troubled when he recognized that Kissinger was not passing him substantive detail.[63] His government had participated marginally at best in the working up of negotiating positions. But it was largely unaware of the terms of the draft agreement, which had been reached by the Americans and the North Vietnamese alone, until Kissinger showed Thieu the completed text. It was now up to him, backed by Nixon and assisted by Bunker, to persuade the president and his colleagues to accept it.

Bunker had been informed about the existence of the secret talks from the time they began in 1969. Summaries of the talks were sent to him in Saigon, and he was instructed to share an abbreviated version of them with Thieu, who had agreed to the secret sessions at the Midway conference a couple of months before they began. Bunker also received transcripts of some of the earlier exchanges, and Kissinger briefed him when they met in Washington and elsewhere.

Bunker was at least partly in the loop long before almost everyone else not directly involved. According to Kissinger, Secretary of State Rogers was not told of the talks until well into 1971. Thus, Kissinger noted, "we had the curious result that [two] ambassadors [Bunker and David Bruce, head of the delegation to the formal Paris talks] knew more than their nominal chief."[64] Peter Rodman, a key member of Kissinger's NSC negotiating team in the secret talks, has recalled that "Bunker was clued in to almost everything. . . . For Henry, it was extraordinary. He was still at the White House and didn't trust a lot of the [State] Department or most ambassadors. . . . Bunker was an exception. . . . Every time we had a meeting Bunker got a report and advice on what to communicate with Thieu."[65] According to Rodman, only when the negotiations moved forward quickly, as they did in September and October 1972, were Bunker (and Thieu) not kept current. Kissinger himself has acknowledged that the summaries provided Bunker were sometimes "quite selective."[66]

Charles Whitehouse, Bunker's deputy in Saigon when the secret talks reached their climax in 1972, remembered that he and the ambassador both thought they were being told very little. What was not very good got worse in October, he recalled.[67] In Whitehouse's view, Bunker was not happy with this arrangement, but was reluctant to make a fuss about it. He never requested additional information about the talks. This was not because he believed he was getting the full story (which he knew he was not) but because he felt the secret exchanges were a Kissinger operation in which he had only a secondary role. Bunker's chief of staff Charles Hill recalled that for Bunker the most important thing was to do his own job, and not try to get into—or even follow closely—what Kissinger was up to with the North Vietnamese.[68]

Aside from keeping Thieu generally informed of what was going on in the talks and reporting his reactions, Bunker, like other ambassadors in similar situations, was expected to make U.S. actions and proposals as attractive to his host government as he realistically could. He took on his briefing and advocacy responsibilities with his usual care and determination. His files include many examples of the detailed "talking points," based on instructions from Washington, that he would dictate in advance to his secretary Eva Kim for use with the South Vietnamese president in interpreting the U.S. case as persuasively as possible.

Kissinger also asked Bunker for assessments of what Thieu could be brought to accept, how best his acquiescence could be won, and, as negotiations with the South Vietnamese became more difficult, how far Washington should go in twisting his arm. Bunker was "our conscience in U.S. dealings with Thieu," Kissinger recalled telling him in Nixon's presence at a strategy session in Hawaii in August 1972. "If you think this [proposed approach on a negotiated settlement] is unreasonable, we'll change it."[69] How sincere that pledge was is at best questionable.

The part Bunker played in the ticklish and frustrating effort to bring Thieu to accept the proposals Washington and Hanoi had worked out was more limited than his role four years earlier during the Johnson administration's hurried pre-election efforts to persuade the GVN to take part in the Paris negotiations. Unlike October–November 1968, Bunker was often superseded now as chief American contact with Thieu by emissaries from Washington, either Kissinger himself or his NSC deputy, General Alexander Haig. This practice reflected Kissinger's style of operating. It was probably also prompted by Nixon and Kissinger's sense that Thieu could be more readily won over by someone with White House authority who was more intimately involved than Bunker with the twists and turns of the secret negotiations with Hanoi. It did not indicate any lack of confidence in their ambassador in Saigon.

Bunker would occasionally offer advice, usually in response to a specific request, that went beyond ideas about the handling of Thieu and his government. His suggestions ordinarily concerned tactics and appear to have been given serious consideration. His views on broader policy had scant if any influence and he rarely offered them. To the extent that he was aware of them, he seems for the most part to have gone along with the evolving positions Nixon and Kissinger set forth in the secret talks and elsewhere to bring about a negotiated settlement. But he did not play a significant part in shaping them.

His role in the peace process hinged importantly on the relationship he developed with Kissinger both before the negotiations reached their crucial phase in the second half of 1972 and during those last promising but frustrating months. By all accounts, most notably his own, Kissinger continued to think highly of Bunker and to afford him a respect he gave few other ambassadors and senior Foreign Service officers. Without that respect, Bunker is likely to have been largely sidelined much as other ambassadors and senior officials often were by the domineering national security adviser. In an unusually long and admiring tribute in *White House Years*, Kissinger wrote that Bunker "was one of our great diplomats. . . . His values were reflected not in self-serving rhetoric but in the matter-of-fact performance of a high standard of duty. He was a quintessential American in the optimism that made him appear youthful even then [1972], in his late seventies. . . . He performed his chores with gentleness, discipline, and selfless skill."[70]

Officials who worked closely with Kissinger and Bunker attest that the passage genuinely reflected Kissinger's affection and admiration for a man so different in background and style from himself. Charles Hill, who had a front-row seat as the two men interacted in Saigon, maintains that Kissinger was in awe of Bunker in a strange way. "He seemed to Kissinger . . . an unreal specter from the past, . . . an antique figure, American in a primeval way." Kissinger was feared by everyone, Hill recalled, and blew people away. "Bunker couldn't be blown away."[71] Anthony Lake remembered that Kissinger always spoke of Bunker with great respect. "Respect," Lake observed, "was not an outstanding characteristic of Kissinger." But like others, Lake questioned how important Bunker's opinions about Vietnam policy were to Kissinger other than as support for positions he had already developed.[72]

Bunker also had high regard for Kissinger. Although he recognized that Kissinger's style was a major problem in the national security adviser's dealings with Thieu, who came to dislike and distrust him thoroughly, Bunker had high praise for his negotiating skills, conceptual brilliance, vitality, and courage. He enjoyed Kissinger's nervous pomposity and saturnine sense of humor, and had a calm and bemused attitude toward his antics. He was able to work well with Kissinger, as he had with a long string of assertive, unorthodox, and difficult personalities, American and foreign.

It became clear in August 1972 that Thieu could become a major obstacle to a peace settlement. Earlier, he had seemingly gone along with the concessions the Nixon administration made publicly and in the secret talks. The stubbornly negative and, to the Americans, dangerously unhelpful attitude he adopted in mid-1972 toward major elements of the projected compromise agreement was a direct reaction to the softening of Hanoi's long-standing positions on key unresolved elements in the negotiation agenda and the consequent possibility that the talks might actually lead to a settlement. It was one thing for Thieu to take an accommodating line with the Americans during the years when the talks seemed to him, and many others, a lengthy exercise in futility. It was quite another once he recognized that they could produce an agreement that would involve the total withdrawal of U.S. forces from South Vietnam and the continuing presence there of substantial numbers of North Vietnamese troops. His earlier assent was likely "an expedient that appeared to involve no risk, as long as there seemed no possibility that the Communists would meet American terms."[73]

Bunker knew well and had called to Washington's attention the nervousness of Thieu and other anticommunist South Vietnamese when they contemplated political competition with the better disciplined Communists following a peace agreement and the end of the American military presence in the country. He had tried over the years to build up their self-confidence and advocated and implemented policies and programs to bolster it. He recognized Thieu's concern about the prospect of North Vietnamese forces remaining in the South, even though the president had not objected to this major concession when Nixon and Kissinger had offered it in increasingly explicit terms.

Bunker had had problems with the idea himself. In April 1971, asked for his views on a package of terms that the U.S. negotiating team was considering using in the next round of talks, he sent Kissinger a two-step strategy that included total withdrawal of North Vietnamese forces from South Vietnam, Cambodia, and Laos. This should take place, in Bunker's proposal, within six months of the completion of the withdrawal of U.S. troops.[74]

Kissinger had rejected this approach. He cabled Bunker: "We will say [to the North Vietnamese] that [the] peoples of Indochina should discuss this question among themselves but we will not set [a] date."[75] Bunker accepted the revised language but does not appear to have recognized at the time how important the change was or how the softening of the U.S. position in secret, exploratory talks would later lead to a settlement leaving Hanoi's army in full force in South Vietnam. He recalled, accurately, that he had not alerted Thieu to that aspect of the proposals.[76]

In any event, there is no available evidence that he contested the White House decision at any time. He appeared content with the deliberately imprecise language on North Vietnamese military withdrawal that Kissinger crafted, and he repeatedly passed it on without protest to Washington or warning to Thieu. Charles Hill was no doubt correct when he wrote: "Bunker never wavered from his view that the U.S. had an obligation to help bring about the departure of the North Vietnamese army. The fact was, however, that this could not be achieved through a negotiated agreement."[77] Like others in Saigon and Washington who dealt with the issue, Bunker recognized that public and congressional opinion at home and the huge unilateral reduction by the United States of its forces in Vietnam ruled out any negotiated settlement that specifically mandated North Vietnamese troop withdrawal from the South. As he told an interviewer on the eve of his final departure from Saigon in May 1973, "One cannot hope to win at the conference table more than one has won on the field."[78]

Bunker had misgivings about North Vietnamese forces remaining in the South and knew that Thieu was similarly troubled at that prospect. But neither he nor anyone else on the U.S. side seems to have seriously suspected before Hanoi began to make major concessions that the South Vietnamese government would go so far as to refuse to accept a U.S.–North Vietnamese draft agreement based on terms to which it had already consented. However, by mid-August 1972, when Kissinger visited Saigon to review the negotiations with Thieu, Bunker had come to recognize that potentially serious problems were developing. These involved more than North Vietnamese troops in the South or the mandate and composition of an unworkable tripartite body that would play some meaningless role in a political settlement, two matters that Thieu would make key sticking points in opposing the terms of the settlement Kissinger was working out with Hanoi. As Kissinger wrote of his arrival in Saigon on August 17:

> Ambassador Ellsworth Bunker greeted me . . . unflappable as ever. He was convinced that Thieu felt stronger than ever but also that his new-found strength would make him more recalcitrant. Thieu thought that South Vietnam had the upper hand militarily; concessions to which he had agreed in less promising times appeared senseless to him now. He seemed, according to Bunker, genuinely afraid of peace. All his life, he too had known only war; his entire career had been based on American support. A world in which the South Vietnamese would have to stand entirely on their own was full of terrors that his pride would not let him admit.[79]

The ensuing discussions Kissinger had with Thieu quickly showed that Bunker was right. Thieu dug in his heels. To quote the exasperated Kissinger again, "With serious negotiations approaching, his views and ours began increasingly to diverge. . . . He was looking for a retroactive justification to undo the negotiating record of the past three years."[80] The talks proved fruitless and ended on a rancorous note. At a strategy session in Hawaii a few weeks later, Bunker reiterated an impression he had long held: the South Vietnamese "fear that they are not yet well enough organized to compete politically with such a tough disciplined organization [as the Communists]."[81]

Kissinger had instructed Bunker to keep in close contact with Thieu—instructions he hardly needed but which became increasingly difficult to carry out as the Vietnamese president deliberately sought to avoid meeting him. In an assessment he sent Washington on September 16, Bunker stressed that the time had come to be tough with Thieu. "I think we have been understanding and very forbearing in deferring to his views and I believe that we should now be firm in making clear that we also have imperatives."[82] In meetings with Thieu that month Bunker chided him for his negative public comments on the U.S.–North Vietnam negotiations and for his assertion that "Anglo-Saxon pragmatism" seemed to guide the American approach. "Had we wished to be pragmatic," he told Thieu, "we could have settled the war at any time during the last three and a half years. On the contrary, we had supported the GVN at the sacrifice of many American lives as well as treasure because we were deeply committed to the principle of nonaggression and to the search for an honorable peace."[83]

But as he had in 1968 and on many other occasions, Bunker called for a more patient approach to the GVN. We had been going too fast, he wrote, and undue speed could be harmful in dealing with someone of Thieu's suspicious nature.

The first thing we should do, if it can be done in consonance with our strategy between now and the [November U.S. presidential] election, is to slow the pace, to give the GVN more time in which to consider our proposals and to give us more time for persuasion and argument. We clearly cannot be in a position of permitting them to call the tune; we must be firm, but at the same time not let them get the impression that we are attempting to force the pace. We must also not let them paint themselves into a corner as they did in 1968. I think that what will be needed is more painstaking explanation and persuasion, while at the same time letting them know we have our own imperatives which we intend to follow and which indeed are essential if they expect our support.[84]

It was vintage Bunker.

The eagerness of the North Vietnamese to reach a settlement before the elections proved far more telling in determining the pace of the negotiations than did Bunker's advice about taking time to persuade the South Vietnamese. As noted, Kissinger achieved a breakthrough with the North Vietnamese in Paris on October 12. After a brief further round there a few days later to iron out some remaining minor issues, he went to Saigon with the draft in hand to try to bring Thieu along. The South Vietnamese had not seen the text until he showed it to them, in its English version, following his arrival. Nor had Kissinger kept them, or Bunker, more than sketchily informed of what had been going on during the crucial four days of Paris talks preceding agreement. Bunker had been unhappy with this silence. He feared, with good reason, that "with so little of substance to report concerning the developments of four days of meetings, Thieu's apprehensions, not to say suspicions, will be aroused."[85] In response, he was sent only a very limited report for use with Thieu.

Bunker worked closely with Kissinger in the doomed U.S.–South Vietnamese discussions that followed. His good relations with Thieu, which he had cultivated for five years, did not spare him from the angry outbursts and rude behavior of the Vietnamese president and his colleagues. In many respects, it was for him a repeat of 1968: Thieu's unavailability on the flimsiest of pretexts; lengthy, casually explained delays in meetings when they did take place; emotional and vituperative Vietnamese charges of U.S. bad faith and double dealing; the drawing in of other GVN officials as a device to hold up progress. Even Bunker's legendary patience was tried and—for the first time in the recollection of his colleagues—found wanting when he lost his temper after one too many deliberate slights.

But by then he could not have been surprised when, despite his and Kissinger's concerted effort, another deadlock occurred. On the eve of the breakthrough in the Paris talks, he had delivered to Thieu a message from Nixon expressing extraordinary disappointment with GVN reaction to U.S. negotiating proposals and strategy. Thieu had said nothing in that meeting that suggested any change in the GVN's earlier position.[86] A few days later, Bunker forecast what was coming in a letter he sent to Carol while Kissinger was still negotiating in Paris. "I sense increasing nervousness here over the possibility of some agreement between us and the DRV [Democratic Republic of Vietnam, i.e., North Vietnam], which the Vietnamese think they are not ready for, and with which they won't be able to cope. What they fear most is an in-place cease-fire, leaving the enemy in a sizeable number of hamlets and villages, and the political confrontation which would follow, admitting that the Nationalists outnumber the NLF [National Liberation Front] nine or ten to one, but fearful that they haven't the political organization or cohesion for the contest."[87] He found himself reading over memoranda relating to the 1968 negotiations and reported to Kissinger the day after the breakthrough in Paris that he feared a similar situation was developing. "What we see now has a somewhat ominous tone of history repeating itself. I have been trying to get the message across to Thieu that this is no longer acceptable and I think he probably accepts this fact intellectually, but not emotionally; that he thinks a reversion to low level warfare . . . will put him in a position to make a better settlement a year or two from now."[88]

Following the failure of Kissinger's Saigon mission, Nixon instructed Bunker to meet Thieu every day to persuade him that unless he made concessions, political realities at home would make it impossible for the United States to continue to support South Vietnam. This mirrored the line Kissinger had taken with Thieu earlier. Although Thieu had angrily rejected the draft agreement in an October 24 speech, Bunker continued his efforts to bring him to a more accommodating position. As he had in 1968, he tried to convince Thieu that it was in his own interest to participate in the U.S. initiative.

Kissinger's instructions to Bunker were to avoid a public break with Thieu before the upcoming U.S. elections. He used very tough language on this point. "Between now and [Election Day] November 7, we are posed with a most delicate problem. Before November 7, we cannot brutalize Thieu to the point that he will kick over the traces and undertake a public confrontation and break with us. . . . After November 7 full leverage will be applied."[89]

Bunker wove his arguments skillfully, but he was trying to reason with a man who was afraid of peace or at least convinced that the Communists would betray any peace agreement. Bunker stressed—quite accurately— that he was speaking to the president as a friend and admirer who had supported him throughout his time as ambassador to Vietnam. He urged him to maintain a posture of flexibility and avoid the GVN's being singled out in the United States and elsewhere as the sole remaining obstacle to peace.

Bunker also warned Thieu about the danger of a confrontation between Saigon and Washington if he continued to resist signing on.

Bunker tried to allay Thieu's concerns regarding provisions in the agreement that the president claimed were most difficult for him to accept, especially the continuing postwar presence in South Vietnam of North Vietnamese forces and the powers, composition, and nomenclature of the proposed Council of National Reconciliation and Concord. Bunker highlighted the military superiority of the GVN, noting that it had some 1.1 million men under arms as compared to around 143,000 North Vietnamese troops in the South. This disparity would be widened by the agreement's provisions prohibiting replacement of troops who return to North Vietnam, closing the Laotian and Cambodian borders, and barring further infiltration into the South. But he was disingenuous in telling Thieu that Kissinger would take up with the other side the issue of the withdrawal of North Vietnam forces and in asserting that "whether or not this could be resolved to his [Thieu's] satisfaction was difficult to say."[90] Bunker knew full well that Hanoi would not accept such a major change in the draft agreement. Nixon finally put the matter to rest when he told Thieu in January that the United States had become convinced that the North Vietnamese would hold to this position. He assured Thieu that there were so many collateral clauses that impacted on the issue that the continued presence of North Vietnamese troops and introduction of new forces would violate the agreement.[91] In the event most of these provisions proved unenforceable.

In discussing the projected council, Bunker stressed the provisions that made that tripartite body essentially powerless. Any changes in the wording of the Vietnamese text that was needed to clarify this would be made.[92] He urged that Thieu tell his people that the Saigon government was not being dissolved, as the Communists had demanded for so long. Saigon had won, not lost, and Hanoi had given up the political demands it had insisted on during four years of warfare. Bunker also tried to make clear to Thieu the penalties South Vietnam would face if it did not maintain a common front with the United States. If that were to happen, Washington would be unable to continue its support should the other side violate the agreement after U.S. forces had left the country.[93]

Kissinger had at first tried to obfuscate the cause of the delay in moving toward a final settlement with Hanoi. But following Saigon's rejection of the draft, the North Vietnamese published a summary of the text agreed to in Paris in the expectation that this would put pressure on the American side. Kissinger's effort in a celebrated Washington press conference two days later to justify his actions ("peace is at hand") and reassure the North Vietnamese went over well at home but masked the difficulties that lay ahead.

Soon afterwards, to Bunker's great satisfaction, Nixon defeated the Democratic "peace candidate" George McGovern by a huge margin. Bunker regarded Senator McGovern and his views on a Vietnam settlement with utter contempt. They were for him a shameful sellout of American interests and commitments, a "prescription for disaster."[94]

He sent an effusive message of congratulations to the White House that demonstrated once again that for a man who projected the image of a dignified New England Yankee, Bunker could be almost embarrassingly fervid in hailing his leaders' accomplishments: "This has been a great day for the American Mission in Vietnam, civilian and military. We are overjoyed by the overwhelming endorsement of the President and his policies and are heartened by the fact that the great majority of American people have thus registered their approval of his courage and his integrity. It gives us faith in America as well."[95]

The outcome of the congressional elections must have been less to Bunker's liking. It showed an increase in the number of members determined to end U.S. involvement in Vietnam on minimally honorable terms (namely, withdrawal of American troops in exchange for the release of POWs).

Well before his reelection, Nixon had provided Thieu concrete evidence of the support the United States would give Vietnam following a peace agreement. He authorized the large-scale shipment to South Vietnam of military equipment, initially items to replace those lost in repulsing Hanoi's Easter Offensive (the Enhance program), later even more massive deliveries, including sophisticated aircraft, that greatly expanded the South's arsenal both qualitatively and quantitatively (Enhance Plus). This buildup also substantially raised the basis for calculating the allowable replacement of arms, ammunition, and other military material in Saigon's pre-agreement stocks—which the draft agreement itself permitted. These programs, very much in line with what Bunker had urged in pushing Vietnamization over the years, were useful to him as he tried to bolster Thieu's confidence in South Vietnam's postwar military position.

In a series of secret messages, Nixon also sought to reassure Thieu that the United States did not intend to turn its back on South Vietnam following a peace agreement. In *The Palace File*, Nguyen Tien Hung and Jerrold Schecter have reproduced twenty-one letters that Nixon sent in the thirteen months leading to the signing of the Paris Accords in January 1973. Bunker personally delivered almost all of these messages and was one of a handful of American officials fully aware of their contents.

The most sensitive — and important — of Nixon's assurances was his specific pledge to Thieu that the United States would forcefully intervene should Hanoi violate the terms of the proposed agreement. Nixon offered this commitment most definitively in a letter he sent Thieu on November 14, 1972. In it he declared: "You have my absolute assurance that if Hanoi fails to abide by the terms of this agreement it is my intention to take swift and severe retaliatory action. . . . I repeat my personal assurances to you that the United States will react very strongly and rapidly to any violation of the agreement."[96] Bunker welcomed these assurances and wove them into his discussions with Thieu. He believed they were the inducement that eventually brought the South Vietnamese to sign the Paris agreement.

Supported by Nixon's volley of letters to Thieu, which combined promises of support if Thieu accepted the U.S. position and threats of dire consequences if he did not, Bunker tried throughout November and early December to move the South Vietnamese forward and to block unhelpful statements and countermoves on their part that further angered Nixon and threatened to upset the draft agreement. These included a Thieu reference to the agreement as a "surrender document" and a demand for an electoral commission elected in a vote conducted by the United Nations. Under this plan, the composition of the government subsequently formed would reflect the contesting parties' vote.[97] Bunker ruefully told Washington that Thieu's playing on the psychological climate in South Vietnam — "fear of the communists, distrust of the Americans, and apprehension regarding the future" — had brought about greater unity under his leadership than at any time since November 1968. This made progress even more difficult, though Bunker still forecast that Thieu would eventually concur.[98]

In mid-November Alexander Haig again came to Saigon to underscore and strengthen Bunker's efforts. But Thieu continued to balk. He submitted sixty-nine changes that he demanded be made to the draft agreement text. Bunker organized and took part in a U.S.-GVN six-man task force to review the draft and deal with Saigon's problems with it. This group made minimal progress, as the Vietnamese representatives repeated Thieu's 1968 performance and came up with one problem after another.

Bunker soon wrote in exasperation to Kissinger: "It seems to me we have reached that point where we have given the Vietnamese the resources to do the job, that the draft agreement you have worked out gives them the opportunity, and that we have discharged our responsibilities. It is up to them to make it possible for us to support them."[99] Concluding that Thieu would prefer to fight on for two or three years with U.S. support in the hope that the points he was insisting on would eventually be obtained, Bunker urged Kissinger to establish a time frame for the negotiations. In his judgment, Thieu "will decide to go with us when [the time frame] is made clear to him and he realizes there is no viable alternative."[100] He will follow the course that will ensure continued U.S. support, but it was "essential that [he] be made to understand clearly what our limits are. . . . [He] will probably continue to play his old game of waiting until the last minute to decide which way to jump—but, as he has always done, he will opt for survival."[101]

Meanwhile Hanoi, angered at what it suspected was Washington-Saigon connivance, also became tough. It not only turned down the proposed changes, which Kissinger had conveyed to the North Vietnamese in the resumed Paris talks. It also reneged on some of the provisions it had agreed to earlier and made fresh demands. By mid-December the deadlock was complete. Peace no longer seemed at hand.

Aware that weakening support for his Vietnam policy on Capitol Hill would further erode when the new Congress convened in January, Nixon moved dramatically to break the stalemate. On December 18, U.S. B-52s began intensive, sustained attacks on North Vietnam. Soon dubbed the Christmas Bombing, these raids were targeted particularly against military facilities in Hanoi and the port city of Haiphong. Most analysts agree that in ordering them Nixon had two purposes: to frighten the North Vietnamese into submission and to offer Thieu a foretaste of what the United States would do should Hanoi violate the peace agreement. Bunker had been told that drastic action was being contemplated by the White House. He does not appear to have been asked for his opinion, which almost certainly would have been to go ahead.

After ten days of bombing, the North Vietnamese climbed down, sending word on December 29 that they were prepared to renew negotiations.

The raids were then stopped. U.S. and North Vietnamese representatives agreed on a slightly revised text in Paris on January 13 after five days of talks.[102] Nonetheless, Thieu remained adamant. He had been impressed, however, by a further pledge of postwar support from Nixon, spelled out in the final paragraph of a letter delivered by Bunker on January 6. This stated, "Should you decide, as I trust you will, to go with us, you have my assurance of continued assistance in the post-settlement period and that we will respond with full force should the settlement be violated by North Vietnam."[103] William Bundy has concluded that "in the light of the Christmas bombing, the phrase 'full force' clearly strengthened the earlier general promise, implying unmistakably that U.S. military action would be on a similar scale and for whatever length of time might be needed."[104] Interestingly, especially in light of Bundy's comment, the phrase was Bunker's, added at his suggestion to the original text the White House cabled him for delivery to Thieu.[105]

Thieu fought on despite reassurances, blandishments, clarifications, and threats conveyed in letters from Nixon and in person by Bunker and Haig. In a December 30 cable, Bunker forecast: ". . . Thieu will follow the course which will assure him continued U.S. support. But he will continue to procrastinate, temporize and play for time until he is finally brought up against the moment of decision. Until the moment we are ready to say we are definitely going to sign the agreement, with or without him, he will hold off."[106] Nixon made it very clear in a letter he sent Thieu on January 17 that he was prepared to do just that. In the message, Nixon also said that the only alternative to GVN acceptance was a total cutoff of U.S. assistance.[107]

Thieu finally gave up on January 21. Although the letter he handed to Bunker accepting the agreement was argumentative, Bunker reported that the president "made no[further] comment except to say that he had done his best and all that he could do for his country. He appeared resigned but not unfriendly."[108]

Two days later Kissinger and Le Duc Tho initialed the agreement, which was formally signed in Paris on January 27, 1973.

Although he recognized the shortcomings of the Paris agreement and must have foreseen, as many others did, that some of its key provisions could not be enforced, Bunker was convinced that the accord was a reasonable one under the circumstances. Impressed as he was by the economic progress, military strength, and political stability South Vietnam had achieved during the five and a half years he had been ambassador, he did not regard the accord as a stopgap measure that would merely provide a reasonable interval for the United States to salve its conscience before South Vietnam inevitably fell to the Communists. Instead, he was confident that if the United States continued to support South Vietnam as it had promised to do—sending it substantial economic and military aid and remaining prepared to intervene "with full force" should North Vietnam significantly violate the terms of the agreement—the country would survive and could even flourish. "Vietnamization has succeeded," he wrote a few months later. "With continued economic and military aid, we will have done everything that can be reasonably expected of us to ensure the South Vietnamese their political and military independence."[109] That, he argued, had always been America's objective in undertaking its intervention in Vietnam.

The final three and a half months of Bunker's Saigon assignment that followed the signing of the peace agreement must have seemed something of an anticlimax to him after the momentous events leading up to it. But he remained as active and involved as ever. He supervised changes in the U.S. mission that reflected the new situation on the ground following the withdrawal of the last American forces and the closing of MACV. He received Vice President Spiro Agnew in Saigon and accompanied Thieu on a visit to San Clemente and Washington. And he and the mission continued to cable Washington detailed reports of political and military developments.[110]

During this period of frequent cease-fire violations by both sides, which he described on March 30 as "neither peace nor war," Bunker's efforts to improve matters again led to difficult sessions with Thieu. As Arnold Isaacs has written, "Thieu was utterly distrustful of the agreement and of the Communists . . . [and] apparently saw his military advantage as large but temporary, an asset that must be used before it evaporated. His objective after the Paris agreement was exactly what it had been before: the destruction of his Communist enemy."[111] Bunker forcefully pressed Thieu to issue unambiguous commands to his troops to cease all offensive activities, warning him that unless he took strong and clear action to enforce the cease-fire the GVN would lose support in Congress for adequate assistance to South Vietnam. He also called on Thieu to adopt a more cooperative attitude toward the Communist members of the Joint Military Commissions set up to enforce the cease-fire and other provisions of the

Paris agreement.[112] He believed that he had achieved some success on both these fronts.

He was less successful in his efforts to promote progress toward the political settlement envisaged in the agreement. Thieu eventually agreed to hold elections for a body empowered to decide the future of South Vietnam, as demanded by the PRG, rather than a presidential election under the GVN constitution that the Communists were aware they could not win. But he also insisted that North Vietnam withdraw its armed forces from the South before the election, a position that Thieu knew was unacceptable to Hanoi. A few years later, in discussing Vietnam following the cease-fire, Bunker observed that Thieu's most important mistake was his failure to go to elections right after the Paris agreement was signed. He was convinced that the GVN would have won a substantial victory. Given among other factors the superior political organization Thieu had at that time, he is probably right.[113]

Bunker's final report to President Nixon, sent on May 5, 1973, was somber. "[T]here is still no cease-fire and no visible movement toward a political settlement," he found, "[and] the hope many Vietnamese expressed last January that perhaps the long war was coming to an end has given way to resigned acceptance of a situation which is neither war nor peace." He speculated that what was happening was "the slow working out of a balance of forces which, once achieved, could lead to a stable cease-fire." But now, he told Nixon, the cease-fire was at a critical point, and unless a determined effort were made soon the situation could gradually deteriorate into large-scale fighting.

Bunker found Thieu's political position in some respects stronger than ever. His administrative-security apparatus controlled most of the country, and the Communists had made no headway since the cease-fire in changing the situation. The noncommunist opposition was stymied by Thieu's recent restrictions on their political activity and on the press and handicapped by the absence of another leader capable of replacing him. But Bunker found potential dangers beneath the surface calm. No cure had been found for Vietnam's endemic factionalism, nor had corruption been effectively tackled. "The Communists will do their utmost to exploit these deep-seated flaws, using a combination of military pressure and political agitation," he warned. He concluded this final message with a call for continuing U.S. involvement: "I feel confident . . . that if we do all we can to deter Hanoi from again seeking a military solution while at the same time encouraging the GVN to negotiate with the other side in a spirit of compromise and reconciliation, peace will finally come to Vietnam." [114]

Bunker left Vietnam for the last time on May 12, 1973, his seventy-ninth birthday. His departure prompted much journalistic comment about his record since 1967, his personality, and his diplomatic style. The over-all thrust of the articles reflected to some extent the editorial positions of the publications—Fox Butterfield, an admirer of Bunker, told him that his editors had made him rewrite his long piece in the antiwar *New York Times* twice before they would publish it. [115] But most of the assessments were fairly well balanced in citing Bunker's accomplishments and short-comings.

The discussions of Bunker's character were often very insightful. The Saigon correspondent of the *Economist* was very much on the mark in writing: "[Bunker's] dignity and politeness went together with a very cool sort of toughness. . . . If he writes his memoirs, it will come as no surprise to find that he believed entirely in the policy he was charged with carrying out." [116]

Peter Osnos also had it right in his discussion of "Bunker's art" in the *Washington Post*. "To some extent, it was his manner. He seemed an un-flappable man, brisk in the wilting afternoon sun and just as cool in the heat of events. No matter how badly things seemed to be going at any moment and no matter what his private anxiety over the state of military affairs or his personal discouragement with political events, Bunker con-cealed his dismay. . . . This special skill enabled [him] to keep the lid on through a series of crises." [117]

The syndicated columnist Charles Bartlett expanded on this theme. Bunker had left Saigon like Tennyson's Ulysses, he wrote, "strong in will to strive, to seek, to find, and not to yield." He had succeeded with the South Vietnamese "largely because they respected his age, integrity, and stubbornness. He avoided giving orders, but he kept talking to them until they shared his comprehension of the alternatives. He was dealing with excitable people sometimes dismayed by his unflappable poise, but he mel-lowed them with his humanism, friendly respect, and good manners." [118]

Bunker's departure from Saigon's Than Son Nhut airport on a U.S. Air Force plane bound for Kathmandu was a very special occasion.

Carol had come from Nepal to share his last few days in Saigon and participate in the many farewell functions that marked the completion of his assignment. These included a ceremony at which Thieu gave him the GVN's highest decoration, the National Order, First Class. The honor reflected the strong relationship the two men had maintained despite the strains of the 1971 election, the long deadlock over the Paris agreement, and other problems. Bunker also received a warm message from President Nixon: "As you depart Saigon after six years of unparalleled challenge and accomplishment, you have my heartfelt thanks and those of the American people for a job superbly done."[119]

"Both champagne and tears flowed at the airport ceremonies marking the farewell of the sprightly, white-haired Vermonter," George McArthur reported to the *Los Angeles Times*. "His final act in Vietnam, while walking up the stairs to his plane, was to blow a courtly kiss to one of his embassy secretaries waving farewell."[120] Bunker made no formal remarks before turning over charge of the mission to his deputy Charles Whitehouse, who would carry on until the arrival of Ambassador Graham Martin in early July. He had already made a farewell speech to mission staff a few days earlier. One passage summed up what he thought the United States had achieved during his six years in Vietnam:

I believe that history will determine that [what we have done here] has not been in vain. One small country has gained a chance at self-determination. Other nations have gained time to create a more stable Asia. And the great powers of the world have, through this war, evolved a way to replace confrontation with diplomacy. . . . Now that I am leaving this country and this task I simply want to say to you all— Americans and Vietnamese—that I am proud of you and proud to have been one of you in this work we have shared. We have come to the end of a chapter and we have fulfilled our commitment.[121]

With President Sukarno and U.S. Ambassador to Indonesia Howard Jones, 1965.
At Lyndon Johnson's request, Bunker undertook an important mission to Indonesia
at a time of deteriorating U.S.-Indonesian relations. (© Bettmann/Corbis)

Casting a vote as U.S. ambassador to the Organization of American States, 1965.
Bunker played an energetic role in trying to stem the anger of OAS Latin
American representatives after LBJ sent the marines into the Dominican Republic.
(National Archives)

Bringing peace to the Dominican Republic, 1966. As de facto head of an Ad Hoc Committee organized by the Organization of American States, Bunker helped restore peace and stability to the Dominican Republic following the 1965 U.S. military intervention. In picture, from left to right: Fernando von Reigersburg, Bunker, Dominican President Héctor Garcia Godoy, Salvadoran Ambassador Ramón de Clairmont Dueñas, Brazilian Ambassador Ilmar Penna Marinho, and Harry Shlaudeman. (Ambassador Harry W. Shlaudeman)

A surprise wedding in Nepal, 1967. Bunker's marriage to Carol Laise, then U.S. ambassador to Nepal, was a diplomatic bombshell. (Ambassador Harry G. Barnes Jr.)

Presenting his credentials as U.S. ambassador to Vietnam to President Nguyen Van Thieu, 1967. Thieu was Vietnamese head of state throughout Bunker's six years there. Bunker had some major difficulties with him, but believed he was the right man for a tough job. (Barry Zorthian)

Bunker and LBJ *in Vietnam,* 1967. *Johnson relied heavily on Bunker's reporting in pursuing the war in Vietnam.* (LBJ *Library)*

With President Johnson and Averell Harriman at Camp David, 1968. Bunker and Harriman disagreed sharply on Vietnam policy. (LBJ Library)

Aboard Air Force One with President Nixon, early 1970s. Bunker strongly supported and helped implement Nixon's Vietnamization policy. In background from left to right: General Creighton Abrams, Assistant Secretary of State Marshall Green, National Security Adviser Henry Kissinger. (National Archives)

Accompanying President Thieu to San Clemente, 1973. Following the Paris peace agreement, Nixon welcomed the Vietnamese president to his home in San Clemente. Henry Kissinger is on the right. (National Archives)

Farewell to Vietnam, 1973. Bunker left Saigon with Carol for the last time on his seventy-ninth birthday. (Eva Kim)

President Carter announces the successful completion of the Panama Canal negotiations, 1977. Bunker and Sol Linowitz, the American co-negotiators, look on approvingly following their hectic last-minute efforts in Panama. Bunker spent five years negotiating the canal treaties before finally winding up his diplomatic career at the age of eighty-five. (Jimmy Carter Library)

President Carter and Panama's Omar Torrijos sign the treaties, 1977. Between them is OAS Secretary General Alejandro Orfila. The signing set the stage for the effort to sell the treaties to Congress and the American public. Bunker played a major role in that tough struggle. (Jimmy Carter Library)

At Georgetown University, in his role as chairman of the Institute for the Study of Diplomacy, early 1980s. Bunker helped make the institute a successful link between foreign policy professionals and academia. His ability to draw famous names to ISD's programs helped, as Dr. Kissinger's presence at this one suggests. (Institute for the Study of Diplomacy)

At Georgetown in his last days, early 1980s. Bunker is still well remembered at Georgetown, where an endowed fellowship bears his name. (Institute for the Study of Diplomacy)

13
The Panama Canal Negotiations

Many of Bunker's friends expected that after Saigon he would leave public life and live quietly in retirement as Carol continued her Foreign Service career. Instead, he remained a major figure in American diplomacy, serving with distinction for six years as a lead negotiator of the treaties that changed the status of the Panama Canal and playing a small but valuable role in Henry Kissinger's Middle East shuttle diplomacy. He was well over 85 when he left the nation's service in 1979.

Secretary of State Rogers sounded out Bunker for assignment as chief negotiator on the Panama Canal issue soon after he and Carol had returned to the United States. Bunker appears to have accepted the offer without hesitation. The *Washington Post* accurately reported in late June that Carol was also in line for a senior State Department position. "This combination of assignments," the paper commented, "presumably would give the unusual ambassadorial team considerably more time together than they had when Bunker was traveling between Saigon and Nepal when his diplomatic duties permitted."[1] Bunker's appointment to his former position of ambassador-at-large later that summer set the stage for his canal negotiations assignment.

Carol became assistant secretary of state for public and cultural affairs at the same time. This assignment as head of an important State Department bureau reflected her strong standing in Washington's corridors of power. As an assistant secretary, Carol held what was then the highest State Department position occupied by a woman Foreign Service officer. In March 1975, she went on to become director general of the Foreign Service, the department's top personnel position. She was the first woman appointed to that prestigious and powerful post.

The appointment of a top-ranking, well-known senior statesman who had won their confidence and admiration by his performance in Vietnam was read—and no doubt was meant to be read—as strong evidence of Nixon's and Kissinger's determination to make a greater effort to work out fundamental changes in the status of the canal.

In 1973, the treaty arrangements between the United States and Panama governing the operation and defense of the canal basically remained what they had been since the United States began to build the waterway seventy years earlier. Many Americans and virtually everyone in Panama and elsewhere in Latin America had become convinced that the provisions were outmoded colonial relics urgently requiring radical modernization. Bunker was no newcomer to the issue and his experience, talents, and interests made him an obvious choice for what was widely recognized as a complex, politically sensitive assignment.

Bunker had first dealt with the Panama problem as Organization of American States (OAS) ambassador in 1964.[2] His deft diplomacy following the violent "flag riots" that swept Panama that January set the stage for the negotiations the Johnson administration soon launched to change the canal's status. These negotiations, which Robert B. Anderson led for the U.S. side, resulted in 1967 in a package of three separate draft treaties. But premature publicity and domestic U.S. and Panamanian political opposition led the two governments to delay. The texts were never submitted to either nation's congress for ratification.[3]

After Nixon took office in 1969, he was reluctant to deal with the canal issue—"another time bomb left for [him] by the Johnson Administration," as Kissinger later termed it.[4] He was preoccupied during his first term with Vietnam and building new relationships with the Soviet Union and Communist China, and his priorities lay elsewhere. Negotiations did not resume until the summer of 1971. But even then, as William J. Jorden who became U.S. ambassador to Panama later in the 1970s found, "They were a negotiation without a soul . . . and lacked firm policy decisions on the part of both countries that they wanted to go forward and get a treaty."[5] Recalling that period, Kissinger has said that Nixon "was determined to proceed only on the basis of congressional consensus and a united government."[6] Such a timid approach virtually guaranteed that no agreement would be reached with the Panamanians unless the administration made a major push for one. Until 1973, it was not prepared to do so.[7]

The status of the canal thus continued to be based on a treaty hastily negotiated in 1903 by John Hay, Theodore Roosevelt's secretary of state, and Philippe Bunau-Varilla, a French citizen with Panamanian business interests who represented the newly independent Republic of Panama.[8] By any standard, this Hay–Bunau-Varilla Treaty stands out as one of the more egregious examples of big-power imperialism as practiced in the early years of the twentieth century. The new leaders of Panama had accepted it only because Bunau-Varilla persuaded them, quite wrongly, that unless they did so the United States would abandon the fledgling republic. The Roosevelt administration had famously engineered Panama's independence from Colombia only a few months earlier to expedite construction of the canal, and Panamanians who had conspired with the United States could easily imagine what their fate would be under renewed rule from Bogotá.

Despite this reluctant acquiescence, the Hay–Bunau-Varilla Treaty came under fire in Panama almost immediately. And for good reason. Secretary Hay himself had acknowledged in a letter to a U.S. senator that the treaty was "very satisfactory, vastly advantageous to the United States, and we must confess, with what face we can muster, not so advantageous to Panama. . . . You and I know too well," he confided, "how many points there are in this treaty to which a Panamanian patriot could object."[9] Hay's comments became well known and those who wanted a new and more equitable arrangement for the canal often cited them. Bunker quoted them in several speeches he made during the campaign for ratification of the treaties he eventually negotiated to replace Hay–Bunau-Varilla.

Several features of the treaty were especially galling to the Panamanians in 1903 and for the next three-quarters of a century. Panama had been obliged to grant to the United States *in perpetuity* the use, occupation, and control of a ten-mile-wide Canal Zone that cut through the heart of the isthmian country. The United States exercised its authority over this zone "as if it were sovereign," to the entire exclusion of any Panamanian sovereign rights there. The U.S. military was responsible for the defense of the canal and enjoyed the unilateral right to establish bases and station forces in the Canal Zone. Panama received a paltry $10 million for its loss of territory. Additionally, the United States provided Panama an annual subsidy of $250,000, eventually raised to $2.3 million, hardly a generous amount.

After it was completed in 1914, the canal was operated by a U.S. government–owned company in which American citizens held all senior positions. They and other American civilian and military officials and their families enjoyed a privileged, subsidized, segregated life in the Zone that contrasted sharply with the poverty of most Panamanians. Controlled by U.S. laws, judged by U.S. courts, and protected by a U.S. police force, Panamanians who lived in the Canal Zone became second-class citizens in their own country. The harsh racial attitudes many American "Zonians" adopted toward Panamanians individually and as a group made matters worse.

Why did Nixon and Kissinger give priority to Panama after years of neglect? With the direct American military role in the Vietnam War ended by the Paris accords and a new structure of peace at least tentatively in place following the president's historic visits to Beijing and Moscow, the administration had concluded that it needed to do more to promote and strengthen U.S. ties with other parts of the world. For the first time, it had the time and flexibility to do so. Latin America, becoming increasingly restive, was high on its list. Prospects for stronger relations with the Latins would be much improved if the canal no longer stood out as an irritating and provocative throwback to the bad old days of Yankee imperialism.

Growing international pressure also played a role. A strong feeling had arisen in Latin America and elsewhere in the world against the kind of extraterritoriality the United States enjoyed in the Canal Zone. The Panamanian head of government, Omar Torrijos Herrera, a populist, hard-driving general who had seized power in a 1968 coup, made mobilization of this international opinion an important part of his strategy to induce Washington to move forward. At his urging, a special session of the U.N. Security Council was held in Panama in March 1973 to consider the issue. To Washington's dismay, the Security Council voted overwhelmingly in favor of a resolution calling on the United States to conclude a new treaty that would fulfill without delay Panama's demand for full sovereignty over the Canal Zone. Only the United States voted against it. (Britain abstained.)

Although the United States used its veto power to defeat the resolution, the administration recognized, as Kissinger later put it, that "the problem would not become easier; the pressures would grow more difficult to control."[10] Washington understood, too, that unless the treaty was changed the political and security situation in Panama could deteriorate to the point where the operation and defense of the canal might be jeopardized. The canal's locks, dams, and long, narrow cuts through the mountainous isthmian terrain made it vulnerable to sabotage by Panamanian nationalists. This was a far greater threat to its security than attack from outside Panama.

Bunker later said that aside from Vietnam the Panama Canal negotiations had been his toughest assignment. It is not difficult to understand why. For the negotiations comprised a series of prolonged, highly politicized, emotionally charged interactions among many powerful, often antagonistic forces that viewed the issue from very different perspectives.

The formal negotiations themselves involved the governments of the United States—the Nixon (1973–74), Ford (1974–77), and Carter (1977–79) administrations—and the Republic of Panama, which General Torrijos continued to dominate throughout the negotiating period. While these diplomatic exchanges were going on, and even after they seemed to have been completed, further negotiations just as critical for the success of the operation were taking place in which other institutions and individual actors made their presence and power felt.

The most highly publicized of these negotiations were the intricate, often angry interactions between the executive branch and Congress. It was not simply a matter of lobbying by the White House and the State Department for the two-thirds Senate majority the Constitution requires for ratification of treaties. It also involved lengthy administration consultations with the Senate leadership and rank-and-file while U.S.-Panamanian negotiations were still in progress, then bargaining over the amendments, understandings, and reservations individual senators sought to attach to the texts of the draft treaties after the negotiations had been completed.

The House of Representatives also played a role. Its vote was needed for passage of legislation implementing the two canal treaties the Senate had ratified. But House members also tried to get into the act much earlier. For three successive years the House either considered or actually passed amendments to State Department appropriations bills requiring that no money be spent to support treaty negotiations with Panama that might change the status of the canal. Six representatives sought to have the courts halt negotiations on grounds that the Constitution provided that only Congress, not the executive branch, could dispose of U.S. property and territory.[11] Individual members spoke up frequently in the House and elsewhere during the negotiating period and the Senate's consideration of the draft treaties.

Hard bureaucratic in-fighting within the executive branch was also a major feature of the Panama battle. The two departments principally concerned, State and Defense, often took sharply different positions. The State Department generally favored moving forward with new arrangements. Although individual officials in the Defense Department and the armed services sometimes disagreed with one another, the Pentagon's attitude was usually more averse than the State Department's to substantial changes in the status quo. Many in the military feared that the proposed changes would weaken U.S. defense capabilities in Panama and elsewhere in the region.

Closely linked to Congress's role in the negotiations was the battle for public opinion. The effort of senators and representatives to shape the texts of the treaties was influenced as much by worry about the formidable strength of opposition to change among their constituents as it was by rational concern about the impact the modernization of the treaty could have on the operation and security of the canal and broader U.S. foreign and security interests. No legislation in recent times had prompted such a high level of public interest or such prodigious efforts to mobilize popular opinion.

The debate in Congress and elsewhere took place in a highly charged atmosphere. Many opponents of change were incensed by what they considered a deceitful and dangerous sellout of vital American interests. Some became convinced that the abandoning of the Panama Canal status quo was a conspiracy perpetrated by clandestine enemies of the United States. Supporters of change were ordinarily cooler in their approach and used more rational arguments to justify their positions.

The symbolism the canal had come to have for Americans over the years figured importantly in shaping attitudes. As one insightful journalist wrote in 1975, "Many Americans, especially of the older generation, have been brought up to regard the Canal as an engineering marvel which only the United States could have built and run, and as emblematic of an entirely beneficent and successful way to help raise up a less fortunate people. The combination of technology in the service of communication, and power in the service of uplift, stirs deep feelings in the breasts of people who simply do not understand why Panamanians would wish to object."[12] Bunker and others saw a similarity in the emotions evoked by the canal issue and the public fervor aroused by the recent moon landing, another epic U.S. technological feat.

Introduced soon after the Communist victory in Vietnam, the treaties were darkly perceived by opponents as another American retreat from global power. This perception was intensified by the widely held but incorrect conviction that by agreeing to change the status quo in Panama the United States was giving up sovereignty over territory that was as much a part of the country as Alaska or the states carved out of the Louisiana Purchase. The raw anger that the canal issue aroused spilled over into bitter personal attacks against those promoting the treaties. Bunker's stature and age did not spare him from becoming a target of abusive hate mail that questioned his patriotism, his good sense, and even his manhood.

Many detailed accounts of the struggle over the Panama Canal treaties have been written, most of them in the five years after it ended. More recently, Henry Kissinger, who ignored Panama in his earlier memoirs, discussed it in a final volume. The present study focuses on the main features of the lengthy, complex series of actions that culminated in 1979 and assesses Bunker's role in shaping and influencing them.

Bunker took over his Panama responsibilities in late September 1973, at first working out of a small office on the seventh floor of the State Department down a corridor from the suites that housed Kissinger and other department "principals." (Kissinger had replaced William Rogers as secretary of state the same month.) Bunker's staff was minimal and he relied for support on the Bureau of Inter-American Affairs. As William Jorden has commented: "Anyone who saw how Bunker was operating recognized he was a man who did not confuse perquisites with power."[13]

Over the next couple of months, Bunker familiarized himself with the issue and consulted his colleagues at State, old friends on Capitol Hill, and senior civilian and military officials at the Pentagon. He left Washington briefly to accompany Kissinger to New York for a useful meeting at the United Nations with Panamanian Foreign Minister Juan António Tack. In late November, he went to Panama for his first negotiating session.

By that time, several major aspects of the issue confronted the negotiators: jurisdiction over the Canal Zone, defense of the canal, U.S. payments to Panama, and the rights of the two countries should a new sea-level canal be built to replace the existing waterway. Panama demanded that the United States surrender jurisdiction over the Canal Zone in gradual stages within five years. In earlier negotiations, Washington had accepted the principle of a transfer of control, but had insisted on a longer period for implementing it.

The Panamanians also called for the progressive elimination of the U.S. military presence (troops of the Southern Command and their dependents in the Canal Zone totaled about 12,000), a sharp reduction in the area around the canal used by the military, and Panama's immediate participation in its defense. They wanted payment from the United States for the "privilege" of maintaining troops on Panamanian territory. The Pentagon had discouraged the State Department from engaging in any detailed discussion of such military questions. Panama also wanted a role in deciding where and how a sea-level canal should be built and prior agreement on how long the United States could administer it. It demanded a sharp rise in the annual rental that the United States paid.

Earlier in 1973, Foreign Minister Tack had passed to William Rogers a set of eight principles on which he believed a canal settlement should be based. These included abrogation of the 1903 treaty and its replacement by a new treaty with a fixed termination date (instead of the "in perpetuity" clause the Panamanians so resented); termination of U.S. jurisdiction over the Canal Zone; U.S. use of Panamanian land and water areas necessary to operate and maintain the canal and to protect vital installations during the treaty's lifetime; provision for increased Panamanian participation in the operation of the canal and payment to Panama of a "just and equitable share" of canal benefits; and restriction of U.S. military activities to those the new treaty expressly stipulated. The principles also included several that concerned a possible sea-level canal. Tack's principles had subsequently gathered dust in Washington until Bunker found them and decided that they could be useful in moving toward an agreement. Over some opposition, mostly from the Pentagon, he succeeded in making a somewhat revised version of the principles the basis for his initial negotiations with the Panamanians.

These negotiations took place on the island of Contadora off Panama's Pacific coast. Contadora provided just the secluded, informal setting that Bunker preferred for his negotiations. Although the tropical resort bore no resemblance to the manor in the Virginia hunt country that he had used for his negotiations with the Indonesians and the Dutch a decade earlier, the purpose Bunker had in mind was the same: to create a relaxed and friendly mood among the negotiators in which they could win one another's confidence and quietly make progress. "It's a lovely little island," he recalled. "It's small, quite small. One of the great advantages that we had there was that we were out of Panama City and away from the distractions of the city. And away from the press too. So that we could carry out our negotiations privately and quietly." [14]

The negotiators met in sport shirts and slacks and gathered together informally for drinks and dinner, where Bunker could entertain them with his ribald stories. For breakfast, Bunker presented each of the Panamanians with a quart can of maple syrup from his Vermont farm. Later in the day he would take the wheel of a forty-five-foot ketch that Panamanian president Demetrio Lakas had sent over while the other negotiators lolled on deck or fished for mackerel and bonita. The Panamanians made sure Bunker knew that they had confiscated the boat from a couple of American drug-runners.

The Panamanians responded well to what Jorden termed this "Bunker treatment." Even the seemingly stiff and thin-skinned Tack, a nationalist intellectual, began to unwind as the two sides engaged in five days of amiable and easy discussion of the principles he had devised and Bunker had reworked. Bunker and Tack sensibly left most of these negotiations to their subordinates, standing by to intervene when deadlocks arose.

As the negotiators moved toward closure, Bunker—always aware of the importance of keeping Washington on board—returned there to enlist the support of Kissinger and other influential figures for what he had accomplished. Although the Pentagon kept up its rearguard resistance to the efforts Bunker's subordinates continued to press in Panama, he was able in the first week of January to return to the isthmus for a final series of sessions with Tack at which they reached agreement. The thrust of this negotiated text was very similar to Tack's first proposal. The language was changed to give it a more measured tone, largely by removing some of the nationalist rhetoric in the original. What emerged was a document less likely to offend the sensibilities of Americans, but one that Panamanian nationalists could accept.

Bunker consolidated this success by persuading a skeptical Kissinger to come to Panama for the formal signing of the "Kissinger-Tack Principles," as they came to be called. As Bunker knew it would be, the secretary of state's participation in the signing ceremony and his willingness to journey to Panama when he was at the height of his fame and power was seen there and elsewhere as the most dramatic indication yet of the Nixon administration's determination to resolve the canal issue. To give the ceremony further political resonance in the United States, Kissinger included in his delegation several senior members of the Senate and House committees dealing with the canal problem.

The principles were much more than "just platitudes, deliberately designed to be satisfactory to both sides," as Kissinger later described them. In fact, they formed the basic architecture of the treaties that were finally negotiated.[15] But they did leave huge gaps to be filled. Many of the outstanding issues that had been on the negotiating table before Kissinger-Tack were still there. These included such divisive matters as the duration of the new treaty, the timing of the United States' relinquishing its jurisdiction over the Canal Zone, and the extent of the lands and waters that would be needed for the operation and defense of the canal under the new dispensation. A host of definitional problems also remained. How, for example, did jurisdiction relate to continuing U.S. rights to participate in the operation and defense of the canal? The possibility of a new sea-level canal raised a further set of problems.

The Panamanians were soon disabused of their earlier hope that with the principles in hand, the drafting of the treaty would easily and quickly follow. Meeting alternately on Contadora and in Washington, U.S. and Panamanian negotiators spent most of their time compiling detailed lists of issues that needed to be resolved. Both sides were painfully aware of efforts to block progress through legislation that opponents of change introduced in the Senate and House.

Bunker was involved in the Arab-Israeli negotiations during part of this time.[16] He intervened briefly in Panama and Washington and soothed Panamanian sensibilities that had been bruised by belated recognition that work on the treaty still had a long way to go. But it was only at the end of June 1974, almost five months after the adoption of the Kissinger-Tack Principles, that he again took charge of the American team on a regular basis and full-fledged negotiations got under way once more in the relaxed atmosphere of Contadora.

As he resumed regular contact with the Panamanian negotiators, men he found intelligent, able, and tough, Bunker moved quickly to make sure that the White House and the Pentagon agreed with the positions he took. He also did what he could to cover his congressional flanks. In his dealings with the Panamanians he adopted several important tactics. William Furlong and Margaret Scranton describe these succinctly in their excellent study of the negotiations: "First, easier issues on the agenda would be resolved before divisive issues were discussed. Second, basic or conceptual agreements on each major issue would be drafted prior to specific provisions. Once all major issues were resolved at a conceptual level, the package of conceptual agreements would be progressively enlarged with specific details. This would allow the negotiators to bargain over specific provisions within a larger, mutually acceptable basic framework."[17] Michael G. Kozak, a State Department lawyer who was deeply involved in the negotiations for many years, has noted that this technique differed sharply from the traditional approach Anderson had favored in which the two sides exchanged negotiating texts that included large blanks on issues on which no consensus had been reached, then tried to negotiate details.[18] A third Bunker tactic was to offer the Panamanians concrete concessions on the ground in the Canal Zone as the negotiations proceeded. By doing this, he reckoned, he could demonstrate U.S. goodwill and win greater Panamanian recognition of the administration's serious interest in modernizing the canal regime.

Despite a hiatus caused by U.S. annoyance over Torrijos's decision in August to recognize the Castro regime in Cuba, the two negotiating teams made good progress over the next six months in fleshing out three of the Kissinger-Tack Principles and turning them into "conceptual agreements."

Consistent with Bunker's negotiating tactics, the first of these was relatively noncontroversial. The American negotiators agreed with the Panamanians that the United States would retain primary responsibility for canal operations during the lifetime of the new treaty. Panama's participation would increase steadily as its citizens were preferentially recruited and trained to take over the senior positions until then reserved for Americans.

Defense of the canal, an issue of greater concern to the United States, came next. The conceptual agreement gave the United States primary responsibility for defending the canal during the treaty period. Panama would participate increasingly to the extent its capacity would allow and in accordance with the lead U.S. role. This U.S. right could be extended by mutual agreement. Panama and the United States would retain unilateral rights to take action necessary to protect the canal. In a provision Washington considered critical, both parties pledged to maintain the permanent neutrality of the waterway and its nondiscriminatory operation. Ducking the dispute over who would participate in the guarantee—the United States and Panama alone (favored by the Americans) or the United Nations (Panama's preference)—the two sides decided to "make efforts that such neutrality is recognized and guaranteed by all nations."

Negotiations on a third, more sensitive issue—the transfer of jurisdiction over the Canal Zone to Panama—focused on the duration of the transition period and the definition of the territory and government functions to be shifted. Not surprisingly, the American negotiators argued that the United States needed to retain more administrative control and territory to ensure the efficient operation of the canal than the Panamanians were willing to concede. They also wanted a longer transition period for implementing the changes. The issue was eventually resolved by compromise language that postponed important decisions. The Canal Zone government would immediately terminate and the Zone would be abolished. At the same time, Panama would grant the United States the use of territory and facilities necessary for operating the canal. But the specific land and water areas would only be determined during the treaty negotiations. Most Panamanian laws and police powers would be applied inside this agreed territory when the treaty went into effect, but the United States would retain some limited authority there for three years.[19]

To both Bunker and the Panamanians, the completion of this first round of negotiations in November 1974 seemed to presage early agreement on a treaty text. Despite Kissinger's quip to the Panamanian foreign minister that Bunker never completed a negotiation in less than four years, both governments handled the process with increasing urgency, for different reasons.

Torrijos worried about the political challenge of Panamanian leftists, who were becoming increasingly suspicious of U.S. sincerity as the talks went on. The frustration of his countrymen with what seemed to them the slow pace of negotiations significantly figured in the general's decision to recognize the Castro regime. He was well aware of the damage this would inflict on the Panamanian cause in the United States, where opponents of a new treaty had long branded him pro-Communist. Like many others who knew the Panamanian leader, Bunker sharply disagreed with this unfair label and other uncomplimentary descriptions of Torrijos that anti-change forces bandied about, such as drug-runner, anti-Semite, ultranationalist, and advocate of violence. He termed the general "a populist who, perhaps more than any [earlier] ruler of Panama, is interested in the well-being of the ordinary people of the country . . . a shrewd politician, a hard bargainer in defending the interests of his country, but . . . also fair."[20] Bunker recognized that, for Torrijos, establishing diplomatic ties with Castro was important to mollify leftist critics. Unless negotiations moved ahead more quickly they would step up their pressure for more drastic action.

For their part, American negotiators understood that progress on politically sensitive foreign policy issues is inevitably influenced by the presidential election cycle. They knew that if a Panama Canal treaty was not negotiated, signed, and ratified by the Senate before the 1976 campaign season began, it would have to await action by the next administration. Gerald Ford's accession to the presidency and the likelihood that he would be challenged for the Republican nomination made this timing problem even more acute. Ford did not want to enter the primaries while he was battling for a new canal treaty that many influential party leaders as well as rank-and-file members would find objectionable.

Bunker's hope for progress was frustrated by the reluctance of many important Pentagon officials to risk making significant changes in the status quo. After signing the conceptual agreements at Contadora, he and Foreign Minister Tack had optimistically worked out a negotiating schedule they hoped would produce a treaty within four months. Jorden, by then American ambassador to Panama, recalled warning the U.S. negotiating team: "We're going to have more trouble with Washington than we are with the Panamanians. . . . I hope I'm wrong," he added. He was not.[21]

The U.S. and Panamanian negotiators were able to reach agreement on a Status of Forces Agreement in March 1974 after months of what for the American side was unexpectedly hard bargaining. But several major issues still faced them. Bunker had great difficulty in winning Pentagon agreement to his proposed negotiating positions on the lands-and-waters and treaty duration issues. He had moved adroitly to lessen Defense Department and Joint Chiefs of Staff opposition to the positions he favored by establishing a Joint Support Group (JSG) for the negotiations. This group included State Department officials and representatives of the Pentagon offices most concerned with the canal issue. Working as a team, the JSG reached useful compromises that they set out in uncleared drafts. The Pentagon officials then returned to their offices, where they either approved the drafts themselves or played crucial roles in shepherding them through their bureaucracies.

Unfortunately for Bunker, opposition at the Pentagon to his approach to the lands-and-waters issue was so powerful that its representatives on the JSG, who had developed a draft in collaboration with their State colleagues, were instructed to reject their own work. Senior Pentagon officials insisted that the United States retain use of a much larger tract of Canal Zone territory than Bunker and his negotiators believed necessary or acceptable to the Panamanians, who were particularly sensitive on the matter. The JSG thereupon disbanded.

The duration issue, too, caused a State-Pentagon confrontation. Bunker had earlier skirted this ticklish matter when he was negotiating under the guidance the first Nixon administration had prepared in 1971 for Anderson. Those instructions authorized a termination date no earlier than fifty years after the treaty came into effect. Bunker quickly recognized that the Panamanians would not agree to this. In early 1975, he suggested that the treaty terminate at the end of the century, that is in some twenty-five years, the period called for in the failed 1967 draft. The Pentagon accepted this date, but only for U.S. rights to *operate* the canal. It insisted that the United

States retain responsibility for *defending* the canal for the full fifty years. It also wanted an option to extend this period by another thirty years if a sea-level canal were constructed.

Bunker was unable to break these stalemates on the lands-and-waters and treaty duration issues. He had gone to considerable lengths to persuade the civilian and uniformed leaders at the Pentagon that modernization of the treaty was necessary and would enhance, not damage, U.S. security interests in Panama and elsewhere in the region. He was well regarded personally and professionally by the defense establishment. His relations with General Creighton Abrams, in 1973 Army chief of staff, and Air Force general George Brown, who became chairman of the Joint Chiefs in 1974, dated back to Vietnam days. Bunker recalled that Abrams had told him: "If you run into any problems [in the canal negotiations] come over and see me."[22] Brown, too, would be helpful, assigning retired Lt. General Welborn "Tom" Dolvin to the negotiating team that October. Dolvin soon became one of its most valuable members, greatly helping Bunker in his dealings with the Pentagon. Yet in early 1975, Bunker could not overcome a combination of intense Pentagon unease about the implications of major changes in Panama and its concern, similarly overdrawn, that the State Department, including Bunker, was trying to force a treaty through without sufficient participation and input from its side of the Potomac.

Bunker eventually decided to break the deadlock by seeking fresh instructions from the Ford White House. He believed these would reflect his position, not the Pentagon's. He had at least two opportunities to take his case directly to the president and members of the National Security Council (NSC). At an NSC meeting on May 15, he told Ford that a treaty was within reach providing he was given flexibility on the duration and lands-and-waters issues. "We want flexibility so we can bargain as between a duration for operation and a duration for defense: twenty-five years for operations, fifty for defense, if we can get it [from the Panamanians], though I am certain we cannot. Something in between is what is necessary. And then a land[s]-and-water[s] proposal which is sufficient to permit agreement. The present one is not saleable to Panama."

He painted a grim picture of the implications of failure in the negotiations: "It would entail unacceptable risks including negative effects beyond Panama which would disrupt our relations with Latin America, lead to world condemnation, and hamper the operation of the waterway. While we could undoubtedly maintain our control, we would deprive ourselves of what we have gained so far and undermine any future possibility of a reasonable agreement."

Bunker got only limited support from Kissinger, who concluded that the best course might be to sign a treaty but not submit it to the Senate for ratification. Defense Secretary James Schlesinger strongly opposed any further concessions to the Panamanians. "What Ambassador Bunker refers to as flexibility," Schlesinger said, "is no less than . . . an erosion in our position of substantial magnitude." It seemed to him that the United States was reducing its requirements to what it thought Torrijos would accept. In Schlesinger's view, worldwide reaction to a tough U.S. position was likely to be mixed, not the thoroughly negative attitudes that Bunker (and Kissinger) forecast. "When the United States shows strength and determination, it receives respect. When it recedes from its position, it whets appetites."[23]

The meeting was inconclusive, and a second NSC session on the Panama issue took place on July 23. At that time, Bunker concurred with Kissinger's proposal that the negotiations continue but that they be confined to reaching certain conceptual agreements. This strategy would permit the administration to avoid signing a treaty before the end of 1976 (i.e., before the presidential election). Although Schlesinger held to his hard-line position and said he was reluctant to give up sovereign control, William Clements, his deputy at the Defense Department, adopted a more forthcoming attitude. The participants eventually agreed to establish a high-level group that would seek agreement on the duration and lands-and-waters issues. The group was to submit any differences to the president for decision.[24]

Ford finally set out his position in an August 18 National Security Decision Memorandum (NSDM 302). This authorized Bunker to negotiate separate arrangements stipulating the length of time the treaty would remain in effect for the operation of the canal and for its defense. Bunker could agree to terminate U.S. rights regarding canal operations as early as December 31, 1999. He was told to obtain defense rights for fifty years but could reduce this to forty in negotiations. Ford also instructed him to obtain in principle a U.S. right to participate in the defense of the canal following the expiration of the treaty period.[25]

While Bunker welcomed this dual-duration formula, and is credited in some accounts of the negotiations with first proposing it, he knew that even the forty-year fallback position he was authorized to offer on defense would be too long for the Panamanians. But he had been unable to persuade Kissinger to go any lower and, in fact, the numbers reflected the position that the secretary of state had advocated at the July NSC meeting.

The prolonged deadlock within the U.S. government had led to a six-month suspension of Bunker's negotiations with the Panamanians. They did not resume until he returned to Panama in September with instructions that were bound to create another standoff. But this fitted in well with the president's interest in delaying any breakthrough on the negotiations—while avoiding their breakdown—until the election was safely over.

By the autumn of 1975, the campaign preliminaries were already getting under way. The strident anti-treaty stance some of Ford's challengers adopted as they began to position themselves for the spring 1976 Republican primaries no doubt strengthened the president's conviction that he had been correct in deciding not to push for a treaty signing during his current term. The strength of the opposition was also reflected in actions on Capitol Hill, where with some quiet encouragement from Pentagon officials both senators and representatives sponsored legislation that would have effectively shut down the negotiations. Bunker played a major role in the administration's strenuous, ultimately successful lobbying to defeat these bills.

Not surprisingly, General Torrijos had become increasingly worried during the long Washington deadlock over the future of the negotiations. Once again seeking to rally the international community to exert pressure on the United States, the Panamanian leader persuaded the presidents of three nearby Latin American countries to sign a letter to Ford urging action. After winning the Mexican president's agreement as well, Torrijos sought to enlist what he hoped would be even broader support by bringing Panama into the Non-Aligned Movement, then dominated by anti-Western Third World powers. These tactics did little to help the Panamanian cause, but they kept Kissinger and Bunker busy devising countermeasures. Some of these were designed to limit negative reaction in the United States to Torrijos's moves, others to reduce pro-Panama sentiment in the international community.

The situation decidedly improved in early September, just before negotiations were to resume, when General Brown and Deputy Secretary Clements led a team of high-ranking Pentagon officials to Panama, where they assured Torrijos that they would work for a new treaty. This persuaded him to accept the facts of American political life and agree to wait for the next administration to complete the treaty-making process.

Thus during 1976, the negotiations were essentially on hold. Ronald Reagan in particular had discovered early in the presidential primary season how potent an issue the canal could be to the Republican faithful. The former California governor's standard, increasingly familiar line—"We bought it and paid for it.... It's ours . . . [and] we're not going to give it up to some tinhorn dictator"—contributed greatly to a string of primary victories he won over Ford in the spring. Forced on the defensive by Reagan's emotional, often factually incorrect rhetoric, the president waffled in public on the issue and failed to make a strong case for a new treaty. Bunker was told that he should not tackle any of the unresolved matters still pending in the negotiations that could provide more ammunition to Reagan. He was specifically instructed to avoid the duration issue.

As the administration wished, Bunker remained inactive long after Ford had eked out a narrow victory over Reagan at the Republican National Convention in Kansas City in August. He held sessions on Contadora in May with Panama's new foreign minister, Aquilino Boyd, but did not see Boyd again until just before the election. Their deputies met intermittently and made some progress in identifying options. But the negotiations basically remained on dead center while Ford battled for the White House against the Democratic nominee, former governor of Georgia Jimmy Carter.

As he had in fighting off his Republican challengers, Ford adopted a defensive position on the canal after he won the nomination. His Democratic opponent equivocated. At first seemingly in favor of substantial change, Carter later repeatedly declared in his standard campaign speech that he would not give up practical control over the Panama Canal Zone any time in the foreseeable future. Neither candidate wanted to stick his political neck out on Panama.[26]

Torrijos fretfully watched the American presidential campaign. Though he understood the domestic political compulsions for U.S. stonewalling and had told the visiting Pentagon officials that he was prepared to wait out the American electoral season, the general faced a serious challenge from the increasingly restive Panamanian leftists. Whether he would be able or willing to contain it remained unclear.

Meanwhile, Bunker maintained his customary sangfroid. He calmly accepted Kissinger's directives to go slow, and if he was troubled by Ford's public waffling on Panama in the face of Reagan's demagogic onslaughts, he kept his counsel. He reacted to adversity much as he always had. When Ambassador Jorden phoned him in Contadora with news of Reagan's decisive win over Ford in the important Texas primary, he listened quietly, thanked Jorden, put down the phone, looked out the window, and told a staff member "I think I'll go for a swim." [27] Returning to Panama in October for a last meeting with the Panamanians before America voted, he faithfully went through the negotiating motions to keep the process alive though he recognized that his instructions ruled out any progress. As he had foreseen, the session was another futile exercise as the Panamanian negotiators, and everyone else, waited for the outcome of the U.S. presidential race.

The ambivalence, real or feigned, that candidate Carter had shown during the presidential campaign quickly gave way after his election to a much more positive and straightforward attitude toward changing the status of the canal and the Zone.[28] In his autobiography, Carter stated that as he conferred with his foreign policy advisers soon after the elections, he concluded that "if we were going to negotiate seriously with Panama, . . . we would have to begin immediately . . . and the eventual agreement would have to include a phasing out of our absolute control of the Canal, as well as the acknowledgement of Panamanian sovereignty." [29] As early as January 12, eight days before his inauguration, he told a congressional gathering that he planned to resume negotiations immediately after taking office with the goal of completing a treaty based on the Kissinger-Tack Principles by June 1977.

This early decision to go forward on the canal stemmed from the importance the incoming administration gave to Latin America and its interest in making what it regarded as overdue progress in improving hemispheric relations. Commenting on this, Abraham Lowenthal, an authority on U.S. relations with the region, has written: "It took Kissinger years to discover Latin America. The Carter administration *began* with an expressed concern for the region, stressed personally and often by the President himself." [30] Resolving the canal issue in a way that would be welcomed throughout the hemisphere would be an impressive place to start. More broadly, Carter's action reflected his administration's pursuit of a foreign policy that placed greater importance on American values and sought to associate the United States with what the president considered the positive forces of global change.

Cyrus Vance, whom Carter appointed secretary of state, strongly favored giving high priority to the canal problem. Unlike the president, Vance had long been familiar with the issue. As secretary of the army, he had been sent by President Johnson to Panama during the 1964 "flag riots." He later recalled concluding at the time that "almost all Panamanians regarded exclusive U.S. authority over the canal and Zone as an affront to their national dignity and sovereignty." Vance's conviction that "sooner or later Panama would resort to major violence, even to the point of destroying the canal" heightened his sense of urgency.[31] Soon after his appointment, he told an interviewer that Washington could not renege on its commitments gradually to turn over control of the canal to Panama because all of Latin America viewed the negotiations as a barometer of U.S. relations with the region.[32]

President Carter recognized, of course, that he would face massive congressional and public opposition to a policy of change. He calculated that if he moved swiftly to bring the negotiations to a successful conclusion, he could complete the ratification process while his popularity was still high and before the 1978 congressional election further complicated the situation on Capitol Hill. Reflecting this assessment, Carter made the canal the subject of his administration's first foreign policy review and chaired a high-level White House meeting on the issue within a week of taking office.

A Presidential Review Memorandum prepared for that session accurately described the canal as "an aging utility of declining commercial value . . . [whose] strategic significance has diminished while its potential as a source of conflict has increased." Without specifically naming Bunker, the memorandum stated that "our negotiators believe that we can, with continued effort, shortly be within reach of a treaty with Panama that will meet [U.S.] requirements provided both sides are willing to make compromises." It placed these requirements in the context of basic American national interests in Panama, which it defined as "the Canal remain[ing] efficient, secure, neutral, and continuously open to all world shipping at reasonable tolls." Panama's national interests, it found, were similar.[33]

The memorandum offered a couple of options for resuming negotiations. The one clearly favored, and apparently adopted, called for giving negotiators broad flexibility to probe for the basis of an agreement without the advance requirement of a time-consuming review of U.S. positions. This negotiating approach, it argued, would assure Latin America and the Third World of the administration's interest in speedily resolving the canal issue. The drafters of the memorandum optimistically forecast that such an approach could lead to the initialing of a "concept agreement" with Panama by mid-March (only six weeks off), the presentation of a draft treaty to the president for final concurrence by June 15, and a formal signing by July 1. Ambler Moss, a member of the negotiating team in 1977 whom Carter appointed ambassador to Panama the following year, later recalled that Bunker told Vance that the negotiations were roughly half completed and could be finished in another six or seven months. Moss reflected that "in retrospect [the decision to move ahead quickly] emanated not only from a tremendous sense of goodwill but also from an inordinate amount of political naivete as to what the reaction would be in the Senate and in the rest of the country."[34]

Before his inauguration, Carter had decided on Vance's recommendation to make Sol Linowitz chief negotiator. A top-flight lawyer who had been chairman of the board of the Xerox Corporation, Linowitz entered public service in 1966 when President Johnson named him to succeed Bunker as ambassador to the Organization of American States. He was an influential figure in both the Democratic Party and the foreign policy establishment, where he was recognized as an outspoken advocate of durable new arrangements for the canal. The appointment was another clear signal that the new administration meant business on the canal.

Linowitz's views on the canal had recently gained further prominence with the well-publicized release in December 1976 of a report prepared by the Commission on U.S.–Latin American Relations, a prestigious, bipartisan private study group that he chaired. The commission called for a fundamental reorientation of U.S. policy in the hemisphere that would reflect the dramatic changes it argued had occurred over the past decade within the Latin American and Caribbean countries and in their relations with the world. The report termed the Panama Canal the most urgent issue the new administration faced in Latin America and called on Carter to negotiate promptly a new and equitable treaty that would eliminate the "colonial enclave" of the Canal Zone. Only then could a potentially disastrous confrontation be avoided.[35]

Linowitz had an affectionate regard for Bunker, who had gone well beyond the call of professional duty in introducing him to the centers of power in Washington when he came there as a newcomer to public office to undertake his OAS duties. He politely declined Vance's offer to make him chief negotiator in place of Bunker. As he put it in his memoirs, he "was not willing to be the instrument by which Bunker's 30 years of service to his country would come to an end."[36] Linowitz told Vance he was prepared to accept the position of co-chief negotiator providing Bunker consented to that arrangement. Carter agreed to this proposal, and soon afterwards Bunker phoned Linowitz to ask him to join the negotiating team.[37] Bunker said later he recognized that even though he was himself a Democrat the new administration needed someone of its own choosing in the negotiations. There was no one, he recalled, he would rather have had as co-chief negotiator than Sol Linowitz.[38]

Assuming, as the administration evidently (and correctly) did, that Bunker and Linowitz could work successfully together, the decision to retain Bunker was a wise one. Aside from the talent and experience he brought to the negotiations and the battles on Capitol Hill that followed, his continuing presence usefully demonstrated that the Democrats did not intend to disown what had already been achieved. They would instead pick up where the Republicans had left off when the election campaign intervened. Along with the retention of other longtime members of the negotiating team, Bunker's staying on also signaled to the Senate in advance of the ratification struggle that Carter was taking a bipartisan approach that built on the work of the Nixon and Ford administrations.

Although their negotiating styles were different, Bunker and Linowitz were able to form an effective, well-coordinated partnership from the outset of their collaboration. They managed this despite Linowitz's preference for a more aggressive and businesslike approach to the negotiations. Not for him were the leisurely rhythms and easy camaraderie of the Contadora setting that Bunker prized. In a 1992 interview, he spoke of his "admiration and respect for the old fox" and commented on his relations with his co-negotiator:

> Because he was so reserved, people found that there was always a distance between him and a co-negotiator. He never tried to break through that reserve between him and me. . . . [A]s a negotiator, Ellsworth kind of liked the fact that he was held in some awe and with a little fear. He rarely spoke more than a sentence or two at a time. I can't say that we worked out a modus operandi in advance. It just naturally happened

that I took the lead. But he was always listening. Sometimes he would send me a note or whisper something in my ear. For the most part, he was not front and center in the negotiations. . . .

I always felt that his mere presence, his just being there, gave a real significance to the negotiations. The fact that he was who he was and was devoting himself, as he obviously was, to these negotiations, showed they were serious and had the highest foreign policy importance to the United States government.[39]

The revamped U.S. team resumed negotiations with its Panamanian counterpart at Contadora in mid-February 1977, less than a month into the new administration. Remembering his own experiences as the Johnson administration's troubleshooter during the 1967 Cyprus crisis and the 1968 confrontation with North Korea over its seizure of the U.S.S *Pueblo*, Secretary Vance gave the negotiators broad authority to explore various formulations to resolve the remaining issues. The secretary's guidance also reflected the NSC decision to move forward quickly without a lengthy interagency review to map out negotiating positions. As any negotiators would, Bunker and Linowitz welcomed this mandate.

Their initial negotiations focused on three of the big unresolved issues: the duration of a treaty, the neutrality of the canal, and, related to both, the canal's post-treaty defense. The new American team probed to learn whether Panama would accept U.S. requirements for defense if the United States in turn agreed to a treaty that ended by the year 2000, much earlier than the forty-year duration Bunker had offered before. They reiterated Washington's position that Panama and the United States alone should be the guarantors of the canal's permanent neutrality. Bunker and Linowitz also proposed that the two countries reach a mutual defense agreement before the canal treaty expired.

These positions suggested to the Panamanians that the American negotiators were insisting that U.S. forces remain forever in Panama, for them an unacceptable arrangement akin to the loathed "in perpetuity" clause of the 1903 treaty. Their dismay was heightened by their disappointment that the new administration's much publicized desire for a breakthrough had not translated into a more forthcoming U.S. negotiating stance. In fact, aside from the year 2000 expiration date, most of what the Americans proposed on the three core issues and other important matters was a reiteration of positions the Ford administration had put forward. So strong and bitterly expressed was the adverse Panamanian reaction that even Bunker let his irritation show: he used his recently revealed mild deafness to provide a pretext ("what was that you said?") for interrupting the flow of Panamanian invective. Some of the U.S. negotiators wanted to break off the negotiations then and there, but as Linowitz recalled, "Bunker and I thought that was not what the President expected of us."[40]

The negotiators made no progress in subsequent informal discussions at Contadora or at a secret meeting in March at the Panamanian ambassador's residence in Washington. Torrijos then muddied the waters further by visiting Libyan president Muammar Qaddafi in Tripoli, another one of his misguided efforts to impress Americans with the strength of international opinion on Panama's side. Formal sessions did not resume until May. At Linowitz's insistence, they took place in Washington, a more businesslike setting than Contadora and one close to the medical care he needed for an eye problem. These meetings began at the Panamanian embassy but soon shifted to the conference room of the deputy secretary of state on the seventh floor of the State Department.

The negotiators soldiered on there until August. Richard Wyrough, one of the U.S. negotiators, recalled that "a more structured, formal, and efficient style emerged. . . . The five members on each side faced each other across the long polished table that dominates the room. There were the standard simultaneous interpreters and stenographers taking down the full discussion verbatim."[41] Bunker acquiesced in this shift of venue from Contadora, where the next round would ordinarily have been held. He was no doubt pleased that while the setting, form, and pace of the negotiations no longer reflected his customary preferences, the spirit of candor and collegiality that had earlier characterized relations among the negotiators remained intact. "Had that spirit not been present," Ambler Moss later maintained, "it would have been impossible for the two sides to work as a team during the ratification process [that followed] and for the Panamanians to accept the extraordinary baggage of the reservations, understandings, and changes in the spirit of the treaties which they understood had to be accepted in order to get the treaties through the U.S. Congress."[42]

Aside from establishing a more efficient negotiating regime, the Washington setting offered other obvious advantages to the American negotiators. Meeting there made it easier for them to consult specialists on the highly technical issues involved and to draw quickly on government documents and other relevant material. It also permitted them to engage closely in the battling within the civilian and military bureaucracies that remained a major feature of the negotiations. Perhaps most important, it allowed

Bunker and Linowitz to keep members of the Senate and House regularly informed of their progress, explain to the legislators what they were trying to do, and seek their advice. Acutely aware of the looming struggle over ratification that would follow the completion of the negotiations, the last thing either man wanted to do when that battle began was to confront senators and representatives with texts they had not been consulted about earlier.

The Washington meetings went on for over two months, with only a few breaks in the daily negotiating sessions. This was by far the longest round in the fourteen years of intermittent canal talks. Its length and pace reflected the determination of both sides to complete their work. Linowitz took the chair on the U.S. side, according to him with Bunker's consent. Before the new round began, he and Bunker had suggested that in order to break the deadlock over the issue of a continuing U.S. role in the defense of the canal beyond the year 2000, the new termination date the American negotiators had offered, the United States propose two treaties. One would assure the permanent neutrality of the canal, and thus give the United States the right to maintain its security indefinitely. The second would transfer the canal to Panama at the end of the century and provide for an increasing role for the Panamanians in its operation until then. Linowitz conceived the idea of the two separate treaties, and his legal training and ability enabled him to become the principal drafter of the sensitively worded Neutrality Treaty that eventually emerged from it.

This imaginative formula became the basis for the final settlement. Persuading the Panamanians to agree to it was not easy. Reversing Bunker's preference for tackling easier issues before taking up more difficult ones, the American team decided to deal with the matter head on, apparently in the expectation that a breakthrough could pave the way for agreement on other problems. The question of how the two governments would share responsibility for post-2000 canal security was crucial. As Ambler Moss has pointed out, "The real crux of the matter was what rights would the United States have to reopen the Canal if it was closed and to defend it in case it was attacked; and, in particular, what rights would the United States have if the threat to the Canal came from within the Republic of Panama?"[43] The Panamanians eventually accepted the separate neutrality treaty concept with the understanding that the U.S. right of defense would apply only to threats from outside Panamanian territory. The Panamanian government would protect the canal against danger from within the isthmus.

Buoyed by this accomplishment, the negotiators gradually made progress on the remaining issues. Many of these, like the future status of the American employees who operated the canal, the structure of a new organization to replace the U.S. government–owned Panama Canal Company, and the long-standing lands-and-waters dispute, were complicated matters important to both sides that involved decisions covering the most minute details.

The negotiators deliberately left the knotty and emotional problem of U.S. payment to Panama until last, a wise decision in light of the fundamentally different approaches the two sides brought to the matter. When the issue was joined, the Panamanians demanded a large lump sum payment to compensate for all the years in which they had benefited little from the canal. Their opening figure was $1.02 billion. They also wanted a hefty boost in annual payments, to be derived from higher toll rates, for the duration of the Panama Canal Treaty. From the American viewpoint, meeting such demands was out of the question. The U.S. negotiators rightly concluded that were Panama's demands conceded, opponents of the treaties would charge the administration with "paying Panama to take over the canal."

Eventually, thanks in large part to the good sense of their planning minister, Nicola Ardito Barletta, a Chicago-trained economist who later became president of the republic, the Panamanians accepted a more reasonable settlement. This included loan concessions and guarantees, and, more important, a moderate increase of canal tolls and their allocation to Panama. The Panamanians dropped their earlier demand for a bigger rise in tolls when Barletta accepted a toll sensitivity study that showed that bigger boosts in toll rates would lead customers to use transcontinental highways and railroads for shipments in preference to an expensive canal.

By early August, most obstacles including the question of payments had been largely overcome through a variety of compromises supplemented in some cases by deliberately ambiguous language. But the negotiators were able to accomplish this only after Carter had personally met them and sent a message to Torrijos pleading for a resolution of outstanding matters. Nearing the finish line, Bunker and Linowitz then flew to Panama for what they hoped would be a final, breakthrough negotiating session. Linowitz's six-month appointment was about to expire, on August 10, and this gave the negotiations an artificial deadline of sorts. Perhaps seeking to exploit this, the Panamanians suddenly tabled a new draft that reopened a long list of issues already resolved, including the financial settlement. They quickly backed down when they recognized that the Americans would not be moved.

A final marathon negotiating session on August 9 brought about a settlement. Bunker and Linowitz returned triumphantly to Washington with the completed draft treaties the following day. There they were hailed by the president, helped him brief the press, and prepared for the ratification battle.

In his statement of August 12, 1977, announcing the agreement on the draft texts, President Carter declared, almost certainly with more hope than conviction, that he knew that during the ratification process "each senator will give the most careful consideration not only to the treaties themselves but to the positive impact their approval will have in our own country and for our position in the world as a strong and generous nation."[44] The president's statement, the highly publicized September 6 ceremony in Washington at which Carter and Torrijos signed the treaties in the presence of almost all other hemispheric heads of government, and the submission of the texts to the Senate for its advice and consent soon afterwards raised the curtain on what would be one of the longest, toughest, and most intense foreign policy confrontations ever to grip Capitol Hill. The important role that Bunker played in the eventually successful fight was a fitting climax to his years in foreign affairs.

The two treaties Carter sent to the Senate were formally titled "The Panama Canal Treaty" and "The Treaty Concerning the Permanent Neutrality and Operation of the Panama Canal." Although many of the provisions of these treaties have been discussed in the foregoing pages, it would be useful to summarize their principal elements.

What Bunker termed the "basic" Panama Canal Treaty was a lengthy document that explicitly superseded the old 1903 Hay–Bunau-Varilla treaty. Unlike that treaty, it had a termination date—December 31, 1999. Panama, "as territorial sovereign," granted the United States until then the right to operate and defend the canal, with increasing Panamanian participation. The United States was to maintain control over all lands, waters, and installations—including military bases—necessary for these purposes. These areas and facilities were listed in a separate document.

A new U.S. government agency was to operate the canal, ensuring U.S. control of canal operations for the rest of the century. Its board would have a U.S. majority under an American administrator through 1989 and a Panamanian chief for the remaining decade of the treaty period. All American citizens currently employed on the canal could continue in U.S. government jobs until retirement, but within the five years following the treaty's coming into force the number of American staff was to be reduced by at least 20 percent. Lengthy financial provisions included Panama's receiving from future canal revenues a share in tolls (30 cents per ton of shipping), plus $10 million per year, and up to a further $10 million annually if canal traffic and revenues permitted. Outside the treaty, Washington pledged its best efforts to arrange for a generous economic package of loans, loan guarantees, and credits totaling $345 million. On the effective date of the treaty Panama was to assume general territorial jurisdiction over the Canal Zone and could use for its own purposes those portions of the defunct Zone not needed for the operation and defense of the canal. At the end of 1999, Panama would assume control of the canal operations. The two countries agreed to study jointly the feasibility of a sea-level canal. They would negotiate the terms for its construction if both found such a canal desirable.

The neutrality treaty was much shorter. In its first section, the Republic of Panama declared that the canal would be permanently neutral so that in peace or war the waterway would remain open to the ships of all nations on terms of full equality. Panama and the United States agreed to maintain this regime of neutrality without time limit, though following the termination of the Panama Canal Treaty at the end of 1999 Panama alone was to maintain armed forces and military installations on the isthmus.[45] Only U.S. and Panamanian warships were entitled to transit the canal "expeditiously" (later spelled out to mean that they could go to the head of the line in case of need or emergency). An attached protocol, which the United States and Panama were to introduce at the Organization of American States, was designed to allow other hemispheric nations to join the signatories in formally agreeing to respect the canal's permanent neutrality.

The administration faced an uphill battle. Senate head counts and public opinion polls showed the numbers running strongly against ratification. In May, the Opinion Research Corporation stated that opposition to relinquishing "ownership and control" of the canal had reached 78 percent.[46] Aware of this strongly negative opinion in the country and the often passionate feelings of many of those who held it, senators were understandably reluctant to commit themselves to a favorable vote. A survey of senatorial positions taken that same month by the Washington-based Institute for Conflict and Policy Studies showed only thirty-seven of the sixty-seven necessary for the required two-thirds majority in favor of the treaties and twenty-five solidly opposed. The remaining bloc of undecideds had strong misgivings about the economic and national security aspects of any new agreement transferring sovereignty of the canal to Panama.[47]

If Carter was to get the controversial treaties and the implementing legislation passed, he had to bring about a massive shift in public opinion. At the same time, the administration needed to make an intensified and more focused effort to explain and argue its case for the treaties on Capitol Hill. In the Senate, the support, influence, and advice on tactics of such senior members as Majority Leader Robert Byrd, a West Virginia Democrat, and Minority Leader Howard Baker, a Republican from Tennessee, were indispensable. But these powerful figures could not deliver the needed two-thirds for ratification, however much they came to favor the treaties and were willing to work closely with the administration for their acceptance. The hierarchical structure of the Senate had begun to erode, and back-benchers were starting to have more of a role. Moreover, the canal issue was too controversial and visible, and, in the thinking of many senators, too closely related to general disquiet about the global decline of U.S. power for rank-and-file members simply to vote the way party leaders told them to.

The administration found it had to work on an individual basis with large numbers of senators, providing them detailed explanations of the complicated and unusual treaties and dealing with their concerns and misgivings about specific provisions. In many cases it was obliged to grapple with amendments, understandings, and reservations to the treaties sponsored by individual senators. These proposals were often designed as much to provide the senators with a form of protection from vociferous and politically powerful opponents of the treaties as they were to allay the lawmakers' own problems, real and alleged, with the texts. At times, the administration felt obliged to offer senators concessions (critics called them bribes) on unrelated matters in order to assure their support for ratification.

Bunker played an important part in the carefully conceived and meticulously executed campaign to turn the tide. This sustained effort was led by the president and directed and implemented in the senatorial trenches by Deputy Secretary of State Warren Christopher and a dedicated band of State, Defense, and White House officials. Alternating with Linowitz,

Bunker participated regularly in the White House briefing sessions that Carter and other senior civilian and military officials conducted for groups of influential people from states whose senators were uncommitted on ratification. On the Hill, he testified before the Senate Foreign Relations Committee when it began its hearings on September 26, appearing together with Linowitz following Secretary Vance's opening presentation. Bunker was also a lead government witness before other Senate and House committees and subcommittees that held hearings on the treaties.[48] The Bunker-Linowitz approach was for each to testify on specific provisions of the treaties, then to field questions jointly. Linowitz bore the brunt of these.

Continuing and expanding the relations he had developed during the negotiations, Bunker briefed and lobbied many individual senators, supplementing the thirty or so State Department officials assigned to this task. He estimated that between them, he and Linowitz spoke privately to some eighty senators. Sometimes it would be a luncheon for eight or ten, sometimes a call on a single senator in his office. Looking back, Bunker was particularly proud that he had been able to secure "yes" votes from Vermont's two senators, Republican Robert Stafford and Democrat Patrick Leahy, and provide them some needed political cover as he did so. He gave an amusing account of what happened:

> They both telephoned me and asked if I would get in touch with George Aiken [the popular retired Republican Vermont senator] to see if I could get a good statement from him. They made it clear that they were going to support the treaty but they were both getting a lot of flack. So I called up George, and I said Bob Stafford and Pat Leahy would like a good statement from him, that they were going to support the treaty and that would help. "Well, Ellsworth," he said, "whenever anybody asks me about the Panama Canal treaties, I just say I'm a good friend of Ellsworth Bunker." That was George's statement.[49]

Bunker's detailed familiarity with the negotiating process and the terms of the treaty gave him considerable credibility both with senators and outsiders. But perhaps more important was his standing as a respected senior statesman. Douglas Bennet, who as assistant secretary of state for congressional relations helped direct the campaign, recalled that "it was not so much what Bunker said as who he was" that made him an effective lobbyist for the treaties.[50] Bunker's position on Vietnam does not seem to have figured in senators' appraisals of him. He told historian David McCullough that as a general rule "those who supported me in Vietnam were against me on the treaties," and vice versa.[51]

The role Bunker played in the administration's parallel campaign to sell the treaties to the broader public was astounding for a man in his early eighties. Sent out on the stump as one of a team of senior spokesmen, he covered the country from California to New England, where he made his way across Vermont and New Hampshire in the middle of winter, sometimes speaking to crowds as sparse as twenty-five or less. When a heavy snowstorm blanketed the Northeast, closing airports throughout the region, he borrowed a small plane from the Defense Department and delivered a speech in Franconia, New Hampshire, where a small airstrip had been plowed to accommodate him.

By his own count, Bunker made seventy-five speeches in twenty-one states and the District of Columbia and almost as many television and radio appearances. He gave the talks at foreign policy associations, service clubs, chambers of commerce, and wherever else the Washington-based staff directing the public relations aspect of the campaign could find an audience for him. The speeches were carefully prepared and well organized presentations in which Bunker spelled out the main provisions of the treaties, stressed their advantages for the United States, and, probably most important, tried to correct popular misconceptions that ratification opponents had spread about them.

A speech Bunker gave in Des Moines in January 1978 provides good evidence of how much misinformation these opponents had passed out and how he sought to set the record straight. He told his Iowa audience that foes of the treaties were simply wrong in charging that Panama was an unreliable, potentially unfriendly country whose involvement in the canal would threaten efficient operations or lead to its closure. He flouted their claims that the United States needed to perpetuate all its present rights to keep its security interests in the canal intact and their insistence that the generous financial arrangements that had been negotiated meant that the United States was "paying Panama to take the canal." He debunked the long-standing allegations, first popularized by Ronald Reagan, that the United States was surrendering sovereignty over the canal. Finally, he denied that the treaties could lead to a Cuban or Soviet military presence in Panama or in some other manner lead to an increase in Communist influence in the area.[52]

Although Bunker no doubt drew heavily on the prepared texts drafted by the speechwriters the administration had assembled for the ratification campaign, the final product he delivered showed his personal touch. Sometimes this came through in quietly humorous quips. He told a Midwest gathering: "I feel rather like that character in the *New Yorker* cartoon who—not having thought about the Canal for thirty years—finds himself suddenly unable to live without it."[53] No great orator, Bunker was effective with his audiences because they considered him, as his interlocutors in Washington did, a senior statesman who had been deeply involved in the negotiations and would never advocate anything that could harm the country's interests. His style added to his persuasiveness. He offered patient, well-informed responses to hostile questioners and consistently displayed the same courtly and reasonable manner that had long been the hallmark of his diplomatic encounters. He often got ovations from originally cool listeners at the end of his appearances. The State Department published and distributed some of his presentations as pro-ratification pamphlets.

As he spoke in such places as Los Angeles, Boston, and Seattle, Bunker took his share of abuse (though Sol Linowitz has recalled that Bunker was sometimes miffed that Linowitz—probably because he was Jewish—was targeted more often than he was). He recalled for a 1979 audience: "In travelling around the country on behalf of the Panama Canal treaties, I was picketed almost everywhere. In Miami, one large placard caught my eye. It read: 'Archie Bunker [the TV comic character] is smarter than Ellsworth.'"[54] The comparison became a favorite of his. He found other comments less amusing. As he dryly put it, they "often cast doubt on my manhood or suggested that I would be more at home in Red Square."[55] A self-described former neighbor in Vermont wrote him: "You are too old to know what you are doing. You old bastard. Go jump in the river."[56] Bunker said these attacks had not troubled him because he believed that what he was doing was right.

Writing to Harriet's brother Allan Butler on February 8 about the ratification battle after he had spoken fifty-three times on "the sawdust trail," Bunker said: "It has been an uphill struggle but I think we are making progress. I am hopeful that the Senate will approve the treaties, although I see a rough debate ahead of us."[57] His appraisal was accurate. A good deal of progress had in fact been made. By that time, the treaties had been approved by the Panamanian people in an October 23 plebiscite, with 68 percent voting in favor. The Senate Foreign Relations Committee had completed seventeen days of hearings in which no fewer than sixteen administration witnesses (including Bunker) and seventy-five congressional and private witnesses had testified. On January 30, 1978, the committee had sent the Neutrality Treaty to the full Senate in a fourteen-to-one vote. The adoption of "leadership amendments" to the treaty, sponsored by Senators Byrd and Baker, greatly bolstered its willingness to do so. These amendments incorporated into the treaty the language of the Carter-Torrijos memorandum of understanding of the previous October that interpreted the intervention and expeditious passage clauses of the text in a way acceptable to both governments.[58] The full Senate was beginning its debate on the treaty just as Bunker sent his message to Dr. Butler.

During the debate on the Neutrality Treaty and the subsequent consideration of the Panama Canal Treaty, all regular Senate business was suspended. In both debates, the long and often emotional exchanges covered many issues already made familiar by the lengthy and well-publicized committee hearings and, by Bunker and others, in public discussion. (In an interesting study of the negotiations, Timothy Stater has even maintained that, "the arguments pro and con were basically the same—control vs. use of the canal—as those made ever since the 1903 treaty.")[59] Could the canal be effectively operated and defended in the absence of U.S. sovereign rights? Could the United States adequately participate in safeguarding the neutrality of the canal once it had wound up its military presence in Panama at the end of the century? Why should the United States give away an integral part of its territory and pay Panama generously to take it in the bargain? What about the political leanings of the Torrijos regime and its record on human rights and narcotics trafficking? What would be the effect of ratifying or rejecting the treaties on U.S. interests elsewhere in the hemisphere? A quarter century later, the repetitious points often make tiresome reading. But when they were being made, they sparked great excitement and passion on the Senate floor.

The debates were punctuated by the repeated introduction of amendments, reservations, and understandings to the original texts. Some of these were so-called "killer amendments" put forward by ratification opponents. Designed to make the treaties unacceptable to Panama, they were often argued in terms the Panamanians could only find highly insulting. The exchanges on the Senate floor were broadcast, and the Panamanians who tuned in to the Spanish translation listened with mounting anger to the denunciations of their country by foes of the treaties. Torrijos later would show visiting Americans the scars he had made on the walls of his house when in fury he had hurled transistor radios as he monitored the Washington proceedings. Many of the other amendments and conditions were proposed by senators seeking political cover.

As the vote on the Neutrality Treaty neared, neither Bunker nor anyone else in the administration could be confident of the final tally. But on March 16 the Senate passed it by a razor-thin margin of sixty-eight to thirty-two, only one more than the two-thirds needed for ratification, when two uncommitted senators climbed aboard at the last minute.

As adopted, the treaty included a reservation sponsored by Dennis DeConcini, a conservative Arizona Democrat, stating that were the canal closed to shipping, the United States would have the right to use military force to open it. Panama reacted strongly to the DeConcini condition, which the administration had handled badly, and for a while its addition to the Neutrality Treaty seemed to jeopardize prospects for Panama's acceptance and a final settlement. Fortunately, the problem was resolved during the Senate's debate on the Panama Canal Treaty, when on April 14 it approved a reservation sponsored by nine senators, including the majority and minority leaders as well as DeConcini himself, that provided that U.S. action to keep the canal open should not be interpreted as intervention in the internal affairs of Panama. Passage of this reservation, which was acceptable to the Panamanians, ended the crisis.[60] Four days later, the Senate ratified the treaty by the same sixty-eight to thirty-two margin it had earlier given the Neutrality Treaty.

Carter and Torrijos exchanged instruments of ratification in an impressive ceremony in Panama City on June 16, with Bunker in attendance. But the process still had to clear a further hurdle, the enactment of implementing legislation needed to set up a new organization for operating the canal; to establish a retirement program for the canal's American employees; to transfer military facilities, schools, and hospitals; and to carry out the many other provisions of the newly ratified treaties.

The battle over this legislation was fought almost entirely in the House. In that body, the treaties enjoyed far less support than they did in the Senate. Bitter opponents of the canal "giveaway" staged a determined rearguard action that sought to prevent passage of the required legislation or at least to shape it in ways that undercut some of the terms of the treaties.

The fight proved much more difficult and prolonged than the administration had anticipated. As Bunker explained in an oral history interview he gave while the House was struggling over the legislation:

The problem was in part . . . the considerable resentment in the House because they were not involved in the ratification process. . . . There's another element [among representatives] which has never been reconciled to the treaties and to the transfer of the Canal . . . even though it's twenty years away. . . . And they've taken a very aggressive attitude, started a countrywide campaign in favor of legislation that would make it impossible to operate the Canal. So the treaty is going into effect willy-nilly October 1 [1979], and the opponents, the die-hard opponents, will try to pass legislation that will make the treaties actually ineffective, which will lead, I think, to a situation of chaos, because the old treaties will no longer be in existence. The new treaties go into effect, and if no funds are provided for operation, it's going to be a very tough situation.[61]

Faced with this unexpectedly strong opposition, the administration reactivated the task forces it had organized for the Senate ratification effort and undertook another strenuous if belated campaign to win approval of at least minimally acceptable legislation. Its own bill had been pronounced dead on arrival at the House so it was obliged to deal with a version proposed and managed by John Murphy, the chairman of the Merchant Marine and Fisheries Committee, who was an avowed opponent of the treaties.

Bunker was inevitably drawn back into the fray from very brief retirement. In the spring of 1979 he again went from office to office on Capitol Hill, this time to win over House members. Many of these representatives feared that if they supported the legislation they would suffer the same fate in the 1980 congressional elections as many pro-treaties senators had in 1978.[62]

Bunker's return meant that he had to learn the motivations and interests of a cast of characters few of whom he had known during the negotiations with the Panamanians and the Senate ratification battle. He contrasted the House members unfavorably with the senators he had worked with. Dealing with them could not have been easy for Bunker after his long effort to win Senate approval of the treaties, and there is a note of weariness and frustration in his recollections of this final chapter in the Canal saga on the Hill. Both houses eventually passed the much flawed legislation only five days before the treaties went into effect on October 1, 1979.

Many of those who took part in the long battle over the treaties lived to see the control of the canal transferred to the Republic of Panama on December 31, 1999, following a twenty-one-year transition period when, contrary to the claims of ratification opponents, Panama effectively took on increasing responsibility for the waterway's operation and defense.

Bunker, of course, had died long before, but some of the survivors, including President Carter, were appointed to the official U.S. delegation to the ceremony. The Clinton administration then in office was fearful of reviving conservative antagonism toward the transfer by giving great prominence to the event, however, and Clinton and his secretaries of state and defense did not attend. Bunker would not have welcomed Clinton's decision. He had too great a sense of pride and accomplishment in what he and others had achieved in negotiating the treaties and bringing them into force.

His own post-mortem of the long negotiating process was, characteristically, best put in a speech in which he talked about the art of diplomacy. "Creativity [is] an important element in successful negotiation," he told a Duke University audience in November 1979 a few weeks after the treaties had come into effect. "One side may give up an immediate advantage for the sake of a long-term advantage, even while the other side is more concerned with the immediate advantage because of certain requirements of its domestic political situation." In this case, by giving up certain privileges the United States had secured relations of equality and mutuality that had made Panama its partner rather than its colony. "By an act of creative statesmanship we gave up something which in the last analysis was of symbolic rather than practical value . . . and had obtained something of great value, . . . the willing cooperation of Panama without which . . . possession of the Canal would have meant little to us."[63]

It was a fitting way for a skilled practitioner to look at the final episode of his career in diplomatic service.

I4
Final Chapter

Following the Yom Kippur War in October 1973, Henry Kissinger developed a new strategy to disengage Arab and Israeli armed forces and establish at least a tenuous peace. His plan included convening a Middle East conference under American and Soviet auspices to discuss a comprehensive settlement. Kissinger wanted to use this multilateral conference, to be held at Geneva, as a cover for U.S. bilateral diplomacy with several Arab countries and Israel, from which the Soviets would be excluded. As Kissinger wrote in his memoirs, "All of the key actors understood that the sole achievement of the conference would be its opening: the progress that was foreseeable would take place in other forums."[1] In this way, Moscow would be relegated ("doomed" in Kissinger's vivid language) to irrelevance, unable to play a spoiler's role in a sensitive and difficult diplomatic operation.

The United States and the Soviet Union agreed to designate permanent representatives of ambassadorial rank to the conference. These diplomats would attend the ceremonial opening session and then remain in contact with one another following the (supposedly temporary) adjourning of the conference immediately afterwards.

Kissinger asked Bunker to leave the Panama Canal negotiations temporarily and take on the permanent representative assignment. It was a brilliant choice. Bunker had the rank and distinction necessary to persuade the Soviets and others that Washington took the conference seriously and might eventually exercise the option of reconvening it. Alfred L. Atherton Jr., a senior State Department official who had a major role in the negotiations, said later that "Henry wanted to show that [the conference] was not a charade. [He] needed the symbolism of someone like Ellsworth. . . . Ellsworth provided the image of commitment to the process and that was the image that Henry wanted to project."[2] Moreover, unlike many other senior diplomats in similar circumstances, Bunker had no trouble in accepting the irrelevance to which Kissinger's strategy condemned the conference, and hence Bunker himself. As Kissinger wrote later, he "was sure enough of himself so that he would not harass us into a pace incompatible with our plans."[3]

Bunker's laconic style also helped. Harold H. Saunders, another senior State Department negotiator, has noted that "Ellsworth probably had a lot more appreciation than a lot of us do about the importance of being quiet sometimes."[4] In Saunders's view, Bunker's performance at Geneva was a natural way for him to act. What for many others would have been a difficult feat of self-restraint and self-discipline came easily to him.

Bunker seemed to have enjoyed himself during his limited time in Geneva. He occasionally conferred with his Soviet counterpart and otherwise kept himself occupied, often by forays into the neighboring countryside to sample French and Swiss cuisine.

Aside from dawdling in Geneva pretending to wait for the conference to reconvene (it never did), Bunker took part in two of the extended diplomatic shuttles that took Kissinger and his negotiating team back and forth between Israel and Egypt and then between Israel and Syria. This was designed mainly to lead the Soviets further down the garden path by suggesting to them that as a participant in the shuttles Bunker could later feed back information about Kissinger's negotiating efforts to the resumed conference.

Bunker's actual role in the grueling exercise was limited but not insignificant. He sat in on strategy sessions and at all meetings with foreign officials except those in which Kissinger met national leaders privately. He did not ordinarily provide advice on tactics, but focused on the bigger picture. Like most others on the shuttle, he usually spoke up only when asked, and then only when he believed he had a genuine contribution to make. Joseph Sisco, another senior State Department shuttle passenger, recalled that when Bunker intervened, "it was not on marginal matters but on the heart of the issue."[5] Atherton thought Kissinger also saw Bunker as a sounding board, perhaps as a counterweight to the Middle East specialists. "Henry always needed counterweights, and rightly so, since many of us came to the issue with a lot of Mideast history. Ellsworth Bunker didn't have that baggage."[6] By all accounts, Bunker was neither pro-Arab nor pro-Israeli on Middle East issues.

Recalling Bunker's participation years later, his companions on the shuttle spoke of the remarkable stamina and good humor he displayed despite the strains of the long ordeal. Kissinger later maintained that Bunker withstood the exhausting journeys at least as well as staffers fifty years younger. In this Bunker was helped by his ability to catch catnaps without revealing that he was sleeping. "He would sit bolt upright with that New England look and his head never dropped," Atherton remembered, "but suddenly you'd realize that he was sleeping." His risqué Vermont stories provided moments of relaxation to others on the shuttle. The stories featured a couple named Phoebe and Walter, and Bunker told them in an accent that those unaware of his New York background mistakenly considered authentically native.

During the Syrian shuttle Bunker reached his eightieth birthday, on May 11, 1974. To quote Kissinger once more, "In the midst of tensions, discouragements and beginning doubts of the shuttle, [Bunker] united us all at a surprise party that Ambassador [to Israel Kenneth] Keating gave him at [Jerusalem's] King David Hotel." The secretary of state proposed a toast, hailing Bunker as the epitome of the best and most permanent in America—"where we stand as a people and society."[7] It was a fitting, sincere salute by Kissinger to a fellow diplomat whose background, style, and temperament were so very different from his own.

When the Communists took Saigon in April 1975, Bunker was again caught up in the Panama Canal negotiations. Unlike other U.S. officials who had dealt with Vietnam earlier and tried to make themselves useful during the final weeks of South Vietnam's agony, he remained aloof and deliberately avoided any further involvement. He seemed to feel that it was no longer his affair.[8]

He blamed the collapse of South Vietnam on Congress. In his view, its refusal to provide adequate funding had made it impossible for the United States to fulfill the commitments Nixon had given the Vietnamese. He regarded the triumph of the Communists as a tragedy for America and its friends that "created doubt among our allies as to our will and our credibility and [gave] encouragement to our adversaries to pursue their aggressive policies while feeling we will not respond."[9]

In later years Bunker would tell interviewers that he had drawn two important lessons from the Vietnam experience. The first was that a democracy cannot wage war successfully without public support. He was critical of Johnson for failing to explain adequately to the American people what the objectives and the stakes in Vietnam were. But he reserved his harshest scorn once again for "committed journalists" whom he continued to believe had misled the public and turned the country against the war.

Bunker also held that the United States "can't wage a limited war for limited objectives against an adversary whose objectives are unlimited and who has or is given the means to carry on and wage unlimited war."[10] He did not spell out what the implications of this had been on the ground in Southeast Asia during the war except to reiterate his long-standing conviction that the United States ought to have intervened early in Laos to cut off Communist supplies to the South.

Some time after the collapse of South Vietnam, and according to him because of it, Bunker decided to write a book about his Vietnam experiences that would spell out the lessons that could be learned from U.S. involvement. He chose as his collaborator Stephen Young, then an assistant dean at the Harvard Law School, whom he had known when Young was in Vietnam from 1968 to 1971. Drawing on interviews with Bunker and official documents and private correspondence that Bunker made available to him, Young produced a lengthy, fairly rough manuscript in the early 1980s. Neither Bunker nor Carol was satisfied with the draft, titled "Lost Victory," and though Bunker showed portions of it to colleagues for their review and suggestions, it remains unpublished.[11]

Later, Bunker considered collaborating with former *New York Times* Saigon correspondent Fox Butterfield on a book about Vietnam that Butterfield proposed to write in his own name. Bunker was to provide Butterfield with his cables to the president, other official messages, and his letters to Carol, and give him personal interviews. The project, which would have superseded the Bunker-Young collaboration, never materialized.

Thus unlike many other senior American officials who were involved in the war and sought in memoirs to explain and justify their roles in it, Bunker left behind no written account of his Vietnam experiences other than those found in his declassified official reports, several published interviews and talks, his correspondence with Carol, and a few letters to others. History is the poorer for it.

Following Senate ratification of the Panama Canal treaties, Bunker resigned as ambassador-at-large, by his own choice with minimal publicity.[12] Secretary of State Vance hosted a small dinner in his honor but no press releases were issued nor announcements made. According to the media, Bunker was simply listed on Vance's schedule with no further explanation.[13] President Carter, the last of the seven presidents Bunker served, paid tribute to him in a long message that praised his wisdom, judgment, and strength of character and expressed personal appreciation "for what you have given, to me, to the Department of State, and to our Nation."[14]

By then, Bunker was becoming increasingly frail despite the careful attention he always gave to keeping fit. He made good use of his time despite this. He attended receptions and dinners with Carol, who had also retired,[15] and kept in touch with old State Department colleagues. With some of them, he helped set up the American Academy of Diplomacy, an association of retired ambassadors and others, still going strong, that seeks to ensure high standards for diplomatic appointment. Long a member of the board of the Asia Foundation, which fosters democratic leadership and institutions in Asian countries, he helped keep the organization afloat when its U.S. government funding was in jeopardy. According to Haydn Williams, then Asia Foundation president, "No foundation trustee worked harder with [me] than Bunker to hold the foundation together and carry on."[16]

Back in Vermont, Bunker hosted annual Fourth-of-July parties at his Dummerston farm house. They were preceded by a parade in nearby Brattleboro in which Bunker and other old timers rode in open cars and waved to the crowd. Bunker loved these old-fashioned occasions; they appealed to his patriotism and his pride in an older, passing America. He also kept interested in the political scene. Still "a good Democrat" after years of service in both Republican and Democratic administrations, he voted in a town meeting straw poll for Walter Mondale for the 1984 presidential nomination.[17] He and Carol became regular communicants at Brattleboro's St. Michael's Episcopal Church, whose rector came to value him not only as an important parishioner but as a man of deep sincerity and spirituality, "a man of great prayer in dealing with the Lord."[18]

Bunker took a special interest in the newly established Institute for the Study of Diplomacy (ISD), part of Georgetown University's Edmund A. Walsh School of Foreign Service in Washington. In 1976, when the institute had only just been proposed to the school's dean, Peter F. Krogh, Georgetown awarded honorary degrees to both the Bunkers, possibly the only time the old and prestigious Jesuit institution had honored a husband and wife at a single commencement ceremony.[19] This brought them into closer touch with the university and set the stage for Bunker's appointment as ISD's first board chairman.

Krogh recalled that Carol had come up with the idea of Bunker's going to the institute. "She was interested in having [Ellsworth] continue to be engaged in the diplomatic field with all of his experience and stature. She thought ISD would be a great outlet for him and also a way to honor him. . . . Her objective was to be sure that this great man lived out his life with effect and dignity and was appropriately honored while being kept active and engaged so that his life would last as long as possible."[20]

Bunker helped to put the incipient institute on its feet financially and substantively. Leaving most of the day-to-day operation to ISD's able director, former ambassador Martin F. Herz, who had served as his minister for political affairs in Saigon, he made himself available for many different institute activities. He raised money, enlisted new board members, and persuaded prestigious figures such as Henry Kissinger to address institute-sponsored conferences. Following Bunker's death, ISD established a fund in his memory. It still provides stipends to Georgetown undergraduates who work with the institute's professional associates on diplomatic research projects. His most important substantive contribution was his collaboration with two of these associates on monographs about his negotiations to resolve the West New Guinea, Yemen, and Dominican Republic crises. They were among the institute's first major publications.[21]

Thanks in important measure to Bunker's varied activities on its behalf, the institute soon found a place on Washington's crowded think-tank map as Georgetown's window to the world of the foreign policy practitioner. He is still well remembered and honored at the university, where ISD continues to flourish.

On May 11, 1984, Bunker celebrated his 90th birthday at a large party Carol hosted at the F Street Club. Many of the people he had worked with in his diplomatic years were there. Ambassador Philip Habib doubtless spoke for them all in his toast: "When we look back over the greatest figures of our generation, this is one of the greatest."[22] Several newspapers ran stories on the occasion. Bunker must have been particularly pleased with the *San Diego Union*'s report: "Ellsworth Bunker had that spare, pink-cheeked puritan look that puts one in mind of the early American patriots. As he stood receiving applause at his ninetieth birthday party, it was easy to see him as an eighteenth century citizen-diplomat from Vermont."[23]

Soon afterwards, the Bunkers left their apartment in Northwest Washington on what would be Ellsworth's last trip home to Dummerston. On September 13 he became ill and was rushed to Brattleboro Memorial Hospital, where he was found to have a general viral infection. Death came two weeks later from complications attributable to his advanced age.

His funeral was held at St. Michael's Episcopal Church, where Harriet had been eulogized twenty years before. Some 200 people led by Richard Nixon crowded the small church in Brattleboro to pay a final tribute.[24] A memorial service was held later at the Washington National Cathedral in the presence of a large congregation of dignitaries, admirers, and friends. He was buried beside Harriet in the family plot near their Dummerston home.[25]

Bunker's death received major coverage. Many dailies published lengthy obituaries that reviewed his eventful and unusual career as a businessman-turned-diplomat. The accounts gave special prominence to his role in Vietnam, but even those papers that had strongly opposed the policies he advocated and implemented during the war recalled his record in Saigon in a balanced and understanding way. The *New York Times* front-page article highlighted vintage quotes from Bunker interviews. "When the President calls on you to do a job, you do it." "I'm an old-fashioned patriot. I have always assumed that my country was fundamentally right in its dealings with others." "The object of our diplomacy there [in Vietnam], as elsewhere, was the quite proper one of not winning arguments but achieving goals."[26] Many press accounts carried Secretary of State George Shultz's statement about Bunker: "He scored remarkable achievements that have few parallels in American history."[27]

By the time he died, Bunker had become an icon of American diplomacy. In his assignments as ambassador and troubleshooter–special negotiator, he had dealt with problems on four continents. Some of them seemed far removed from America's confrontation with the major Communist powers, the focus of much of postwar U.S. foreign policy. But virtually all of these problems could have seriously jeopardized American interests in regions important to the United States had they not been resolved or effectively managed. His assignments as ambassador to Vietnam and chief negotiator on the Panama Canal treaties, which climaxed his diplomatic career, involved controversial issues at the heart of both America's relations with the world and its domestic politics.

In his twenty-five years as a diplomat, Bunker played three broadly defined roles. In his troubleshooting role he acted as a third-party mediator between hostile governments or civil war factions and as a negotiator representing the United States in bilateral disputes. In his second role he headed three U.S. embassies that carried out essentially conventional diplomatic operations. His responsibilities in Vietnam fell into a third category. As a virtual American proconsul there, he led a mission whose activities went well beyond those of other U.S. overseas posts and were arguably unprecedented in scope and magnitude in American diplomatic history.

Bunker's personality and skills served him well in all these roles. He had a sure understanding of the principles of classic diplomacy and practiced them with a skill that brought him the admiration of both his colleagues and his negotiating partners. His unusual ability to win the trust of U.S. and foreign leaders and his presence and manner were key to his diplomatic success.

It was in his troubleshooter–special negotiator role that Bunker made his most important contributions to U.S. diplomacy. He achieved his greatest success in resolving the Dominican Republic crisis after other envoys of the United States and the Organization of American States had failed. The settlement he worked out rescued the Johnson administration from a major foreign policy embarrassment that was damaging U.S. interests throughout the hemisphere. It also produced changes in the Caribbean republic that proved of lasting benefit to the Dominican people. Few American statesmen other than Bunker had the originality and sensitivity required to fashion the terms of a settlement that the contentious Dominican rivals would accept. And almost none enjoyed standing at the White House sufficient to tackle the problem largely free of the outside interference that could otherwise have impaired the negotiating process.

Bunker lucidly spelled out and, in the Dominican Republic and elsewhere, personally practiced the principles a good negotiator should follow. These principles largely conformed to the maxims set out by classic commentators on Western diplomatic practice as updated to take account of twentieth-century political changes.

Bunker held that every negotiation is different. But several common techniques stand out in his third-party and bilateral efforts. The most distinctive hallmark of a Bunker-led negotiation was his tactic of creating an informal atmosphere in which the contending parties could develop easier personal relations, preferably in a pleasant and secluded setting. Another was his practice of putting forward early in the negotiating process a set of draft proposals that became the terms of reference for the bargaining that followed. Thus in the Panama Canal negotiations he adapted ideas formulated earlier by the Panamanian foreign minister, shrewdly renamed them the Kissinger-Tack Principles, and made them the centerpiece for further negotiating. In the West New Guinea negotiations he tabled the Bunker Plan and in Santo Domingo his OAS Ad Hoc Committee's "Proposal for a Solution of the Dominican Crisis," with the same purpose. The teams that he set up to assist him were somewhat unusual for American diplomacy. They were almost always small so that they could move swiftly and decisively to develop fresh approaches before others could second-guess them.

Despite the importance top officials in Washington attached to the issues Bunker dealt with, he enjoyed a remarkable degree of independence in developing tactics and strategy in his negotiations. The confidence of the White House was a great boon to him. It helped restrain the bureaucracy from its normal penchant to micromanage negotiations from Washington. Harry Shlaudeman's comment about Bunker—"Ellsworth didn't throw his weight around; he didn't have to"—had relevance beyond the Dominican crisis. Only in the canal negotiations did he become more involved in bureaucratic infighting. But given the stakes, the large number of powerful actors involved, and the sharp differences of view on this highly emotional national issue, that was inevitable. He proved himself adept both in dealing with the bureaucracy and then, in a new role in his diplomatic experience, in selling the treaties he had negotiated to Congress and the American people.

In Argentina, Italy, and India, Bunker played the role of a modern American ambassador far more in the manner of a seasoned career professional than as a talented amateur. He correctly saw his job in these countries as an exercise in state-to-state relations, not as an opportunity to promote his own ideas or a popularity contest. This meant interpreting for Washington the motives and concerns of his host governments, especially as their policies affected U.S. interests. Equally important, it meant promoting and explaining U.S. global, regional, and bilateral policies in ways that made them acceptable or at least plausible to his hosts. He carried out both these functions effectively. His skill in developing strong professional relations with the local leadership—in Perón's Argentina as strong, that is, as he thought appropriate—was important in enabling him to do so.

In his sober, elegant way, Bunker made friends for America. He traveled a good deal outside national capitals and got to know something of his host countries. But his was a rather detached and impersonal style. He did not see himself as a "cultural bridge," as some other successful ambassadors have, and developed only a limited interest in the culture, traditions, and history of these countries. He brought his business experience to the management of his embassies and also used it to de-demonize modern capitalism among those who considered multinational business organizations immoral and dangerous. He followed a relaxed management style. He gave his deputies responsibility for the day-to-day operation of his missions and interfered relatively little in the work of individual embassy offices.

Bunker recognized that public affairs and economic assistance had come to stay as important mission functions. Although his public style was rather formal, he tried with considerable success to reach out to different sections of society. He had no interest in "going native." His character and his deep roots in American life helped make him an excellent spokesman for the United States. He keyed some of his public appearances to economic assistance programs, which he strongly supported but was careful not to micromanage.

Bunker's relationship with the Washington bureaucracy was strong and mutually supportive. He had little interest in the gamesmanship familiar in the corridors of the State Department and elsewhere in Washington. On his visits home he cultivated Congress, most notably in lobbying to win higher levels of economic assistance for India. His effectiveness on Capitol Hill dated back to his years as a spokesman for the sugar industry, and he was always well regarded there.

Bunker largely accepted the objectives and strategy of U.S. policy toward the countries in which he served. His recommendations to Washington were mainly designed to advance those policies, not to challenge them, and he offered few original proposals on broader issues. In Italy and India, countries with which the United States enjoyed friendly relations, his policy recommendations often included calls for greater economic assistance and, in India as its rift with China deepened, for supply of military hardware. This reflected the "clientitis" that afflicted many ambassadors in those Cold War days, and still does. Bunker kept such special pleading within limits, and it did not undermine his credibility in Washington.

Bunker displayed no special interest in the domestic political issues in the countries in which he served except as they demonstrably affected U.S. interests, especially in the economic development sphere. In Italy and India, he shared Washington's satisfaction with the current political dispensation and made only marginal efforts to tinker with it. But this diffidence did not rule out clandestine efforts to thwart local communist parties. He unapologetically supported such activity, as did other American diplomats during the Cold War.

As already noted, Bunker is still regarded in India as one of the finest American ambassadors to serve in New Delhi. Circumstances over which he had no control ruled out any similar appreciation for him in Rome. A review of Argentine writings about U.S.-Argentine relations in the 1940s and 1950s suggests that his work in Buenos Aires also passed largely unremarked, certainly as compared to the activities of Spruille Braden and other more interventionist American ambassadors of the time. Considering that Bunker was sent to Buenos Aires to pursue a policy of masterful inactivity, that is not too bad a tribute.

Bunker's role in Saigon differed sharply from the one he played in Buenos Aires, Rome, and New Delhi. It had to. United States involvement in Vietnam was so momentous and comprehensive that the conventional diplomatic business American embassies elsewhere perform was inadequate for U.S. purposes. Bunker would have shunned the title of American proconsul or viceroy. But in effect that is what he was in his six years in Saigon.

Bunker's policy preferences and recommendations on Vietnam policy made him one of the most outspoken hawks on the war in the top ranks of the U.S. government. His advice to Washington often reflected his view that the war should be waged more vigorously, especially through actions designed to choke off the movement of troops and supplies through privileged sanctuaries in Laos and Cambodia.

But he recognized that the American people would not indefinitely support a conflict of the scale the war had reached in the year he came to Saigon. This helped make him a strong supporter of Vietnamization, which he believed could successfully transfer the defense of South Vietnam from American to local forces. He enthusiastically welcomed Nixon's making the concept central to his administration's withdrawal strategy. Yet it seems fair to conclude that had the president not moved in that direction, Bunker would have loyally supported whatever other policy Washington developed.

Bunker's major influence on Vietnam policy was most evident in his first year in Saigon. President Johnson carefully read his special weekly messages. These cables, and other messages sent from Embassy Saigon, probably had a greater impact in shaping administration policy than any specific recommendations on strategy or tactics that Bunker made. As good ambassadors recognize, carefully crafted messages supported by convincing evidence play a powerful role in establishing the policy environment in which decisions are taken. Bunker rightly gave these reports his special attention and made them the vehicle for his assessments of major developments and their implications for the future. Along with other sanguine embassy reporting, the excessive optimism of his weekly cables to the White House misled Washington and eventually damaged his credibility, especially among those who had misgivings about current policy.

As the massive U.S. stake in Vietnam required, Bunker and his mission involved themselves in all facets of South Vietnamese political and economic life in ways that went far beyond the more limited approach he had adopted in his previous ambassadorial assignments. In his dealings with Thieu and other Vietnamese leaders, his guiding principle was to persuade the Vietnamese to recognize the advantages to themselves of policies the United States recommended, not to impose those policies on them. He relentlessly tried, with limited success, to convince Washington to be more forthcoming with Saigon in disclosing what it was trying to accomplish in the negotiations with the North. Thieu and others in his government seemed to recognize and welcome Bunker's approach, and gave him much respect. But even Bunker's careful ministrations were insufficient to bring Thieu around at crucial points. Some Americans and Vietnamese argue that had Bunker taken a tougher, less accommodating line with the evasive and indecisive Vietnamese president, things might have been different. But this must remain tantalizingly speculative.

To the end of his foreign affairs career, Bunker remained a diplomatic craftsman, not a "big thinker" or foreign policy intellectual. His focus was always on resolving or managing immediate issues to meet current U.S. foreign policy objectives. He never sought senior jobs in Washington that would have placed him in a position to frame broad policy, and turned down President Kennedy's offer of one. He accepted the conventional Cold War wisdom of his times. If he had any philosophical approach to American foreign policy, it was a generally Wilsonian view that included a strong emphasis on the right of self-determination and the improvement of the lot of ordinary people.

In his later years, Bunker came to typify and symbolize the old-fashioned American who was ready to shoulder arduous, difficult, sometimes dangerous tasks in the country's service. He never questioned America's greatness or the values that he thought had made it great, and came across to foreigners and compatriots alike as an authentic American in the best sense of that term. Henry Kissinger's reported awe for Bunker as an unreal specter from the past, an antique figure, American in a primeval way, rings true. Beneath his adopted cool New England exterior, Bunker was a passionate patriot who was proud to be an American and never reluctant to say so.

With his passing, only a few remained of the remarkable band of statesmen born around the turn of the last century who played key roles in shaping and implementing America's foreign policy in the Cold War years. Some of them had climbed the career ladder as professional Foreign Service officers. Others came to diplomacy as a second calling. They all shared a sense of service to the country and believed they had an obligation to America that they could fulfill by taking on major foreign policy responsibilities.

Bunker's character and personality set him somewhat apart from his colleagues. In an increasingly hurried age, he maintained a deliberate calm in all of his diplomatic roles. His sure sense of who he was and a recognition in his diplomatic years that he had nothing to prove to himself or others helped explain his success. This self-assurance reflected a robust inner strength that served him and the nation well.

At the end of his days, Bunker was serenely pleased in his quiet way that he had been able to serve the United States when it could use his talents to carry out its new global responsibilities. Although he was troubled by the erosion, in a changing America, of old-time values he cherished and upset by the debacle that had undone his accomplishments in Vietnam, he remained the contented and self-confident man he had been for so long. He dedicated his skills to the diplomat's trade, often in trying circumstances, in keeping with the country's best patriotic tradition. From its beginning, America's survival has depended on the few who, like Ellsworth Bunker, were prepared to set aside their private concerns to serve the nation.

NOTES

Abbreviations Used in Endnotes

BC	Bunker Collection, LBJ Library, Austin, Texas
CIA	Central Intelligence Agency
DDE	Dwight D. Eisenhower
EB	Ellsworth Bunker
EUCOM	European Command
FRUS	*Foreign Relations of the United States*
GVN	Government of Vietnam
IAPF	Inter-American Peace Force
NA	National Archives, Washington, D.C.
NATO	North Atlantic Treaty Organization
NSF	National Security File
OAS	Organization of American States
PRG	Vietcong Provisional Revolutionary Government
U.N.	United Nations
USUN	U.S. Mission to the United Nations
WHCF	White House Central Files
YAR	Yemen Arab Republic

Chapter 1

1. EB letter to Carol Laise Bunker (hereafter Carol), July 21, 1972, privately held. All EB letters to Carol cited hereafter are also privately held unless otherwise specified.

2. Moran, *Bunker Genealogy*, 25.

3. Letter to EB from Edward Eaton Chapin of Noank, Connecticut, n.d., 1962, BC.

4. EB address to the Royal Navy Officers' Dining Club, Buenos Aires, October 19, 1951, BC.

5. Good accounts of the development of the sugar business and the role in it of the National Sugar Refining Company can be found in Eichner, *Emergence of Oligopoly*, and Catlin, *Good Work Well Done*.

6. EB Oral History interview, Columbia University, 13.

7. EB letter to Carol, March 22, 1972.

8. Ibid.

9. EB letter to Katherine Parsons, October 26, 1968, BC.

10. EB Oral History interview, Columbia University, 19.

11. EB letter to Katherine Parsons, May 12, 1954, BC.

12. EB comments on the occasion of the Yale Bowl Award, May 14, 1975, BC.

13. In its citation, Yale accurately stated: "You have combined intelligence, thorough knowledge, and integrity of character with humor, unassuming modesty and personal charm. Your career bears witness to your concern for the nation and the welfare of your fellowmen."

14. EB letter to (grandson) Jamie Bunker, January 30, 1983, BC.

15. EB letter to Mathilda Tyler of New Haven, December 2, 1961, BC.

16. EB remarks at Davenport College, Yale University, October 25, 1961, from handwritten notes, BC.

17. Special interview of Herman Von Holt by Michaelyn Chou, Honolulu, March 9, 1987, BC.

18. For an account of the Warner purchase, see *New York Times*, January 20, 1927.

19. For Bunker's 1934 testimony, see House Committee on Agriculture, *Hearings before the Committee on Agriculture*, 169–77, and Senate Committee on Finance, *Hearings before the Committee on Finance*, 148–63.

20. Catlin, *Good Work Well Done*, 212.

21. EB address to the American Beet Sugar Industry, "A Post War Program for Sugar," January 12, 1944, 3, BC. Bunker gave the speech in his capacity as chairman of the U.S. Cane Sugar Refiners' Association.

22. Ibid., 8–9.

23. A parallel organization representing the beet sugar refining industry was set up at the same time, with Frank Kemp as its chairman.

24. See, for example, *New York Times*, January 3, 1938, and House Committee on Agriculture, *Sugar Legislation: Hearing before the Committee on Agriculture*, 123–34.

25. EB Oral History interview, Columbia University, 36.

26. Samuel Bunker, interview by author, February 1992.

27. Catlin, *Good Work Well Done*, 255.

28. *Boston Globe*, September 4, 1982.

29. Minutes of meeting of Executive Committee of the General Finance Committee, held at Hotel Biltmore, September 9, 1936, BC.

30. Minutes of meeting of Executive Committee of the General Finance Committee, held at Hotel Biltmore, October 22, 1936, BC.

31. By comparison, Republican senator George Aiken had won in 1956 with almost two-thirds of the vote.

32. See EB interview by Sanford Ungar for *Foreign Policy*, January 1978, and EB letter to Mrs. Erwin N. Griswold of Washington D.C., n.d., BC.

33. Samuel Bunker, interview by author.

34. Unidentified and undated newspaper clipping in BC. The text suggests that it was taken from a local newspaper and printed in 1983.

35. Quoted in the *Boston Globe*, September 4, 1982.

36. Address by U.S. Senator (former Secretary of Agriculture) Clinton Anderson, University Club, New York, March 2, 1951, BC.

37. *Business Week*, June 10, 1944.

38. Catlin, *Good Work Well Done*, 255.

39. *New York Times*, July 25, 1947.

Chapter 2

1. EB letter to Dean Acheson, January 11, 1953, Acheson Papers, Box 4.

2. David Acheson, interview by author, June 1993.

3. Acheson, *Present at the Creation*, 589.

4. Bunker reciprocated this feeling. Writing from Buenos Aires when he learned that Miller would be staying on as assistant secretary to the end of Truman's second term in 1953, Bunker reflected, "As you know, my decision to come here was in great part determined by my admiration for the work which you were doing and the way in which you were doing it and the feeling that if I could pitch in in any way and help, it was an obligation to do so." (EB letter to Miller, January 10, 1952, Lot 53, D26, Miller Files.)

5. Many of these letters are in the Miller Files.

6. EB Oral History interview, Duke University, 2.

7. Acheson, *Present at the Creation*, 589.

8. In a speech he gave at a testimonial dinner hosted by his sugar industry colleagues, Bunker described it as coming out of a clear sky. "As you know," he said, "I have never been in the diplomatic service, I have never been to Argentina, and to date I really know nothing about my job. Perhaps some would say that represented a typical set of qualifications for a government job." (EB address, University Club, New York City, March 2, 1951, BC.)

9. Henry Dearborn, interview by author, June 1991.

10. See the exchange of letters, Acheson to EB (December 4, 1950) and EB's reply to the secretary (December 8, 1950), Acheson Papers, Box 3.

11. EB Oral History interview, Duke University, 3. The remark obviously delighted Bunker. He also recounted it in two other oral history interviews.

12. EB letter to Earl Wilson, January 23, 1951, BC.

13. EB Oral History interview, Duke University, 4.

14. Policy Statement, October 26, 1951, *FRUS*, vol. 2, 1123. For a useful discussion of Perón's attitude toward the Argentine press and his closing of *La Prensa*, see Blanksten, *Perón's Argentina*, 199–216.

15. Page, *Perón*, provides a good review of the Argentine president's career.

16. Tulchin, *Argentina and the United States*, 107–11.

17. Perón exploited Braden's maneuvers against him to appeal to Argentine anti–United States nationalism. He told the voters they had to choose "Perón or Braden." Not surprisingly, they chose Perón, who won by a 2–1 margin over the opposition candidate in what was regarded as a fair ballot. Harold F. Peterson studies this unusual episode in *Argentina and the United States*, 450–54.

18. Whitaker, *United States and Argentina*, 210.

19. James Bruce, an executive of the National Dairy Products Company (1947–49), and Stanton Griffis, a partner in the investment banking firm of Hemphill, Noyes and Company (1949–50). Griffis had been ambassador to King Farouk's Egypt and left Argentina in November 1950 to become ambassador to Franco's Spain.

20. Warren, "Diplomatic Relations."

21. Acheson, *Present at the Creation*, 589.

22. Mallory letter to Miller, March 22, 1951, Miller Files.

23. Policy Statement, October 26, 1951, *FRUS 1951*, vol. 2, 1112–13. The statement was drafted by Henry Dearborn. It listed five principal U.S. objectives in Argentina: realization by Argentina that its traditional neutralism is not feasible in the world of today and that in U.S.-Argentine relations Argentina needs the United States more than the United States needs Argentina; Argentine collaboration in the maintenance of international security, especially in the western hemisphere; Argentine adoption of policies which will strengthen those forces striving for peace and a democratic way of life; creation and maintenance of a favorable climate of opinion among the Argentine people toward the United States and its policies; and encouragement of healthy bilateral economic relations and protection of U.S. enterprises carrying on Argentine operations.

24. "It is going to require little short of diplomatic acrobatics to play our self-imposed role of 'masterly inaction' while at the same time performing what is one of our basic roles, namely that of representing U.S. interests in Argentina," the assistant secretary had advised Bunker. (Miller letter to EB, May 22, 1951, Miller Files.)

25. EB letter to Miller, June 14, 1951, Miller Files.

26. Embassy Buenos Aires despatch 1755, Enclosure 1, May 10, 1951, State Department Files, POL 27 Argentina, NA.

27. EB letter to Henry Dearborn, May 18, 1951, State Department Files, POL 27 Argentina, NA.

28. EB letter to Miller, June 14, 1951, Miller Files. Bunker wrote at least twice to Miller on June 14. This quote is from the shorter message.

29. Miller letter to EB, August 16, 1951, *FRUS 1951*, vol. 2, 1107.

30. EB letter to Miller, December 13, 1951, *FRUS 1951*, vol. 2, 1138. Miller letter to EB, December 28, 1951, *FRUS 1951*, vol. 2, 1139.

31. EB letter to Dearborn, May 18, 1951, State Department Files, POL 27 Argentina, NA.

32. Embassy Buenos Aires despatch 1084, January 10, 1952, State Department Files, POL 27 Argentina, NA.

33. EB letter to Miller, June 14, 1951, Miller Files.

34. EB letter to Dearborn, May 18, 1951, State Department Files, POL 27 Argentina, NA.

35. Mallory became ambassador to Jordan and Guatemala.

36. Harriet Bunker letter to Katherine Parsons, May 27, 1951, BC.

37. Miller memorandum to Under Secretary James Webb, November 26, 1951, Miller Files.

38. EB letter to Miller, January 7, 1952, Miller Files.

39. Acheson, *Present at the Creation*, 589.

40. EB letter to Miller, March 1, 1952, Miller Files.

41. See Embassy Buenos Aires despatch 1351, March 6, 1952, State Department Files, POL 27 Argentina, NA.

42. EB memorandum, "Suggestions for Argentine Policy," March 11, 1952, *FRUS 1952–54*, vol. 2, 400–406.

43. See "Notes of the Secretary of State's Staff Meeting, . . . March 20, 1952, *FRUS 1952-54*, vol. 2, 407-9.

44. See above (Acheson, *Present at the Creation*, 589).

45. Dean Acheson letter to the Board of Governors of the Metropolitan Club [of Washington], February 4, 1954, Acheson Papers, Box 3.

46. Lester Mallory letter to Miller, November 28, 1951, Miller Files.

Chapter 3

1. The 1962 Dutch-Indonesian negotiations were the only other time Bunker dealt significantly with European diplomats.

2. *New York Times*, May 7, 1952.

3. For a discussion of the details of the EDC proposal as introduced by the French government and later modified by Washington, see Brogi, *Question of Self-Esteem*, 123-24.

4. With 305 seats, the Christian Democrats alone had a parliamentary majority. Of the other parties of the democratic center which from time to time had participated in de Gasperi's center coalition, the Liberals had 19, the Republicans 9, and the Social Democrats 33.

5. EB Oral History interview, Duke University, 146-47.

6. For an extensive discussion of these developments, which set the stage for Bunker's ambassadorship, see Smith, *United States, Italy, and NATO*. Brogi, *Question of Self-Esteem*, 132-33, is especially useful on de Gasperi's evolving positions on regional security and economic organizations.

7. Brogi, *Question of Self-Esteem*, 137.

8. "Implementation of NSC 67/3, 'The Position of the U.S. With Respect to Communism in Italy,'" National Security Council report, November 1, 1952 (FOI Document).

9. See Kogan, *Political History of Italy*, 164-65. Kogan's study of the overall political situation in the first decade after the war (chapters 1-4) is useful in understanding the situation Bunker and other American ambassadors of the that era faced (and tried to influence).

10. Acquired by Italy from Austria-Hungary following World War I, Trieste was claimed by Yugoslavia at the end of the World War II. The port city and its environs were made a Free Territory by the 1947 Italian Peace Treaty and divided into two zones of military administration, "A" under the British and Americans and "B" under the Yugoslavs.

11. The term used by Walter Isaacson and Evan Thomas as the title of their 1986 study of the architects of American postwar diplomacy. The book includes passing reference to Bunker, mostly in connection with his role as ambassador to Vietnam, but the authors did not include him among their Wise Men.

12. Nathaniel Davis, interview by author, June 1991; William Knight, interview by author, June 1991; Elbridge Durbrow, interview by author, July 1991.

13. EB letter to Katherine Parsons, December 28, 1952, BC. It is worth noting, but hardly surprising, that studies written later of U.S.-Italian relations in the early

and mid-1950s often include numerous references to Mrs. Luce's activities. By contrast, Bunker receives scant attention. (See, for example, Wollenborg, *Stars, Stripes,* and Andreotti, *U.S.A. Up Close.*)

14. See Embassy Rome telegram 5067, May 20, 1952, *FRUS 1952-54*, vol. 6, 1574, and Embassy Rome despatch 2588, May 6, 1952, Embassy Rome general records, 1950-52, 350-350.1, Box 74.

15. The embassy reported that "Taking last year's results [of the local elections in the north] together with those this year to have nationwide picture, CDs [Christian Democrats] and minor allies polled 51 percent of total vote compared to 62 percent in 1948 giving them 64 percent of Chamber seats while Social-Communists polled 35 percent and Rightists 12 percent. Signs are not that Center coalition is currently in full retreat but that center's vote-getting power fell back from phenomenal 1948 peak very soon after that voting and has now more of less stabilized at level indicated by 1951-52 results." (Embassy Rome telegram 88, July 8, 1952, *FRUS 1952-54*, vol. 6, 1581-84.) In 1953 the center coalition parties polled just slightly under 50 percent of the popular vote. De Gasperi, unable to form another government, fell from power in July 1953 after seven and a half years as premier. He died a year later.

16. Hughes, *United States and Italy*, 196. Norman Kogan has pointed out that although the Christian Democrats suffered large overall losses, changes in the election law enabled them in coalition with other centrist parties to hold or gain control of several major cities in northern and central Italy, including Rome (Kogan, *Political History of Italy*, 62).

17. For example, he told a high-level congressional delegation visiting Rome in October 1952 that "because of these coming elections, . . . political considerations are of first importance in determining policy, so that 'we will not be left to pick up the pieces for years to come.'" (Embassy Rome memorandum of conversation with Congressman James Richards and others, October 1, 1952, Embassy Rome general records, 1950-51, 320.1, Box 64.)

18. See EB Oral History interview, Duke University, 153. Bunker had no regrets about the program, pointing out to his interviewer that the Communists were well funded by Moscow.

19. Elbridge Durbrow, interview by author.

20. EB letter to Homer M. Byington Jr., September 18, 1952, *FRUS 1952-54*, vol. 6, 1591.

21. EB letter to Harriman, November 12, 1952; Embassy Rome memorandum of conversation, October 1, 1952; EB letter to Italian Minister of Defense Randolfo Pacciardi, March 30, 1953-55, Embassy Rome general records 1953-55, 320.1-350, Box 254. For Bunker's role in the well-publicized ceremonies marking the first U.S. purchase for delivery to the Italian army of Italian-produced equipment, three-quarter ton FIAT trucks, in Brindisi on September 30, 1952, see Embassy Rome despatch 928, November 5, 1952, Embassy Rome general records 1950-52, 310-320.1, Box 252. A similar message describes his participation in the celebration of the first U.S. offshore purchase for the use of the Italian navy, two mechanized landing craft, in February 1953. (Embassy Rome telegram 128 to the European Command (EUCOM), repeated

to the State Department, February 13, 1953, Embassy Rome general records 1953–55, 320.1–350, Box 254.)

22. Embassy Rome telegram to Paris 25, repeated to the State Department, July 9, 1952, *FRUS 1952–54*, vol. 6, 1584.

23. See Rabel, *Between East and West*, 143–47; Eden, *Full Circle*, 195–209; and EB Oral History interview, Duke University, 155. The port city of Trieste went to Italy, most of the environs to Yugoslavia (and eventually to Slovenia).

24. Embassy Rome telegram 2277, November 19, 1952, Embassy Rome general records, 1950–52, 765.5, Box 3446.

25. See Embassy Rome telegrams 3944, March 10, 1953, *FRUS 1952–54*, vol. 5, 756–57; 4062, March 18, 1953, *FRUS 1952–54*, vol. 5, 776–77; and 4115, March 23, 1953, *FRUS 1952–54*, vol. 5, 778–80.

26. See article by Joseph Lash in the *New York Post*, January 27, 1957.

27. Nathaniel Davis, interview by author; Davis was with Bunker as the results came in.

28. *Chicago Daily News*, November 25, 1952; *Rome Daily American*, January 14, 1953.

29. "Memorandum of [Secretary of State Dulles's] Conversation with Amb. Bunker," January 31, 1953, Box 2, General Correspondence and Memoranda Series, Dulles Papers.

30. Premier de Gasperi's Valedictory Toast to EB, n.d. [March/April 1953], BC.

31. EB remarks at final staff meeting, Rome, n.d. [April 1953], BC.

Chapter 4

1. According to George Elsey, who was his executive assistant during Bunker's time as American Red Cross president, Bunker did in fact continue to interest himself in the sugar industry's dealings with the U.S. government during his years in Washington in the mid-1950s. He was in close touch with Malcolm Baldrige, the cane sugar refining industry's chief Washington lobbyist. Baldrige, later secretary of commerce in the Reagan administration, had been associated with Bunker earlier in the U.S. Cane Sugar Refiners' Association. (George Elsey, interview by author, February 2000.)

2. E. Roland Harriman letter to Mrs. John Stanley Hipp, Executive Secretary, Douglas County Chapter, Lawrence, Kansas, December 2, 1953, American Red Cross records.

3. EB statement before the Committee on Banking and Currency, House of Representatives, February 10, 1956, reproduced in EB letter to senior officials of the American Red Cross, February 24, 1956, American Red Cross Files.

4. EB letter to Katherine Parsons, September 27, 1955, BC.

5. EB speech delivered at the American National Red Cross Convention, Atlantic City, N.J., 1955.

6. EB, interview by Sanford Ungar, January 1978, BC.

7. EB letter to Katherine Parsons, December 10, 1954, BC.

8. EB, interview by Ungar, BC.

9. The information about the Gruenther-Bunker relationship was provided to me by George Elsey in a February 2000 interview. As Bunker's executive assistant at the Red Cross, Elsey had accompanied him on the European trip in 1956. He later became Red Cross president himself, from 1970 to 1982.

10. *New York Times*, November 14, 1956.

11. EB letter to Eisenhower, November 13, 1956. Eisenhower letter to EB, November 14, 1956. Both are in Official File 69, Box 278, Dwight D. Eisenhower Library.

Chapter 5

1. Dulles memorandum of conversation with Eisenhower, August 6, 1956, Box 4, John Foster Dulles Papers.

2. Gopal, *Jawaharlal Nehru*, 41.

3. Henry Grady (1947–48), Loy Henderson (1948–51), Chester Bowles (1951–53), George V. Allen (1953–55), and John Sherman Cooper (1955–56). Brands, *Inside the Cold War*, 195–210, and Schaffer, *Chester Bowles*, 42–112, provide detailed accounts of Henderson's and Bowles's ambassadorships.

4. U.S. interest in keeping the air base in the Azores it leased from Portugal, and the alliance relationship between the two NATO countries, led Washington to avoid taking any steps to pressure the authoritarian government of António Salazar to turn over Goa and other enclaves to India. Soon after his arrival, Bunker suggested to Nehru that India might purchase Goa from Portugal in the same way the United States bought Louisiana from France. As Nehru's biographer S. Gopal points out, "This ingenious proposal presumed what was far from being the case, Portugal's willingness to part with Goa." Bunker was almost certainly speaking without instructions from Washington. (See Gopal, *Jawaharlal Nehru*, 191.) The Indians eventually took Goa and the other enclaves by force in December 1961, nine months after Bunker left India. The United States spoke out sharply against the armed action, and Bunker privately criticized it. (See Chapter 6.)

5. For a good study of the impact the U.S. alliance with Pakistan had on U.S.-Indian relations, see McMahon, *Cold War on the Periphery*, 213–31. It is part of a chapter McMahon appropriately calls "Paying the Costs [of the Alliance] 1954–57."

6. For a very insightful study of the power of stereotypes in influencing U.S.-Indian relations, see Isaacs, *Scratches on Our Minds*.

7. Jagat Singh Mehta, letter to author, April 4, 2002.

8. EB Oral History interview, Columbia University, 83–86.

9. When Bunker gave the interview in 1979, Mrs. Gandhi was out of office and was still largely discredited among American friends of India for imposing an authoritarian regime on the country during the 1975–77 "Emergency." Bunker's views probably reflect the times. He had earlier been on very friendly terms with Mrs. Gandhi.

10. "Statement of Policy on U.S. Policy [*sic*] Toward South Asia," *FRUS 1955–57*, vol. 8, January 10, 1957, 29–43.

11. EB letter to Frederic Bartlett, Director of the Office of South Asian Affairs, Department of State, December 9, 1958, *FRUS 1958–60*, vol. 15, 473.

12. Memorandum of conversation, June 4, 1957, "Indian Financial Problems," 891.00/6-457, NA.

13. EB letter to Secretary Dulles, November 19, 1957, 791.5 MSP/11-1957, NA.

14. Merrill, *Bread and the Ballot*, 156.

15. New Delhi telegram 473 to the State Department, August 26, 1958, 791.5 MSP/8-2658, NA.

16. EB letter to Dulles, November 19, 1957.

17. Memorandum of conversation (EB and President Eisenhower), April 25, 1960, "U.S.-Indian relations," Ann Whitman Files, DDE Diary Series, Box 49, Dwight D. Eisenhower Library.

18. The issue of U.S. assistance to the steel mill was resolved during President Kennedy's administration. Kennedy favored financing but was obliged to drop the project because of opposition in Congress. The mill, at Bokaro in eastern India, was eventually built by the Soviets. For an excellent discussion of the way the issue was handled in the Eisenhower administration, see Merrill, *Bread and the Ballot*, 158–59.

19. Memorandum of Discussion at the 416th Meeting of the National Security Council, Washington, August 6, 1959, *FRUS 1958-60*, vol. 15, 32. Bunker, on home leave at the time, was invited to the meeting. It had been called to discuss a paper on U.S. policy toward South Asia.

20. Papers of Wharton Hubbard, Guilford, Connecticut (privately held).

21. Memorandum of conversation, "General Discussion of India-Nepal Political and Economic Developments," June 15, 1959, 791.00/6-1959, NA.

22. New Delhi telegram 1538 to the State Department, January 8, 1959, 791.5-MSP/1-859, NA.

23. For a discussion of Eisenhower's thinking and his struggles with his administration colleagues and Congress over economic assistance to India, see Ambrose, *Eisenhower*, 379.

24. For a study of Bowles's ideas on this and other aspects of Indian economic development, see Schaffer, *Chester Bowles*, 63–79.

25. See, among Rostow's many studies on the subject, *Eisenhower, Kennedy, and Foreign Aid*. The book provides a summary of the influential recommendation Rostow and Millikan made in their 1957 *A Proposal: Key to an Effective Foreign Policy*. Kaufman, *Trade and Aid*, 95–112, has an excellent assessment of the role of the two MIT professors and other aspects of the Eisenhower administration's approach to U.S. economic relations with India.

26. See New Delhi telegrams 1206 and 1207 to the State Department, October 3, 1959, Box 13, Don Paarlberg Records, 1954–61, Dwight D. Eisenhower Library.

27. Embassy New Delhi telegram 452 to the State Department, August 22, 1957, *FRUS 1955-57*, vol. 8, 144.

28. Memorandum of Eisenhower-EB conversation, April 25, 1960, *FRUS 1958-60*, vol. 15, 535.

29. See letter of Assistant Secretary G. Lewis Jones to EB, July 13, 1960, *FRUS 1958-60*, vol. 15, 545.

30. For a good discussion of the Sidewinder issue, see Kux, *Estranged Democracies*, 168–70.

31. New Delhi telegram 3723 to the State Department, May 5, 1960, *FRUS 1958–60*, vol. 15, 538.

32. Politically and personally close to the prime minister, Krishna Menon remained defense minister until strong opposition to him within the Congress Party following the Indian debacle in the 1962 Sino-Indian border war forced a reluctant Nehru to drop him.

33. New Delhi telegram 2726 to the State Department, April 3, 1957, *FRUS 1955–57*, vol. 8, 130.

34. Ibid.

35. New Delhi telegram 1355, November 22, 1957, *FRUS 1955–57*, vol. 8, 154.

36. See Gopal, *Jawaharlal Nehru*, 85, which cites Eisenhower's letter to Nehru of May 14, 1958; Nehru's conversation with EB May 16, 1958; and Nehru's reply to Eisenhower, June 7, 1958. *FRUS 1958–60*, vol. 15, 75–131, carries a selection of State Department, Embassy New Delhi, and Embassy Karachi messages on the failed package proposal. The Bunker message quoted is among them (New Delhi telegram 3137, June 8, 1958, 119–23).

37. New Delhi telegram 3164 to the State Department, June 11, 1958, Dwight D. Eisenhower Library (FOI document).

38. Memorandum for the Operations Coordinator (O'Connor) to the Assistant Secretary of State for Near Eastern and South Asian Affairs (Jones), August 5, 1959, *FRUS 1958–60*, vol. 15, 512.

39. EB memorandum to Eisenhower, December 7, 1959, "Your Conversations with Mr. Nehru," Dwight D. Eisenhower Library (FOI document).

40. See EB Oral History interview, Columbia University, 100–101. Bunker was asked if he agreed with B. K. Nehru, a former Indian ambassador to the United States, that India needed a tougher, tighter, and more authoritarian system than the West was accustomed to. His answer recalled his views of Argentine politics almost thirty years before. It may also have reflected his more recent experience in Vietnam: "Yes, I think it may well be. I think we have a tendency here to feel because our system works for us that it ought to work everywhere in the world. That's been one of the problems of our foreign policy, that there's a tendency to feel that Western-type democracy is good for us and it's good generally. . . . But when you consider Asian traditions and Asian culture, a family-oriented society that exists in Asia, entirely different traditions, history, religion, cultures, the problem of trying to impose a Western-style democracy becomes pretty difficult. It poses many problems, and I'm not sure that it can work as we see it without modification."

41. Kux, *Estranged Democracies*, 145.

42. Moynihan, *Dangerous Place*, 41.

43. For a good assessment of Mrs. Gandhi's role in the dismissal of the Kerala Communists, see Malhotra, *Indira Gandhi*, 63–70. Gopal, *Jawaharlal Nehru*, 53–74, discusses Nehru's evolving position on the Kerala issue and his interaction with Mrs. Gandhi in its resolution. Lieten, *First Communist Ministry* provides a useful study of events leading to central government intervention and the dismissal of the state administration.

44. *New York Times*, May 8, 1979.

45. EB Oral History interview, Columbia University, 76–78.

46. EB, speech at a farewell dinner hosted by Indian Foreign Secretary Subimal Dutt, New Delhi, March 6, 1961, handwritten notes, BC.

47. EB, speech at a farewell party given him by the American and Indian press, New Delhi, March 17, 1961, BC

48. Eugene Rosenfeld, interview by author, June 1992.

49. See, for example, EB memorandum to Eisenhower, December 7, 1959, "Your Conversations with Mr. Nehru," Dwight D. Eisenhower Papers, 1953–61.

50. Eisenhower described his visit in his autobiography, *Waging Peace*, 499–504. See also Ambrose, *Eisenhower*, 552–53.

51. See Kaufman, *Trade and Aid*, 198.

52. New Delhi telegram 2179 to the State Department, December 18, 1959, Dwight D. Eisenhower Library (FOI document).

53. See EB Oral History interview, Columbia University, 64–65, and EB Oral History interview, Duke University, 65–66.

54. Harriet Bunker letter to John and Katherine Parsons, January 8, 1960, BC.

55. Harriet Bunker letter to her children, March 14, 1957, BC.

56. Harriet Bunker letter to Katherine Parsons, March 24, 1957, BC.

57. EB letter to John Wilcox, Madison, Conn., September 8, 1962, BC.

58. Until November 1959, when Henry Stebbins was assigned as resident ambassador.

59. Harriet Bunker letter to her children, March 14, 1957, BC.

60. Harriet Bunker letter to Katherine Parsons, April 30, 1958, BC.

61. Harriet Bunker letter to Katherine Parsons, March 24, 1957, BC.

62. Ibid.

63. Handwritten notes, April 17, 1961, BC.

64. Associated Press, New Delhi, March 23, 1961.

65. Quoted in the *New York Times*, March 22, 1961.

66. Quoted by the Associated Press, March 23, 1961.

67. *Hindu*, March 22, 1961.

68. *Eastern Economist*, March 24, 1961.

Chapter 6

1. EB letter to Mrs. John Glascock Baldwin, Woodside, Calif., June 13, 1961, BC.

2. EB letter to Edward E. Chapin, Noank, Conn., September 10, 1962, BC.

3. EB letter to Desai, September 1, 1961, BC.

4. EB letter to C. Tyler Wood, July 8, 1961, BC. Wood headed the U.S. economic assistance program in India.

5. EB letter to Dr. Bennett (not otherwise identified), October 1961, BC.

6. EB letter to Katherine Parsons, January 18, 1962, BC.

7. The following remarks are taken from EB's address at Duke University, February 27, 1979, BC. They track very closely with comments he made elsewhere.

Chapter 7

1. Lijphart, *Trauma of Decolonization*.

2. Markin, "West Irian Dispute," 6.

3. Among the more important of the personnel changes was the appointment in November 1961 of the politically well-connected and operationally savvy W. Averell Harriman, Bunker's onetime Yale rowing coach, as assistant secretary for Far Eastern affairs.

4. Briefing Book for Sukarno Visit to Washington, April 24–25, 1961, Box 113, NSF, JFK Library.

5. State Department telegram, December 8, 1961, Box 113, NSF, JFK Library.

6. State Department telegram to USUN, January 18, 1962, Box 205, NSF, JFK Library.

7. A moderator's role is the lowest level of direct third-party involvement in negotiations. Unlike arbitrators, who can impose decisions on the conflicting parties, or mediators, who suggest specific proposals to them, moderators are only expected to create a congenial atmosphere for talks and, when appropriate, develop a framework for discussion that can help the parties work out their disagreements by themselves (see Markin, "West Irian Dispute," 103).

8. State Department telegram to The Hague, March 2, 1962, Box 206, NSF, JFK Library.

9. State Department memorandum of conversation, "Dutch Government Reaction to Arrangements for Secret Preparatory Talks," March 6, 1962, Box 206, NSF, JFK Library. See also State Department telegram, March 6, 1962, Box 206, NSF, JFK Library, which instructed embassies at The Hague and Djakarta to "stress [Rusk's] view that Bunker would be absolutely first class." In an April 1991 interview, Rusk told me that he had been blessed as secretary of state to have a man of Bunker's negotiating skill to turn to on West New Guinea and other problems.

10. See Jones, *Indonesia*, 207 n. 5.

11. See State Department telegram, March 10, 1962, Box 206, NSF, JFK Library.

12. See EB letter to Harriman, May 31, 1962, BC.

13. He tried to keep Harriet amused. According to one of his associates, "After he was appointed, [Bunker] briefed Harriet on West [New Guinea] and the Papuans [and] included pictures of Papuan males from the *National Geographic*, naked except for spectacular codpieces tied with thongs. Harriet observed that males in all cultures were prone to showing off in that department" (Michael Newlin, letter to the author, March 2000).

14. For example, the memoranda of conversation that were prepared by Bunker's aide, a State Department official, were sent only to the department and not to U.N. headquarters in New York.

15. Markin, "West Irian Dispute," 143–44.

16. Michael Newlin, letter to the author.

17. Komer memorandum to National Security Adviser McGeorge Bundy, February 16, 1962, Box 206, NSF, JFK Library.

18. Memorandum of conversation, "West New Guinea Problem," March 2, 1962, Box 206, NSF, JFK Library.

19. The account of the negotiations that follows is largely drawn from official documents available at the John F. Kennedy Library and elsewhere and from several published and unpublished studies, most of which had been prepared before the documents were released. The most comprehensive of these earlier studies are Henderson, *West New Guinea: The Dispute and Its Settlement* and McMullen, *Mediation of the West New Guinea Dispute*, 1962. McMullen prepared his study in close collaboration with Ambassador Bunker. Another useful work is James Thorwald Hermanson's 1965 Georgetown University M.A. dissertation: "The Role of Good Offices and Mediation in Settling an International Conflict: Ellsworth Bunker and the West Irian Dispute." A valuable later, more comprehensive and detailed study that draws both on newly available material and interviews with surviving Dutch, Indonesian, and American participants in the negotiations is Markin's previously cited Johns Hopkins University Ph.D. thesis, "The West Irian Dispute."

20. See State Department telegram, March 22, 1962, Box 206, NSF, JFK Library, for the text of Bunker's proposal.

21. State Department telegram March 27, 1962, Box 206, NSF, JFK Library.

22. See State Department telegram, March 28, 1962, Box 113, NSF, JFK Library.

23. Stressing once again the dangers to "free world" interests of a war for West New Guinea, Kennedy spelled out for Prime Minister de Quay a new version of the domino theory for Southeast Asia. "Only the Communists would benefit from such a conflict," the president maintained. "If the Indonesian army were committed to all-out war against The Netherlands, the moderate elements within the army and the country would be quickly eliminated, leaving a clean field for communist intervention. If Indonesia were to succumb to communism in these circumstances, the whole non-communist position in Vietnam, Thailand, and Malaya would be in grave peril." State Department telegram March 31, 1962, Box 143, NSF, JFK Library. In his reply, de Quay seems to have indulged in a little domino theorizing of his own in contending that appeasing Sukarno by giving him West New Guinea would only make him more aggressive. Sukarno's triggering of the Indonesian "confrontation" with Malaysia soon after the West New Guinea settlement lends credence to the Dutch prime minister's assessment.

24. State Department telegram, April 2, 1962, Box 206, NSF, JFK Library. The particular formulation ". . . the Papuans, when able to obtain a full understanding of the Indonesian position, will opt to join Indonesia" was a U.S. effort to pick up on a long-standing Indonesian contention that the Dutch had been able to tutor Papuan opinion since Indonesian independence, and the Indonesian government must be given an opportunity to work with the Papuans before they decided on their future. It seems likely that the formulation was read in Djakarta as a license to the Indonesians to manipulate Papuan opinion, which is of course exactly what they did once they had gained control of West New Guinea.

25. State Department telegram, May 2, 1962, Box 206, NSF, JFK Library.

26. McMullen, *Mediation*, 42.

27. State Department telegram May 26, 1962, Box 206A, NSF, JFK Library.

28. See State Department telegram, August 2, 1962, Box 206A, NSF, JFK Library. The Kennedy-Subandrio confrontation came on the same day that Ambassador Jones reported his conclusion that "the Indonesians intend a major military punch in early August unless agreement has been reached with the Dutch prior to that time." (Embassy Djakarta telegram, July 26, 1962, Box 206A, NSF, JFK Library.)

29. EB letter to Kennedy, August 29, 1962, BC. The letter was in reply to Kennedy's congratulatory note to Bunker, August 24, 1962, also in BC.

30. U.S. Mission Geneva telegram, July 25, 1962, Box 206A, NSF, JFK Library.

31. The territory recently returned to world attention in the 1990s when an armed movement broke out there calling for Papuan independence from Indonesia. The movement's supporters denounce what they accurately allege has been Djakarta's oppressive rule and call attention to Indonesian economic exploitation and colonization programs that have made the Papuans a minority in their own land. They scathingly (and correctly) characterize the 1969 U.N.-conducted "Act of Choice" as an "Act of No Choice."

32. *New York Times*, August 16, 1962.

33. Embassy Djakarta telegram, August 3, 1962, Box 206A, NSF, JFK Library.

34. The phrase is drawn from Embassy The Hague telegram, August 11, 1962, Box 206A, NSF, JFK Library. Van Roijen told Michael Newlin years later that he thought the agreement had been unfair.

35. Van Roijen letter to EB, August 16, 1962, BC.

36. Kennedy letter to EB, August 24, 1962, BC.

37. Embassy Djakarta telegram, August 23, 1962, Box 206A, NSF, JFK Library.

38. "Another 'Bunker' Hill," *Brattleboro Daily Recorder*, August 3, 1962.

39. Markin, "West Irian Dispute,"439.

40. Ibid., 440.

Chapter 8

1. For a valuable discussion of Nasser's decision to intervene, see Rahmy, *Egyptian Policy*, 81–107.

2. Despite the Syrian withdrawal, Egypt continued to call itself the United Arab Republic.

3. For a discussion of Faisal's 1962 visit to the United States, see Hart, *Saudi Arabia and the United States*, 114–16.

4. The strain the Yemeni coup and the Saudi government's reaction to it put on the Saudi military was reflected in the defection to Egypt, in early October, of several Saudi aircraft crews with planeloads of arms intended for the royalists. On taking the reins of government from the ailing King Saud later that month, Faisal shook up the military command to safeguard internal security.

5. See Page, *Soviet Union and the Yemens*, 5–6, and Badeeb, *Saudi-Egyptian Conflict*, 67.

6. See "President's Talk with Crown Prince Faisal," October 5, 1962, *FRUS 1961–63*, vol. 18, 165.

7. For the text of Kennedy's proposal, which he sent in identical messages to Nasser, Faisal, Sallal, and King Hussein, but not to the deposed imam, Mohammed al-Badr, see *FRUS 1961-63*, vol. 18, 228.

8. State Department telegram 198 to Jidda, October 25, 1962, *FRUS 1961-63*, vol. 18, 198.

9. For a discussion of the recognition issue, see Rusk-Kennedy memorandum, "U.S. Recognition of Yemen," November 12, 1962, *FRUS 1961-63*, vol. 18, 218, and McMullen, *Resolution of the Yemen Crisis*, 3. Bunker cooperated with McMullen in the preparation of this useful book and gave him access to his files.

10. The administration feared that with Egyptian support YAR forces might move southward into British-controlled territory that Yemen had long claimed. The territory included Aden, a major U.K. military base at the entrance to the Red Sea that played a key role in the security of the Persian Gulf and the western Indian Ocean.

11. This is indeed what happened after the Egyptians withdrew from Yemen in 1967. See Stookey, *Yemen*, 232-38.

12. Gause, *Saudi-Yemeni Relations*, 58.

13. Embassy Jidda telegram 122 to the State Department, December 28, 1962, *FRUS 1961-63*, vol. 18, 282.

14. Gause, *Saudi-Yemeni Relations*, 62.

15. State Department telegram 2028 to USUN, January 28, 1963, *FRUS 1961-63*, vol. 18, 331.

16. Telephone conversation, January 22, 1963, *FRUS 1961-63*, vol. 18, 331 n. 4.

17. Parker T. Hart, manuscript for *Saudi Arabia and the United States*, chapter 13. Hart made the manuscript available to me.

18. Memo from Komer to McGeorge Bundy, February 7, 1963, *FRUS 1961-63*, vol. 18, 339.

19. National Security Action Memorandum no. 227, February 27, 1963, "Decisions Taken at President's Meeting on Yemen Crisis, 25 February 1963," *FRUS 1961-63*, vol. 18, 366.

20. At Ambassador Hart's suggestion, "suspension" was used in place of termination. It implied that if, as Faisal suspected he would, Nasser did not carry out his parallel obligation to withdraw his forces, the Saudis could resume their support for the royalists.

21. Stevenson letter to Rusk, March 20, 1963, State Department Files, POL 27 YEMEN, NA. In the letter, Stevenson said that the way U Thant had been treated made his own job at the United Nations more difficult.

22. Thant insisted that Bunche meet only officials of the YAR, which represented Yemen at the United Nations, and avoid the royalists. Faisal was not prepared to receive a United Nations emissary under those conditions.

23. Badeau had been president of the American University in Cairo before Kennedy made him ambassador to Egypt as part of his effort to improve relations with Nasser. Hart was a senior professional Foreign Service officer trained in Arabic who had served in many diplomatic posts in the Near East and was familiar with Yemen, to which he was also accredited.

24. Talcott Seelye, interview by author, September 1994.

25. Hart, *Saudi Arabia and the United States*, 169.

26. Hart letter to author, November 17, 1994. Hart and others have also called attention to the useful roles played in the Faisal-Bunker talks by Omar Saqqaf, the Saudi deputy foreign minister, and Isa Sabbagh, the public affairs officer at the U.S. embassy in Saudi Arabia. Saqqaf, close to Faisal, was a strong advocate of Saudi disengagement and privately briefed Bunker and Hart about how best to approach the crown prince to win his acceptance of their ideas. Sabbagh, a Palestinian who had become a naturalized American citizen, acted as interpreter for the Bunker mission in the talks with Faisal. Bilingual and bicultural, he seemed to have had a particular talent for translating across the language and culture gap in ways that made what one side said to the other more palatable and comprehensible yet did not misrepresent it.

27. The points are listed in *FRUS 1961-63*, vol. 18, 404.

28. State Department telegram 583 to Jidda, March 14, 1963, *FRUS 1961-63*, 427.

29. State Department telegram 2719 to USUN, April 30, 1963, State Department Files, POL 27 YEMEN, NA.

30. McMullen, *Resolution*, 42. The quote, which appears in varying versions in some of Bunker's oral history accounts, is not included in the record of the negotiations documented in State Department messages.

31. Memorandum of Rusk meeting with Saudi Ambassador Abdullah al-Khayyal, February 23, 1963, State Department Files, POL 26 YEMEN, NA.

32. Consulate General Dhahran telegram 181 to State Department, March 8, 1963, *FRUS 1961-63*, vol. 18, 404.

33. State Department telegram 583 to Jidda, March 14, 1963, *FRUS 1961-63*, 427.

34. McMullen, *Resolution*, 33.

35. Embassy Cairo airgram A-733, April 6, 1963, State Department Files, POL 27 YEMEN, NA. Bunker did return to Cairo and bothered Nasser again, but not about this issue.

36. For the terms of the settlement, see Embassy Jidda telegram 219, April 7, 1963, *FRUS 1961-63*, vol. 18, 456.

37. The vote was 10-0. The Soviets abstained.

38. "The plan was never really carried through essentially because the Russians blocked it. The United Nations delayed in getting observers there." EB, interview by Sanford Ungar for *Foreign Policy*, January 1978, BC.

39. Von Horn, *Soldiering for Peace*, 354. Interestingly, Nasser also thought this was the case, or at least said he did. At a meeting in Cairo on July 11, he told Ambassador Badeau that "the heart of the difficulty [regarding Egyptian withdrawal from Yemen] lay in the unexpected lag between the acceptance of the disengagement proposals and the beginning of UN operations." Nasser complained that during that period the problem had been aggravated by assistance coming to the royalists from the Saudi side of the border. He claimed that immediately after disengagement, the Egyptians had brought some troops home in the hope that they need not be replaced, "but continuation of outside help to the royalists and [renewed] tribal fighting led to troop rotation instead of withdrawal." (Embassy Cairo telegram 121, July 11, 1963, *FRUS 1961-63*, vol. 18, 639.)

Chapter 9

1. Lincoln Gordon, former ambassador to Brazil, and Walt Rostow, former head of the Policy Planning Staff, interviews by author (telephone), June 2001.

2. EB, interview by William J. Jorden, March 26, 1979, BC.

3. Organization of American States, *Report of the Secretary General*, 6.

4. See Chapter 13.

5. *New York Times*, April 20, 1964.

6. Johnson telegram to EB, April 22, 1964, Name File, Box 570, LBJ Library.

7. Already excluded from the inter-American system, Cuba had allegedly supported an armed rebellion against the Venezuelan government. Other significant OAS issues that arose during Bunker's first year as U.S. representative included the re-admission of Bolivia to the organization and the controversial problem of the admission of newly independent Caribbean states whose territory was claimed by existing members.

8. Mehta letter to author, April 4, 2002.

9. Ball proposed the Bunker assignment to the president on March 18 (*FRUS 1964–68*, vol. 26, 251–52). In a meeting two months earlier with a White House representative, Rusk and Ball concluded that Bunker should be appointed ambassador to Indonesia to replace Jones. (John Macy, Memo for the Record, January 17, 1965, Office Files of John Macy, LBJ Library.) Although nothing came of the idea at that time, Ball revived it in his March 18 memorandum, suggesting that the president might want to make the assignment after Bunker reported his conclusions. A few days before Ball sent his memorandum to the White House, Jones had recommended that Johnson meet Sukarno in Washington or Hawaii. He suggested as a fallback sending to Indonesia a presidential envoy, who in his view would have to be Vice President Hubert Humphrey, bearing with him a letter from Johnson. No evidence is available that Johnson ever seriously considered a personal meeting with Sukarno or a Humphrey mission. The president did give Bunker a letter for Sukarno, but it was less outgoing than the text Jones suggested. (Jones made his suggestion in Embassy Djakarta telegram 1850, March 13, 1965. The Johnson-Sukarno letter that Bunker took to Indonesia is dated March 26, 1965. Both are in NSF Country Files, Indonesia, vol. 4, Box 247, LBJ Library.)

10. Embassy Djakarta telegrams, especially 2087 (April 1, 1965), 2116 (April 5), 2127 (April 6), 2138 (April 7), 2207 (April 13), and 2224 (April 14) provide detailed reports of Bunker's conversations and his assessments of his progress. They are all in NSF Country Files, Indonesia, vol. 4, Box 247, LBJ Library.

11. Embassy Djakarta telegram 2127, April 6, 1965, NSF Country Files, Indonesia, vol. 4, Box 247, LBJ Library.

12. Embassy Djakarta telegram 2239, April 15, 1965, NSF Country Files, Indonesia, vol. 4, Box 247, LBJ Library. See also *New York Times*, April 12, 1965. No complete text of Sukarno's diatribe is available.

13. EB, interview by Sanford Ungar for *Foreign Policy*, January 1978, BC.

14. EB speech, St. Michael's College, *New York Times*, April 12, 1965.

15. Embassy Djakarta telegram 2224, April 14, 1965.

16. Embassy Djakarta telegram 2222, April 14, 1965, NSF Country File, Indonesia, vol. 4, Box 247, LBJ Library.

17. The text of Bunker's report, submitted to President Johnson on April 23, 1965, is in Indonesian-U.S. Political Affairs and Relations, State Department, Central Files, 1964–68, Box 2327, NA. The brief summary of the report McGeorge Bundy sent Johnson is in *FRUS 1964–68*, vol. 26, 251–52. In this memorandum, Bundy went on to discuss Johnson's possible interest in naming Bunker as ambassador to Indonesia replacing Howard Jones, who planned to leave Djakarta to become chancellor of the East-West Center in Hawaii. Bundy noted that Bunker himself had recommended Henry Byroade, a senior diplomat then ambassador to Burma. Bundy added: "On Bunker himself, I continue to think that if he were interested, he would give a stature and coherence to [the State Department's] European Bureau that it has never had in many years, even under Foy Kohler [a much respected career Foreign Service officer then ambassador to the Soviet Union]." To replace Jones, Johnson chose Marshall Green, a senior career officer who had held several important positions in East Asia and the Far East bureau of the State Department.

18. Embassy Djakarta telegram 2239, April 15, 1965, NSF Country Files, Indonesia, vol. 4, Box 247, LBJ Library.

19. Masters letter to the author, May 2, 2001.

20. McGeorge Bundy–Johnson memorandum, October 22, 1965, *FRUS 1964–68*, vol. 26, 336–37.

21. The president's motives for dispatching them and the activities and policy recommendations of U.S. officials in the four days between the outbreak of the pro-Bosch revolution and the landings have been the subject of numerous studies. Among the more important of them are Draper, *Dominican Revolt*; Slater, *Intervention and Negotiation*; Lowenthal, *Dominican Intervention*; Palmer, *Intervention in the Caribbean*; Gleijeses, *Dominican Crisis*; Mansbach, *Dominican Crisis, 1965*; Wiarda and Kryzanek, *The Dominican Republic, A Caribbean Crucible*; and Yates, *Power Pack*. Most analysts agree that it was Johnson's dread of a "second Cuba" that was the driving force behind his decision to intervene. They cite in particular the fact that the marines were sent to Santo Domingo only after the tide of battle had turned in favor of the pro-Bosch side, which many senior U.S. officials were convinced was increasingly falling under Communist domination. But there is a sharp difference of view among these commentators, as there was at the time, as to whether this fear of a Communist takeover had any basis in fact, or, if it did, if a massive military intervention was the best way to deal with the problem.

22. EB Oral History interview, LBJ Library, part 3, 26. Bunker added that he could not recall his immediate reaction.

23. EB Oral History interview, Duke University, 100. Washington had difficulty winning the required two-thirds majority for a key resolution it proposed after the intervention, and obtained it only with the questionable support of the Dominican representative, an appointee of the ousted triumvirate.

24. For the texts of the more important of Bunker's intercessions, see *Department of State Bulletin* 52, no. 1351 (May 17, 1965): 738–47.

25. These other envoys were John Bartlow Martin, who had been ambassador to the Dominican Republic earlier in the 1960s, and Abe Fortas, a justice of the U.S. Supreme Court to whom Johnson often turned for political advice and assistance.

26. *New York Times*, September 28, 1984. The article was an obituary of Bunker.

27. Bunker spelled out the advantages of his OAS role in a memorandum he sent to the White House in December 1965 when he was being considered as a replacement for Bennett as U.S. ambassador. He stressed that his dual role as a member of the Ad Hoc Committee and special emissary of the president put him in a stronger position to speak for the hemisphere as a whole, give direction and guidance to the IAPF, and limit charges that Washington was trying to pressure the Dominican government. (See EB memorandum, "Dominican Republic," December 9, 1965, NSF Country File, Dominican Republic, vol. 13, Box 45, LBJ Library). The administration accepted Bunker's recommendation. Secretary Rusk wrote the president, "So long as Ambassador Bunker is 'our man' in full charge in Santo Domingo, it seems to me that our central purpose is achieved" (December 9, 1965, NSF Country File, Dominican Republic, vol. 13, Box 45, LBJ Library).

28. Harry Shlaudeman, interview by author, October 1992.

29. The mandate called on the committee "to proceed with the work . . . of making its good offices available to all the [Dominican] parties with a view to creating an atmosphere of peace and conciliation which will enable the democratic institutions of the Dominican Republic to operate and make possible its economic and social recovery." (Documents of the OAS Tenth Meeting of Foreign Ministers [MFM Documents], Document 131, Minutes of the Tenth Session of the General Committee, June 2, 1965.)

30. Harry Shlaudeman has recalled that at one point in a well-attended press conference at the embassy before Bunker came to the Dominican Republic, one of the some 100 reporters present had asked if it was true that Johnson was sending McGeorge Bundy to the island. Just as the spokesman replied in the negative, Bundy's plane was landing at a nearby airport. (Shlaudeman letter to the author, April 10, 1995.)

31. In a half-humorous, half-serious speech on the occasion, James Pringle of Reuters remarked that "First impressions were somewhat intimidating. . . . Mr. Bunker reminded me a bit of the fire and brimstone Scottish Presbyterian minister who terrorized my early youth." He went on to characterize Bunker's relations with the press as "helpful and unhypocritical. . . . Considering the way we badgered him, I feel he has always treated us with politeness and regard." Bunker was very pleased. (Speech delivered by James Pringle, June 5, 1966, General Records of the Department of State, Records of Ambassador at Large Ellsworth Bunker, and EB letter to Everett M. Woodman, June 9, 1966, box 6, NA.)

32. Harry Shlaudeman letter to the author, June 15, 1998.

33. For an excellent account of earlier diplomatic efforts to resolve the crisis, see Slater, *Intervention and Negotiation*, 86–95. The Slater book is one of the few that discusses not only the intervention and its immediate aftermath but also the lengthy efforts leading to a settlement. Slater is admiring though not uncritical of Bunker's role. Bunker later recalled that he had corresponded with Slater, and said he found

his account "excellent, accurate, complete and readable. He clearly did a thorough research job and has given a very useful record of the whole episode" (EB, interview by Sanford Ungar for *Foreign Policy*, January 1978, BC). Bunker's role is also carefully detailed in Bracey, *Resolution of the Dominican Crisis, 1965*. Bracey worked closely with Ambassador Bunker, who was the chairman of the sponsoring institute's board and made his files available to her.

34. Embassy Santo Domingo telegram 2323, June 10, 1965, NSF, Files of Gordon Chase, "Bunker Activities," Box 3, LBJ Library.

35. See Department of State telegram 1427 to Santo Domingo, June 11, 1965, NSF Bundy Files, vol. 11, Box 3. The message stressed the urgency of a political solution and again made clear that avoidance of the establishment of a Communist regime on the island remained a sine qua non of administration policy. Bunker was working within that context, of course, and though he did not spell out the goal in his cable he implied it when he spoke of "a formula which would meet our requirements."

36. Shlaudeman letter to Martin Herz, Institute for the Study of Diplomacy, Georgetown University, June 6, 1980. A copy of the letter, which analyzes the way Bunker dealt with his Dominican Republic mission, was made available to me by Ambassador Shlaudeman.

37. The document, dated June 18, 1965, was signed by the three members of the Ad Hoc Committee. It was conveyed to Washington in Embassy Santo Domingo telegram 2484, NSF Bundy Files, vol. 11, Box 3.

38. See Embassy Santo Domingo telegram 2485, June 18, 1965, NSF Bundy Files, vol. 11, Box 3. Bunker subsequently apologized to Johnson for presenting the proposal to the Dominicans before the president had had an opportunity to review it in detail. He blamed the urgency on the rapid deterioration of the political and military situation on the ground. Bunker's willingness to move without full Washington concurrence reflected the confidence he enjoyed in the Johnson White House. (See Embassy Santo Domingo telegram 2513, June 19, 1965, NSF Country File, Dominican Republic, vol. 6, Box 40, LBJ Library).

39. Embassy Santo Domingo telegram 2475, June 17, 1965, NSF, Files of Gordon Chase, "Bunker Activities," Box 3, LBJ Library.

40. In this connection, note the first paragraph of the message he sent (with Bennett) to Washington on August 1: "We fully share the department's impatience for definitive solution and concern over attitudes of government officials and public in [Latin America], as well as over trend of public opinion in the United States. Unfortunately, it is difficult to convey to those not intimately involved here just what a slippery and complex situation this is and what a cross-hatching and interrelation of competing pressure there are. As [the] department is aware from previous attempts to settle the Dominican problem, there are key elements on both sides who do not want a solution." (Embassy Santo Domingo telegram 310, August 1, 1965, NSF Country File, Dominican Republic, vol. 10, Box 43, LBJ Library.)

41. See, for example, Embassy Santo Domingo telegram 76, July 8, 1965, NSF Country File, Dominican Republic, vol. 6, Box 40, LBJ Library.

42. Bunker was always careful to say that he was not "imposing" Garcia Godoy and had no mandate to do so. He took the line "that after finding that candidates

proposed by each side were unacceptable to the other, the committee felt within its mandate to suggest Garcia Godoy [as someone] meeting necessary qualifications." (See Embassy Santo Domingo telegram 115, July 11, 1965, NSF Country File, Dominican Republic, vol. 6, Box 40, LBJ Library.)

43. Slater, *Intervention and Negotiation*, 131.

44. Embassy Santo Domingo telegram 525, August 25, 1965, NSF Country File, Dominican Republic, vol. 6, Box 40, LBJ Library.

45. Bunker's report of his final conversation with Imbert provides a good example of the negotiating tactics he was at times obliged to use. He told the Dominican leader that "the constitutionalists had been defeated in all their major demands," which he defined with artful selectivity. "However," Bunker went on, "although defeated, it is always essential to give a beaten adversary some way by which he can accept defeat. . . . The constitutionalists had had substantial support in the country and hemisphere, and although their image has been tarnished by association with the Communists, it could be revived if the Government of National Reconstruction delayed agreement on [the installation of] the Provisional Government." (Embassy Santo Domingo telegram 512, August 24, 1965, NSF Country File, Dominican Republic, vol. 6, Box 40, LBJ Library.)

46. Slater, *Intervention and Negotiation*, 134.

47. At one point Bunker had favored the appointment of a special OAS representative who would take over most of the functions of the Ad Hoc Committee. But Garcia Godoy had insisted that he and his two ambassadorial colleagues carry on during the provisional government's tenure, and Bunker agreed.

48. Harry Shlaudeman letter to the author, April 10, 1996.

49. Embassy Santo Domingo telegram (number not available), October 12, 1965, NSF Bundy Files, vol. 15, Box 5.

50. Embassy Santo Domingo telegram 1108, October 27, 1965, NSF Country Files, Dominican Republic, vol. 12, Box 45, LBJ Library.

51. Embassy Santo Domingo telegram 1115, October 27, 1965, NSF Country Files, Dominican Republic, vol. 12, Box 45, LBJ Library.

52. Bundy memorandum to Johnson, January 6, 1966, NSF Bundy Files, vol. 18, Box 6.

53. Many of these are now available in the NSF Country Files for the Dominican Republic at the LBJ Library.

54. Embassy Santo Domingo telegram 1846, February 9, 1966, NSF Country Files, Dominican Republic, vol. 14, Box 46, LBJ Library.

55. Embassy Santo Domingo telegram 1674, January 16, 1966, NSF Country Files, Dominican Republic, vol. 13, Box 45, LBJ Library.

56. Castelo Branco was the great-uncle of Bunker's son-in-law, Fernando Gentil. Ellen Bunker recalls that the private and informal meeting took place in the Rio apartment of Gentil's sister.

57. As noted, General Palmer later wrote a book about the Dominican crisis. He was one of the more intellectually gifted U.S. army officers of his time. To Bunker's great satisfaction, the two men served together a few years later in Vietnam.

58. *New York Times*, May 31, 1965. In an editorial it ran on June 3 after the ballot-

ing, the *Times* credited the successful election to Bunker and Garcia Godoy, "whose diplomacy and fairness paid off."

59. See Embassy Santo Domingo airgram A-16, July 9, 1966, NSF Country File, Dominican Republic, vol. 16, Box 47, LBJ Library.

60. *New York Times*, June 19, 1965.

61. Samuel Huntington in Pfeffer, *No More Vietnams?*, 2–3.

62. Palmer, *25-Year War*, 47.

Chapter 10

1. EB letter to Johnson, October 10, 1966, Office Files of John Macy, LBJ Library.

2. Carol Laise Bunker, interview by Charles Stuart Kennedy, April 17, 1989, Association for Diplomatic Studies and Training, Foreign Affairs Oral History Program.

3. Ellen Bunker, interview by author (telephone), May 2000.

4. See Johnson's January 3, 1967 letter to EB and Carol, WHCF Name File, Box 570, LBJ Library. Ellsworth had written Secretary Rusk in late November or early December telling him of their decision to marry, and Rusk had passed the note on to Johnson at that time. The president wrote to Bunker on December 5 congratulating him and Carol for this "pleasant surprise." (ibid.)

5. Harry Barnes letter to author, June 11, 2000. Bhekh Thapa, a senior Nepalese government official who worked closely with Carol and was a personal friend, attended the reception. Thirty-five years later, he still vividly recalled how completely dumbfounded he and the other uninformed guests were by Carol's casual announcement. (Bhekh Thapa, interview by author, March 2002.)

6. EB letter to Ellen Bunker, February 1, 1967, BC.

7. See Lodge, *The Storm Has Many Eyes*, 219. In a note he sent at the time to the president, Rostow stressed Lodge's concern for his own safety: "He actually feels that overstaying his time increases the odds of physical harm — he's a nut on security." (*FRUS 1964–68*, vol. 4, 883–84.)

8. Blair, *Lodge in Vietnam*, 152–53.

9. See Gibbons, *U.S. Government and the Vietnam War*, 575.

10. Memorandum to the President from Katzenbach, February 11, 1967, NSF Rostow Files.

11. Memorandum for the President from Bundy, February 27, 1967, NSF Rostow Files.

12. A copy of the president's letter to Rusk dated March 2, 1967, was sent to Bunker by Richard Hunt, a Department of the Army historian who found it while researching at the LBJ Library. The copy and the covering letter from Hunt to Bunker are in BC.

13. Bunker learned about the ambassador-at-large proposal only much later, years after he had completed his Saigon assignment, when Hunt sent him the copy of the president's letter. Bunker told Hunt that the arrangement would not have worked and that he would not have been willing to accept the assignment on those terms. (EB letter to Richard Hunt, June 22, 1981, BC.)

14. Johnson, *Vantage Point*, 259. EB Oral History interview, LBJ Library, Part 1, 2.

15. Walt Rostow, interview by author, July 1992.

16. In November 1966, Bunker's name had come up at the White House in a Vietnam context when Johnson considered sending him to several countries, mostly in Asia, to conduct a systematic assessment of what they could do to support the Vietnam effort. Nothing came of the idea. (*FRUS 1964-68*, vol. 4, 828.)

17. White House memorandum, January 20, 1967, WHCF Name File, Box 570, LBJ Library. President Kennedy had offered the position to Bunker in 1960 (see Chapter 7).

18. Johnson letter to Laise, March 24, 1967, WHCF Name File, Box 570, LBJ Library.

19. Gibbons, *U.S. Government and the Vietnam War*, 607.

20. The *New York Times* carried the full text of Johnson's speech in its March 16 issue.

21. Ibid.

22. *Newsweek*, March 27, 1967.

23. Diem, *In the Jaws*, 188.

24. *Pentagon Papers*, 425.

25. The senators do not appear to have been concerned that Bunker had taken part in the conference before they had confirmed him. Nowadays, any appointee found to be exercising his new responsibilities before the Senate had approved his appointment would find himself in deep trouble on Capitol Hill.

26. Senate Committee on Foreign Relations, *Report of Proceedings . . . Nominations*, 99.

27. Ibid., 95.

28. Ibid., 107.

29. Ibid., 121.

30. Ibid., 116.

31. According to Galen Stone, an American Foreign Service officer who served in senior positions in both New Delhi and Saigon during Bunker's Vietnam ambassadorship, this was the sarcastic term used by officials at the Indian Ministry of External Affairs when the U.S. embassy in New Delhi sought clearance for the plane to fly over Indian territory. It quickly caught on in Saigon and Kathmandu. Bunker regularly made seats on the flights available to mission staff, who shared his pleasure at getting away to the Himalayas. (Stone letter to the author, January 26, 2000.)

32. *New York Times*, April 12, 1967.

33. Embassy Saigon telegram, May 3, 1967 (Pike, *Bunker Papers*, 7).

34. Bunker drew these conclusions on many occasions in interviews he gave in the late 1970s. See, for example, his interview with Sanford Ungar for the January 1978 issue of *Foreign Policy*.

35. In his LBJ Library oral history interview, Bunker recalled Johnson telling him: "You can have anybody you want. If there's anybody there that you don't want, he'll be on his way home in twenty-four hours." Bunker noted that in the six years he was in Saigon, he had asked for the removal of only one officer. (EB Oral History interview, LBJ Library, Part 1, 9-10.)

36. Colby, *Lost Victory*, 208.

37. Richard Eder, "A Quiet American Goes to Vietnam," *New York Times Magazine*, March 26, 1967.

38. EB Oral History interview, LBJ Library, Part 1, 4.

39. EB Oral History interview, Duke University, 50.

40. See EB letter to Carol, March 23, 1968.

41. Ibid.

42. Sorley, *A Better War*, 19.

43. Westmoreland, *A Soldier Reports*, 217.

44. Sorley, *Thunderbolt*, 286. Sorley, *A Better War*, 10.

45. George McArthur letter to author, November 15, 1999. These warm and supportive relations between Bunker and the military no doubt contributed to his winning two prestigious awards: the Sylvanus Thayer medal, presented to him in May 1970 by the Association of Graduates of the United States Military Academy, and the George Catlett Marshall medal, given him by the Association of the United States Army in October 1974.

46. Embassy Saigon telegram 16600, January 22, 1968, Ambassador Bunker Files, Box 1. Locke had graduated from Yale Law School in 1940 and was an officer of its Alumni Association.

47. Beech, *Not Without the Americans*, 236.

48. For an admiring account of Samuel Berger's career, see the biography written by his brother Graenum Berger, *A Not So Silent Envoy*.

49. Roger Kirk, interview by author, February 1992.

50. Galen Stone, interview by author, August 1992.

51. Eva Kim, interview by author, February 1992.

52. EB letter to Carol, March 17, 1968.

53. EB letter to Carol, March 25, 1968.

54. Carol letter to Katherine Parsons, July 11, 1967, BC.

55. Saigon telegram 14169, December 23, 1967, Ambassador Bunker Files, Box 1.

56. Fred Z. Brown letter to author, December 9, 1999.

57. Barry Zorthian letter to the author, January 2, 2000.

58. EB Oral History interview, Duke University, 50.

59. Embassy Saigon telegram 26467, May 23, 1967, General Records of the Department of State, 1967–69, POL 14 VIET S, Box 2757, NA.

60. For Bunker's negative attitude toward a possible Minh candidacy, see Embassy Saigon telegram 620, July 9, 1967, Box 65, NSF Country File, Vietnam, LBJ Library.

61. Ky, *Twenty Years and Twenty Days*, 155.

62. State Department telegrams 198950, May 21, 1967, and 204933, May 30, 1967, Box 65, NSF Country File, Vietnam, LBJ Library.

63. Westmoreland, *A Soldier Reports*, 218–19.

64. Bunker-Rusk cable sent through CIA channels, quoted by Gibbons, *U.S. Government and the Vietnam War*, 768.

65. Diem, *In the Jaws*, 197.

66. Ky, *Twenty Years and Twenty Days*, 135, 168.

67. Robert Shaplen has a graphic description in the *New Yorker*, later reproduced

in *Road from War*, 156–57. The best account in English of the run-up to the election written by a Vietnamese insider is probably in Diem, *In the Jaws*, chapters 23 and 24. Both Shaplen and Diem use the term "coup de théâtre" to describe the outcome of the military commanders' crucial meeting. See also Embassy Saigon telegram, July 5, 1967 (Pike, *Bunker Papers*, 72), and Embassy Saigon telegram 29258, June 30, 1967, in General Records of the State Department, 1967–69, POL 14 VIET S, Box 2757, NA.

68. Embassy Saigon telegram 27074, May 30, 1967, General Records of the State Department, 1967–69, POL 14 VIET S, Box 2757, NA.

69. Embassy Saigon telegram, July 5, 1967 (Pike, *Bunker Papers*, 69).

70. Embassy Saigon telegram 80, July 1, 1967, General Records of the Department of State, 1967–69, Pol 14 VIET S, Box 2758, NA.

71. Embassy Saigon telegram, July 26, 1967 (Pike, *Bunker Papers*, 92).

72. EB letter to Katherine and John Parsons, September 12, 1967, BC. Bunker's special bête noire among the *Times*'s correspondents was R. W. "Johnny" Apple, a seasoned correspondent who went on to an outstanding career on the newspaper. According to Barry Zorthian, Bunker had probably been particularly angered by Apple's criticism of U.S. policy in his story, "Vietnam: The Signs of Stalemate," which appeared in the paper on August 7, 1967. (Barry Zorthian, interview by author, May 2002.)

73. Barry Zorthian, interview by author.

74. Embassy Saigon telegram, January 13, 1968 (Pike, *Bunker Papers*, 284).

75. Richard Harwood, "The War Just Doesn't Add Up," *Washington Post*, September 3, 1967. Harwood's article, a thoughtful assessment of the reasons for the pronounced differences between American journalists and senior civilian and military officials about developments in Vietnam, was reproduced in the anthology *Reporting Vietnam*, vol. 1, 484–89. Volume 2, pages 394–407, of the anthology includes a useful article on "The Military and the Press," written from Saigon five years later by Sydney H. Schanberg for the *New York Times Magazine* of November 12, 1972. Schanberg complained that "Reporters can, from time to time, obtain interviews from all the top American officials [including] Ambassador Ellsworth Bunker . . . but none will speak for the record. No names can be used. No one accepts personal responsibility for what he says. What this means is that these men can get things in print as the official American view—sometimes outrageous things—and never have to answer for them personally if events prove their analyses totally wrong." A careful study of the American media and the Vietnam War, Wyatt, *Paper Soldiers*, concludes that "an examination of how the press actually covered the war in Vietnam makes it clear that not politics [or ideology] but the demands of journalism, motivated reporters in Vietnam and their superiors back in the United States" (216).

76. Beech reciprocated Bunker's regard and considered him the most influential ambassador the United States ever had in Saigon. But he also concluded in a description of his dealings with the ambassador that "to arrive at his destination, Bunker could be as devious as Machiavelli, as ruthless as Genghis Khan." (Beech, *Not Without the Americans*, 235–42.)

77. For the text of President Johnson's letter to Thieu and Ky, see State Depart-

ment telegram 22160, August 17, 1967, General Records of the State Department, 1967–69, POL 14 VIET S, Box 2757, NA. In the letter, Johnson took a mild approach. After reiterating the by then familiar U.S. call for free and fair elections, he concluded "I am writing you now not to offer advice but simply to say that I am following events in Vietnam with interest, sympathy, and great respect for you both, for your colleagues in the government, and—above all—for the gallant people of your country." Bunker liked the message: "In recent weeks," he told the president, "I have had to put a good deal of pressure on them about the elections and I think at this point they need a little encouragement." (Embassy Saigon telegram 3330, August 17, 1967, General Records of the State Department, 1967–69, POL 14 VIET S, Box 2757, NA.)

78. EB Oral History interview, LBJ Library, Part 1, 15.

79. In the earlier of his two autobiographies, Ky wrote, "It is unjust to call the election rigged. The public knew that I was extremely powerful and could have easily won with sixty or seventy percent of the votes if I wanted to cheat. . . . [But] there was no reason to cheat in favor of Thieu and get the blame, when I had given up my own chance for the presidency." (Ky, *Twenty Years*, 157.) According to Ambassador Bui Diem, Ky told him: "The government had given no formal instructions to provincial authorities about influencing voters in any way. On the other hand, he said, there was of course a tacit understanding about the kind of vote he and Thieu would like to see. As a result, there was no doubt that some pressure had been applied where local authorities were especially zealous and well organized. But the result showed a very uneven pattern and consequently a relatively clean election." (Bui Diem, *In the Jaws*, 207 n.)

80. Embassy Saigon telegram 3721, August 22, 1967, General Records of the State Department, 1967–69, POL 14, VIET S, Box 2759, NA.

81. Embassy Saigon telegram 4885, September 4, 1967, LBJ Library. After the election, Dzu led an unsuccessful effort to persuade the National Assembly to invalidate the election results. He was jailed for five days, apparently to remove him from that campaign, then released. In October 1967 he was sentenced to nine months in prison and payment of a substantial fine for bad check and illegal currency transactions. Bunker reported that the judicial procedure that was followed was fully in accordance with Vietnamese practice. He concluded that Dzu's jailing was "a matter which we can leave to the courts to handle." (Embassy Saigon telegrams October 4, 1967 and October 25, 1967 [Pike, *Bunker Papers*, 194, 221–22]).

82. Embassy Saigon telegram 4885, September 4, 1967, LBJ Library.

83. Ibid.

84. Embassy Saigon telegram, November 29, 1967 (Pike, *Bunker Papers*, 246).

85. See EB Oral History interview, LBJ Library, Part 1, 31.

86. *Pentagon Papers*, vol. 4, 517.

87. Embassy Saigon telegram, January 24, 1968 (Pike, *Bunker Papers*, 310–11).

88. Barrett, *Uncertain Warriors*, 91.

89. Pike, *Bunker Papers*. The Asia Foundation was also associated with the project.

90. Gilbert Sheinbaum, interview by author, April 1999.

Chapter 11

1. Embassy Saigon telegram, January 13, 1968 (Pike, *Bunker Papers*, 284–88).

2. For a discussion of General Westmoreland's assessment, which was similar to Bunker's, see MacGarrigle, *United States Army in Vietnam*, 431–43. Questioning in particular the general's conviction that the North Vietnamese were nearing exhaustion, MacGarrigle noted that "Westmoreland ignored the fact that an estimated 200,000 North Vietnamese males reached draft age each year, far more than the number killed on the battlefield, which enabled Hanoi to replace its losses and match each American escalation" (439).

3. Gibbons, *U.S. Government and the Vietnam War*, 896.

4. "Address to Overseas Press Club, New York, November 17, 1967," *Department of State Bulletin* 57, no. 1485 (December 11, 1967): 781–84. For the text of Bunker's November 13 press conference at the White House, in which he made similar points, see *Department of State Bulletin* 57, no. 1484 (December 4, 1967): 748–51.

5. *New York Times*, November 20, 1967. In the same interview, Westmoreland declared that it might be possible for the United States to start withdrawing its troops from Vietnam in two years or less. Bunker made no such predictions. In his White House press conference, he had declined to forecast how long the United States military would need to remain in the country.

6. U.S. Congress, Senate Committee on Foreign Relations, unpublished executive session transcript, November 16, 1967, made available to me by committee staff.

7. Rostow back-channel message to EB, December 12, 1967, Ambassador Bunker Files, Box 1. Bunker liked the idea, but preferred separate TV appearances for himself and Westmoreland.

8. By then the phrase had, of course, come into common, if often ironic use. A few months earlier, Bunker had used it without irony in a September 10, 1967 interview on *Face the Nation* when he stated that "I think we are beginning to see light at the end of the tunnel." He then wisely resisted efforts to get him to say how long the tunnel might be. (*Department of State Bulletin* 57, no. 1475 [October 2, 1967]: 416–21).

9. Embassy Saigon telegram, October 4, 1967 (Pike, *Bunker Papers*, 188).

10. Allen Wendt, interview by author, February 2002. The classic study of the Tet offensive and its aftermath is Oberdorfer, *Tet!*.

11. Peter Braestrup's lengthy study, *Big Story*, provides an excellent assessment of the way the American press and television reported and interpreted the Tet crisis and its aftermath. Braestrup found media reporting distorted. But unlike Bunker, he found "simple 'ideological' explanations of media flaws gravely insufficient." In Braestrup's view, "the distortions at Tet resulted from the impact of a rare combination of circumstances on the various habits, incentives, economic constraints and managerial and manpower limitations peculiar to each of the major U.S. news organizations. Tet sharply illuminated these limitations" (xi). In *Paper Soldiers*, Clarence Wyatt came to a similar conclusion (180–88). Wyatt argued that Americans came to believe that the cost in lives and treasure was simply too great to sustain without some

successful conclusion in sight. "The Tet Offensive, despite its drama and intensity, was but one important milestone on the road to that realization" (188).

12. EB Oral History interview, LBJ Library, Part 2, 9.

13. Embassy Saigon telegram 20928, March 1, 1968, Ambassador Bunker Files, Box 1.

14. Ibid.

15. Embassy Saigon telegram 22548, March 20, 1968, NSF Country File, Vietnam, Box 127, LBJ Library.

16. Embassy Saigon telegram 21733, March 11, 1968, NSF—NSC History, Box 48, LBJ Library.

17. EB letter to Carol, April 1, 1968.

18. EB back-channel message to Johnson, April 2, 1968, Ambassador Bunker Files, Box 1.

19. Embassy Saigon telegram 23612, April 1, 1968, LBJ Library.

20. Embassy Saigon telegram 23912, April 4, 1968, Ambassador Bunker Files, Box 1.

21. EB letter to Carol, April 7, 1968.

22. Embassy Saigon telegram, September 27, 1967 (Pike, *Bunker Papers*, 183).

23. Humphrey, *Education of a Public Man*, 349. Bunker reported that the mission had made suggestions to Thieu for a number of speeches, including the inaugural address. He noted that the president had not stuck to the mission's script. (Embassy Saigon telegram, October 12, 1967 [Pike, *Bunker Papers*, 197]).

24. Embassy Saigon telegram, October 4, 1967 (Pike, *Bunker Papers*, 188).

25. Embassy Saigon telegram, January 24, 1968 (Pike, *Bunker Papers*, 302).

26. EB back-channel message to Walt Rostow, February 1, 1968, Ambassador Bunker Files, Box 1.

27. Ibid., February 2, 1968.

28. Embassy Saigon telegram, March 14, 1968 (Pike, *Bunker Papers*, 372).

29. EB letter to Carol, March 23, 1968.

30. Embassy Saigon telegram 24147, April 6, 1968, Ambassador Bunker Files, Box 1.

31. Hung and Schecter, *Palace File*, 18.

32. Diem, *In the Jaws of History*, 276.

33. EB letter to Carol, April 21, 1968.

34. Embassy Saigon telegram, June 13, 1968 (Pike, *Bunker Papers*, 469).

35. EB letter to Carol, September 10, 1968.

36. EB letter to Carol, October 22, 1968.

37. Embassy Saigon telegram, October 19, 1968 (Pike, *Bunker Papers*, 607).

38. EB Oral History interview, LBJ Library, Part 3, 10.

39. Notes of the President's Meeting at Camp David, April 9, 1968, Meeting Notes File, Box 2, LBJ Library.

40. EB message to Rostow, April 30, 1968, Ambassador Bunker Files, Box 1.

41. Embassy Saigon telegram 29841, June 13, 1968, Ambassador Bunker Files, Box 2.

42. Karnow, *Vietnam*, 581.

43. EB letter to Carol, June 24, 1968.

44. EB letter to Carol, June 11, 1968.

45. Embassy Saigon telegram, May 9, 1968 (Pike, *Bunker Papers*, 434).

46. Embassy Saigon telegram 31594, July 4, 1968, Ambassador Bunker Files, Box 1.

47. Bunker's animus was also directed at another member of the Kennedy family, Senator Edward Kennedy of Massachusetts. A speech that Senator Kennedy gave on returning to the United States from a visit to Vietnam in early 1968 particularly angered him. The senator had called on the administration to withdraw U.S. forces to population centers, cease offensive military activities, and threaten to leave Vietnam altogether if the GVN failed to take energetic action against corruption and waste. In a thirty-five-page telegram that detailed Kennedy's alleged errors, Bunker called the speech "a most unfortunate statement, apparently based in large part on incomplete, biased or false information. It appeals heavily to the emotions, and is in no sense a sober evaluation of our policy, our tactics, and our progress in Vietnam." (Embassy Saigon telegrams 17179 and 17180, both January 28, 1968, Ambassador Bunker Files, Box 1.)

48. EB letter to Carol, June 24, 1968.

49. EB letter to Carol, October 15, 1968.

50. See Embassy Saigon telegrams 39602, October 6, 1968 and 40121, October 13, 1968, both in LBJ Library.

51. Embassy Saigon telegram, October 19, 1968 (Pike, *Bunker Papers*, 602).

52. Bunker discussed this in his Columbia University Oral History interview, 118: "It's a way of life in Asia. A way of life because it's a family-oriented society. In these countries, in those societies, there's no social security institutions . . . such as we have. The family is the social security institution. A man's first duty is to look out for the family. . . . So whatever he has to do to support that family is justifiable in their view. Consequently, there's a more tolerant view of corruption in that whole area than there is in our more advanced societies."

53. Clifford, *Counsel to the President*, 550–51.

54. Ibid.

55. EB letter to Carol, July 22, 1968.

56. Embassy Saigon telegram 33628, July 26, 1968, Ambassador Bunker Files, Box 2. In this message, Bunker wrote: "The strong and unqualified reaffirmation of our support for South Vietnam, plus the statement about the GVN role in the peace negotiations, appear to have come as a very welcome surprise."

57. Clifford, *Counsel to the President*, 553.

58. Embassy Saigon telegram 34163, August 1, 1968, Ambassador Bunker Files, Box 2.

59. EB letter to Carol, August 18, 1968.

60. EB letter to Carol, September 10, 1968.

61. See Dallek, *Flawed Giant*, 586–88, and Bundy, *Tangled Web*, 35–45. Bundy's well-informed reconstruction of Chennault's role is especially persuasive. In his auto-

biography, published in 1971, Johnson had concluded that Nixon himself was not involved (*Vantage Point*, 516). For a well-informed Vietnamese view, see Diem, *In the Jaws of History*, 235–46.

62. Embassy Saigon telegram 40178, October 13, 1968, Ambassador Bunker Files, Box 4.

63. Embassy Saigon telegram 41768, November 3, 1968, Ambassador Bunker Files, Box 4.

64. *New York Times*, November 2, 1968.

65. Clifford discusses the negotiations and Bunker's role in them in *Counsel to the President*, 573–95.

66. Abramson, *Spanning the Century*, 670–71.

67. Bunker's faithful adherence to his instructions has often been noted by staffers who worked with him, for example Roger Kirk, who participated in Bunker's discussions with Thieu on the peace talks earlier in 1968. Kirk recalled: "I would write talking points from the detailed messages we received, and Bunker would literally read what I had written to Thieu. It was almost scary; . . . you wanted to be very sure you did not make a mistake." (Roger Kirk, letter to author, November 8, 1999.)

68. Postscript to an undated letter from William Bundy, Ambassador Bunker Files, Box 6. Berger's name does not appear as the addressee, but internal evidence suggests Bundy sent it to him, probably early in 1969. At the end of the postscript, Bundy wrote, "Share this with Ellsworth if you want. I am sure that his stock of compassion would be equal to it."

69. Embassy Saigon telegram, January 16, 1969 (Pike, *Bunker Papers*, 643).

70. Pike, *Bunker Papers*, 644.

Chapter 12

1. William Rogers, interview by author, May 1998.

2. Bundy, *Tangled Web*, 54.

3. *Washington Post*, January 8, 1969.

4. See EB letters to Katherine Parsons, September 25, 1968, and Ellen Bunker, October 2, 1968, BC. In these messages to his sister and daughter, Bunker indicated that he expected Nixon would win and that he would therefore leave the embassy soon after the first of the year.

5. EB letter to Katherine Parsons, January 14, 1969, ibid.

6. See EB letter to Carol, January 6, 1969.

7. EB letter to Under Secretary of State for Political Affairs U. Alexis Johnson, February 1, 1969, Ambassador Bunker Files, Box 6.

8. Anthony Lake, interview by author, August 1997. Lake was on the Kissinger-led National Security Council staff in 1969–70.

9. In this connection, see Bunker's letter to Carol, June 1, 1971: "The observation by George McArthur in the *Los Angeles Times* article that I might stay here through the U.S. election [of November 1972] was entirely his own idea, certainly not mine. When I got your telegram, I assumed this is what troubled you and so I wanted to

reassure you that no such thought had entered my head. Enough is enough in Kathmandu and Saigon and we have both had it."

10. Palmer, *25-Year War*, 47. See also EB Oral History interview, LBJ Library, Part 1, 3. In this interview, Bunker stated: "My recollection is that the President emphasized the fact that he wanted to see the training of the Vietnamese accelerated and speeded up to enable us to more quickly turn the war over to them, which was our main objective, of course, to enable the Vietnamese to defend themselves."

11. Embassy Saigon telegram, July 16, 1969 (Pike, *Bunker Papers*, 713).

12. Embassy Saigon telegram, August [n.d.] 1969 (Pike, *Bunker Papers*, 717).

13. Embassy Saigon telegram, March 27, 1970 (Pike, *Bunker Papers*, 763).

14. Embassy Saigon telegram, November 18, 1969 (Pike, *Bunker Papers*, 726).

15. Embassy Saigon telegram 2830, February 12, 1969, Ambassador Bunker Files, Box 7. In this message, Bunker also reported that he had found the Abrams briefing "impressive in its pinpointing of COVSN headquarters and [it] also shows our capacity to use B-52s without hitting the nearest Cambodian villages or army outposts."

16. Washington considered this shelling a violation of one of the understandings that had made possible the cessation of U.S. bombing of North Vietnam and the beginning of "serious" peace talks in Paris.

17. See, for example, his March 27 message to Nixon: "The situation in Cambodia will bear close watching. While the present situation has in it promising elements and a potential favorable to achieving our objectives, it could also develop in a way adverse to our interests. Either a reversion to a government less favorable than the present one [Lon Nol's] appears to be or a descent into civil war in Cambodia itself would present us with new problems here and there." (Embassy Saigon telegram, March 27, 1970 [Pike, *Bunker Papers*, 762].)

18. See Saigon telegram 4622, March 28, 1970, Ambassador Bunker Files, Box 7. For a summary of events in Cambodia during the month following Sihanouk's ouster, see Kosut, *Cambodia and the Vietnam War*, 71–87.

19. See Kissinger, *White House Years*, 501.

20. See Bundy, *Tangled Web*, 157–61, for an excellent assessment of the military and political fallout of the 1970 Cambodian intervention.

21. Hill letter to author, January 20, 2000.

22. For a detailed account of Lam Son 719, see Nolan, *Into Laos*.

23. Embassy Saigon telegram, January 30, 1971 (Pike, *Bunker Papers*, 807).

24. Ibid.

25. For more a recent example, see Bundy, *Tangled Web*, 226–28. In his biography of Abrams, Robert Sorley provides an interesting review of the criticism leveled against the general for his role in planning and helping carry out the operation (*Thunderbolt*, 303–16). Sorley also discusses Abrams's role in his later book, *A Better War*, 228–71.

26. Embassy Saigon telegram 4508, March 28, 1971, Ambassador Bunker Files, Box 4.

27. Embassy Saigon telegram 4876, April 2, 1971, Ambassador Bunker Files, Box 4.

28. EB letter to Norman Hannah, April 25, 1983, BC.

29. EB letter to Carol, March 29, 1971. For an account of U.S. press reporting of Lam Son 719, see Wyatt, *Paper Soldiers*, 196.

30. Sorley, *Better War*, 266.

31. Embassy Saigon telegram 4929, April 3, 1971, Ambassador Bunker Files, Box 4.

32. Embassy Saigon telegram 1515, January 1, 1970, Ambassador Bunker Files, Box 4.

33. Embassy Saigon telegram, January 30, 1971 (Pike, *Bunker Papers*, 818).

34. Embassy Saigon telegram, August 26, 1970 (Pike, *Bunker Files*, 789).

35. James Nach, interview by author, March 1994.

36. Embassy Saigon telegram 307, January 8, 1971, State Department, Central Files, POL 14 Viet S, Box 2811, NA.

37. Ibid.

38. Ibid.

39. State Department telegram 64107, April 15, 1971, State Department, Central Files, POL 14 Viet S, Box 2811, NA.

40. A main source on this issue is Frank W. Snepp III, then a CIA officer in Saigon. According to Seymour Hersh, Snepp told him in an interview that the CIA station was deeply involved in bribing members of the Vietnamese National Assembly to ensure that Vice President Ky would be unable to contest (Hersh, *Price of Power*, 437). In his own book, *Decent Interval*, Snepp alleges more generally that the CIA provided funds to the Thieu government to be used to cow and neutralize its opposition (15). In his biography of Ted Shackley, the CIA chief of station in Saigon during the 1971 election, David Corn reported that when *Los Angeles Times* reporter George McArthur asked Shackley how much money the station was spreading around to support Thieu's reelection, he was told "You're a damn fool to ask me that question" (Corn, *Blond Ghost*, 218).

41. Bundy, *Tangled Web*, 296.

42. EB letter to Carol, July 30, 1971.

43. A State Department analyst proficient in Vietnamese examined the document. He concluded that it "is far less sinister than Thieu's opposition would have us believe. It calls for thorough analysis of the voters and a coordinated campaign to expand the bloc of pro-GVN voters, but it does not, in my view, call for anything fraudulent." (Memorandum from State Department Executive Secretary Theodore Eliot to Dr. Kissinger, August 20, 1971, State Department, Central Files, POL 14 Viet S, Box 2811, NA.) Seymour Hersh writes that in an interview, Bunker told him that "my feeling was that it was not authentic. . . . It wasn't necessary to write it. [Thieu] had control of the apparatus of government anyway." (Hersh, *Price of Power*, 437.)

44. The allegations were reported in the *New York Times*, September 4, 1971.

45. Richard Thompson, interview by author, May 1999. The charges surfaced again in Snepp's *Decent Interval*. Snepp wrote that the bribe attempt "would have worked—Bunker made his overture with typical diplomacy—had not Minh ultimately concluded that three million dollars offered him for his campaign was less

compelling than the prospect of assured defeat." (Snepp, *Decent Interval*, 11.) In a written deposition in Snepp's subsequent trial, a CIA official acknowledged that the agency had tapes "in which Ambassador Bunker offered to finance (deleted) race for the presidency." The omitted name, it was obvious, was Minh's. The deposition said the official "noted that the amount of $3 million was not mentioned in that conversation, although the basic report by Snepp is true." Bunker, who had denied the Snepp allegation, declined to comment on the disclosure of the deposition since the case was still in court. (Deposition of Norman Jones, United States of America vs. Frank W. Snepp III, Case No. 78–92a, U.S. District Court for the Eastern District of Virginia, *New York Times*, May 27, 1978.) In *The Palace File*, Nguyen Tien Hung and Jerrold L. Schecter state that "President Thieu had proof that Minh transferred funds to Paris from his account in the Bank of Tokyo in Saigon. When it became apparent to Minh that he could not beat Thieu, he kept the money and did not run" (12–13). This finding seems to be based on a 1985 interview with Thieu as well as information provided by Hoang Duc Nha, who had been Thieu's special assistant in 1971. Neither Thieu nor Nha can be considered a reliable source on this matter. Hung and Schecter also cite Snepp's account in *Decent Interval*. They fail to note that the two accounts are quite different. In the Vietnamese version, Minh accepted the money, in Snepp's he did not (12, 481–82).

46. Ky, *Twenty Years*, 194. Ky wrote that Bunker told him: "A one man show will not be a good example for the rest of the world." Ky was even more explicit in his later biography, *Buddha's Child*. He claimed that Bunker offered him $2 million to run against Thieu.

47. EB letter to Carol, September 23, 1971.

48. EB letter to Carol, September 30, 1971.

49. White House message WHS1109 to Saigon, October 2, 1971, Gerald R. Ford Library, NSC Convenience Files, Copies of Materials from the U.S. Embassy, Saigon: 1963–75, Box 1. General Haig, Kissinger's deputy, had recently visited Saigon, where he had discussed with Thieu proposed strategies for the secret U.S. negotiations with North Vietnam. The "game plan" almost certainly refers to a formulation Haig gave Thieu for an election arrangement following a political settlement.

50. Embassy Saigon message 0485 to the White House, October 4, 1971, Gerald R. Ford Library, NSC Convenience Files, Copies of Materials from the U.S. Embassy, Saigon: 1963–75, Box 1.

51. In its comments on the election, Embassy Saigon reported that the vote "demonstrated that the GVN exerts thorough administrative control over the population of the country and can effectively execute major tasks that it considers of great importance. Although largely unenthusiastic and skeptical over the uncontested election, people trooped to the polls in record numbers, moved probably by a combination of civic duty, fear of harassment by the authorities, and the absence of widespread dissension." The embassy doubted that the Vietnamese would point with pride to the election. "Most will be glad it is over and relieved to turn their attention to other subjects." (Embassy Saigon telegram 15933, October 5, 1971, State Department, Central Files, POL 14 Viet S, Box 2812, NA.)

52. EB Oral History interview, Duke University, 51.

53. EB letter to Carol, August 29, 1971. Carol herself was incensed by what she called "the seemingly unnecessary blow that Thieu gave to the hope for a fair test of his political leadership . . . I regarded it," she wrote Ellsworth's sister, as "[a] betrayal of the confidence we had placed in him and of Ellsworth in particular. In such a situation I did not see why Ellsworth should continue to be a party to such a farce." (Carol letter to Katherine Parsons, September 23, 1971, BC.)

54. This was in his Embassy Saigon telegram 485 to the White House, Privacy Channel, October 4, 1971, October 5, 1971, State Department, Central Files, POL 14 Viet S, Box 2812, NA: "While there has been naturally some disappointment at failure to hold a contested election, I think there is a general awareness that we cannot expect too much of a country as new to the practice of the constitutional process as Vietnam."

55. Assistant Secretary of State for Congressional Relations David Abshire—Lester Wolff letter, October 19, 1971, State Department, Central Files, POL 14 Viet S, Box 2812, NA. The file includes the text of Wolff's letter.

56. For a caustic Vietnamese account of this cease-fire in place proposal, see Tan Van Don, *Our Endless War*, 195: "[It is] rather like a policeman interrupting a robber holding up a candy store. Under the principle agreed to by the United States, the law enforcement officer would leave the robber pointing his weapon at the frightened store owner instead of hauling him off to jail in handcuffs."

57. Embassy Saigon telegram 163 to the White House, September 16, 1971, Privacy Channel, Gerald R. Ford Library, NSC Convenience Files, Copies of Materials from the U.S. Embassy, Saigon: 1963–75, Box 1.

58. Karnow, *Vietnam*, 654. The description of the Easter offensive that follows draws on Karnow's account.

59. EB letters to Carol, April 30, May 3, and May 23, 1972.

60. EB letter to Carol, May 3, 1972.

61. EB letter to Carol, May 23, 1972.

62. EB letter to Carol, April 30, 1972.

63. Hung and Schecter, *Palace File*, 17.

64. Kissinger, *White House Years*, 448.

65. Peter Rodman, interview by author, February 1999.

66. Kissinger, *Years of Renewal*, 80.

67. Charles Whitehouse, letter to author, November 30, 1999.

68. Charles Hill, letter to author, January 20, 2000.

69. Kissinger, *White House Years*, 1327.

70. Ibid., 1366–67.

71. Charles Hill, interview by author, November 1998.

72. Anthony Lake, interview by author, August 1997.

73. Isaacs, *Without Honor*, 41.

74. Bunker's proposal was forwarded in Embassy Saigon telegram 270 to the White House, Privacy Channel, April 17, 1971, Gerald R. Ford Library, NSC Convenience Files, Copies of Materials from the U.S. Embassy, Saigon: 1963–75, Box 1.

75. White House telegram WHS1047 to Saigon, Bunker Channels, May 25, 1971,

Gerald R. Ford Library, NSC Convenience Files, Copies of Materials from the U.S. Embassy, Saigon: 1963–75, Box 1.

76. See Embassy Saigon telegram 144 to the White House, Privacy Channel, June 3, 1971, Gerald R. Ford Library, NSC Convenience Files, Copies of Materials from the U.S. Embassy, Saigon: 1963–75, Box 1. In this message, Bunker reported that in a meeting with Thieu, "I did not go into details of our package proposal, but said that we in general followed the lines of President Nixon's proposal last October, i.e. cease-fire in all Southeast Asia, international supervision of cease-fire, prisoner exchange, withdrawal of our troops and eventual withdrawal of all foreign troops from Indochina."

77. Letter to the *Wall Street Journal*, February 6, 1996. Hill sought to refute an earlier allegation by Stephen B. Young (*Wall Street Journal*, January 23, 1996), who had collaborated closely with Bunker after the war, that Kissinger "never disclosed to Thieu the implications of the May 1971 'modification' of Bunker's proposal." (Young wrote to me on February 27, 2000 that Bunker, too, was unaware until Kissinger came to Saigon that U.S. policy was to let Hanoi's troops stay in South Vietnam.)

78. *U.S. News and World Report*, May 21, 1973.

79. Kissinger, *White House Years*, 1320.

80. Ibid., 1323.

81. Ibid., 1324.

82. Embassy Saigon telegram 158 to the White House, Privacy Channel, September 16, 1972, Gerald R. Ford Library, NSC Convenience Files, Copies of Materials from the U.S. Embassy, Saigon: 1963–75, Box 2.

83. "Meeting with President Thieu, September 23, 1972" and Embassy Saigon telegram 169 to the White House, Privacy Channel, September 9, 1972, both in Gerald R. Ford Library, NSC Convenience Files, Copies of Materials from the U.S. Embassy, Saigon: 1963–75, Box 2.

84. Embassy Saigon telegram 181 to the White House, Privacy Channel, October 5, 1972, Gerald R. Ford Library, NSC Convenience Files, Copies of Materials from the U.S. Embassy, Saigon: 1963–75, Box 2.

85. Embassy Saigon telegram 185 to the White House, Privacy Channel, October 12, 1972, Gerald R. Ford Library, NSC Convenience Files, Copies of Materials from the U.S. Embassy, Saigon: 1963–75, Box 2.

86. Embassy Saigon telegram 180 to the White House, Privacy Channel, October 5, 1972, Gerald R. Ford Library, NSC Convenience Files, Copies of Materials from the U.S. Embassy, Saigon: 1963–75, Box 2; EB Talking Points for his October 5, meeting with Thieu, ibid.

87. EB letter to Carol, October 10, 1972.

88. Embassy Saigon telegram 186 to the White House, Privacy Channel, October 13, 1972, Gerald R. Ford Library, NSC Convenience Files, Copies of Materials from the U.S. Embassy, Saigon: 1963–75, Box 2.

89. White House telegram to Saigon WHS2298, Bunker Channels, October 25, 1972, Gerald R. Ford Library, NSC Convenience Files, Copies of Materials from the U.S. Embassy, Saigon: 1963–75, Box 2.

90. Embassy Saigon telegrams 242 and 243 to White House, Privacy Channel, October 31, 1972, Gerald R. Ford Library, NSC Convenience Files, Copies of Materials from the U.S. Embassy, Saigon: 1963–75, Box 2.

91. Nixon-Thieu letter, January 21, 1972, Gerald R. Ford Library, NSC Convenience Files, Copies of Materials from the U.S. Embassy, Saigon: 1963–75, Box 4.

92. U.S. negotiators had been sloppy in their use of the Vietnamese language in describing the nature of the council. The South Vietnamese had been upset that the Vietnamese phrase the U.S. side had meant to signify "administrative structure" actually meant government. Characteristically, Thieu saw the differences between the English and Vietnamese texts in a sinister light and alleged that the council would be a coalition government. Bunker told Kissinger that his own embassy translators confirmed that the term did indeed mean government. Bunker had often commented on the importance Vietnamese of all factions attached to the issue of legitimacy, and GVN sensitivity on the wording issue again demonstrated this.

93. See EB's Talking Points for his October 31, 1972 meeting with Thieu, Ambassador Bunker Files, Box 7.

94. EB letter to Sam Berger, July 16, 1972, Ambassador Bunker Files, Box 7.

95. Embassy Saigon telegram 0255 to the White House, Privacy Channel, November 8, 1972, Gerald R. Ford Library, NSC Convenience Files, Copies of Materials from the U.S. Embassy, Saigon: 1963–75, Box 3.

96. A photocopy of the letter appears in Hung and Schecter, *Palace File*, 488.

97. See Embassy Saigon telegram 15591, November 1, 1972, Gerald R. Ford Library, NSC Convenience Files, Copies of Materials from the U.S. Embassy, Saigon: 1963–75, Box 3.

98. Embassy Saigon telegram 252 to the White House, Privacy Channel, November 7 1972, Gerald R. Ford Library, NSC Convenience Files, Copies of Materials from the U.S. Embassy, Saigon: 1963–75, Box 3. The message also included an interesting suggestion Bunker made to help bring Thieu along by having him visit the United States. As originally conceived in Washington, and eventually carried out, Thieu was to make this visit after the agreement was signed. Bunker proposed that the visit be scheduled before rather than after the signing. He argued that "Thieu would be able to say that the commitment of continued support which he had received from the President gave adequate assurance that the Vietnamese people could look forward to a future of peace and progress."

99. Embassy Saigon telegram 282 to the White House, Privacy Channel, November 27, 1972, Gerald R. Ford Library, NSC Convenience Files, Copies of Materials from the U.S. Embassy, Saigon: 1963–75, Box 3.

100. Embassy Saigon telegram 286 to the White House, Privacy Channel, December 1, 1972, Gerald R. Ford Library, NSC Convenience Files, Copies of Materials from the U.S. Embassy, Saigon: 1963–75, Box 3.

101. Embassy Saigon telegram 300 to the White House, Privacy Channel, December 18, 1972, Gerald R. Ford Library, NSC Convenience Files, Copies of Materials from the U.S. Embassy, Saigon: 1963–75, Box 3.

102. For the complete text of the Paris agreement, see White House press release,

January 24, 1973, reprinted in the *Department of State Bulletin* 68, 175 (February 12, 1973): 169–88.

103. Hung and Schecter, *Palace File*, 392.

104. Bundy, *Tangled Web*, 362.

105. See Embassy Saigon telegrams 315, January 5, 1973 and 317, January 6, 1973, to the White House, both Privacy Channel. They are in Gerald R. Ford Library, NSC Convenience File, Copies of Materials from the U.S. Embassy, Saigon: 1963–75, Box 3.

106. Embassy Saigon telegram 313 to the White House, Privacy Channel, December 30, 1972, Gerald R. Ford Library, NSC Convenience File, Copies of Materials from the U.S. Embassy, Saigon: 1963–75, Box 3.

107. Hung and Schecter, *Palace File*, 393.

108. Embassy Saigon telegram 348 to the White House, Privacy Channel, January 21, 1973, Gerald R. Ford Library, NSC Convenience File, Copies of Materials from the U.S. Embassy, Saigon: 1963–75, Box 3.

109. Embassy Saigon telegram, May 5, 1973 (Pike, *Bunker Papers*, 858).

110. See, for example, Embassy Saigon telegram 386 to White House, Privacy Channel, March 2, 1973, and EB, "Vietnam: Assessment of the Cease-Fire at X + 60," March 30, 1973, both in Gerald R. Ford Library, NSC Convenience File, Copies of Materials from the U.S. Embassy, Saigon: 1963–75, Box 3.

111. Isaacs, *Without Honor*, 101.

112. The first of these Joint Military Commissions was a four-party body comprising the United States, North Vietnam, the GVN, and the Provisional Revolutionary Government. As the agreement provided, it was succeeded sixty days after the cease-fire by a two-party body consisting of representatives of the GVN and the PRG. Other than their important success in supervising the withdrawal of U.S. and allied troops and the return of POWs, neither of the commissions carried out the responsibilities assigned to them. As Bunker candidly reported, all of the Vietnamese parties were guilty of hamstringing their operations. A basic problem was the unwillingness of the Vietnamese members to delineate the areas controlled by the contending forces. Without such a delineation, a cease-fire and many of the provisions connected with it could not work.

113. EB, Remarks at 85th Birthday Dinner, May 16, 1979, BC.

114. Embassy Saigon telegram, May 5, 1973 (Pike, *Bunker Papers*, 852–62). This was Bunker's ninety-third message to the White House. It followed a long lapse in the series, which was largely superseded by his back-channel messages to Kissinger. The ninety-second message had been sent more than fifteen months earlier, on January 26, 1972. Not surprisingly, Bunker professed greater optimism in a long interview he gave the same day to *U.S. News and World Report*. "Vietnam is now on the threshold of a new era which we hope will become an era of durable peace," he declared. "The cease-fire agreement is basically a good agreement that will work, if the parties who signed it abide by it. I think they will."

115. The article, appropriately headed "Bunker, Personification of U.S. Role, Leaves Vietnam," appeared in the *New York Times* on May 12, 1973. Yet despite its

antiwar position, the *Times* had earlier run an appreciative editorial about Bunker which concluded: "Only when the diplomatic record is open to view will it be possible to judge Mr. Bunker's influence and vision in the making of policy. But now, on his departure, few who knew him would deny that he carried out his difficult role with the dignity and grace that for the past two decades have marked his distinguished career in the service of his country." (*New York Times*, April 1, 1973.)

116. *The Economist*, May 12, 1973.

117. *Washington Post*, May 12, 1973.

118. Bartlett article, probably May 1973, Ambassador Bunker Files, Box 6.

119. The message was transmitted to Saigon in State Department telegram 88718, May 10, 1973, Ambassador Bunker Files, Box 6. Bunker's reply was equally effusive: "Had it not been for your courage and your willingness to take the risks of tough decisions at critical moments, none of the accomplishments you so generously ascribe to my mission could have been achieved." (Embassy Kathmandu telegram 2104, May 16, 1973, Ambassador Bunker Files, Box 6.)

120. *Los Angeles Times*, May 13, 1973. The secretary was Eva Kim, Bunker's indefatigable assistant, who later married McArthur.

121. Ibid.

Chapter 13

1. *Washington Post*, June 30, 1973.

2. See Chapter 7.

3. For the texts of the three draft treaties, see *Background Documents Relating to the Panama Canal* (Washington: U.S. Government Printing Office, 1977), 1149–1370.

4. Kissinger, *Years of Renewal*, 711.

5. William J. Jorden in Bendahmane and McDonald, *Perspectives on Negotiation*, 11.

6. Kissinger, *Years of Renewal*, 713.

7. Nixon's disinclination to do much about the treaty during his first administration was heightened by his attitude toward Robert Anderson, whom he had kept on as chief canal negotiator. Eisenhower had briefly considered Anderson as a replacement for Nixon as his vice-presidential running mate in 1956. Although nothing came of this idea, Nixon typically harbored a grudge and as president exacted his revenge by ignoring Anderson (despite having reappointed him).

8. Subsequent revisions, to Panama's advantage, agreed to in 1936 and 1955, were largely cosmetic.

9. McCullough, *Path Between the Seas*, 392.

10. Kissinger, *Years of Renewal*, 715.

11. Article IV, Section 3, Clause 2 of the Constitution states: "The Congress shall have Power to dispose of and make all needful Rules and Regulations respecting the Territory or other Property belonging to the United States." The Supreme Court dismissed the suit. See Furlong and Scranton, *Dynamics of Foreign Policymaking*, 135.

12. Stephen Rosenfeld in *Foreign Affairs* 54 (October 1975).

13. Jorden, *Panama Odyssey*, 207.

14. EB, interview by Sanford Ungar for *Foreign Policy*, January 1978, BC.

15. Kissinger made the comment at a National Security Council meeting convoked by President Ford in May 1975. (NSC Meeting of May 15, 1975, Gerald R. Ford Library, National Security Adviser, NSC Meetings File, 1974–77, Box 1.)

16. See Chapter 14.

17. Furlong and Scranton, *Dynamics of Foreign Policymaking*, 69.

18. Michael G. Kozak in Bendahmane and McDonald, *Perspectives on Negotiation*, 13.

19. For the texts of the Conceptual Agreements, see *Congressional Record*, 94th Cong., 1st sess., October 6, 1975, 121: 31, 874–76.

20. EB letter to Mark Zashin, April 19, 1978, BC.

21. Jorden, *Panama Odyssey*, 265.

22. EB, interview by David McCullough, October 8, 1981, BC.

23. All quotes are drawn from NSC Meeting of May 15, 1975, Gerald R. Ford Library, National Security Adviser, NSC Meetings File, 1974–77, Box 1.

24. NSC Meeting of July 23, 1975, Gerald R. Ford Library, National Security Adviser, NSC Meetings File, 1974–77, Box 1.

25. For the text of NSDM 302, see Records of the National Security Council, Presidential Review Memorandum, Box 1, NA. The extension of the U.S role in the defense of the canal was to be agreed upon by the two parties not less than one year prior to the treaty's expiration. To obtain this right of further negotiation, Bunker was authorized to offer a reduction of the duration period applicable to canal operations to a period of not less than twenty years.

26. In their foreign policy debate on October 6, the two candidates took very similar, notably cautious positions. Carter said he would not give up "practical control" of the canal but would favor continued negotiations. Ford replied that the United States must retain "complete access" to the canal and that the negotiations should continue. (See *New York Times*, October 7, 1976.)

27. Jorden, *Panama Odyssey*, 321.

28. In his study of the Carter administration's approach to the Canal issue, George Moffett argues that the position that candidate Carter took during the campaign stemmed from a recognition of the strong public opposition to treaty reform and did not reflect his real intentions. (Moffett, *Limits of Victory*, 51–53.)

29. Carter, *Keeping Faith*, 155.

30. Abraham F. Lowenthal, "Jimmy Carter and Latin America: a New Era of Small Change," in Oye et al., *Eagle Entangled*, 291. Emphasis in original.

31. Vance, *Hard Choices*, 141.

32. *New York Times*, December 6, 1976.

33. Records of the National Security Council, Presidential Review Memorandum, Panama, January 26, 1977, Box 1, NA.

34. Ambler H. Moss Jr. in Bendahmane and McDonald, *Perspectives on Negotiation*, 17.

35. *New York Times*, December 19, 1976. *United States and Latin America*.

36. Linowitz, *Making of a Public Man*, 150.

37. According to Linowitz, "It didn't seem in any way unreasonable, [Bunker]

said, that the President would want his own man in such negotiations, especially if the administration planned to make a strong push for a new treaty. In addition to picking up much of the load, I would symbolize for the Panamanians the President's seriousness in seeking a balm for this long-standing hemispheric irritation" (Ibid., 151). Because he wished to carry on with his business interests and law practice, Linowitz served in the position as a presidential appointee without Senate confirmation. His appointment was therefore limited to six months. So technically, he ceased to be Bunker's co-negotiator in August 1977, a few weeks before the treaties were signed and long before they were ratified by the Senate. In practice, the expiration of Linowitz's appointment made little or no difference, and the Bunker-Linowitz tandem continued to operate after August 1977 as it had earlier.

38. EB, interview by David McCullough, September 5, 1981, BC.

39. Sol Linowitz, interview by author, July 1992.

40. Linowitz, *Making of a Public Man*, 157. Both Linowitz and Jorden have vivid accounts of the Bunker-Linowitz team's first sessions with the Panamanians. For Jorden's very detailed description, see *Panama Odyssey*, chapter 14. The two accounts are similar on all significant points.

41. Richard Wyrough in Bendahmane and McDonald, *Perspectives on Negotiation*, 28.

42. Ambler Moss in ibid., 30.

43. Ambler Moss in ibid., 22.

44. *New York Times*, August 13, 1977.

45. The arrangement was made more specific in an agreement between Carter and Torrijos reached in October 1977 and subsequently made part of the treaty. This agreement stated that "the correct interpretation of the principle [of U.S. and Panamanian shared responsibility] is that the two countries shall, in accordance with their respective constitutional processes, defend the Canal against any threat to the regime of neutrality, and consequently shall have the right to act against any aggression or threat directed against the Canal or against the peaceful transit of vessels through the Canal. [But] this does not mean, nor shall it be interpreted as the right of intervention of the United States in the internal affairs of Panama. Any U.S. action will be directed at insuring that the Canal will remain open, secure, and accessible, and it shall never be directed against the territorial integrity or political independence of Panama."

46. Moffett, *Limits of Victory*, 44.

47. Ibid., 74.

48. Four full committees and one subcommittee held hearings in the Senate, three full committees and one subcommittee in the House.

49. EB, interview by William J. Jorden, March 26, 1979, BC.

50. Douglas Bennet, interview by author, September 1992.

51. EB, interview by McCullough, September 5, 1981.

52. Curiously, this last charge was repeated in post–Cold War terms when the canal was handed over to the Panamanians at the end of 1999. It was noised about at that time that the Panamanian government's award of a contract to a Hong Kong–

based engineering firm to operate harbor facilities at either end of the canal would result in a dangerous Communist Chinese foothold on the isthmus.

53. "Panama Canal Treaties: A Negotiator's Perspective," speech given by EB before the Des Moines Chamber of Commerce and Rotary Club, January 26, 1978, Department of State, Bureau of Public Affairs, Office of Public Information, Washington, D.C.

54. EB remarks, December 17, 1979, BC.

55. EB letter to Brooke Shearer, October 16, 1978, BC.

56. EB letter to Edward G. Janeway, May 25, 1978, BC.

57. EB letter to Dr. Allan Butler, February 8, 1978, BC.

58. See note 45, above.

59. Timothy Stater in Summ and Kelly, *Good Neighbors*, 76.

60. Bunker does not appear to have had a role in resolving the DeConcini problem. He stated later that the original DeConcini reservation, to the Neutrality Treaty, clearly went beyond what Panama could have accepted. (Moffett, *Limits of Victory*, 104.)

61. EB Oral History interview, Columbia University, 1.

62. Of the twenty senators up for reelection in 1978 who supported the treaties, six did not run and only seven won. Eleven more who had voted for the treaties were defeated in 1980.

63. EB speech at Duke University, November 29, 1979, BC.

Chapter 14

1. Kissinger, *Years of Renewal*, 794.

2. Alfred Atherton, interview by author, July 1992.

3. Kissinger, *Years of Renewal*, 795.

4. Harold Saunders, interview by author, August 1992.

5. Joseph Sisco, interview by author, July 1992.

6. Alfred Atherton, interview by author.

7. Kissinger, *Years of Renewal*, 1072.

8. But he did pay a call in 1980 on Thieu, who had fled Vietnam and was living in exile outside London. It was a sad experience for Bunker. "[Thieu] told me he made a mistake in leaving the country when he did," Bunker reported. "He [said he] could have gone to the delta and continued fighting, and the Americans would have come to his aid. But it was wishful thinking." (*Boston Globe*, September 4, 1982).

9. EB letter to Thom Piel, December 3, 1981, BC.

10. Bunker noted these conclusions on a number of occasions. The quote is drawn from his interview with Sanford Ungar for the January 1978 issue of *Foreign Policy*, BC.

11. Bunker's son Sam gave me a copy of the full text of the manuscript. As others who went through it also found, the draft seems to reflect Young's views as much as Bunker's. Since Bunker never authorized publication, *Lost Victory* is not cited in

this book. In 2001, Young completed another book, published in Vietnamese, whose translated title is "From the Documents of Ellsworth Bunker."

12. The resignation became effective June 30, 1978. As noted in Chapter 13, Bunker was called back to help win House passage of the legislation implementing the Panama Canal treaties. But he did not formally resume his ambassadorship at that time.

13. *New York Times* News Service, July 11, 1978.

14. Carter letter to EB, July 12, 1978, BC.

15. Carol left the Foreign Service in 1977 when she turned 60. As the service's director general, she had urged older officers to make way for younger talent and wanted her early retirement to set a good example for them.

16. Haydn Williams, interview by author, September 1992.

17. See *New York Times*, May 11, 1984.

18. Rev. Paul M. Thompson, interview by author, May 1992.

19. Bunker was made a Doctor of Law, *honoris causa*. His citation stated: "He is a man for all seasons whom six [sic] Presidents have called to national service. Without regard to party, in the waning tradition of selfless service to country, he has accepted and accomplished some of the Nation's least thankful tasks."

20. Peter Krogh, interview by author, September 1992.

21. The publications are Christopher J. McMullen, *Resolution of the Yemen Crisis, 1963* and *Mediation of the West New Guinea Dispute, 1962*, and Audrey Bracey, *Resolution of the Dominican Crisis, 1965*. All three monographs were useful in the preparation of this biography and have been cited in preceding chapters.

22. *San Diego Union*, May 18, 1984.

23. Ibid.

24. Nixon's presence caused quite a stir when his Secret Service detail felt obliged to go through every prayer book and hymnal in the church looking for possible letter bombs. (Rev. Thompson, interview by author.)

25. When Carol died on July 25, 1991 at age seventy-three from bone cancer, her funeral was also held at St. Michael's, followed by interment in the family plot. Like Ellsworth, she was remembered at a service at the National Cathedral.

26. *New York Times*, September 28, 1984.

27. *Washington Post*, September 29, 1984.

BIBLIOGRAPHY

Manuscript Collections

Abilene, Kansas
Dwight D. Eisenhower Library
　Dwight D. Eisenhower Papers
　John Foster Dulles Papers

Ann Arbor, Michigan
Gerald R. Ford Library

Austin, Texas
LBJ Library
　Bunker Collection
　National Security File
　　McGeorge Bundy Files
　　Walt W. Rostow Files
　Office Files of John Macy

Boston, Massachusetts
JFK Library
　John F. Kennedy Papers
　　National Security File

New Haven, Connecticut
Yale University Library
　Dean Acheson Papers

Washington, D.C.
National Archives
　Ambassador Ellsworth Bunker Files
　Edward G. Miller Files
　Embassy Rome General Records
　State Department, Central Files

Oral Histories

Austin, Texas
LBJ Library
　Interviews with Ellsworth Bunker: (1) December 9, 1980; (2) December 12,
　　1980; (3) October 12, 1983

Durham, N.C.
Duke University, William R. Perkins Library

Special Collections
  Interview with Ellsworth Bunker, March 2, 1979

New York, N.Y.
Columbia University
  Interview with Ellsworth Bunker, June 18, July 17, 1979

U.S. Government Publications

Background Documents Relating to the Panama Canal. Washington, D.C.: U.S. Government Printing Office, 1977.
Department of State Bulletin, various issues.
Foreign Relations of the United States (FRUS), various volumes (Department of State publication).
U.S. Congress. House. *Hearings before the Committee on Agriculture.* 73rd Cong., 2nd sess., February 19–23, 1934.
U.S. Congress. House. *Sugar Legislation: Hearing before the Committee on Agriculture.* 76th Cong., 3rd sess., April 10–12, 1940.
U.S. Congress. Senate. *Hearings before the Committee on Finance.* 73rd Cong., 2nd sess., February 23–26, 1934.
U.S. Congress. Senate. *Report of Proceedings, Hearings Held before the Committee on Foreign Relations, Nominations.* 90th Cong., 2nd sess., April 4, 1967.

Other Primary Sources

Organization of American States. *Report of the Secretary General to the Council of the Organization, January 1, 1963–June 30, 1964.* Washington, D.C.: Pan American Union, 1964.

Secondary Sources

Abramson, Rudy. *Spanning the Century.* New York: William Morrow, 1992.
Acheson, Dean. *Present at the Creation.* New York: W. W. Norton, 1969.
Ambrose, Stephen E. *Eisenhower: The President.* New York: Simon and Schuster, 1984.
Andreotti, Giulio. *The U.S.A. Up Close: From the Atlantic Pact to Bush.* New York: New York University Press, 1992.
Badeeb, Saeed M. *The Saudi-Egyptian Conflict over North Yemen.* Boulder, Colo.: Westview Press, 1986.
Ball, George. *The Past Has Another Pattern.* New York: W. W. Norton, 1982.
Barrett, David M. *Uncertain Warriors: Lyndon Johnson and His Vietnam Advisors.* Lawrence: University Press of Kansas, 1993.
Barrett, David M., ed. *Lyndon B. Johnson's Vietnam Papers.* College Station: Texas A&M Press, 1997.
Beech, Keyes. *Not Without the Americans.* Garden City, N.Y.: Doubleday, 1971.

Bendahmane, Diane B., and John W. McDonald Jr., eds. *Perspectives on Negotiation*. Washington, D.C.: Department of State, n.d.

Berger, Graenum. *A Not So Silent Envoy*. New Rochelle, N.Y.: J. W. B. Hampton Publishing, 1992.

Blair, Anne E. *Lodge in Vietnam*. New Haven, Conn.: Yale University Press, 1995.

Blanksten, George I. *Perón's Argentina*. Chicago: University of Chicago Press, 1953.

Bosch, Juan. *The Unfinished Experiment*. New York: Praeger, 1965.

Bracey, Audrey. *Resolution of the Dominican Crisis, 1965: A Study in Mediation*. Washington, D.C.: Institute for the Study of Diplomacy, 1980.

Braestrup, Peter. *Big Story*. Boulder, Colo.: Westview Press, 1977.

Brands, H. W. *Inside the Cold War*. New York: Oxford University Press, 1991.

Brogi, Alessandro. *A Question of Self-Esteem: The United States and the Cold War Choices in France and Italy, 1944-1958*. Westport, Conn.: Praeger, 2002.

Bui Diem. *In the Jaws of History*. Boston: Houghton Mifflin, 1987.

Bundy, William P. *A Tangled Web: The Making of Foreign Policy in the Nixon Presidency*. New York: Hill and Wang, 1998.

Carter, Jimmy. *Keeping Faith*. New York: Bantam Books, 1982.

Catlin, Daniel, Jr. *Good Work Well Done: The Sugar Business Career of Horace Havemeyer, 1903-1956*. New York: n.p., 1989.

Clifford, Clark, with Richard Holbrooke. *Counsel to the President: A Memoir*. New York: Random House, 1991.

Colby, William, with James McCargar. *Lost Victory: A Firsthand Account of American's Sixteen-Year Involvement in Vietnam*. Chicago: Contemporary Books, 1990.

Corn, David. *Blond Ghost: Ted Shackley and the CIA's Crusades*. New York: Simon and Schuster, 1994.

Dallek, Robert. *Flawed Giant*. New York: Oxford University Press, 1998.

Draper, Theodore. *The Dominican Revolt: A Case Study in American Policy*. New York: Commentary, 1965.

Eden, Anthony. *Full Circle*. Boston: Houghton Miflin, 1960.

Eichner, Alfred S. *The Emergence of Oligopoly: Sugar Refining as a Case Study*. Westport, Conn.: Greenwood Press, 1978.

Eisenhower, Dwight D. *Waging Peace*. Garden City, N.Y.: Doubleday, 1965.

―――. *The White House Years*. Garden City, N.Y.: Doubleday, 1963.

Furlong, William L., and Margaret E. Scranton. *The Dynamics of Foreign Policymaking*. Boulder, Colo.: Westview Press, 1984.

Gause, G. Gregory III. *Saudi-Yemeni Relations*. New York: Columbia University Press, 1990.

Gibbons, William Conrad. *The U.S. Government and the Vietnam War, Part IV*. Princeton, N.J.: Princeton University Press, 1995.

Gleijeses, Piero. *The Dominican Crisis*. Baltimore: Johns Hopkins University Press, 1978.

Gopal, S. *Jawaharlal Nehru*. Vol. 3. Cambridge, Mass.: Harvard University Press, 1984.

Hart, Parker T. *Saudi Arabia and the United States: Birth of a Security Partnership.* Bloomington: Indiana University Press, 1998.

Henderson, James Thorwald. "The Role of Good Offices and Mediation in Settling an International Conflict: Ellsworth Bunker and the West Irian Dispute." M.A. thesis, Georgetown University, 1965.

Henderson, John. *West New Guinea: The Dispute and Its Settlement.* South Orange, N.J.: Seton Hall University Press, 1973.

Herring, George. *America's Longest War.* New York: Wiley, 1979.

———. *LBJ and Vietnam: A Different Kind of War.* Austin: University of Texas Press, 1994.

Hersh, Seymour. *The Price of Power: Kissinger in the Nixon White House.* New York: Summit Books, 1983.

Hughes, H. Stuart. *The United States and Italy.* Cambridge, Mass.: Harvard University Press, 1979.

Humphrey, Hubert H. *The Education of a Public Man: My Life in Politics.* Garden City, N.Y.: Doubleday, 1976.

Isaacs, Arnold R. *Without Honor: Defeat in Vietnam and Cambodia.* Baltimore: Johns Hopkins University Press, 1983.

Isaacs, Harold R. *Scratches on Our Minds.* Westport, Conn.: Greenwood Press, 1958.

Isaacson, Walter, and Evan Thomas. *The Wise Men.* New York: Simon and Schuster, 1986.

Jayakar, Pupul. *Indira Gandhi: An Intimate Biography.* New York: Pantheon Books, 1992.

Johnson, Lyndon B. *The Vantage Point: Perspectives of the Presidency, 1963-1969.* New York: Holt, Rinehart and Winston, 1971.

Jones, Howard P. *Indonesia: The Possible Dream.* New York: Harcourt Brace Jovanovich, 1971.

Jorden, William J. *Panama Odyssey.* Austin: University of Texas Press, 1984.

Karnow, Stanley. *Vietnam: A History.* New York: Penguin, 1984.

Kaufman, Burton I. *Trade and Aid: Eisenhower's Foreign Economic Policy 1953-1961.* Baltimore: Johns Hopkins University Press, 1982.

Kissinger, Henry A. *White House Years.* Boston: Little, Brown. 1979.

———. *Years of Renewal.* New York: Simon and Schuster, 1999.

Kogan, Norman. *A Political History of Italy: The Postwar Years.* New York: Praeger, 1983.

Kosut, Hal, ed. *Cambodia and the Vietnam War.* New York: Facts on File, 1971.

Kux, Dennis. *Estranged Democracies.* Washington, D.C.: National Defense University Press, 1993.

LaFeber, Walter. *The Panama Canal: The Crisis in Historical Perspective.* New York: Oxford University Press, 1989.

Lieten, Georges Kristoffel. *The First Communist Ministry in Kerala, 1957-59.* Calcutta: K. P. Bagchi and Company, 1982.

Lijphart, Arend. *The Trauma of Decolonization.* New Haven, Conn.: Yale University Press, 1966.

Linowitz, Sol. *The Making of a Public Man*. Boston: Little, Brown, 1985.

Lodge, Henry Cabot. *The Storm Has Many Eyes*. New York: W. W. Norton, 1973.

Lowenthal, Abraham. *The Dominican Intervention*. Cambridge, Mass.: Harvard University Press, 1972.

MacGarrigle, George L. *The United States Army in Vietnam, Combat Operations, Taking the Offensive, October 1966 to October 1967*. Washington, D.C.: Center of Military History, United States Army, 1998.

Malhotra, Inder. *Indira Gandhi*. London: Hodder and Stoughton, 1989.

Mansbach, Richard M., ed. *The Dominican Crisis*. New York: Facts on File, 1971.

Markin, Terrence. "The West Irian Dispute." Ph.D. diss., Johns Hopkins University, 1996.

Martin, John Bartlow. *Overtaken by Events: The Dominican Crisis from the Fall of Trujillo to the Civil War*. Garden City, N.Y.: Doubleday, 1966.

McCullough, David. *The Path between the Seas: The Creation of the Panama Canal, 1870-1914*. New York: Simon and Schuster, 1977.

McMahon, Robert J. *The Cold War on the Periphery*. New York: Columbia University Press, 1994.

McMullen, Christopher J. *Mediation of the West New Guinea Dispute, 1962*. Washington, D.C.: Institute for the Study of Diplomacy, 1981.

———. *Resolution of the Yemen Crisis, 1963*. Washington, D.C.: Institute for the Study of Diplomacy, 1980.

Merrill, Dennis. *Bread and the Ballot: The United States and India's Economic Development, 1947-1963*. Chapel Hill: University of North Carolina Press, 1990.

Millikan, Max F., and W. W. Rostow. *A Proposal: Key to an Effective Foreign Policy*. Westport, Conn.: Greenwood Press, 1976.

Moffett, George. *The Limits of Victory: The Ratification of the Panama Canal Treaties*. Ithaca, N.Y.: Cornell University Press, 1985.

Moran, Edward C., Jr. *Bunker Genealogy*. Rockland, Maine: n.p., 1965.

Moynihan, Daniel Patrick. *A Dangerous Place*. Boston: Little, Brown, 1978.

Nguyen Cao Ky. *Twenty Years and Twenty Days*. New York: Stein and Day, 1976.

——— with Marvin J. Wolf. *Buddha's Child: My Fight to Save Vietnam*. New York: St. Martin's Press, 2002.

Nguyen Gregory Tien Hung and Jerrold L. Schecter. *The Palace File*. New York: Harper and Row, 1986.

Nolan, Keith William. *Into Laos*. Novato, Calif.: Presidio Press, 1986.

Oberdorfer, Don. *Tet!*. Garden City, N.Y.: Doubleday, 1971.

Oye, Kenneth A., Donald Rothchild, and Robert J. Lieber. *Eagle Entangled*. New York: Longman, 1979.

Page, Joseph A. *Perón, A Biography*. New York: Random House, 1983.

Page, Stephen. *The Soviet Union and the Yemens*. New York: Praeger, 1985.

Palmer, Bruce B., Jr. *Intervention in the Caribbean*. Lexington: University of Kentucky Press, 1989.

———. *The 25-Year War: America's Military Role in Vietnam*. Lexington: University of Kentucky Press, 1984.

The Pentagon Papers, Senator Gravel Edition. Boston: Beacon Press, 1969.

Peterson, Harold F. *Argentina and the United States, 1810-1960*. Albany: State University of New York, 1964.

Pfeffer, Richard M., ed. *No More Vietnams?* New York: Harper and Row, 1968.

Pike, Douglas, ed. *The Bunker Papers: Reports to the President from Vietnam*. Berkeley: Institute of East Asian Studies, University of California, 1990.

Rabel, Robert Girgio. *Between East and West: Trieste, the United States and the Cold War, 1941-1954*. Durham, N.C.: Duke University Press, 1988.

Rahmy, Abdul Ali Rehman. *The Egyptian Policy in the Arab World*. Washington, D.C.: University Press of America, 1983.

Reporting Vietnam. 2 vols. New York: The Library of America, 1998.

Rostow, Walt W. *Eisenhower, Kennedy, and Foreign Aid*. Austin: University of Texas Press, 1985.

Rusk, Dean, as told to Richard Rusk. *As I Saw It*. Edited by Daniel S. Papp. New York: Norton, 1990.

Schaffer, Howard B. *Chester Bowles: New Dealer in the Cold War*. Cambridge, Mass.: Harvard University Press, 1993.

Schandler, Herbert. *Lyndon Johnson and Vietnam: The Unmaking of a President*. Princeton, N.J.: Princeton University Press, 1983.

Shaplen, Robert. *The Road from War*. New York: Harper and Row, 1970.

Shawcross, William. *Sideshow: Kissinger, Nixon, and the Destruction of Cambodia*. New York: Simon and Schuster, 1979.

Sheehan, Neil. *A Bright and Shining Lie: John Paul Vann and America in Vietnam*. New York: Random House, 1988.

Slater, Jerome. *Intervention and Negotiation: The United States and the Dominican Revolution*. New York: Harper and Row, 1979.

Smith, E. Timothy. *A Political History of Italy: The Postwar Years*. New York: Praeger, 1983.

———. *The United States, Italy, and NATO, 1947-52*. New York: St. Martin's Press, 1991.

Snepp, Frank W., III. *Decent Interval: An Insider's Account of Saigon's Indecent End*. New York: Random House, 1977.

Sorley, Lewis. *A Better War: The Unexamined Victories and Final Tragedy of America's Last Years in Vietnam*. New York: Harcourt Brace and Company, 1999.

———. *Thunderbolt: General Creighton Abrams and the Army of His Times*. New York: Simon and Schuster, 1992.

Stookey, Robert W. *Yemen: The Politics of the Yemen Arab Republic*. Boulder, Colo.: Westview Press, 1978.

Summ, G. Harvey, and Tom Kelly, eds. *The Good Neighbors: America, Panama, and the 1977 Canal Treaties*. Athens: Ohio University Center for International Studies, 1988.

Summers, Harry G. *On Strategy: A Critical Analysis of the Vietnam War*. New York: Dell, 1984.

Tran Van Don. *Our Endless War*. San Raphel, Calif.: Presidio Press, 1978.

Tulchin, Joseph S. *Argentina and the United States: A Conflicted Relationship.* Boston: Twayne, 1990.

The United States and Latin America: Next Steps: A Second Report by the Commission on United States—Latin American Relations. New York: Center for Inter-American Relations, 1976.

Vance, Cyrus R. *Hard Choices: Critical Years in American Foreign Policy.* New York: Simon and Schuster, 1983.

Von Horn, Carl. *Soldiering for Peace.* New York: David McKay, 1966.

Warren, Harris G. "Diplomatic Relations between the United States and Argentina." *Inter-American Economic Affairs* 18 (Winter 1954): 63–82.

Westmoreland, William. *A Soldier Reports.* Garden City, N.Y.: Doubleday, 1976.

Whitaker, Arthur P. *The United States and Argentina.* Cambridge, Mass.: Harvard University Press, 1954.

———. *The United States and the Southern Cone.* Cambridge, Mass.: Harvard University Press, 1976.

Wiarda, Howard J., and Michael J. Kryzanek. *The Dominican Republic, A Caribbean Crisis.* Boulder, Colo.: Westview Press, 1982.

Wollenborg, Leo. *Stars, Stripes, and Italian Tricolor.* New York: Praeger, 1990.

Wyatt, Clarence R. *Paper Soldiers: The American Press and the Vietnam War.* New York: W. W. Norton, 1993.

Yates, Lawrence P. *Power Pack: U.S. Intervention in the Dominican Republic, 1965–66.* Fort Leavenworth, Kans.: Combat Studies Institute, 1988.

INDEX

Page numbers in *italics* indicate illustrations.

Boyd, Aquilino, 285

Braden, Spruille, 27, 29, 314, 319 (n. 17)

Braestrup, Peter, 343 (n. 11)

Brandon, Henry, 179

Brands, H. W., 54

Brazil: and Dominican crisis, 140, 156–57; EB trips to, 22, 25, 128, 130, 163; U.S. strategic study of, 128–29

Brown, George, 282, 284

Bruce, David K. E., 33, 243

Bruce, James, 319 (n. 19)

Buenos Aires. *See* Argentina

Bui Diem, 170, 181, 184, 203, 342 (n. 79)

Bunau-Varilla, Philippe, 270–71

Bunche, Ralph, 115–16, 125

Bundy, McGeorge, 138, 140, 141, 155, 164, 165, 255, 334 (n. 17), 335 (n. 30)

Bundy, William, 216, 218, 231

Bunker, Arthur (brother), 5, 7

Bunker, Ellen (daughter), 5, 16, 22, 25, 32, 76, 117, 130, 131, 161

Bunker, Ellsworth: as ambassador-at-large, 160–63, 269, 306, 307; as ambassador to Argentina, 1, 4, 22, 23–24, 28–36, 39, 43, 45, 49, 52, 71, 74, 77, 179, 312, 314, 319 (nn. 4, 8); as ambassador to India, 1, 16, 50–74, 78, 85, 114, 131–32, 162, 179, 312–14, 324 (n. 4); as ambassador to Italy, 1, 33–36, 38–45, 71, 74, 179, 312–14; as ambassador to Nepal, 1, 72, 161–62; as ambassador to OAS, 129–31, 140–42, 160, 261–62, 270, 333 (n. 7), 335 (n. 27); as ambassador to Vietnam, 1, 2, 9, 16, 128, 159, 163–259, 263–66, 310, 314–15, 337 (n. 57), 339 (n. 31), 340 (n. 45), 341 (nn. 72, 75, 76), 342 (n. 81), 345 (n. 47), 346 (n. 67), 352 (n. 98), 353 (n. 112); American Red Cross presidency, 1, 45–50, 77, 323 (n. 1), 324 (n. 9); arthritis attack, 11, 14–15, 18; church membership, 17, 308; civic

activities, 21–22; death of, 309–10; as diplomatic troubleshooter, 85–88, 106–9, 114, 117, 127, 129, 141–43, 145, 158, 160, 166, 181, 310; and Dominican crisis, 1, 107, 129, 140–59, 165, 166, 261–62, 309–12, 335 (n. 27), 337 (nn. 45, 47); education, 6–10, 25, 75; family background, 3–7; first marriage, 16–19; foreign language skills, 7, 23, 31, 43; in foreign policy organizations, 83, 85; honorary degrees, 7, 308, 318 (n. 13), 358 (n. 19); Indonesia mission, 132–38, 261, 333 (n. 9), 334 (n. 17); and Medal of Freedom, 128; and media relations, 69, 143, 185–87, 196–97, 207–8, 211, 306, 335 (n. 31), 341 (nn. 72, 75); and Middle East shuttle diplomacy, 69, 304–6; oral history interviews with, 57–58, 70–71, 345 (n. 52); Panama Canal treaties role, 1, 108, 130, 267, 269–70, 272, 275–86, 288–94, 296–303, 310, 312, 355 (n. 37); and 1964 Panama crisis, 129–30; as parent, 18, 76; personal qualities, 1–3, 5–6, 9, 14, 19–20, 24, 35, 36, 46, 56, 94, 106–7, 141–42, 158, 165, 175, 176, 181, 258, 299, 305, 308, 312–13, 315–16, 335 (n. 31), 341 (n. 76); political party affiliations, 14–16, 24, 36, 45, 46, 51, 52, 207, 289, 308; public service career overviews, xi, xii, 1–2, 51, 163, 166, 310–16; in retirement, 308–9; second marriage, 160–63, 263, 338 (nn. 4, 5); sense of humor, 143, 181, 276, 299, 306, 328 (n. 13); sources on, xi–xiv, 57–58, 215; as sugar industry lobbyist, 12–15, 19, 21, 22, 313, 323 (n. 1); as sugar refining industry executive, 4, 7, 10–14, 16–18, 20–22, 75, 84, 85, 181; in U.N. General Assembly, 51; and U.S. foreign policy, 2, 9, 51, 84–85, 142, 192, 228, 315–16, 326 (n. 40);

Cold War: and Argentine politics, 27; in the Caribbean, 139; and "clientitis," 228–29, 313; EB roles in, 310, 313–16; in Europe, 37–39; and Indonesia, 93; and Red Cross planning, 47–48; and U.S.-India relations, 53–55, 57, 69; and Yemen crisis, 112. *See also* Communism; Soviet Union

Colonialism, Western, 89. *See also* Goa; West New Guinea dispute

Commission on U.S.-Latin American Relations, 288

Committee to Defend America by Aiding the Allies, 15

Communism: as economic development option, 84–85; and Middle East, 111; as post-WWII threat to peace, 37–39, 53, 54, 58, 59, 60, 64, 92, 96, 310; in Southeast Asia, 173. *See also* Communists

Communist China. *See* China, People's Republic of

Communist Party of India (CPI), 67

Communists: in Cambodia, 222; in Cuba, 139, 145, 159; in the Dominican Republic, 138–40, 144–47, 149–53, 155, 157–59; in India, 67, 181, 313–14; in Indonesia, 90–93, 96, 97, 100, 106, 133, 137–38; in Italy, 313–14; in Vietnam, 168, 169, 173, 176, 182, 188–90, 193–99, 204, 205, 208–9, 211, 221–22, 228, 236, 306–7, 329 (n. 23). *See also* Communism; National Liberation Front; Vietcong

Conant, James B., 51

Constitutionalists (Dominican political faction), 144–57, 337 (n. 45)

Contadora negotiations, 276–78, 281, 285, 286, 289–91

Cooper, John Sherman, 50, 61, 172

Corn, David, 348 (n. 40)

Council of National Reconciliation and Concord, 241, 251

Council on Foreign Relations, 83

Covington and Burling (law firm), 23

Cuba: Castro regime in, 139, 145, 159, 279, 280; EB visit to, 7; OAS sanctions against, 131, 333 (n. 7); and Panama Canal treaties, 298; sugar exports, 11, 13

Cuban missile crisis, 112

Cuthell, David, 134–35

Dearborn, Henry, 24, 25, 28, 30, 31, 320 (n. 23)

Deconcini, Dennis, 301

De Gasperi, Alcide, 37–44

Democratic Party: EB ties to, 14–16, 24, 36, 45, 46, 51, 207, 289, 308; and 1968 presidential race, 207–8

De Quay, J. E., 99, 107, 329 (n. 23)

Desai, Morarji, 73, 80, 84

Diem, Bui. *See* Bui Diem

Diem, Ngo Dinh. *See* Ngo Dinh Diem

Dillon, C. Douglas, 61

Diplomacy: EB background for, 13; EB techniques in, 276–79, 311–12; requisites for success in, 1–2, 86–88, 303, 311

Dolvin, Welborn "Tom," 282

Dominican crisis (1965–66), 138–39; EB role in resolving, 1, 107, 129, 140–59, 165, 166, 261, 262, 309–12, 335 (n. 27), 337 (n. 45)

Dominican Republic: political instability in, 138–39; U.S. interventions in, 131, 138–40. *See also* Dominican crisis

Dueñas, Ramón de Clairmont, 141, 262

Dulles, Allen, 45

Dulles, John Foster, 13, 23, 44, 45, 51, 58–59, 61

Dummerston, Vt.: EB farm in, 18–19, 20, 22, 76, 82, 83, 84, 131, 308, 309

Dunn, James, 33

Duong Van Minh ("Big Minh"), 183, 230–34, 237, 348 (n. 45)

Hay–Bunau-Varilla Treaty (1903), 270–71, 276, 294, 300
Henderson, Loy, 56
Hersh, Seymour, 348 (nn. 40, 43)
Herter, Christian, 83
Herz, Martin F., 309
Hill, Charles, 223, 243, 245, 247, 351 (n. 77)
Hoang Duc Nha, 349 (n. 45)
Ho Chi Minh Trail, 169, 190, 221, 224–25
Holmes, Oliver Wendell, Jr., 44
Honolulu summit conference, 210–11
Hotel Embajador (Santo Domingo), 143–44
Hughes, H. Stuart, 40
Humphrey, George, 61
Humphrey, Hubert H., 61, 158, 160–61, 193, 195, 201, 208, 213, 215, 333 (n. 9)
Hung, Nguyen Tien. See Nguyen Tien Hung
Huntington, Samuel, 158–59
Huntland Estate (Middleburg, Va.), 95, 96, 107, 276. See also Middleburg talks
Huong, Tran Van. See Tran Van Huong
Hussein (king of Jordan), 111

Imbert Barrera, António, 144, 147–50, 337 (n. 45)
India: Bowles ambassadorship to, 53, 56, 61; and China, 54, 61, 63, 73, 85, 313, 326 (n. 32); EB ambassadorship to, 1, 16, 50–74, 78–81, 144, 162, 179, 312–14, 324 (n. 4); EB continued interest in, 84–85; and Pakistan, 54, 62–63, 161; U.S. relations with, 53–70, 73–74, 84–85, 324 (n. 4), 325 (n. 18), 326 (n. 40). See also Goa; Kashmir dispute; Kerala
Indochina, 57, 90, 236, 237, 242, 246. See also Cambodia; Laos; Vietnam,

Democratic Republic of; Vietnam, Republic of
Indonesia: Communist influence in, 90–93, 96, 97, 100, 106, 133, 137–38, 329 (n. 23); EB mission to, 132–38, 261, 328 (nn. 7, 13); nationalist movement, 89, 90–91; and Papuan independence movement, 330 (n. 31); U.S. relations with, 92–93, 100, 106, 109, 132–38, 329 (n. 24). See also West New Guinea dispute
Indus Waters dispute, 65
Institute for Conflict and Policy Studies, 296
Institute for the Study of Diplomacy (ISD), 268, 308–9
Inter-American Peace Force (IAPF), 140, 145–49, 151–52, 154, 156–58, 335 (n. 27)
International House (Washington, D.C.), 83
International Movement for Atlantic Union, 83
Iraq, 118
Isaacs, Arnold, 256
Israel, 160, 304–6
Italian Social Movement (MSI), 40
Italy: and Cold War political issues, 37–38; EB ambassadorship to, 1, 33–36, 38–45, 49, 71, 74, 179, 312–14; postwar elections in, 39–40, 42–44, 321 (n. 4), 322 (nn. 15, 16); U.S. economic assistance to, 40–41, 43. See also Trieste dispute

Janeway, Edward, 52
Johnson, Eric, 84
Johnson, Lyndon B.: and aid to India, 62; and Dominican crisis, 138–43, 150, 151, 155, 158, 165, 261, 311, 335 (n. 25); and EB ambassadorship to Vietnam, 163, 165–68; EB cables to, 185–86, 189, 191–93, 195, 196, 200–203, 208–9, 213–14, 216, 314–15;

EB consultations with, 203–4, 244, 264–65; and EB Medal of Freedom, 128; and EB OAS ambassadorship, 129; and EB wedding, 161, 338 (n. 4); and Indonesia, 132–34, 136–38, 261, 333 (n. 9), 334 (n. 17); and Linowitz OAS ambassadorship, 288; and Panama, 130; praise for EB, 131, 158, 165, 167, 168, 219; refusal to seek reelection, 199–200; and Vietnam, 164, 165, 167–68, 170, 175, 179, 182, 184, 187, 190, 191, 193, 197, 199, 210, 213–16, 219, 264, 306, 339 (n. 16); and women ambassadors, 160

Johnson administration: and Dominican crisis, 148–52, 158–59; EB as troubleshooter for, 127; and Indonesia, 134–35; and Panama, 270, 287; Vance as troubleshooter for, 290; and Vietnam, 163, 166, 174, 201, 209, 210, 212–13

Jones, Howard, 94, 105, 133, 135, 137, 261, 333 (n. 9), 334 (n. 17)

Jones-Costigan Act (1934), 12

Jordan: and Yemen crisis, 111, 112

Jorden, William J., 270, 275, 277, 281, 286

Kaiser, Robert, 187

Kashmir dispute, 54, 64–66

Kathmandu. See Nepal

Katzenbach, Nicholas, 165, 207

Keating, Kenneth, 306

Kemp, Frank, 318 (n. 23)

Kennedy, Edward M., 345 (n. 47)

Kennedy, John F.: and aid to India, 61, 73, 84, 325 (n. 18); foreign policy approach, 92; and Medal of Freedom ceremony, 128; and Nasser, 331 (n. 23); relations with EB, 83, 106, 107, 114, 128, 129, 207, 315; and West New Guinea dispute, 93, 97, 99, 100–103, 329 (n. 23); and Yemen

crisis, 111–15, 119, 121–23, 127. *See also* Kennedy administration

Kennedy, Robert F., 94, 207

Kennedy administration: and Dominican Republic, 139; and Indonesia, 92; and Vietnam, 164; and West New Guinea dispute, 93–101, 103; and Yemen crisis, 111, 112, 126, 331 (n. 10)

Kent State University: war protests at, 223

Kerala: CIA intervention in, 67–68

Kim, Eva, 178, 180, 244, 354 (n. 20)

Kim Il Sung, 135

Kiphuth, Robert J. H., 128

Kirk, Roger, 346 (n. 67)

Kissinger, Henry, xii–xiii, 218, 265–66; at ISD, 268, 309; and Middle East diplomacy, 269, 304–6; and 1971 elections in Vietnam, 231, 233–35; and Panama Canal treaties, 270, 271, 275, 277, 283, 284, 286; relations with EB, 244–45, 305–6, 316, 351 (n. 77); and secret peace negotiations, 219, 236–37, 240–52, 254, 255, 351 (n. 77)

Kissinger-Tack Principles, 276–79, 286, 311–12

Kohler, Foy, 334 (n. 17)

Komer, Robert, 96–97, 114, 168, 178, 189, 190, 208

Kontum: siege of, 238, 239

Korea, 57

Korean War, 54

Kozak, Michael G., 278

Krishna Menon, V. K., 63–64, 326 (n. 32)

Krogh, Peter F., 308–9

Kux, Dennis, 67

Ky, Nguyen Cao. See Nguyen Cao Ky

Laird, Melvin, 219

Laise, Carol (second wife), xi, xiii; death of, 358 (n. 25); EB courtship of, 131, 132, 144, 161; and EB departure from Saigon, 259, 266; EB letters to, 176, 179, 180, 195, 200–203, 206, 208, 210–11, 226, 232, 234, 235, 238–40, 249–50, 307; and EB visits, 172, 181, 206, 218, 238, 339 (n. 31); and Georgetown University, 308–9; letter from LBJ, 167; marriage, 160–63, 167, 180–81, 218–19, 263, 338 (nn. 4, 5); State Department career, 131–32, 160–61, 180, 219, 263, 269, 308; and unpublished EB book, 307

Lakas, Demetrio B., 276

Lake, Anthony, 219, 223, 245

Lam Son 719 (military operation), 224–26, 230

Landon, Alfred M., 15

Laos: Communist seizure of, 173; 1971 ARVN incursion into, 224–26, 230, 236; North Vietnamese infiltration through, 169, 190, 209, 314; peace provisions concerning, 236, 242, 246, 251; U.S. ambassador to, 178; U.S. reluctance to invade, 190–91, 197, 307, 314

La Prensa (Argentine newspaper), 26, 27–28, 31

Latin America: as Carter administration priority, 286–88; and Dominican crisis, 140, 143, 158, 261; EB exposure to, 7, 13–14, 25, 53, 181; EB views on, 30–31, 34; and Nixon administration, 272. *See also* Argentina; Brazil; Cuba; Dominican Republic; Mexico; Panama; Panama Canal treaties

Laughton, Ransom, 18

Leahy, Patrick, 297

Le Duc Tho, 236, 255

Lijphart, Arend, 90

Linowitz, Sol, 267, 288–94, 296–97, 299, 355 (n. 37)

Lippmann, Walter, 168–69

Locke, Eugene, 168, 177, 178, 189

Lodge, Henry Cabot, 163–64, 166, 168, 170, 172, 187

Lon Nol, 222, 347 (n. 17)

Lovett, Robert, 8, 41

Lowenthal, Abraham, 286

Luce, Clare Boothe, 36, 38–40

Luns, Joseph, 92, 94, 97, 100–101

Luns Plan, 92, 93

MacDonald, Malcolm, 58

Malaya, 329 (n. 23)

Malaysia, 133–36, 329 (n. 23)

Malik, Adam, 95, 98, 103

Mallory, Lester, 28, 32, 35

Mann, Thomas, 152

Marinho, Ilmar Penna, 141, 262

Markin, Terrence, 95, 106, 107

Marshall Plan, 37

Martin, Graham, 172, 259

Martin, John Bartlow, 335 (n. 25)

Masters, Edward E., 137

McArthur, George, 176–77, 259, 348 (n. 40), 354 (n. 20)

McCarthy, Eugene, 207

McCormick, Anne O'Hare, 36

McCullough, David, 297

McGhee, George, 114

McGovern, George, 242, 252

McMullen, Christopher, 101, 119, 123

McNamara, Robert, 164, 179–80, 191, 209

Medal of Freedom presentation (1963), 128

Mehta, Jagat Singh, 56, 132

Merrill, Dennis, 59

Mexico: EB experiences in, 13–14

Middleburg talks, 95, 96–99, 102–7

Middle East: Kissinger diplomacy in, 269, 304–6; U.S. objectives in, 111–13, 121, 122, 126–27. *See also* Yemen crisis

Military Assistance Command, Vietnam (MACV), 164, 170–71, 186, 189, 193, 229, 256

Miller, Edward G., Jr., 23–25, 28–33, 39, 83, 319 (n. 4), 320 (n. 24)

Millikan, Max, 61

Minh, Duong Van. *See* Duong Van Minh ("Big Minh")

Miterev, G. A., 48, 49

Moderators: role in negotiations of, 328 (n. 7)

Mondale, Walter, 308

Monnet, Jean, 128

Mora, José, 141

Moreno, Miguel, 130

Morse, Wayne, 171

Moss, Ambler, 288, 291, 292

Moynihan, Daniel Patrick, 67

Murphy, John, 302

Mysore, maharajah of, 71, 84

Nach, James, 228

Narcotics: sales to U.S. troops of, 227, 228

Nasser, Gamal Abdel, 110–13, 116–26, 331 (n. 23), 332 (n. 39)

National Liberation Front (NLF), 168, 204–7, 212–14, 216

National Security Council (NSC) report 5701, 58

National Security Decision Memorandum (NSDM 302), 283–84

National Sugar Refining Company, 4, 10–13, 16, 17, 18, 20, 21, 22, 23, 25, 46, 51, 84

Nehru, B. K., 326 (n. 40)

Nehru, Jawaharlal, 1, 52–58, 63–66, 70–73, 79, 80, 84, 85, 131, 324 (n. 4), 326 (n. 32)

Nepal: EB ambassadorship to, 1, 72, 161–62; EB visits to, 206, 263; Laise ambassadorship to, 160–63, 263

Netherlands. *See* West New Guinea dispute

Netherlands East Indies, 89, 90, 103. *See also* West New Guinea dispute

Neutrality Treaty, 292, 294, 295, 300–301. *See also* Panama Canal treaties

New Delhi: Eisenhower arrival in, 70–71, *80*; living conditions in, 71, 72, 79. *See also* India

Newlin, Michael, 330 (n. 34)

Ngo Dinh Diem, 164, 183, 203, 230

Nguyen Cao Ky, 170, 179, 183–85, 187–88, 230–34, 342 (n. 79), 348 (n. 40)

Nguyen Tien Hung, 203, 253, 349 (n. 45)

Nguyen Van Thieu: and Cambodian incursions, 191, 222; and cease-fire period, 256–57; and Easter Offensive, 239; EB relations with, 170, 179, 181, 183, 195, 201–3, 227–30, 259, 263, 315, 344 (n. 23), 346 (n. 67), 352 (n. 98), 357 (n. 8); in exile, 357 (n. 8); and Honolulu conference, 210–11; and Lam Son 719, 225–26; and 1967 elections, 183–85, 187–88, 201–2, 342 (n. 79); and 1971 elections, 230–35, 237, 259, 348 (nn. 40, 43, 45); and Paris peace talks, 203–6, 210, 212–17; and post-Tet initiatives, 197–98, 200–203, 208; and secret peace negotiations, 236–37, 241–55, 259, 314, 351 (n. 77); and Vietnamization, 220–21; visit to U.S., 266, 352 (n. 98)

Nixon, Richard M., 265–66; and bombing raids on North Vietnam, 254; and Cambodia, 222–24, 347 (n. 17); and China, 270, 272; and EB, 191, 208, 218–19, 226–27, 259, 347 (n. 17); at EB funeral, 310, 358 (n. 24); election of, 211, 213, 216; and Lodge, 164; and Panama Canal negotiations, 270, 271, 273, 277, 281, 289, 354 (n. 7); and peace negotiations, 245, 246, 249–55, 306; reelection of, 242, 250, 252; and Soviet Union, 270, 272; and Vietnam cease-fire, 174, 257; and Vietnam War, 220, 232, 235–42, 244, 265, 270, 314

Vietnam, Republic of: EB ambassadorship to, 1, 2, 9, 16, 128, 159, 163–259,
310, 337 (n. 57), 348 (n. 45); EB appraisals of, 181–82, 226–30, 235,
248, 257–58, 326 (n. 40); fall of,
172–74, 274, 306–7, 316; government corruption in, 209, 226–28,
239, 240, 257, 345 (nn. 47, 52);
military forces, 169, 170, 176, 178,
183–85, 190, 191, 193, 194, 196, 197,
199, 202, 208–9, 220–26, 228, 235–
40, 251, 252; 1967 elections in, 170,
182–85, 187–88, 193, 201, 232, 342
(nn. 79, 81); 1971 elections in, 230–
35, 237, 348 (nn. 40, 43, 45), 349
(n. 51); pacification program in, 178,
188–90, 193, 194, 202, 208, 219–21,
224, 227, 231, 235, 236; U.S. forces
in, 169, 188, 190, 198–99, 211, 220,
225, 235–40, 246, 247, 256; U.S.
policies toward, 170–72, 176, 178,
182–84, 210–12, 215–18, 229, 235;
wartime objectives of, 256
Vietnam War: cease-fire period, 256–
57, 353 (nn. 112, 114); critics of, 16,
171, 182, 194, 198, 199, 207–8, 223,
227–28, 232, 234, 235, 252, 315, 341
(n. 72), 345 (n. 47); and Dominican
invasion, 139, 158, 159; and EB reputation, 2, 9, 163; EB views on, 163,
166, 173–74, 182–83, 192–94, 197–
99, 204, 209, 219–30, 236, 238–39,
256, 259, 265, 297–98, 306–7, 314–
15; Guam conference on, 168–71,
182, 201; media coverage of, 185–
87, 194, 196–97, 208, 223, 226–28,
306, 341 (nn. 72, 75), 343 (n. 11);
negotiations to end, 199, 202, 204–
5, 209–17, 219, 235–37, 240–55, 351
(n. 77); North Vietnamese forces
in, 169, 171, 172–74, 190, 193, 194,
204–5, 212, 220–21, 236–40; and
Panama Canal treaties, 274; unfinished EB book on, 307; U.S. military

strategies in, 176, 178, 190–91, 193,
219, 221–22; U.S. objectives in, 238,
256; "Vietnamization" of, 176, 178,
193, 199, 210, 219–21, 224–28, 235–
39, 252, 256, 265, 314. *See also* Easter
Offensive; Tet offensive
Von Holt, Herman, 9–10
Von Horn, Carl, 126
Von Reigersburg, Fernando, 262

Watts, William, 223
Webb, James, 32–33
Weller, George, 43
Wendt, Allan, 195
Wessin y Wessin, Elias, 154
Westmoreland, William, 164, 165,
168–71, 175–76, 178, 184, 189–91,
193–97, 199
West New Guinea dispute, 88–109; EB
role in resolving, 1, 88, 94–109, 114,
129, 133, 309, 312, 328 (n. 7); and
1990s Papuan independence move-
ment, 330 (n. 31); U.S. positions on,
92–97, 99–101, 329 (nn. 23, 24)
Wheeler, Earle, 164, 199
Whitaker, Arthur, 27
White, William Allen, 15
Whitehouse, Charles S., 178, 243, 259
Wilder, Thornton, 128
Williams, Haydn, 308
Wolff, Lester, 235
World Bank, 61, 65
World War II: Argentine policies dur-
ing, 27; EB activities during, 17,
20–21; EB stance toward, 15–16
Wyatt, Clarence, 343 (n. 11)
Wyrough, Richard, 291

Xuan Thuy, 236

Yale University: alumni contacts with,
84; EB family ties to, 4, 7; and EB
honorary degree, 7, 318 (n. 13); EB
undergraduate years at, 1, 7–10, 23,